WHEN YOU MARRY

Evelyn Millis Duvall, Ph.D.

Reuben Hill, Ph.D.

WITH CHAPTERS

IN COLLABORATION WITH

Sylvanus M. Duvall, Ph.D.

D. C. HEATH AND COMPANY

WHEN YOU MARRY

REVISED EDITION

Cartoons drawn by

WYNCIE KING and HUGH DEVINE

WHEN the original *When You Marry* appeared in 1945 it set the style for functional education for marriage and family life that has been followed by many other texts since. By *functional education* we mean the education that begins with the interests, needs, and known readiness of the student, geared to assist him in finding answers to his questions. As his interests grow, so does the breadth of coverage, in ever-widening circles. Functional education is clearly distinguished from the traditional academic approach which customarily starts with the historical backgrounds of the problem and the theoretical concepts employed, only incidentally getting around to the student's current interests and questions — and usually late in the course sequence if at all.

Our philosophy, expressed in the content and the format of both editions of *When You Marry*, is that love, marriage, and family life does not need to be dull. We gear into the motivations that lie latent in the universal interest in men and women, their loves and problems, their interactions and plans in dating, courting, getting married, and raising a family. From the lift of the kick-off cartoon and its human interest questions through every chapter, written to be readable with frequent illustrations, graphic presentations, and subtitles, the design is *reader-centered*. Check tests are located to help the reader check his comprehension of the material as he goes along. Teachers report that new units of work are effectively introduced by the stimulus of such a self-test device, and/or an appropriate illustration. Each cartoon depicts a problem situation that the student may view more objectively for having caught it visually. Flashed on a screen or copied on a blackboard, they become live material for discussion.

The rapid development of the marriage and family field is vividly seen in the quality and amount of new material that re-enforces the entire second edition. New census data, several national conferences, new research have required whole new sections in every chapter, and have contributed significantly to the two new chapters.

By this time our debt to others who have blazed the trails that we follow and who have encouraged us in our pioneering is too great to spell out in detail. We appreciate more than we can enumerate the thousands of colleagues, friends, and students who have encouraged, assisted, and prodded us through the years. Their criticisms arising out of their experiences in using the first edition have played a major role in the focusing of the revised edition of *When You Marry*.

Specifically we gratefully acknowledge permission to use a number of charts from *Children and Youth at the Midcentury — A Chart Book* prepared by the Midcentury White House Conference on Children and Youth; published by Health Publications Institute, Inc., copyright, 1951, by Health Publications Institute, Inc., 216 North Dawson Street, Raleigh, North Carolina.

We reaffirm our faith in the collaborative process; it is truly creative for those rugged enough to take it. Again, as in the earlier volume, not only the entire book, but every chapter in it, has been thought through, worked over, written, and rewritten by both Duvalls and Hills. In general, Evelyn Duvall is responsible for chapters 1, 2, 3, 6, 9, 16, 17, 18, and 20; Reuben Hill for chapters 4, 5, 7, 8, 10, 12, 13, 14, 15, and 21; Sylvanus Duvall for chapters 11 and 19 and for some of the content and focus of Chapter 7. The revised edition is much the richer for the more mature contributions of both growing families that in the interval between the two editions have completed several stages of the family life cycle and have brought a wealth of family living to point up our professional orientation.

When You Marry represents the active participation of two whole families who jointly dedicate this book to growing families everywhere.

Evelyn Millis Duvall
Reuben Hill

FOREWORD TO THE FIRST EDITION

THIS book, exemplifying the functional approach to teaching marriage and family living, is timely. American youth by the hundreds of thousands are concerned as never before with problems of adjustment. The hasty marriages of wartime, disturbing wartime experiences, and separation of husbands and wives have created problems of personal and marital readjustment which are taxing all our resources of knowledge, research, and skill in education and counseling. Equally important are the problems arising from the great number of marriages, as hostilities cease, of couples already engaged and of others who have postponed marriage.

While there are several excellent books already available on preparation for marriage, this new volume combines several distinctive features which make it particularly helpful. First, it presents the findings of recent research in several pertinent disciplines as they have practical application to the many adjustments to marriage and family living. Each chapter begins with the questions young people raise in the area to be discussed, and the material that follows is organized in the light of these concrete problems rather than in the traditional fashion. Any valid research finding, regardless of the specific scientific field of its origin, is applied to that particular problem in personal-family adjustment which it is most helpful in solving.

Second, the readable and lively style of the book makes it usable not only for students of the family but also for all young people personally interested in getting married. Illustrations as visual aids are especially helpful in clarifying the material discussed and in focusing attention on major concepts. Numerous tests throughout the book are designed to assist the reader in self-checking his progress in comprehension. All in all, the book is admirably designed as an integral course in a program of general education; for use in discussion classes in colleges, schools, churches, settlements, and young people's associations; or as part of a community program of education for marriage and family living.

Third, the book is exceptional in its wide coverage of interrelated fields and in their synthesis into a new educational approach. This quality derives from the interweaving of the backgrounds of experience of the authors and from the unique beginnings of the book in the combined thinking of many educators.

This volume has an interesting and significant history. Its conception occurred in the spring of 1943 when a committee of the American Council on Education was charged with developing a design for general education to meet the interests and the needs of men and women in the armed services.[1] This committee defined general education as "the type of education which the majority of our people must have if they are to be good citizens, parents, and workers,"[2] and it included in the fourteen courses proposed as a basic offering in general education one on Marriage and Family Adjustments.

All fourteen courses were planned to be functional in the triple sense that they were devised to meet felt needs of the individual in preparing him for life, that they had a social emphasis in enabling him to discharge the privileges and obligations of citizenship in a democracy, and that they stressed integration of different fields of knowledge in application to significant life situations.

The Subcommittee on Marriage and Family Adjustments appointed to outline the course in this area consisted of Mrs. Duvall, Dr. Hill, Dr. Oliver Ohmann, then of Western Reserve University, and the writer as chairman. The functional approach undertaken by our committee may be illustrated by quoting from the published report of the statement of objectives of the proposed course on Marriage and Family Adjustments:[3]

General education should lead the individual as a citizen in a free society to think through the problems and to gain the basic orientation that will better enable him to make a satisfactory family and marital adjustment. In order to accomplish this purpose, the student should acquire the following:

A. *Knowledge and understanding of*
   1 The ways in which the American family differs from families in other countries and in earlier times

[1] A *Design for General Education for Members of the Armed Forces*, A Report of the Committee on a Design for General Education (Washington, D. C., American Council on Education, 1944).

[2] Quoted in the report from Earl J. McGrath, "General Education in the Postwar Period," *The Annals of the American Academy of Political and Social Science*, Vol. 231 (1944), p. 74.

[3] A *Design for General Education for Members of the Armed Forces*, pp. 36–38.

2 The trends in American society affecting the structure and functions of the family and the role of women and children in our society

3 The personality make-up of the individual as it affects his relationships to friends and to members of the family

4 The ways in which experiences in family life determine the personality development of the child

5 The effects of the war on love, courtship, marriage, and family life

6 The factors making for success in marriage

7 The development of relationships of friendship and affection: dating, courtship, engagement, and marriage

8 Major family crises and conflicts, and ways of meeting them

9 The biological aspects of reproduction and of prenatal and postnatal care

10 Problems involved in earning and spending the family income

11 Available resources for premarital, postmarital, and family counseling and education

B. *Skills and abilities*

1 Skill in meeting and cultivating members of the opposite sex in wholesome relationships

2 Skill in resolving conflicts, hostilities, rejections, and overattachments

3 Habits of discussion and cooperative planning in family situations

4 Ability to relate oneself and family to the broader relationships of social life, and to become identified with larger causes

5 Ability to discharge parental responsibilities in child rearing

6 Skill in planning ways of meeting the problem of in-laws and other relatives

7 Skill in household management, including the budgeting and spending of the family income

C. *Attitudes and appreciations*

1 Realization and happiness in marriage and family life as a significant value, the achievement of which may be aided by preparation

2 Appreciation of companionship as an essential element in the success of a marriage

3 Recognition of democracy as a way of life to be realized in the family in relations of husband and wife and of parents and children

4 Appreciation of family members as persons with needs and interests of their own

5 Awareness of the importance of the prevention, early recognition, and treatment of marital discord and of behavior problems of children

6 Appreciation of the role of religion in personal and family living

The authors of this book, who had already served as two of the members of the committee that prepared the outline of the course, were asked to prepare a workbook to be used in conjunction with a textbook as the basis of a prospective course in the United States Armed Forces Institute. Although a course in Marriage and the Family has not yet been included in the program of the Institute, the authors were encouraged, by indications of widespread interest in a course with the same objectives for all young people preparing for marriage, to write the present volume.

The authors of *When You Marry* are unusually well qualified by their training and experience to prepare a volume meeting the present pressing needs and concerns of young people. Evelyn Millis Duvall has a thorough background in biology, and has completed her residence requirements for the doctor's degree in the field of human development, which is an integrated program of study including pertinent courses in anthropology, biology, economics, nutrition, psychiatry, psychology, and sociology. As director for eight years of the Association for Family Living she gained an understanding of the problems of young people of all social classes, and of ways of working with them in the discussion of their questions. Dr. Reuben Hill had his graduate training in sociology. Organizer and director for four years of the interdepartmental courses in marriage at the University of Wisconsin, with further experience in the University of South Dakota, Iowa State College, and numerous informal collegiate situations, he has intimate knowledge of the problems of college youth and experience and skill in methods of teaching adapted to their interests.

The authors have brought together their combined training and experience in a collaboration that, through collective thinking, has produced what may be considered a new integration both of material and of point of view. The book possesses a vital down-to-earth quality and, at the same time, scientific soundness and thoroughness that would not otherwise be possible.

Ernest W. Burgess

UNIVERSITY OF CHICAGO

CONTENTS

PART *3*   THE MAKING OF A FAMILY

PART *4*   FAMILY LIFE YESTERDAY, TODAY, AND TOMORROW

CHAPTER ONE

He didn't learn that out of a book!

WHAT YOU BRING TO MARRIAGE

What makes you YOU?

How can children born and raised in the same family be so different?

Can you hope to reform the person you marry?

How does the past influence the present in your life?

*W*HEN YOU COME TO MARRIAGE, WHAT DO YOU BRING? A NEW wardrobe? A nest egg in the bank? Some furniture you've inherited? A dependent relative or two? A good job and the prospect of advancement? Whatever your tangible assets or liabilities are, there is something even more important: that is *you* as a *personality*, the way you act toward people and the attitudes which you bring to marriage.

The kind of marriage you make depends upon the kind of person you are. If you are a happy, well-adjusted person, the chances are your marriage will be a happy one. If you have made adjustments so far with more satisfaction than distress, you are likely to make your marriage and family adjustments satisfactorily. If you are discontented and bitter about your lot in life, you will have to change before you can expect to live happily ever after.

There was a time when people thought that unhappiness in marriage resulted primarily from a poor choice of a marriage partner, from some mysterious incompatibility in sex adjustment, from money troubles, or in-laws, or religious mix-ups, or some other chance circumstance. Sex is important. Whom you marry also makes a difference. Money troubles and in-law interference and religious differences all are part of the picture. We'll look them all over soon. Right now let's get at the most important consideration, the personality bases for marriage.

What Is Personality?

Personality is not just an endowment which some people have and others lack. You are not born with a good or a bad personality. The attractive sparkle or the unfortunate habits which make you stand out from others are not a coincidence or a gift of the gods. The many aspects of every personality are not accidental, but have causes and often elaborate histories. What makes you *you* depends upon years of responding to life's situations. Your personality is made up of many things: the kind of body you started with, the type of home you were born into, the sort of people you have associated with, the way you have been brought up and the things you have learned, and most important of all, how you have felt and acted about them. Your personality is the sum total of the characteristic ways of feeling, responding, and behaving which determine your place in society.

What You Started With. Although you were not born with a ready-made personality, many of the potentials of your personality were already established at birth. You were born with a certain kind of body: it was fat or thin, strong or weak, active or quiet, responsive or relatively insensitive. Your personality is affected greatly by such factors as energy output, drive, push, and indefatigability. There is a physical basis to personality.

People are born with a capacity for responding to situations with varying degrees of mental alertness. Environment can do little for idiots and similar defectives, but even the poorest surroundings cannot black out the brilliance of a genius. Even though the great majority of us fall somewhere between these two extremes, our capacities are usually so much greater than our use of them that we can get little scientific encouragement for attributing our personal failures to a low IQ. Recent studies have indicated that these native talents of ours are greatly influenced by the stimuli for growth they receive and by our active willingness to cultivate them.

You were born a boy or a girl. This fact has far more than a biological significance. Whether you are going to grow up to be a man or a woman, a husband or a wife, a father or a mother, does not mean nearly as much as does your early acceptance of yourself for what you are. An American girl of today no longer needs to apologize for her sex. In certain societies, however, being born a girl would have meant the end

of her right then and there. Even now, the fifth girl born in a family
of girls longing for a boy cannot be guaranteed the welcome and the
feeling of importance and personal security that a long-sought girl baby
in another family might have. Being born a girl in a family where
mother finds womanhood satisfying, or a boy in a family where father
relishes being a man, adds to the biological heritage of sex the important element of sex acceptance that is so vital for good personal and
marriage adjustment.

Oldest, Youngest, or in Between. You were born into your family with
a special place all your own. No other brother or sister came into and
grew up in the same family constellation that you entered. If you were
the oldest you had a unique place in your parents' life for a period of
time. When younger brothers or sisters came along you were faced
with your first powerful threat of deprivation. You had to share your
parents and your home with the newcomers. Were you the youngest
in a large family? Then yours was inevitably the place of the baby of
the family, with all the others ahead of you in age and size and power
and protectiveness. If you were somewhere between the oldest and the
youngest, yours was the problem of stretching ahead to the older ones,
while you hung back at times to play with those younger than you.
Only children, although not as spoiled as popular opinion so often gen-
eralizes them to be, live in an entirely different family set-up from the
youngster who shares his home life with brothers or sisters. Children
who arrive long after the parents' marriage come into a far more stable
but rigid family than do those who come while parents are still getting
acquainted and getting used to the idea of being married. Where and
when you came into your family gave you a unique place with its own
assets and liabilities.

Your Status in the Community. You were born with a place in the community. By being a member of your family, you shared their status in
the neighborhood, the community, and the world. As a child in a
minister's home in the Middle West, or of a tenant farmer's family in
Georgia, or of an old-line Boston family, you took on the distinctive
marks of their particular way of living and became a citizen of their
world. Being born across the tracks or on the hill, being born a Negro
or a white, an Oriental or an Indian, coming from parents whose home-
land is far away or from folk whose forebears migrated to this country

several generations ago, makes a difference in the status of the individual within the community.

SOME SOCIAL CLASS DIFFERENCES

Working class people drop out of school earlier [1]
Middle class people get more education [1]

Working class people go to work sooner [2]
Middle class people start work later at more highly skilled levels [2]

Working class people wean babies at later ages [2]
Middle class people wean babies earlier [2]

Working class people toilet train babies later [2]
Middle class people toilet train babies earlier [2]

Working class people expect their children to be neat, clean, and "mannerable" (traditional conception) [3]
Middle class people more frequently want their children to grow at own rate, to learn, to be happy (developmental conception) [3]

Working class people believe mother's job is to wash, cook, clean, and keep house [3]
Middle class people more often say that a good mother should put emphasis on development of children and self [3]

Working class people have fewer troubles but weather them less well [4]
Middle class people have more troubles but weather them better [4]

Working class people are more promiscuous before marriage [5]
Middle class people have less premarital sex intercourse [5]

Working class people are more direct in sex response [5]
Middle class people have less direct sex response, more petting [5]

[1] W. Lloyd Warner, Robert J. Havighurst, and Martin Loeb, *Who Shall Be Educated?* (New York: Harper, 1944).
[2] W. Allison Davis and Robert J. Havighurst, *Father of the Man* (Boston: Houghton Mifflin, 1947).
[3] Evelyn Millis Duvall, "Conceptions of Parenthood," *American Journal of Sociology* (November, 1946), LII, No. 3, pp. 193–203.
[4] Earl Lomon Koos, "Class Differences in Family Reactions to Crises," *Marriage and Family Living* (Summer, 1950), XII, No. 3, pp. 77–78.
[5] Alfred C. Kinsey, Wardell B. Pomeroy, and Clyde E. Martin, *Sexual Behavior in the Human Male* (Philadelphia: Saunders, 1948), Chap. 10.

With Better Home, School, Medical Care,
Johnny Could Have Been Jimmy

From *The Races of Mankind* by Ruth Benedict and Gene Weltfish (Public Affairs Committee, Inc.)

Research studies such as those reported in sum on page 6 have been numerous in the twentieth century. They show clearly that each of us has a given status in the community that we recognize and that those who know us place us in; and that furthermore, much of what we do and think and feel and want and become is determined in part by the social class to which we belong.

Many of us become aware early in childhood of distinctions in status and try to better our situation. The wife who nags her husband to make something of himself, the husband who insists upon his wife getting into a smart social set, the couple sacrificing to get ahead, all are driven to be better off than they are. Often the reason for selecting a certain marriage partner may be little more than that he or she is a means of stepping up the social ladder, as those who joke about marrying the boss's daughter so well recognize. The drive to climb the social ladder is a motivating force and is often the basis of ambition and the source of conflict.

Becoming Human. We learn the fundamentals of social living through interaction with other people. We learn from them how to get and eat food, how to get around, to use tools and machines, to respond to people and act appropriately in many situations. These learnings would not be possible, of course, without the essential biological equipment which it takes to be human. Consider the house cat — he lives for years in close association with people, yet he grows old and dies — still a cat. Even though a fond mistress dubs him one of the family, he is forever limited by the fact that his own parents were feline and is thereby classed forever in the cat family regardless of his residence.

Many of our assets as persons come to us as members of the human family. We walk upright; our hands have amazing dexterity; our eyes and the flexibility of our bodies make it possible for us to know what is going on; we have voices that are the last word in communication and ears that are built for good reception; we have good heads on our shoulders and a long childhood in which to learn the complexities of human behavior. All these and more are ours, simply because we were born with human potentialities.

But it takes more than biological inheritance to make us truly human. Studies of children reared away from human society reveal that we obtain a great many of our characteristics from associating with other human beings. Gesell [6] has told us of a baby girl who strayed from her mother early in her infancy and lived for years in a friendly wolf den. When she was brought back to human society, she could not walk upright or talk or laugh or express affection or carry on any of the human activities which we take for granted in human children. She howled and prowled like a wolf in the stillness of the night and until her death acted more like a wolf than a child.

Another study [7] indicates that isolation from human companionship results in marked backwardness and deprives the child of the opportunities of learning those roles and habits which we think of as making up personality: the ways of responding to situations, the habits and feelings which make human personality unique. Such evidence supports the established theory of personality development, that personality develops mainly through contact and communication with other persons. [8]

You bring to marriage the particular set of habits and customs of your home-town folk. A child of the Tennessee mountains learns the ways of the hills and brings those patterns to marriage. The city child

[6] Arnold Gesell, "Biography of a Wolf-Child," *Harper's Magazine* (January, 1941).

[7] Kingsley Davis, "Extreme Social Isolation in a Child," *American Journal of Sociology*, Vol. 45, pp. 554–565.

[8] This concept of personality development has been developed through the first four decades of the twentieth century by a number of students, notably, C. H. Cooley, *Human Nature and the Social Order* (1902), *Social Organization* (1909); John Dewey, *Human Nature and Conduct* (1922), *Experience and Nature* (1925); George H. Mead, *Mind, Self, and Society* (1934); and Ellsworth Faris, *The Nature of Human Nature* (1937).

learns another set of folkways and operates in conformity to them. By and large the freer the communication with the greater number of people, the more elaborate is the personality development and the more complex the marriage relationship.

CHECK YOURSELF There are correct and incorrect ways of using the term "personality." Check each of the following statements as true or false according to the description of personality used by the authors in this chapter.

_____ 1 Personality is a kind of inherited charm.

_____ 2 Anyone who wants to can be a fascinating personality.

_____ 3 Some people are born with personality.

_____ 4 Your personality is the sum total of the characteristic ways of behaving, feeling, and responding that determine your place in society.

_____ 5 Everyone is born with the same chance for developing a lovely personality.

_____ 6 Brothers and sisters should rightly have the same kind of personality since they are born into the same family.

_____ 7 If you had been born a member of the other sex you would still have had your same personality.

_____ 8 In the last analysis every personality is self-made.

_____ 9 Personality grows out of family living and rubbing elbows with people outside the family.

_____ 10 All you have to do is take a course in charm to become the kind of personality you would like to be.

★ KEY   True: 4, 9   False: 1, 2, 3, 5, 6, 7, 8, 10 ★

Who Am I?

As soon as a child learns the difference between "I" and "others," he begins to explore the question, "Who am I?" [9] This adventure into the self continues throughout the lifetime of the person, coloring many of his actions and determining much of his personality. When the child is still very small he learns that he feels different in different situations, and that people expect him to behave and to be different as the occasion demands. He may be messy with his sand but not with his pudding. He may hit a ball but not his baby sister. He may urinate but only in prescribed places. Although there is some agreement among

[9] For more extensive treatments of the rise of the self, see Kimball Young, _Personality and Problems of Adjustment_ (New York: Crofts, 1940), Chap. 9, and Erik Erikson, _Childhood and Society_ (New York: Norton, 1950).

his family about such things, in other areas he finds a considerable variety of treatment. He may be mother's darling baby and be expected to be sweet, cuddly, and affectionate when he is with her. His father may expect him to be a little man, keeping a stiff upper lip when he is hurt, not being soft or mushy but showing a sturdy self-control. To his older sister he may be a pest who will very probably be naughty, get into her things, and play the role of general nuisance. To his Sunday school teacher he may be the little angel who passes the hymn books and sings on key. The children next door may run when they see him coming because he is so rough when he plays with them. To each of these people he is a different person. All of these roles are part of his rapidly developing personality. This multiplicity begins early in his development, and its elaboration as he grows older makes for the familiar contradictions of personality. These earlier impersonations, assumed in the child's first experience with people in the family, set the general outlines of the behavior which he brings to marriage. If his family love him and make him feel like a big boy capable of doing great things and being a fine acceptable person, he will be able to make a more successful adjustment in his marriage. If, on the other hand, in his early experiences he is made to feel that he is dirty, bad, inferior, he may carry these feelings of unworthiness right into marriage and beyond, unless he is helped along the way to a more adequate acceptance of himself.

Masculinity-Femininity Learnings. You were born male or female, but you learn to be masculine or feminine.[10] The first are biological inheritances; the second are ways of behaving as a member of a sex group. The masculine or feminine habits are learned first in childhood and become more and more complicated as the child grows into adulthood and gets ready to be married.

People used to say that children imitate adults. Now it seems that something stronger than imitation is at work impelling them so wholeheartedly to take over the behavior of others. As an individual finds people who embody the characteristics that he is seeking for himself, he tends to become deeply attached to them and tries out their ways of behavior. This process of identification starts very early in childhood. As the little boy admires the superior strength and power of his father,

[10] See Amram Scheinfeld, *Women and Men* (New York: Harcourt, Brace, 1944), and Margaret Mead, *Male and Female* (New York: Morrow, 1949).

he identifies himself with him and acts out his own interpretation of the grown-up man. He throws out his chest and struts like his daddy. He wears his father's hat and rubbers. He sits in daddy's chair with daddy's pipe in his mouth. He opens the door for his mother as he sees his father do, kisses her good-by, plays the man of the house as he senses the part to be, and acts out through the years the patterns of masculinity he sees his father following.

Similarly, little girls trot around after their mothers, wanting to wipe dishes when mother does, helping to sweep and dust, talking over the telephone in the same tone of voice, and often telling the same little stories that they hear mother telling. A little girl goes through the many motions of being a mother as she disciplines her dolls, dresses up, goes calling, and puts on tea parties. She takes over many of her mother's attitudes toward the man of the house and often openly welcomes her mother's absence so that she can set the table and take care of father. All this time she is building the basic attitudes of her role as a woman which she is to bring to marriage.

In childhood we begin to practice being the kinds of men and women we are to become, and at the same time begin to formulate our ideas and feelings about what we can expect of others. A girl who is fond of her strong, protective daddy develops a faith in men parallel to the fear of men which is learned by the girl whose father is harsh. The boy whose mother is kind, encouraging, and loving is a great deal more likely to appreciate women than is the man who fears them because his masculinity was undermined by a mother too ready to punish him. We learn out of our experience with these first adults both what seems to be expected of us as members of our sex and what we feel we can expect of people in general.

People do what is expected of them, if they can. The lad who is told that little boys don't cry when they are hurt, that boys must fight for their rights, who sees his father confirming these lessons in his actions, is learning what it means to be a man. If his father is a ne'er-do-well and if his mother and other influential persons try to teach him to be different by scolding him for being "just like your father," he faces the difficult task of choosing which type of man he is going to be — the type he has been identifying himself with, his real father, or the type he is being urged to become, the opposite of his father.

Our conception of the ideal woman is changing so rapidly girls can't be blamed for being confused. The girl who sees her mother getting what she wants by crying for it, and being comforted in her tears, learns that it is all right for a girl to cry; indeed, that it is the way to get along as a woman. Then as she grows older and begins to admire other women who get their satisfactions through rugged determination or more straight-forward approaches, she perceives other ways of playing the feminine role. Her choice of the kind of woman she is to become depends first of all on the type of person she is, where her deepest satisfactions lie, and how she is rewarded and punished as she tries first one and then another pattern. Many girls find it impossible to select from the contradictory alternatives a feminine role with which they can be happy. Happy is the girl who knows the kind of woman she wants to be before marriage, because it is in marriage that femininity receives its greatest test.

Our Human Needs

Certain universal hungers run through the course of human living. So powerful and so insistent are these that they cannot be denied without distorting or impoverishing the personality. These needs have been widely discussed and frequently catalogued. Whatever they are called or however they are listed, they remain the great universal needs that are sought by human beings everywhere.

Our physical needs announce themselves so specifically and unmistakably that they are widely recognized. The need for food is recognized immediately by feelings of hunger. Need for water manifests itself promptly in thirst. Organic demands for rest, exercise, elimination, relief from pain and tension, tolerable temperature, and oxygen vary in the intensity and specificity of their manifestations, yet are quite generally understood. Our attitude toward these physical needs is one of general acceptance. When we are hungry we eat, when tired we sleep, when thirsty we drink, all without embarrassment or defense.

Emotional requirements are neither so well recognized nor so accepted. Deprivations of emotional satisfactions may not show up immediately, and when they do they may appear in any one of many highly individual forms. Behavior directed toward satisfaction of emotional needs is often subtly indirect rather than obviously direct. It usually looks toward *persons* rather than toward *things*. Hence, it is more difficult to understand and to accept.

A hungry man eats without question. But an affection-starved fellow may aggressively demand attention, or he may hit his child who seems to be directing his wife's attention away from himself, or he may sulk or argue or slam out of the door or throw a temper tantrum; he may refuse to eat, or, rarely, he may take the more direct approach and cuddle up to be kissed. Any or all of these behavior expressions of his needs may be unrecognized or ignored by all but the highly sensitive wife. Indeed, he may be further deprived by being punished for actions not acceptable to his wife. So his hunger goes unsatisfied, and he, just as needful as before, makes his adjustment around his deprivation. Prolonged or intense neglect of emotional hungers distorts the personality. Patterns of hostility or discouragement or both develop when the person feels chronically that he must fight for what he wants in a hostile world.

Learning to recognize and meet satisfactorily the emotional needs of each other is a challenge for married couples. Although there are differences among individuals, two types of emotional needs are so universal that they are common to all of us: the need for love and the need for a sense of personal worth.

We Need Love. Love is not just an adornment of life about which we sing and toward which we turn as we begin to go dating. We need love throughout all our lives. Love is as necessary for us as is sunshine and fresh air for the tomato. With love and full acceptance we flourish, and grow strong and happy; without them we develop fears and other symptoms of ill health. As Dr. Benjamin Spock says [11] "this is not just sentimental talk. It is a fact that infants who have long been starved for company and affection . . . may wither in body and spirit. They lose all joy in doing things and seeing people. . . . Such tragedies are rare. But they prove that love is as vital as calories. . . ."

Children recognize many ways of being loved. They warm to mother's words of approval and try even harder to be worthy of her love. They watch for signs of affection on the faces of those around them and direct most of their activities toward winning and holding adult com-

[11] Benjamin Spock, M.D., Keynote Address, Midcentury White House Conference on Children and Youth, Washington, 1950.

mendations. Their need for reassurance is most evident, however, when they have done something wrong or when they are sick or hurt.

The need for love is so strong that half-way measures rarely satisfy. We often hear a mother tell her child, "Mother loves you when you are good." She little realizes when she does this that she is threatening the child with the withdrawal of her love. Vulnerable as he is, the child will hang on tenaciously or abandon his struggle for her love completely, since it is withdrawn so easily. Actually, every child needs the affection of his parents whether or not he has earned it. When he is bad or when he displeases them he needs their love more than ever. Being loved for what he *is* rather than for what he *does* makes him feel included and reassures him that he belongs no matter what.

Adolescents pass through many love-hungry days yearning for a more adult variety of love than is available. The satisfactions of earlier days are no longer so accessible. As legs grow long, the snuggling and cuddling forms of loving are no longer feasible. Adolescents dodge their mother's caresses at the time when they want them most, and protest their sister's kisses with a vigor which implies their need for love. Yet it will be years before they are permitted the full affectional responses of adults in marriage. Adolescence is a period of striving for affection and acceptance characterized by inconsistency and frustration. (See the discussion of adolescent-parent interaction in Chapter Seventeen.)

Adults are more fortunate in finding the means of satisfying their need for love. Within the intimacies of marriage and in the parent-child relation there is opportunity to supply the strongest wishes for intimate response. There is, however, a two-way quality to love that is essential for complete fulfillment. It isn't enough to be loved; one must feel free to love others without fear of being rebuffed. Members of the minority groups in America, Negroes, Indians, Orientals, and others, may be loved by their intimate friends but find themselves so inhibited in affectional expressions outside their own circles that they feel chronically deprived. Likewise, unattractive persons fight the haunting fear of not being fully acceptable and may suppress their friendly tendencies toward others after many uncomfortable rebuffs. Men and women fearing that their expressions of interest in the other sex may be misinterpreted as philandering suppress them so completely that their full needs for response often go unsatisfied. A few unusually emancipated persons respond so forthrightly to others that they are able to express their affection for many persons without being misunderstood or misinterpreted.[12]

These patterns of affectional response are learned throughout a person's lifetime. The general outlines are laid down in childhood when the person first begins to respond to others. If his responses are accepted and reciprocated he learns that it is safe and good to love and be loved, and as he grows older his skills in being warm and friendly increase. As he is neglected or abused or ignored or repelled, he shrinks back into himself or lashes out toward others in ways that protect his hurt ego but fail to satisfy his need. Later reassurances from friends, sweethearts, and mate can gradually rekindle his desire to respond fully and freely again, but the retraining period is often long. The emotionally starved individual is rarely a good marital risk; for even though he needs love desperately, he has been without it so long that his own defenses are apt to repudiate it. The art of loving is learned through years of practice in loving and being loved. And like the starving man who cannot assimilate a full meal at once but must be fed slowly, in small quantities, so the emotionally deprived must be patiently reconditioned to full adult love. Grandmother recognized that she shouldn't marry a man to reform his habits. Today it is known that marrying an unhappy, lonely person in the hope of making him or her happy is equally discouraging. The old patterns of adjusting are so deeply entrenched that only exceptional skill and infinite patience can bring about satisfactory reconditioning.

In summary, we see that we all need to love and to be loved. The expression of this need changes as we mature and as we learn more satisfying ways of meeting it. We may or may not express directly the desire to be loved. Our affectional hungers often go unmentioned and unsatisfied only to betray themselves in inappropriate tantrums and excessive demands on others. But the ability to love fully and genuinely is so important that those married partners who have mastered it find fundamental satisfactions in their marriage that other less skilled persons lack, regardless of how well they may be matched otherwise.

We Need a Sense of Personal Worth. A need which parallels the need for love is the desire to feel that one is worthy of respect. Other people

[12] This problem is discussed in considerable detail in Chapter Seven, "Does Morality Make Sense?" pp. 129–149. See especially section on "Responsive Integrity."

set the standards by which self-appraisal is made, but it is pretty much up to the individual to say which of the goals shall be his to attain. Whatever the realm of achievement may be, he needs to feel that he is a growing, progressing person.

In infancy there is ample evidence of rapid growth and motor development. The first undirected leg and foot movements are preliminary to those which propel the baby across the floor in creeping movements. That first thrilling moment when, by holding onto a chair, he first stands erect and looks his world over from the vertical rather than the horizontal plane is but the threshold of the adventure of learning to walk. Motor development is remarkable — creeping, walking, jumping; riding a tricycle, a scooter, a bicycle; then the first exciting attempts at the wheel of the family car!

Building skills also bring their satisfactions. Whether the media be cookie dough or soft pine lumber, clay or engine parts, erector sets or radio equipment, the satisfaction of making something spurs us on and brings to many a keen sense of progress. While one child finds his satisfaction in using his hands and in getting around, another may find greater pleasure in precocious mental achievements. The Quiz Kids are not only unusually bright youngsters; every one of them has grown up in a home where learning has brought unusually keen satisfactions.

Evidence of the need to feel growth is seen in the popularity of such mental sparring games as quiz shows, popular versions of psychological tests, and crossword puzzles. The reason that many men keep golf scores so religiously is that the opportunity to measure their present performance with some past achievement gives them pleasure. To feel the power of growth within oneself is a magnificent sensation. To look over the past five or ten years and see how far one has come in the ability to get along with people, in the development of a satisfying hobby, in performance in one's business or profession, gives keen satisfaction that is its own reward.

The lack of this sense of personal worth is seen in the multitude of weary-eyed wanderers who, losing faith in themselves, lose faith in others and in life itself. The beaten, hangdog attitude which anticipates failure more often than not finds it. On the other hand, the man who brings to marriage the rewards of years of achievement and growth brings with him the faith that he can work out marriage adjustments as they arise, an attribute to weigh heavily in married life.

Modes of Adjusting to Unmet Needs. Methods of meeting unmet needs are so standardized that psychologists have given them the name *mechanisms.* These modes of adjustment are for the most part substitutive, and rest on willingness to accept something less than the real thing. There are two general types, escape and the defense mechanisms.

The *escape mechanisms* are all characterized by displacement of attention away from the unhappy situation which produced the frustration, and are most frequently carried over from childhood patterns of adjustment. The schoolboy expresses the values of escape when he chants, "He who ducks and runs away lives to duck another day." The trouble is that running away becomes a habit and takes up more time and emotional energy than the original situation warranted. There are some crises from which one should escape, but they are far fewer than our poorly trained emotions would have us believe. Standing up to life, understanding what the problem is and accepting it, develops the mental stamina which is needed in marriage. Escape mechanisms enable the individual to alleviate the pain of frustration temporarily but do nothing about meeting his long-time needs. There are many forms of escape, the most frequent of which are:

1 Daydreaming or fantasy, in which the problem is solved by forgetting it; building air castles in which there are no problems of any consequence.
2 Walking out on the problem or running away from it, refusing to talk about it, passing the buck.
3 Retiring into oneself, being with the group but not of it, developing seclusiveness, withdrawing from contacts.
4 Regressing to infantile levels, backsliding to simpler or earlier forms of behavior which brought attention and satisfaction: bed-wetting, thumb sucking, temper tantrums, refusal to eat, and so on.
5 Becoming sick, developing illnesses that come from mental more than physical causes: headaches, stomach troubles, tics, and other troubles which enable the afflicted to run away from some difficulty.

The *defense mechanisms* are modes of adjustment by which the person bolsters himself when he feels threatened or inadequate. The individual is faced with a need, but as he reaches out to satisfy it he is frustrated by an obstacle or force which proves too great for him. Instead of making a direct attack on the obstacle he allows himself to be maneuvered into taking something less than the real thing; he may pretend he didn't want the need satisfied anyway, or may even deny the existence of the need. The defense mechanisms all have one generic factor in common: they all enable the individual using them to prove to himself that there is nothing wrong with him and that the entire blame for his difficulties can be placed elsewhere. The defense mechanisms most frequently observed include:

1 Compensation, making up for a lack by overworking one's strengths, attaining satisfaction by enjoyment in a substitutive activity.
2 Rationalization, giving "good" excuses for one's behavior instead of the real ones, justifying and defending mistakes as if they were wise decisions. Rationalization is accomplished in a variety of ways:
   a. Being a Pollyanna, pretending that everything is wonderful.
   b. Taking a sour-grapes attitude, pretending you don't want to succeed.
   c. Projecting your failure on others, seeing in them the weakness you are trying to cover up in yourself.
3 Negativism, resisting domination, a common form of defending oneself.

These mechanisms, sometimes conscious, sometimes unconscious solutions to problem situations, are rarely effective, because they are modes of adjustment by subterfuge and substitution and do not really bring the craved satisfactions. Pretending that you don't like boys when you don't have a date doesn't give you a partner for the evening nor prepare you to be more winsome another time. Nor is there any gain in blaming your lack of popularity on your mother, your clothes, or your roommate. Staying in and dreaming about being a pin-up girl with men flocking around you may be one way to spend the evening, but it doesn't get you a date to the prom. Similarly, every other mechanism tends to dodge the really effective ways of reaching the goals that you are striving to attain.

Confident persons develop the conviction that problems lend themselves to solution and choose direct ways of satisfying their needs. They are able to admit to themselves that they are hungry or lonely or angry and then deal with the situation in an acceptable way. The direct approach is learned through success in past forthrightness; it not only brings release for the moment but also establishes the habit of direct satisfaction that assures good marriage adjustment.

Growing Up as a Person

How grown up are you? Are you mature enough for marriage? You may be legally of age, but how about your emotional age? You grow up in many different ways, physically, mentally, and emotionally, and the rate of growth is not uniform. Some growth is regular, predictable, and almost unalterable, whereas some is sporadic and irregular.

Chronologically, one year from today we will be exactly one year older, regardless of what happens. We may suffer a severe illness, move across the country, get married, or just stay put, but nothing will change the regularity of our chronological aging.

Physically our growth within certain broad limits is regular and predictable. Taking into consideration wide individual differences, human development experts can accurately plot the whole timetable of growth from conception through senility. Heredity gets the ball rolling, diet and other environmental circumstances keep it going. Speaking of physical growth only, no man can add a cubit to his stature by willing it.

Mentally we move forward with new experiences and then settle onto plateaus of learning which break as we move on to the next level of growth. This staircase type of development seems to be far more rapid in our infancy when we are busy mastering the fundamentals of communication, locomotion, and general exploration than it is later on. Studies indicate that even while we are at the preschool age, mental growth is affected by our feelings about ourselves and the nature of our surroundings.[13] As we find life challenging and feel that we are able to master it, we learn rapidly and maintain a sustained pattern of mental growth. When we feel stumped or frustrated we may quit trying and stagnate at a level below our true capacity. The indications are that native intelligence is greatly influenced by position in society, by assured opportunities, by where we live and how we interpret life's opportunities. Thus the lower class lad with a high native IQ may not achieve the intellectual growth of an upper middle class fellow with very average native ability, because of the limitations in the values, expectations, and opportunities under which he operates.

Emotionally our growth is highly individual. No other area of growth is more irregular and unpredictable. Some adults are more in-

[13] George Stoddard, *The Meaning of Intelligence* (New York: Macmillan, 1943), pp. 343, 347-392.

fantile emotionally than children whole generations younger. Some emotional responses may develop far ahead of others because habits of responding to situations grow out of experience. Where there are opportunities for learning how to handle a specific situation in competent fashion, the person builds satisfactory emotional habits with regard to it. Because emotional development comes through contacts with others, it can be traced through the stages of social growth that follow.

Stages in Social Growth. As infants we were limited to the hazy world of feelings and sensations. We hadn't been anywhere yet. Our eyes focused poorly. We didn't understand what we heard. All was strange and new and unknown. Our own bodies occupied us entirely at first. We felt hungry and cold and uneasy and lashed out with kicks and screams, our whole squirming body expressing our uneasiness. We expressed our pleasure over food and warmth and a sense of well-being by cooing, gurgling, and kicking out with lusty enthusiasm.

1 *Receiving.* All this time we were entirely on the receiving end of things. We swallowed the milk that was put into our mouths. We slept and wakened and thrashed about without direction or purpose. When we became hungry we were quite intolerant, entirely unaware of the circumstances that made for delays in our feeding. Those first responses to life were explosive. By uncontrolled outcries we demanded our own satisfactions without regard for others. Many of us could point out situations in adult life which evoke the self-centered "gimme" attitude of the infant.

2 *Manipulation.* We were not many weeks old before we learned that there was a relationship between what we did and the satisfactions we enjoyed. We learned that our cries brought mother to comfort us. We discovered that our coos brought father in to play with us. By trial and error we found out what it took to get others to yield to our demands. A little later we developed elaborate systems of teasing, bribing, and coaxing as means of getting people to do what we wanted them to do. One baby learned to depend upon her dimples and sweet ways, while another, feeling less sure that her world was a friendly one, lashed out in temper tantrums when things didn't go her way. The child is supported in any of his manipulations if it is apparent that satisfactions are regularly forthcoming.

Too often adults try to get more of what they want by getting around friends and influencing people. This childish mode of emotional and social adjustment is everywhere apparent both in public and private life, and is evident in the many efforts husbands and wives make to manipulate and control their partners. Fortunately, many children outgrow these attempts to manage others, and before they reach school age are already practicing more grown-up forms of adaptation.

3 *Compromise.* When we were old enough to get hold of toys that belonged to others we trod on their rights, and trouble was brewing. The baby tricks that brought the family to our cradle lost their potency in the rough and tumble of more grown-up family interplay. Mother showed her disapproval of continual wet panties, so we tried to win her smile and avoid her scowl by keeping dry. We sensed the size and strength of our all-powerful parents and tried to win their favor by the kind of behavior they asked of us. Our brothers and sisters had to be won over by some recognition of their rights. If we wanted to play with Jimmy's fire engine, he must be convinced of the desirability of playing with our Kiddie Kar. This familiar "you do this for me and I'll do that for you" type of compromise is more mature than simple manipulation, since it recognizes the values and interests of the other. It is widespread in adult society and runs through much of marital adaptation. Yet it leaves much to be desired in comparison with more cooperative patterns of interaction such as sharing and creative cooperation.

4 *Sharing.* When Jimmy with his fire engine and Johnny with his Kiddie Kar join forces and wheel noisily down the walk in a two-man parade, they are already feeling something that is more fun than merely taking turns and exchanging their equipment. They are beginning to find the satisfactions of sharing which will be rediscovered in games, sports, and other activities that revolve around common values. Playing farmer in the dell and drop the handkerchief may not sound like fun to an adult, but such games were once exciting entrees into sharing with others, a variety of social enjoyment that is not found in solitary activities.

Sharing as a method of social adjustment starts in the family circle and continues on into adulthood. As we learn to note and respect the needs of others and to pool our resources with theirs in the pursuit of mutually satisfying values, we are beginning to enjoy the full richness of interrelationships that may be achieved by emotionally mature adults.

5 *Creative Cooperation.* Beyond the satisfactions of personal sharing lie the rewards of joining forces with others for the pursuit of interests that are bigger than any one of the cooperating partners. The couple that has found the joy of working together in community affairs taps deep wells of satisfaction that quench the thirst of loneliness. The family that lives for something beyond its own immediate wants and throws its resources into creative social projects not only gets more out of life as it goes along, but also helps each of its members attain the kind of maturity that assures them of successful human interrelationships.

Phil and Mary were such a couple. When they finished medical college they married and moved to a Southern mountain community, where they set up a much-needed hospital and clinic service. They worked shoulder to shoulder through the years. As their children came, they too became part of the project. Personal and family disputes were ironed out relatively easily, because there were always more serious things to be done together. One by one the children grew up and went on to college, into marriage, and on into their own vocations. Scattered around the world, they still keep in touch with each other and with the home folks. Phil and Mary had built their marriage on the basis of interest in and devotion to a common purpose. Their children grew up prepared in turn to establish sound marriages, and they found, in the example of their parents, that success in marriage comes from throwing themselves wholeheartedly into meaningful programs outside themselves. Seven new families now carry on the tradition of creative cooperation of losing themselves in something bigger than themselves.

Self-centered people often expect marriage to be a case of "they lived happily ever after." They frequently demand personal satisfactions to the exclusion of the larger needs of the marriage and of themselves. They are often too infantile to lose themselves in values larger than those of the immediate present. Professor Terman [14] in a study of the most frequently mentioned grievances of husbands and wives found most of them to be of the infantile order of social-emotional responses: "selfish and inconsiderate," "complains too much," "not affectionate,"

[14] Lewis M. Terman and associates, *Psychological Factors in Marital Happiness* (New York: McGraw-Hill, 1938), p. 105.

"insincere," "criticizes me," "argumentative," and so on. We conclude from the foregoing that socialization needs to be carried to the level of sharing and creative cooperation to produce personalities that will be best equipped for marriage. Marriage is not child's play but requires the values, habits, and attitudes of adults, and its satisfactions are for those who are emotionally ready to enjoy them.

Fulfillment of Needs through Changing Appetites. Maturity doesn't mean that we are all set. As long as we live we continue to grow. As we develop, our adjustments to others change, as we have just seen. We tend to give more of ourselves and to demand less of others. Yet throughout the whole life span we have needs that other people satisfy.

All living things have to get substances and energies necessary for growth from their surroundings. A tomato plant must have the proper soil and sun and moisture in order to grow at its best. A puppy must be given plenty of chance to suck and to chew, and must be kept warm and allowed to sleep and play, if it is to develop into a healthy, comfortable animal. Children as well as older people have needs that must be satisfied if they are to be healthy, strong, and happy. Many of these needs continue for a lifetime and are common to all people everywhere. Other needs are modified as the person grows older. Food, for instance, is a necessity for everyone, but the form in which it is needed changes with the years. The baby needs carefully prepared milk products that would scarcely satisfy a hungry man who craves a steak. The infant is satisfied with its feeding without table adornments, such as flowers, silver service, candlelight, or linens. The adult builds around his elemental needs for food the need for certain embellishments which tends to become part of the basic requirement. He wants not only the steak, but all the fixings.

The table that follows indicates the way our personality needs change as we develop through childhood and into adulthood. Following the need for intervals of solitude as infants, we develop needs for companionship. To our two or three companions of preschool days we add many more as we get into school; then as adolescents we mingle freely among a great many friends. Similarly our activity needs change from those of the rudimentary interaction of the nonsocialized child to those of the team play and sharing of grown-up activities. Our love needs grow from love of mother to deepening friendships of adolescence by

way of the affection within the family and the group loyalties characteristic of the school years. Our needs for attention change, too, from the
more or less constant care required in infancy. By adolescence we are
ready for the more grown-up forms of attention, such as encouragement,
and reassurance that we can carry on with a minimum of supervision.
The schematic outline of changing needs shown in the accompanying
chart is not to be interpreted rigidly but should be understood as de-
scriptive merely of the stages we attain as personality develops. Likewise, the process of developing from receiving through to cooperating
with others is one that is not determined by age alone. Adults still resort to exchange. We all like to lie back and passively receive at times.

HOW NEEDS CHANGE WITH GROWTH

Infant	Preschool Child	School Child	Adolescent	Adult
		SIGNIFICANT PEOPLE		
Family, espe-cially mother	Two or three playmates and family	Many compan-ions and family	Friends of own age group	Wide variety
		TYPES OF CONTACT		
Solitude and one or two at time	Parallel play	Group games, active play	Boy-girl activities	Many forms
		REQUIREMENTS FROM OTHERS		
Nurturing care (Dependence)	Supervision	Guidance	Encourage-ment in inde-pendence	Affirmation through inter-dependence
		RESPONSE		
Receiving	Exchanging	Sharing	Accommodat-ing	Cooperating

Marriage: The Union of Two Unique Personalities

Preparation for your marriage started before you were born. The planning and the anticipating of your parents had a part in setting the stage
for the kind of personality you have since developed.

As soon as you were born you began to learn about life and about
yourself. You learned that you were important and that people cared
about you by the fondling and attention you received. Your efforts to
grow and do things and become somebody were recognized and encour-

aged. Your mistakes were usually corrected with respect for your need of self-esteem. Your love for mother and father was returned in full measure, and the early jealousies of brothers and sisters gradually diminished. Your talents and abilities were duly pointed out, and your efforts to make something of them were praised. You learned that life was rewarding, and you developed faith in yourself and in your ability to meet it without escape or defense. That aspect of you will approach marriage with courage and eagerness.

There is, however, another part of you as a personality which is not so pleasant. Not all of your life has been equally satisfying and rewarding. You have met defeats and disappointments that have left you feeling small, insignificant, and unworthy. Eating problems in childhood may have left you convinced that you have a weak stomach. Training episodes early in your toddler days have left residues of inadequacy, rebellion, and dirtiness. You received some punishments in your youth which you didn't deserve. A baldheaded neighbor teased you about your hair until you developed a phobia about bald heads and a permanent aversion for those tresses of yours. Your mother was sometimes tired and cross and failed to notice all your hard-earned triumphs. Your father never seemed satisfied with what you did. Your sister was smarter than you and lots quicker, and you never did catch up. You nearly drowned one summer at the lake, and you prickle with fear to this day when you get near water. And so it goes. Some of these situations you recognize and understand and have already learned to take without sidetracking. Others have left their scars without any helpful indication to you of their origin, and they account in part for quirks in your personality that will make married living interesting but difficult.

Marriage is a union of two unique personalities, each with a background and a history. Your marriage partner comes with a peculiarly personal set of patterns and habits for meeting life situations that he has learned in his parental family and elsewhere. He is courteous and pulls out your chair at the table for you, because his mother made so much of such gentlemanly manners when he was younger. But he honks the horn of the car in front of the house like a drugstore cowboy, the pattern he picked up from the fellows at the fraternity house whom he idealized as a frosh. He is a whiz in chemistry; his father and he tinkered with chemistry sets in his basement from the time he was nine. But he's like a big bull in the kitchen, because little boys didn't have any business there when he was most teachable. Add all this together and put in all the other highly individualized responses to people and problems, and do you have your Bill? No, not quite.

Each of you is greater than the sum of all your habits and responses. Each of you operates around a core of feelings and beliefs about yourself. Each of you has a highly individualized personality all your own. Each of you has had a unique childhood and has been influenced in a special way by all the people who have mattered to you since then.

What do you bring to marriage? You bring to marriage all that you have ever been. You bring to marriage your needs and hopes and goals. You come prepared to mean a great deal to your chosen one. Success in your marriage relationship is dependent on bringing to the union the habit of happiness and the capacity to love and to be loved. These are attributes of an emotionally mature personality — the best possible dowry you can bring to marriage.

CHECK YOURSELF   Mrs. B. wants a new fur coat badly. She might use any of several methods to get it from her husband, depending on her stage in the socialization process. Write in for each of the methods listed the levels of socialization represented. Is it *receiving, manipulation, compromise, sharing,* or *creative cooperation?*

———— 1 John dear, you said you wished I would fix your favorite desserts oftener. Well, I want a new fur coat so badly I'll make them every night for two months if you'll get me one.

———— 2 We both need new coats this winter, dear. Since our budget is a little tight right now, what do you say if I earn enough extra money to get us each one?

———— 3 I just had to have a new fur coat right away, so I bought one on your account this afternoon.

———— 4 If we budget carefully we could have our new baby this year. We both want one much more than I want that new fur coat we were looking at last week.

———— 5 Other husbands are proud of the way their wives look. Have you seen that beautiful mink coat Mrs. Jones is wearing? Her husband gave that to her just last week. Of course I know that you don't make as much as Harry Jones, but my tastes are so simple. Just a sheared beaver would satisfy little me.

★ KEY   4 Creative cooperation   5 Manipulation
           1 Compromise   2 Sharing   3 Receiving

Selected Readings

DUVALL, EVELYN MILLIS, *Family Living* (New York: Macmillan, 1950), chaps. 1–4, 7, 8.

FOSTER, ROBERT G., *Marriage and Family Relationships* (New York: Macmillan, 1949), Part I.

HILTNER, SEWARD, *Self-Understanding* (New York: Scribner, 1951).

LANDIS, JUDSON T., AND LANDIS, MARY G., *Personal Adjustment, Marriage and Family Living* (New York: Prentice-Hall, 1950), Chap. 1.

LEVY, JOHN, AND MUNROE, RUTH, *The Happy Family* (New York: Knopf, 1938), Chap. 1.

MOORE, BERNICE MILBURN, AND LEAHY, DOROTHY M., *You and Your Family* (Boston: Heath, 1948), chaps. 1, 2, 5, 6.

PRESTON, GEORGE H., *The Substance of Mental Health* (New York: Rinehart, 1943).

TRAVIS, LEE, AND BARUCH, DOROTHY, *Personal Problems of Everyday Life* (New York: Appleton-Century, 1941), Part I.

Technical References

DAVIS, KINGSLEY, "Extreme Social Isolation in a Child," *American Journal of Sociology*, Vol. 45, pp. 554–565.

DAVIS, W. ALLISON, AND HAVIGHURST, ROBERT J., *Father of the Man* (Boston: Houghton Mifflin, 1947).

DUVALL, EVELYN MILLIS, "Conceptions of Parenthood," *American Journal of Sociology* (November, 1946), LII, 3, pp. 193–203.

ERIKSON, ERIK, *Childhood and Society* (New York: Norton, 1950).

GESELL, ARNOLD, "Biography of a Wolf-Child," *Harper's Magazine* (January, 1941).

KINSEY, ALFRED; POMEROY, WARDELL; AND MARTIN, CLYDE, *Sexual Behavior in the Human Male* (Philadelphia: Saunders, 1948), Chap. 10.

KOOS, EARL L., "Class Differences in Family Reactions to Crises," *Marriage and Family Living* (Summer, 1950), XII, 3, pp. 77–78.

MEAD, GEORGE H., *Mind, Self, and Society* (Chicago: University of Chicago Press, 1934).

MEAD, MARGARET, *Male and Female* (New York: Morrow, 1949).

SCHEINFELD, AMRAM, *Women and Men* (New York: Harcourt, Brace, 1944).

STODDARD, GEORGE, *The Meaning of Intelligence* (New York: Macmillan, 1943).

TERMAN, LEWIS M., AND ASSOCIATES, *Psychological Factors in Marital Happiness* (New York: McGraw-Hill, 1938).

WARNER, W. LLOYD; HAVIGHURST, ROBERT J.; AND LOEB, MARTIN, *Who Shall Be Educated?* (New York: Harper, 1944).

YOUNG, KIMBALL, *Personality and Problems of Adjustment* (New York: Crofts, 1940), Part I.

CHAPTER TWO

"How can it be love at first sight?"

IT'S LOVE!?

How do you know it's love?

Can you tell whether it will last?

What about love at first sight?

What are the principles of attraction?

What is the difference between love and infatuation?

$\mathcal{E}$VERYONE HAS IDEAS AND NOTIONS ABOUT LOVE. NOT ALL OF these opinions jibe, however, with what authorities have found about love feelings; so let's pull out what you think you know and see how right you are. Check each of the following statements which you believe to be true. Then compare your replies with those of the authors. If you agree with most of them, you will enjoy the contents of this chapter. If you don't agree with what the investigators believe to be true, read on and see what it is that they are driving at.

? ? ? ? ? ? ? ?   HOW DO YOU KNOW IT'S LOVE   ? ? ? ? ? ? ? ?

_____ 1 When love hits you, you know it.
_____ 2 It is possible to sometimes dislike a person whom you love at other times.
_____ 3 Puppy love is not a real love feeling.
_____ 4 When you are really in love, you just aren't interested in anyone else.
_____ 5 When you fall head over heels in love, it's sure to be the real thing.
_____ 6 There is only one kind of love feeling.
_____ 7 It is quite normal for a person to love several different people at once.

———— 8 You never love two people in quite the same way.

———— 9 Love that grows slowly over a long time is not as satisfying as the sudden thunder-and-lightning variety.

———— 10 Love doesn't make sense. It just *is*.

———— 11 Once two people find that they love each other, that settles it; they should marry as soon as possible, no matter what.

———— 12 Love without marriage is a serious tragedy and will probably ruin one's life.

———— 13 Loving someone besides the one to whom you are married need not wreck your marriage.

———— 14 Before the average person becomes an adult, he will have loved many people.

———— 15 Love isn't anything you can study or know anything about; it's too emotional.

Here are the facts:

1 (*Incorrect.*) Love feelings are of many kinds and only rarely are of the sudden, sure nature indicated in the statement.

2 (*Correct.*) Not only is it possible, but it is also extremely likely that people who are loved will be disliked in some situations. Human nature has too many facets to be expected to show only the best one at all times. Disliking loved ones in some situations is a common experience.

3 (*Incorrect.*) Although puppy love may not be a mature type of love, it nevertheless is a love feeling. The only trouble with puppy love feelings is that, taken too seriously, they may lead to a dog's life.

4 (*Wrong.*) Being in love tends to make other persons and things more rather than less lovable. The truly loving person loves and is interested in most of the people he or she knows well. If love cut off all other interests, wouldn't it tend to become monotonous? We'll never know, because love doesn't operate that way. We have heard, "All the world loves a lover." The converse is also true, "Lovers love all the world."

5 (*Wrong.*) Undergoing such tremendous emotional excitement as is referred to in the popular concept of "falling head over heels in love" is not the best indication that the feeling is true and lasting love. Later in this chapter we will discuss some more reliable love yardsticks. Will you wait until then for more on this?

6 (*No.*) Of course not. There are many, many kinds of love feelings: tenderness, passion, mother love, ecstasy, peaceful security, etc., to name just a few of the contrasting kinds of love feelings.

7 (*Correct.*) It is normal to love several people at once. In fact, it is one of the ways that normality is gauged. Mate love tends to be sexually exclusive, but love in its broader sense is richly inclusive. Love begets love and normally fosters love feelings.

8 (*Correct.*) Just as no two persons are identical, so no two combinations of persons can be the same. The love feelings we have for dear old

friends may be quite different from those we have in an exhilaratingly new relationship. Love for grandpa's sweetness is quite different from the vigorous mate love we feel for a marriage partner, and so on and on through the multitude of combinations possible in a lifetime of warm relationships with hundreds of people.

9 (*Wrong.*) *Satisfying* is the catch. Truly satisfying love relationships are far more apt to be of the long-term, growing variety than of the whoop-whoop-hurrah kind, which frequently dies out like fireworks after a very pretty show.

10 (*Incorrect.*) Generally love makes sense. It is governed by the same natural laws that determine all life. A love has a history that is socially determined and that modifies and directs its present and its future. The person in love may not know why he fell for this particular girl, any more than he may be aware of why he likes certain foods, or what happens to them after he has eaten them, or why they make him strong or sick or fat. But to the scientist, most of these processes are becoming increasingly understandable. So, to some extent, is this mysterious thing called love. Science, which began with a study of the stars in the skies, now is making headway in understanding the stars in lovers' eyes. Investigations tend to show that the laws of attraction are reasonable, reliable, and capable of being understood.

11 (*Incorrect.*) The popular belief in this fallacy is one of the big reasons for so much unhappiness and discord in marriage. There are so many kinds of love feelings that a person who takes this position seriously finds himself in emotional hot water most of the time. Chasing down every tempting trail after a new marriage partner is an exhausting experience.

12 (*Nonsense.*) Can you see why from the answer to the previous question? And isn't it slightly dreary to think that all of life outside of marriage must be completely devoid of warmth?

13 (*Correct.*) We've really been answering this all along, haven't we? Marriages are not so often wrecked by love as by the lack of it!

14 (*Surely.*) We all begin to love before we are out of our cradles; our own toes and fingers, our mothers, our dads, our sisters and brothers, the boy next door, the kindergarten teacher, the scout master, the new girl in second grade, Uncle Louis-who-always-brings-candy, the cub scout troop (all nineteen of them), the girl in the pink sweater, the boy who walked us home from the party — all these and many more have come in for a share of our loving. Indeed, by the time most of us are adults, we are old hands at the game of love!

15 (*No!*) If it were true, why bother with a study like this? Many successful investigations have been carried out and a great deal of information has been made available already. And that's what the rest of this chapter is going to deal with. Besides, who said that emotions cannot be understood? The way we feel about things makes some sense when we know something of the principles of human behavior in the same way that the workings of electricity become predictable to the engineer who knows what to expect. So let's see what we know about love. . . .

What Is Love?

Love is not easy to define. It is a word that covers many feelings. We may feel good, or we may feel very blue, all because we are in love. We may be tenderly protective or lustily aggressive; we may work furiously or daydream for weeks; we may worship devotedly or exploit hungrily; we may give or we may take — all in the name of love!

Love may look like its opposite, hate, when its face is distorted with vanity, possessiveness, or jealousy. One big difference between love and hatred is that love is an irradiation. It flows outward from the loving person in a warm current of feeling toward others generally. Hate, on the other hand, tends to focus on the hated one with heavy concentration. There are no more perfect loves than there are perfect persons. But, as Sidney Harris [1] says, it is the direction and not the degree that is most important. Love turned outward can always grow. Turned inward or concentrated too intensely on one object, love cannot survive its own stagnation. It seems to be this growth factor in love that assures its permanence. As Magoun so ably defines love:

Love is the passionate and abiding desire on the part of two or more people to produce together conditions under which each can be and spontaneously express his real self; *to produce together an intellectual soil and an emotional climate in which each can flourish,* far superior to what either could achieve alone." [2] (Italics ours)

Love then is fulfillment through healthy growth with and for another. It is self-realization in an atmosphere conducive to human growth. It is an emotional response to others who meet our basic personality needs.[3] Two people in love so mutually meet each other's needs that they both thrive in their "togetherness" more fully than could either alone. In this sense love grows as the personality develops, and is capable of ever-changing, ever-deepening, ever-widening involvement.

Self-Love and Outgoing Love. The Greeks had two words for love — *eros* and *agape.* *Eros* tends to center in sexual love. It is that love for another that comes spontaneously and longs to be reciprocated.[4] It is

[1] Sidney Harris, "Strictly Personal," *Chicago Daily News* (February 2, 1952), p. 10.
[2] F. Alexander Magoun, *Love and Marriage* (New York: Harper, 1948), p. 4.
[3] Robert Winch, *The Modern Family* (New York: Holt, 1952), Chap. 15.
[4] Esther Adams, "Eros and Agape," *Marriage Guidance* (August, 1950), pp. 6–7.

possessive and demanding. We have called it the "orange squeezer" type of love that is implied when one says "I love oranges," in which the emphasis is on one's own appetite and not concerned with the fate of the orange! Erotic love wants something in return and if frustrated may turn to hate. This is the "hell has no fury like a woman scorned" [5] brand of love . . . primarily self-love.

Agape, in contrast, cannot be frustrated because it is not demanding. It is outgoing, overflowing joy in fellowship. Its pleasure is in being and in giving. It releases the freedom of cooperation that people find in thinking, yearning, developing, and achieving together. This is the kind of love that inspires the full giving of oneself freely to causes and purposes beyond oneself. It is close to the truth that Jesus described when he said, "He who loses his life shall find it." (Matthew 10:39)

There are satisfactions of personal needs in every marriage, often rich and intense. But if there is nothing more to it than satisfying selfish needs, the marriage will not and cannot endure; for as soon as someone else appears who seems able to give more satisfaction, the partner is tossed out like last week's newspaper. Love that lasts involves a real and genuine concern for others as persons, for their values as they feel them, for their development and growth. As time goes by, those we love become increasingly dear to us. We watch their progress with joy. We are saddened by their sufferings and disappointed with them in their mistakes. Because we love them, we are able to lose some of our petty selfishness in thoughts and actions directed beyond ourselves. This outgoing type of love has capacities for infinite variety and for satisfying deep hungers within us. This is the love that builds a strong, enduring marriage.

Principles of Attraction. Very few of us know just why we like the people to whom we are attracted; our likes and dislikes are not rational or planned. The people we like are not always the folk that the social scientist would recommend for us as companions, either for a lifetime or for a few months. Yet these little-understood forces of personal attraction wield a mighty weight in the process of falling in love and getting married, and often overshadow more rational and sensible considerations in the choice of a wife or husband.

[5] "Heaven has no rage like love to hatred turned,
  Nor hell a fury like a woman scorned."
    Congreve — *The Mourning Bride*, Act III, Scene 8.

Some of the unconscious tendencies that determine our preferences for people are these:

1 We tend to like the people and the things that remind us of pleasant and comfortable experiences in our past, many of which go way back into our early childhood and are forgotten except for the powerful, unconscious role they continue to play in our choices. "I loved him the minute I set eyes upon him."

2 We tend to be repulsed by the people and the things that are associated with uncomfortable and unpleasant experiences in our past. The original painful experience may be no longer remembered, but its influence continues to deflect us from anything and anybody that resembles some aspect of that unhappy situation. "Don't ask me why, I just don't like her."

3 We tend to be attracted to those people who reassure us, do not make us feel less worthy or less able or attractive than we like to think we are. "She's just too smart to suit me," or "I can't stand him, he's always so *superior*," and "She makes me feel as though I am somebody."

4 We tend to seek the people who are considered attractive by those around us and to leave the unsought alone. "I want the kind of girl the other fellows will whistle at."

5 We tend to like those who satisfy some particularly hungry spot in our make-up. The boy who has not had as much mother love as he wanted may be strongly attracted to a mother type of girl. "I don't know why I love her. She just gives me all I need."

6 We tend both to reproduce and to repudiate the relationships in which we grew up. A boy may be attracted to anyone who reminds him of his mother and who can reproduce the feeling of the old parent-child relationships. A girl may be unable to tolerate anyone who even remotely reminds her of her father, a repudiation of the former parent-child relationships. "I want a girl just like the girl who married dear old dad," or "I can't stand her. Who does she think she is, my mother?"

The Course of Love. The girls that Ellis studied [6] reported that they first fell in love with or became infatuated with a man or boy when they were near twelve years of age. They also indicated that between the ages of twelve and eighteen they had been in love with or infatuated with more than six different men or boys. Although further research is needed in this area, general observation corroborates this finding that young people do tend to experience specific love feelings early and to be attracted

[6] Albert Ellis, "Questionnaire Versus Interview Methods in the Study of Human Love Relationships. II, Uncategorized Responses," *American Sociological Review* (February, 1948), XIII, No. 1, pp. 62–64.

to a variety of love objects of the other sex throughout the entire second decade of life.[7]

Two other investigators have shown graphically that college students are able to plot the course of their love affairs between four levels of involvement: love, attraction, indifference, dislike. The most frequently reported curve was regular, beginning with indifference, moving slowly or precipitately upward through attraction to love and then (a) dropping again to indifference (indicating that the affair had terminated), or (b) remaining at a high level of love in ongoing affairs. About one-fifth of the students both male and female reported irregular courses of love, while a somewhat smaller group showed the course of love as they had known it to be vacillating or "cyclical" (see typical graphs and percentages reporting each below).

There is nothing absolute about the data below. They are merely indications of the variable nature of love emotions among young people.

PROFILES OF LOVE EXPERIENCE *

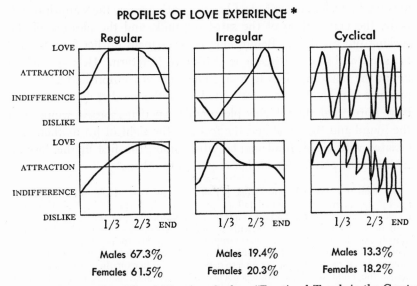

	Regular	Irregular	Cyclical
Males	67.3%	19.4%	13.3%
Females	61.5%	20.3%	18.2%

* Clifford Kirkpatrick and Theodore Caplow, "Emotional Trends in the Courtship Experience of College Students as Expressed by Graphs with Some Observations on Methodological Implications," *American Sociological Review* (October, 1945), X, No. 5, pp. 619–626.

[7] Evelyn Millis Duvall, *Facts of Life and Love* (New York: Association Press, 1950). Based on thousands of questions asked by teen-age young people of both sexes.

Such findings reaffirm the importance of two other questions now to be discussed: 1. how does the capacity to love develop? and 2. how can you tell that you are in love?

Learning to Love

Love does not come as a sudden answer to life's basic needs. We develop the capacity to love gradually through years of interaction with other people. We learn to love just as we learn to eat and to walk and to read. The native tendencies and potentialities are there from the beginning. Given favorable opportunities, these capacities develop and flower; and as in all learning, first experiences set the stage for later responses. Therefore, to trace the development of the ability to love and to be loved, we must go back to the early days of infancy.

Developing the Capacity to Love. In his mother's arms the baby receives his first lessons in learning to love. As she holds him close in nursing, he feels the comfort of her supporting arms, the warmth of her body, the gratification of the satisfying milk, and the pleasure of the sucking process itself. Before long his eyes focus on her face, he sees her smile and soon manages one of his own in return. He coos back to her as she talks and sings to him. The glow of comfort he feels in her presence quickly becomes associated with the mother herself, as the baby learns that these highly pleasurable experiences arrive wrapped in the sound and the smell and the feel and the sight of his mother. Associated with all his fundamental satisfactions, this first mother-love establishes the pattern for further responses to others.[8]

[8] Robert F. Winch, *The Modern Family* (New York: Holt, 1952), especially pp. 396–400, develops in some detail the process by which the child effects this transfer of affection from the parents, more usually the mother, to successive substitutes until he settles on an age mate with whom he experiences "companionship love." Winch explains the process as maturation of the capacity to love without "leaning" dependently on another. From the extremely dependent love of the infant for the mother, based on the infant's complete dependence on her for the gratification of his needs, the child develops self-dependence in many areas of his life, diffuses his "needs-meeting" among many individuals outside the family, and eventually does not need to have all his needs met through one all-consuming love. By means of trial-and-error he discovers persons whose needs to gratify others complement his needs to be gratified. His parents become alternates in his love life, and companionship love of an interdependence-of-peers sort is experienced with one or more age mates. In marriage, this love, based on complementary needs, becomes a solidifying factor, particularly if the love patterns keep abreast of the changing needs of the partners throughout their marriage cycle.

If the child is frustrated in this first important relationship, he may come to feel that he is living in a hostile world in which he must fight for what he needs; or if the outlook is too discouraging, he may lapse into the listless lethargy described so vividly by Ribble.[9] If he is neglected, handled harshly, or fed too little, the unfortunate child develops irritability instead of the glow of the happy child. He feels frustration in continued hunger, and he misses the cuddling support and warmth of the mother. He whimpers his discontent, lashes about in his discomfort, cries out in distress, and if no relief is forthcoming he may lapse into troubled, discouraged apathy.

The neglected child has been deprived of the first opportunities of feeling and responding warmly to another. He starts life, therefore, either like a bully with a chip on his shoulder or like a puppy with his tail between his legs. Years later as an adult he may attempt to compensate for his childhood deprivations by excesses and undue personal demands upon others. His early protests may continue into marriage in the form of unpredictable, little-understood aggressions toward his wife and children.

Diffusion of Love to Others. Mother may be the first love, but she is not the last! Father often enters into the affectional set-up very early. As he helps bathe and dress the child, as he comes in for a frolic before bedtime, as he tucks the infant under the covers, he too becomes an object of the child's love. Soon his voice and his step are awaited with eagerness, and his presence brings peculiarly satisfying meanings to the child. The child now responds to both father and mother with love.

The baby learns still another type of love response from children. Their play with the child is less tender; their laughter is a bit more spontaneous, their voices louder and their touch a little rougher. With them the baby learns a new type of love, hearty and carefree. The familiar roughhouse of the typical household finds the baby the gleeful center. Now he's beginning to feel one of the gang. It took mother to nurse him through early infancy. It took father to teach him that men are good and very much a part of his life. Brothers and sisters round off his early emotional education by helping him feel that he belongs, that he is one of them — a part of the family.

[9] Margaret A. Ribble, *The Rights of Infants* (New York: Columbia University Press, 1943). See also our earlier discussion of the basic love needs of children, pp. 13–15, 23–24.

Early in the child's life come other adults to strengthen and to modify the feelings built up toward parents. Relatives, neighbors, and teachers become substitute parents as the youngster tries out his parent-learned responses on them. These adults play important roles in the lives of children, giving them the comforting security so needed by youngsters growing away from early parent-child relationships. Baruch gives a particularly clear illustration from a nursery school in the following episode:

. . . a two year old is having trouble making his adjustment in the new situation. He has been raised by his grandmother, and now his grandmother has gone to work. He sulks at the teachers and shrugs away. But, after a while, he navigates into the kitchen, settles himself there on a chair, and does not wish to budge. The head-teacher, observing, suddenly realizes, "It's the cook." As she said later, "The rest of the staff was so much younger than the only mother he had ever known. But not the cook. She's an elderly, comfortable, grandmotherly soul. So, we suggested that she take over and that she give him some loving between paring carrots and potatoes. He spent two days sitting in the kitchen, dragging the toys in under her feet, until he got the feeling of anchorage and belongingness, and could wander further apace." [10]

Most of us remember the warm friendly adults who made us feel important back in those days when we went exploring for new relationships. Unfortunately, not all adults were equally friendly, and some of us also remember the shame and ignominy of early experiences with sarcastic, blaming persons, some of whom were teachers who shamed and ridiculed us and rebuffed our struggling efforts to please. All too few educators realize the importance of selecting leaders and teachers who can take the place of parents in the molding and directing of love responses of growing children. Teachers especially should be persons who are themselves emotionally mature enough to guide the affectional as well as the intellectual development of their charges. The typical experience of the youngster falling in love with his scout leader or teacher should be a happy one, guided and understood by the adults involved. It is a further step in the direction of the mature, heterosexual love which unites people in marriage.

Some young people become fearful of social intercourse and avoid the very gatherings that they most crave. Others mask their insecurity

[10] Dorothy W. Baruch, "Are Teaching Techniques Meant for Children?" *Journal of Consulting Psychology*, Vol. 8, No. 2 (March–April, 1944), p. 111.

by a pretense at sophistication and play the bravado role of a "wolf." They may go in heavily for petting rather than explore the fuller personal meanings of boy-girl relationships. The trauma and the disappointment of many of these blind-alley experiences affect the ability to love and seem to be related to later marital unhappiness.

Teen-age young people who have had a hearty experience in loving and being loved in a happy family circle make these adjustments relatively successfully. There are two reasons for their success: 1. they have parents who are adequate examples of people in love, and 2. they have had years of practice in learning to respond with affection and consideration to loved ones.

Learning to Express Affection Takes Practice. Families differ widely in the ways in which their members express affection for one another. In some homes loving words and gestures are rare; in others, the children grow up from babyhood surrounded by warm assurances of love. Some married couples hide their love for each other behind a wall of reserve, while others continue to show their affection by all the small meaningful signals that develop through years of close association. Children growing up in a home where father kisses mother good-by in the morning and returns affectionately to her side in the evening learn that "papa loves mama." Children who have been taught how to express their feelings for others as they grow up, reach marriage with the fundamental skills required for living intimately with another person. On the other hand, the youngster who has never known the meaning of demonstrated love is apt to be clumsy in his efforts to express his feelings.

Elsie was such a person. Her mother died when she was very young, and she was raised by her father and his unmarried sister. Her father so mourned for his young wife that he dared not express the feeling that he had for the little girl who so closely resembled her. The maiden aunt was also bottled up, with no outlets save mournful love ballads. For years the little girl didn't know the meaning of being kissed or fondled. As she grew up and realized that other people were more overt in expressing their affection, she was shocked and vowed that no man would ever fuss around her. In the course of time Elsie found herself involved in a friendship with a fine young man whom she respected highly. They became engaged without having had closer contact than an occasional handclasp. Two weeks before their marriage they still

♡♡♡♡♡♡♡♡♡♡♡♡♡♡♡♡♡♡♡♡♡♡♡♡♡♡♡♡♡♡

DIFFERENCES BETWEEN LOVE AND INFATUATION

Love

1 Tends to occur first in late teens and in the twenties [1]

2 Attachment simultaneously to two or more tends not to be frequent [1]

3 Most cases last over a long period of time [1]

4 More slowly develops again after a love affair has ended [1]

5 Often used to refer to present affair [1]

6 Object of affection is more likely a suitable person [2]

7 Parents tend to approve [2]

8 Broadly involves entire personality [2]

9 Brings new energy and ambition, and more interest in life [3]

10 Associated with feelings of self-confidence, trust, and security [3]

11 Accompanied by kindlier feelings toward other people generally [3]

12 Joy in many common interests and an ongoing sense of being alive when together precludes boredom [4]

13 Relationship changes and grows with ongoing association, developing interests, and deepening feelings [4]

14 Accompanied by willingness to face reality and to tackle problems realistically [5]

---

[1] Albert Ellis, "A Study of Human Love Relationships," *Journal Genetic Psychology* (1949), No. 75, pp. 61–71.

[2] Paul Popenoe, "Infatuation and Its Treatment," *Family Life* (March, 1949), IX, No. 3, pp. 1–2.

[3] Albert Ellis, "A Study of the Love Emotions of American College Girls," *International Journal of Sexology* (August, 1949), pp. 1–6.

♡♡♡♡♡♡♡♡♡♡♡♡♡♡♡♡♡♡♡♡♡♡♡♡♡♡♡♡♡♡♡♡♡

AS REVEALED IN CONTEMPORARY RESEARCH STUDIES

Infatuation

1 Tends to be more frequent among young adolescents and children under teen age [1]

2 Simultaneous attachments to two or more tends to be frequent [1]

3 Tends to last but a short time (only a few weeks in most cases) [1]

4 More quickly reoccurs soon after a given involvement has ended [1]

5 Is often the term applied to past attachments [1]

6 Tends to focus more frequently on unsuitable person [2]

7 Parents more often disapprove [2]

8 Narrowly focused on a few traits; mostly physical thrill [2]

9 Less frequently accompanied by ambition and wide interests [3]

10 Feelings of guilt, insecurity, and frustration are frequent [4]

11 Tends to be self-centered and restricted [4]

12 Boredom is frequent when there is no sexual excitement or social amusement [4]

13 Little change in the relationship with the passing of time [4]

14 Problems and barriers are often disregarded; idealization may have little regard for reality [5]

---

[4] Joe McCarthy, "How Do You Know You're in Love?" *McCall's Magazine*, Reprint, pp. 26–27, 88–90.

[5] Stephen Laycock, Director of Mental Hygiene, Canada (informal communication).

had not kissed each other. In panic the girl, now a young woman of nearly twenty-five, came to a marital guidance center for help. She shivered as she told of her fears in anticipating her marriage, of her desire to be kissed and loved by this man who meant so much to her. Yet she felt impelled to fight off his advances, felt herself freeze whenever he came near. The counselor recommended postponing the marriage until the couple could build up a more satisfactory mode of expressing their affection. After several months, the counselor with step-by-step guidance was able to open up the affectional outlets that would prepare them for the married happiness they both wanted. Elsie and her husband, even so, will probably never be as free in expressing their love for each other as couples whose childhood experiences in loving were adequate. Learning to express affection takes practice.

How Can You Know?

Love is a highly variable sentiment. It may be superficial and trivial or it may be splendid and deep. Love may be a transient appeal that disappears after a few heavy dates, and again it may foster a relationship which will become stronger with the years. It would be folly to decide whether or not to marry by the quality of the love sentiment at a given moment. In some instances the very intensity of the feeling may be a danger signal. How can you know that it's the type of love on which happy marriages are based? One of the first steps is to distinguish between love and infatuation. (See table on pages 40–41.)

Seven Ways to Tell If Your Love Will Last. There is no magic daisy petal test by which you can measure the extent or the depth or the permanence of your love feelings. Yet, if you are going to try to base your marriage upon your love for each other, you must have some criteria by which to judge whether yours is the kind of love that may be expected to last in marriage. Here are some ways to help you tell.

LASTING LOVE . . .

> #### has *many facets:*
> tender, passionate, comradely, protecting, highly specific in its focus, widely general in its diffusion.
>
> #### is *outgoing:*
> radiating out in its values, concerns, and interests to others' happiness and well-being.

is *motivating:*
releases energy for work, is creative, brings an eagerness to grow, to improve, to work for worthy purposes and ideals.

is *sharing:*
what one has and what one is strive to be shared; thoughts, feelings, attitudes, ambitions, hopes, interests, all are sharable.

is *a we-feeling:*
thinking and planning are in terms of "we"; what *we* want, how *we* feel, what *we* will do, rather than "I" centeredness.

is *realistic:*
faults, weaknesses, and problems are faced together as part of reality; willingness to work on building the relationship.

changes and grows with time:
time is the surest test — if the relationship has grown through many emotional climates, further association, developing interests, and deepening feelings, the chances are that it will continue to grow as long as the persons do.

By gaining insight into ourselves and into the nature of our past and present involvements, we may learn in some measure how to appraise the depth and the strength of a particular relationship. If we can love another deeply enough to subordinate ourselves to the relationship and lose ourselves in values common to both of us, we have love enough to marry on.

Selected Readings

CHRISTENSEN, HAROLD, *Marriage Analysis* (New York: Ronald Press, 1950), Chap. 7.

DUVALL, EVELYN MILLIS, *Facts of Life and Love* (New York: Association Press, 1950), chaps. 9, 10, 13, 14.

DUVALL, SYLVANUS M., *Before You Marry* (New York: Association Press, 1949), Chap. 1.

FOLSOM, JOSEPH K., *The Family and Democratic Society* (New York: Wiley, 1934, revised, 1943), Chap. 11.

MAGOUN, F. ALEXANDER, *Love and Marriage* (New York: Harper, 1948), Chap. 1.

MERRILL, FRANCIS E., *Courtship and Marriage* (New York: Sloane, 1949), chaps. 2, 3.

POPENOE, PAUL, "Infatuation and Its Treatment," *Family Life* (March, 1949), pp. 1–2.

WINCH, ROBERT F., *The Modern Family* (New York: Holt, 1952), chaps. 12–15.

Technical References

DYMOND, ROSALIND, "Personality and Empathy," *Journal of Consulting Psychology* (October, 1950), XIV, No. 5, pp. 343–350.

ELLIS, ALBERT, "A Study of Human Love Relationships," *Journal of Genetic Psychology* (1949), No. 75, pp. 61–71.

——, "A Study of the Love Emotions of American College Girls," *International Journal of Sexology* (August, 1949), pp. 1–6.

——, "Questionnaire Versus Interview Methods in the Study of Human Love Relationships. II, Uncategorized Responses," *American Sociological Review* (February, 1948), XIII, No. 1, pp. 61–65.

——, "Some Significant Correlates of Love and Family Attitudes and Behavior," *Journal of Social Psychology* (1949), No. 30, pp. 3–16.

KIRKPATRICK, CLIFFORD, AND CAPLOW, THEODORE, "Emotional Trends in the Courtship Experience of College Students as Expressed by Graphs with Some Observations on Methodological Implications," *American Sociological Review* (October, 1945), X, No. 5, pp. 619–626.

PRESCOTT, DANIEL, "Role of Love in Human Development," *Journal of Home Economics* (March, 1952), pp. 173–176.

WALLER, WILLARD, AND HILL, REUBEN, *The Family: A Dynamic Interpretation* (New York: Dryden, revised 1951), Chap. 7.

WINCH, ROBERT, "Some Data Bearing on the Oedipus Hypothesis," *Journal of Abnormal and Social Psychology* (July, 1950), Vol. 45, No. 3, pp. 481–489.

CHAPTER THREE

"Well . . . Can't you say something!"

DATING: PRACTICE MAKES PERFECT

What makes a person popular?

How about petting as a pastime?

Why are some folks so slow starting to date?

What is there to do on a date besides the same old stuff?

What can you do about the fast ones?

*W*HEN YOU MARRY, YOU MARRY SOMEONE YOU ALREADY KNOW. The strange prince who dashes up and carries the blushing damsel away on his white horse is no more in evidence today than is his prancing charger. Couples find each other in contemporary society through a variety of associations that precede courtship and marriage. These paired contacts between the sexes go by the name of dating.

What Is a Date?

Young people themselves usually think of a date as a mutually agreed upon association of a boy and a girl, or a man and a woman, for a particular occasion or activity. Dating today differs from courtship, as it used to be defined, in that young people now can date each other without either of them or their parents assuming that because they date they are seriously interested in each other. They may be. But just the fact of their dating each other does not commit them in the future.

As such, dating is a phenomenon of the twentieth century. Before then it was usual for the boy to request permission of the girl's parents to "court" her before any paired association took place. Courtship implied in the eyes of the couple, the parents, and the community a responsibility for the future that the greater freedom of current dating does not.

Dating is defined differently by some observers than by others. Willard Waller observing college young people, after World War I in the East, took a pessimistic view of dating as largely exploitative and competitive. Margaret Mead and Geoffrey Gorer have since echoed these reflections. Students of the family such as Burgess and Locke, on the other hand, have seen dating as preliminary to courtship and as having functions preparatory to courtship and marriage. A third concept of dating formulated by persons working closely with large numbers of high school and college students is that dating is a value in itself both in personality development and in education for future stages of involvement and commitment. These three concepts of dating are outlined below.

HOW DATING IS DEFINED [1]

Dating as a dalliance: a time-filler [2]	Prestige in rating
	Status in peer group
	Excitement in pretended involvement
	Pursuit of a thrill
	Exploitative
	Capacity to love impaired
	Many are hurt
	Poor education for marriage
Dating as preliminary to courtship [3]	Opportunity for association with other sex
	Variety of social experience
	Range of social contacts
	Selection of compatible pairs
	Opportunities for choice of potential mate

---

[1] See Samuel Harman Lowrie, "Dating Theories and Student Responses," *American Sociological Review* (June, 1951), Vol. 16, No. 3, pp. 334–340.

[2] See especially, Willard Waller, "The Rating and Dating Complex," *American Sociological Review* (October, 1937), No. 2, pp. 727–734; *The Family, a Dynamic Interpretation* (New York: Cordon, 1938), pp. 222–235; and Margaret Mead, *Male and Female* (New York: Morrow, 1949), pp. 281–295; also, Geoffrey Gorer, *The American People* (New York: Norton, 1948), pp. 106–132.

[3] Ernest W. Burgess and Harvey Locke, *The Family* (New York: American Book, 1945), pp. 382–393.

Dating as a social
value in itself [4]

Enriched personality development
Broad experience
Wide acquaintance
Skills in mixing socially
Poise and self-confidence
Rational selection of friends among other sex
Prestige among associates
Satisfaction of social goals

Some Do Not Date

Those who take the "dating is dalliance" point of view might consider the young person who does not date as fortunate. He is not wasting his time in a time-filler that leads to nothing but pain. Apparently young people themselves do not consider the lack of dates as an advantage. Indeed one of the most frequent problems that both boys and girls raise is that of not having enough contact with the other sex through dating. The Purdue University Opinion Panel for Young People, in a systematic country-wide analysis of representative young people from 12 to 20 years of age, reports that students in senior high schools, in significant percentages, indicate their concern for the lack of dating opportunities and skills.[5]

SOME YOUNG PEOPLE REPORT THEY DO NOT DATE

	BOYS	GIRLS
Seldom have dates	48%	39%
Don't have a girl (boy) friend	41	30
Don't know how to keep girls (boys) interested	25	33
Are bashful about asking girls for dates	34	
Don't know how to ask a girl for a date	26	
Wonder whether anything is wrong with going places "stag"	23	
Wonder whether it is all right to accept "blind dates"		29

[4] Lowrie, *op. cit.*, p. 337; also, Evelyn Millis Duvall and Reuben Hill, *When You Marry* (New York: Association Press, 1945), Chap. 3; and Evelyn Millis Duvall, *Facts of Life and Love* (New York: Association Press, 1950), Chaps. 5, 6.

[5] H. H. Remmers and Benjamin Shimberg, *Examiner Manual for the SRA Youth Inventory*, Form A, Science Research Associates, 228 So. Wabash Avenue, Chicago, Illinois (August, 1949), p. 4.

"I don't think boys are half as girl-crazy as people say they are."

The problem is greater for younger than for older youth. But there is evidence that a considerable number of out-of-school young people and college students still are not dating. More than a third of the university students in one study [6] reported inadequate opportunities for meeting members of the other sex. Attempts to analyze why some young people do not get dates uncovers a number of traits and characteristics that seem to be handicaps. Physically unattractive, geographically isolated, academically insulated, emotionally immature, and psychologi-

[6] Clifford Kirkpatrick and Theodore Caplow, "Courtship in a Group of Minnesota Students," *American Journal of Sociology* (September, 1945), LI, No. 2, p. 117.

cally unstable young people of both sexes seem to have more difficulty securing the favorable attention of the other sex than do the attractive, accessible, mature, and socially skilled young people.

Preferences in Dates. A nation-wide sample of thousands of high school students paralleling previous studies of college youth reports that there is general agreement among young people as to who is preferred as a dating partner. The seven characteristics rated highest are in the table below, in order of rank.[7]

THE PREFERRED DATE . . .

is physically and mentally fit
is dependable, can be trusted
takes pride in personal appearance and manners
is clean in speech and action
has pleasant disposition and a sense of humor
is considerate of me and others
acts own age, is not childish

Both sexes have certain patterns of conduct objectionable to the other sex. In general, boys are criticized for being less inhibited and more careless, thoughtless, disrespectful, sex-driven, and loud than their partners in dating. Girls are characterized as being less natural, more touchy, money-minded, unresponsive, childish, and flighty than the boys they date.[8]

At What Age Does Dating Begin?

Many factors seem to operate to determine the age at which dating begins.

What Your Folks Expect of You. Dating practices vary widely from family to family. There are still some fathers and mothers who so protect their girls that any man walking their daughter home is subjected to a full inquiry of his intentions. A considerable number of fathers forbid their daughters dating privileges. Other parents expect young

[7] Harold Christensen, "Dating Behavior as Evaluated by High School Students," *American Journal of Sociology* (May, 1952), LVII, No. 6, p. 580.
[8] Christensen, *op. cit.*, pp. 581–582.

people to "couple off" very early, with no questions asked or eyebrows raised. In fact, many parents encourage both their sons and daughters in their first dating.

ATTITUDES OF PARENTS TOWARD FIRST DATING [9]

Attitude of Parents as Reported by Students	Father toward		Mother toward	
	Son	Daughter	Son	Daughter
Prohibited or disapproved	8.5%	18.0%	7.3%	9.5%
Indifferent	70.7	62.3	57.6	39.6
Encouraged	20.8	19.7	35.1	50.9

Where You Come in the Family. Studies of the age at which young people begin to have dates indicate that their position in the family is a very important factor. Only children and oldest children are usually a little slower in getting started than are the younger members of the family. The oldest boy or girl has to break the ice among the younger set in the neighborhood. In addition, he must get the parents accustomed to the idea that going out is all right. This is especially difficult when customs are changing from one generation to the next as they are today. Parents who lived in the times when no nice girl was out after dark with a man the family didn't know well, take some plain and fancy reconditioning to be brought up to date. The older children in the family perform a real service to their younger brothers and sisters in winning the parents over to the idea of modern dating. The younger fry then come along and take advantage of all the spade work which has been done. The result is that they begin dating earlier and know more about it than their older brothers and sisters.

It is not uncommon for younger brothers and sisters to get some practice on the friends of those just ahead of them in the family. Kid brother may be a pest when he hangs around the sofa when the boy friends come calling, but he is also getting some very good tips on what to do in such a situation and how a girl whom he knows as well as he does that sister of his acts when she is on a date. Little sisters haven't quite the reputation of little brothers for having to be bought off by visiting suitors, but they usually stick around long enough to get in a few licks of practice on their sister's boy friends, and thus smooth over

---

[9] Adapted from Clifford Kirkpatrick and Theodore Caplow, "Courtship in a Group of Minnesota Students," *American Journal of Sociology* (September, 1945), LI, No. 2, p. 115.

some of their own rough edges before they try out their techniques on a boy who really matters. Going along for the ride with the set just a notch older is of great help in improving these skills and in getting in on the social activities about town. "Has she got a sister?" is a boost that gives many a kid sister a start.

How Friendly You Are. Friendly people make friends. In no area is this more true than in dating. The person who has learned to enjoy being with people, to be sensitive to what they do and do not like, and who has developed the skills of being attractive to others is off to a head start when it comes to getting along with the other sex. These skills are specifically learned. The little wolf child whom you have read about wouldn't have the slightest idea of what to do on a coke date . . . she couldn't even sit up to the table! Shy Sam who got his feelings hurt in second grade and hasn't talked to a girl since may be in an awkward spot when it comes to facing the terrors of a high school dance. Smooth Sue who has gone around with many friends of assorted sizes and sexes from the time she first held Jimmie's hand in nursery school has probably learned what it takes to be friendly and comfortable with all kinds of boys. In this sense, being a person of experience is quite acceptable.

Learning to be friendly is every bit as complex an attainment as learning to swim or to ride a bicycle, and maybe a little more so. You can't learn to swim without getting some water up your nose and being sure that your next breath may be your last! If you can take these first uncomfortable moments, you are soon paddling around, wondering what the early fuss was all about and feeling sure you could do a swan dive if you practiced. It is practice that makes for the poise and skills that are so universally envied in dating too.

What You Consider a Date. It would be hard for some young adults to remember when they had their first real date. Young people of both sexes mingle so freely in some of our communities that they have literally been doing things together since before they could toddle. It is becoming more and more common for grade school boys to take girls in their classrooms to a Saturday afternoon movie, or a children's symphony, or the zoo, in a pattern of behavior that has many of the aspects which in older circles is known as dating. In some neighborhoods, however, a girl is not allowed to go anywhere with a boy until she is sixteen or older, and then under supervision, and the event is regarded by the family and friends as quite an occasion. So the age at which you begin to date, as such, depends on whether you define a date as something special, over and beyond the child's play of early friendship, or whether you are willing to call any sortie of a couple a date, no matter what the maturity of the participants may be.

When You Become Mature. Recent studies of the rate and pace at which children become adults show that there is a great difference in the speed with which individuals do grow up. Generally speaking, most girls mature a little earlier than boys do, causing some tension between the sexes, especially at the awkward age along about junior high school time. Not only are the girls physically more mature than the boys of their own age, but they are ready for grown-up activities before the boys are. We know definitely that these grown-up interests, such as getting special pleasure out of being with those of the other sex, taking an interest in one's personal appearance, enjoying love stories and romantic movies, etc., follow the physical maturing of the boy or girl. The girl who is beginning to look like a woman wants to act like one. The boy who is as tall as his dad will very soon be seeking the more grown-up roles he has seen his dad and other men play. This sequence of development of the person is more important by far than his or her chronological age. In careful work at the University of California, it has been shown that as much as five years' difference may be found in the age at which boys begin to develop. Some youngsters of ten are already in the puberal cycle (period of change from childhood to adulthood, physically speaking), while others of nearly fourteen haven't yet started.[10] And the age at which boys complete their physical growth is not the same for all boys. Some are through the growth period before they are fifteen, while others may be out of high school before they achieve maturity. These individual differences are important to recognize, so that we won't expect all seventeen-year-old boys to be alike in their readiness for dating, for dancing, or any other adult activity. Girls show much the same personal variation in their development, and by the seventh or the eighth grade we find two thirds of the girls on their way to becoming young ladies — one of the reasons why they vote for long dresses and a graduation dance. Two thirds of the boys in their classes, how-

[10] Lois Hayden Meek and associates, *The Personal-Social Development of Boys and Girls with Implications for Secondary Education* (New York: Progressive Education Association, 1940), p. 34.

ever, haven't yet started on the cycle of growth that is to carry them into manhood.

This general tendency for girls to grow up before the boys of their own age leads to another interesting occurrence — girls usually date boys a little older than themselves. Boys, conversely, prefer girls younger than themselves as friends and dates. This tendency carries right through the dating, mating, engagement, and marriage periods and is

STAGES IN DATING DEVELOPMENT

Hit-and-Miss Childhood Groups

Determined largely by family, neighborhood, and community opportunities, the geographical "range" to roam provided, and the amount of supervision.

Gang Groups

Cliquelike groups formed by both boys and girls for which they feel deep loyalty but which change in nature and membership very readily.

Fleeting Affinities

The coke date, the "being walked home from school" involvements characteristic of the junior high school and high school age, types of temporary try-outs with each other across the sex line on a couple basis, called "playing the field" by some.

Going Together

A recognizable couple formation in which a boy and girl show preference for each other over a period of time, perhaps for just a few weeks, the "Jane is going with Jim" stage.

Mixed Couple Formations

Constellations of several previously identifiable couples who start going round together in groups of several couples, attending basketball games together, coming to the proms together, visiting one another's homes as a group — the "sets" we see in every community.

Going Steady

Couples who find their own status as a couple taking precedence over other alignments.

Choosing "The One"

Selection of a permanent partner with the "understanding" that engagement and marriage will develop naturally.

known as the "age gradient." Unfortunately, few of our schools and communities have made adequate provision for this mingling of the sexes of different age groups, making dating more difficult than it is where young people of different ages have ready access to each other in everyday work and play situations.

When a person starts to date is not nearly as important as *how* he begins. The factors determining the onset of his dating practice operate in many ways to influence the progress of dating for him. But more important by far is his willingness and ability to learn the rules and skills by which success is attained, because no one is born popular. Social success is a learned art, and learning is hard and long for most of us. In the last analysis, then, the ability to understand and accept the whole dating scheme is more important than the age of starting.

Although the forms and patterns of dating vary widely in different sections of the country, there is a general pattern of development that is interesting. It appears in tabular form in the table on page 55.

How Many Kinds of Dates Are There?

We not only go through a process of several stages in our dating experiences, but we have many kinds of dating relationships within any one period. These experiences are distinguished by the meanings and feelings they arouse, as we shall see in the following analysis:

Old-shoe familiarity is characteristic of dates with old pals and friends who are enjoyed as comrades, with very little of the excitement of novelty or the thrill of "being in love." She is just "good old Lillian" to him and is taken for granted in much the same way he takes his sister or his maiden aunt.

Glamor dates are made of different stuff. They are something of an achievement. Being seen with a "glamor girl" is a feather in his cap. Similarly, a girl is envied as having made a "catch" if she is seen with someone who rates high among her friends.

Blind dates and **pick-ups** are more scary, in a sense. There's the feeling of being on your guard at the same time that you probe around to see how far you can go. There's the disadvantage of being afraid to be stuck with a dud, but the advantage of being able to try out your skills on someone who doesn't have to remind you of possible failures later. They are good experiences but risky on the whole, both in feeling tones and in results.

Difficulties arise when romantic ideas press you to look for the "one and only" behind every blind date, with the consequence of disillusionment and disappointment, and inability to enjoy the real situation for what it is worth.

Growing friendships deepen and widen their bases through the opportunities of dating. The couple get to know each other, and discover new aspects of their own changing relationship that give the date more meaning and charge it with an increasing depth and variety of feeling. This kind of date usually leads to something, though not always the altar. It may be just the basis for a lifelong friendship.

Where to Go and What to Do on a Date

Keeping dates from becoming monotonous is one of the difficulties of modern dating. "Where can we go?" "What can we do?" "What can you do?" "What can you do that's fun at home?" are pressingly urgent questions for many young people. Few of our cities and towns have provided the kinds of facilities most young folk enjoy. All too often there is nothing but the movies, the pool halls and taverns, and the dance halls open for the casual dater. In some communities Teen Canteens, Community Centers, Teen Towns, etc., have sprung up as hangouts and recreation centers for the young people of the town. There with a juke box, soft drinks, ping-pong tables, and a kitchenette, young people of dating age dance, drink cokes, pop corn, and swap lines, and develop the skills that are necessary to get along with each other. But for the town without such a community hangout, what is there for young people to do when they get together?

For the outdoor girl and boy there are many possibilities: skating, hiking, the walkie-talkie date, cycling, swimming, gardening, hunting for nature specimens of all kinds, picnics, to say nothing of all the outdoor games and sports from croquet and tennis to golf and horseback riding. Making equipment for a favorite sport is great fun. The couple that spent all one summer building a little rowboat got a thrill that will make boating forever afterwards exciting. Setting up an archery set in the back yard may be as interesting as using it afterwards. There are innumerable pursuits which the creative-minded couple can explore together.

Stay-at-home dates can be made interesting by the couple who can think of home as encompassing more territory than just the davenport.

Scrapbook of Army-Navy Humor

"Since you're new at this, Anderson, maybe you'd better
just tag along and watch."

The kitchen has real possibilities for group or couple dating. Making up a batch of spaghetti, trying out a recipe for Hungarian goulash, or beating up an old-fashioned coffee cake have been known to keep dating young people interested for several hours at a time. There is nothing dull in the clowning around and deciding what to make, or the who-will-do-what that precedes the actual culinary endeavor itself. Refreshments are no problem when friends make their own. Even the cleaning up is fun with big Arthur behind the best chintz apron, and everybody behind plans for next time. It's no wonder that some groups of young people have worked their way through the United Nations Cookbook in a series of kitchen dates around the calendar.

Attics yield materials for parades in costume and impromptu plays and skits. The dining room table is just the spot for a series of group table games where several couples can participate at once. Games suggested by such agencies as the National Recreation Association and the publishers of *Handy* are especially good.

Living rooms adapt themselves well to a variety of dates. Piano games, singing old favorites and new hot numbers, amateur orchestras, parlor games of the more grown-up varieties such as Elsa Maxwell so ingeniously devises and which are described from time to time in popular magazines, reading aloud, and a galaxy of other activities around common projects can be fascinating. One couple entertained friends by providing a large cotton square which they were all to decorate with gaudy block printing made from cut potato halves (each person making his own design) dipped in a fabric paint. It took all evening, but was it fun! And you should see the table cloth that resulted. . . .

Radio to the imaginative couple will suggest not just listening, nor even dancing to its rhythms, but also working out slogans and sending in questions to stump the experts. A dozen other ventures into creative twosomeness can be interesting and rewarding, even if the sponsor doesn't come across with a check by return mail. A person armed with such ideas will be welcomed into almost any home. He will find that dating this way can be great fun, and that he doesn't have to be the center of attention to have a good time.

Where to go and what to do depends not only on the wealth of local resources but even more on the ability of those who date to make use of what they have. Going to the museum doesn't have to be stuffy. Going to a concert isn't necessarily prosaic. What takes any activity out of the area of the humdrum is to give it focus. "You must see *this*," "Don't miss *that*," are quite different in interest appeal from the lackadaisical, unfocused suggestion, "Do you want to go downtown?" or "Would you like to make something?" This pepping up of the dating activities comes with experience and learning as does everything else. Take your time. Plan your campaign. And have fun!

What about Petting?

Do you have to pet to be popular? No question is more universally asked by young people who want to rate and to date and yet are interested in a variety of dating activities beyond the sheer sex-exploration level. To answer the question wisely, a categorical "Yes" or "No" is not adequate. Rather, let us look for answers to certain subquestions, an understanding of which will give direction to the final personal choice.

Why Do Young People Pet? Young people discussing this problem give the following reasons for premarital petting:

It seems to be expected of you.
The rest of the crowd are all doing it.
You need some assurance that you are desirable.

Where else can you get a little loving? Most young folk are too old to be fondled by their parents any more, and too young to enjoy the caresses of marriage.

It's exciting.

Sure it's sex, but what's wrong with that?

It's something to do . . . most dates are a bore without it.

How else can you know you are compatible?

What's Wrong with Petting? There seems to be some agreement among both young people and understanding adults that too frequent and too promiscuous petting has hazards that most folk like to avoid. Briefly listed, these difficulties are:

Petting often rules out other activities.

It tends to overemphasize the physical aspects of the relationship.

It may limit the choice of companionship.

It may give rise to feelings of shame and guilt (our own early training and the standards of the communities in which we live see to this).

It rouses sex feelings and then leaves them unsatisfied.

It leads too often into premarital sex intercourse with the threats of unwanted pregnancy and feelings of regret.

It makes good marriage adjustment difficult, especially when the petting has been too promiscuous and too deeply established as a pattern of behavior.

Although there are very real dangers of going too far in the petting game before marriage, few people are so constituted that they can refrain from expressing affection when they feel it. Between people who love each other deeply and who are sharing rich and meaningful experiences, some physical expression of the love each feels for the other is desirable. When these expressions of affection become sex-tinged they need not terrify the intelligent couple, but should merely serve to indicate the potency of the force which attracts them to each other.

Occasionally a young person may be so strictly brought up that he develops feelings of disgust and comes to avoid all physical contact with others. Elsie (p. 39) was such a person. She came within weeks of marriage without ever having been kissed by either her lover or any other man. Consequently, she was in panic over the prospect of the impending intimacies of marriage. The counselor she consulted had to recommend a postponement of the marriage until the couple had paved the way more adequately for the marriage that was to come. Such a case is unusual, but aspects of it are sufficiently common, especially among exceedingly nice girls, to make one aware of the dangers of too much prudery as well as of an excess of license in the sex field.

Do You Have to Pet to Be Popular? No, you do not! Popularity that rests on a reputation for petting is not as satisfying as popularity which comes from the attraction of a pleasing personality. Popularity is a nebulous concept involving all the complexities of what makes a person attractive to others: appearance, abilities, responses, attitudes, charm, and specific skills. In dating success all of these play a part, but large numbers of young people from all sorts of settings agree that the element of friendliness is of primary importance. The person who has developed the habit of being friendly, who is genuinely interested in people and eager to know them better, who sees girls as interesting personalities to explore and understand as whole personalities, who likes boys for what they are, who has had many pleasant experiences with a wide variety of people in the past so that he meets new ones with eagerness and anticipation rather than with fear and hostility, who feels that people like him and that they will like him better when they know him better — this is the type of person, old or young, boy or girl, who will enjoy popularity. This kind of person makes people feel comfortable when he is around; he doesn't threaten or antagonize; he enjoys people and they enjoy him, and he will always be a welcome companion. His friendliness is all he needs to get through to other people.

A person with skills also has alternatives to petting. The girl who can do things goes places. If she can swim and dance and play a decent game of tennis and bridge, or can sing or play an instrument and carry on a live conversation, she is invited out more often, goes to more places, meets more people. Such skills are developed by the processes of learning and are worth the effort for the person who would be a popular, successful dater.

When They Are Either Too Slow or Too Fast

What do to with the "dumb bunny" who answers in monosyllables and leaves the whole burden of the date on you is a puzzler. One constructive possibility is to take the situation as a challenge and see what your social skills and insights can do to help the other person have a good time. Loosening up a shy, reserved girl to the place where her eyes are shining and she's having a good time with you brings rewards that even the Smooth Suzy can't guarantee. Girls as USO hostesses and YWCA volunteers have done an excellent job of making lonesome, reserved, and uncomfortable boys feel at home.

Dealing with the fast ones is quite another thing.[11] Wolves don't always go in packs or pick on the Three Little Pigs. There are she-wolves who are dynamite and Lone Wolves of both sexes who can cause plenty of trouble when allowed to roam too fast or too far. Everyone can develop protective devices and methods of rechanneling the on-slaughts of such exploitive folk. The dangers are not great for the young person who has had some previous understanding of the existence of such exploitation across the sex line, and who has been able to arrive at a decision as to the values worth holding. The greatest danger in dealing with a fast worker is that young people aren't sure themselves just how far they are willing to go. A song of a generation ago phrased it clearly if not too prettily when it moaned, "Her lips tell me 'No, No,' but there's 'Yes, Yes' in her eyes." This inner indecision is what causes the trouble; a preconceived set of values will carry one over many emergencies. The temptations of the moment are effectively met only when they are not desirable in terms of what they will cost. Today this holds for both sexes. There was a time, not too long ago, when it was the girl who was expected to uphold the standards for both of them. Now, when many girls are so open and active in their dating relationships, boys too have to learn the skills of holding to the line in the face of vigorous campaigns.

Boys are often baffled by the lack of understanding shown by girls. As they put it, "Why do really nice girls lead you on so far and then aren't willing to do anything about it?" Woman's sexual response is so general and diffused that frequently she does not even know that she is being aroused, and even more frequently is quite unaware that her behavior is arousing the boy beyond the boundaries which she herself would wish to maintain. It therefore falls to the boy, who is more quickly and recognizably awakened, to share the responsibility for control. Needless to say, there are elements of mutuality here that the couple who care for the long-time relationship will perfect with practice.

[11] See especially, Evelyn Millis Duvall, *Facts of Life and Love* (New York: Association Press, 1950), chaps. 6, 11, 12.

Going Steady

Couples go steady for a number of reasons. In many sets, it's the only way to get around. You must have a steady in order to rate invitations to the activities of the young crowd. Then there is a certain "social security" in knowing that you can count on someone when things come along for which you need a partner. Many girls find that going steady insures them getting to the season's games and dances with far more reliability than comes with "playing the field." A sense of personal security in having someone to belong to means a great deal to some people. Others find that getting and holding a steady is a way of showing himself and others that he can do it: it tends to be a symbol of achievement. Going steady is a good way to get to know each other. Moods and manners change as contacts multiply. Each member of the couple can see how the personality of the other reacts to the ups and downs of daily living far better when going steady than in more fleeting contacts. The reason for going steady most frequently assumed is that the couple love each other and would rather go together than with any other possibility. But behind the story of many steadies lies an element of accident that the couple itself often senses clearly. Ray took Betty to a couple of movies and then to the school prom. By that time friends of both had them paired off in their thinking. Sally gave a party and expected Ray to bring Betty. Soon the habit of going together was so well fixed and expected that they were going steady without the benefit of any particular choice or decision in the matter. All too often the members of such accidental relationships go all the way to the threshold of marriage with a minimum of interests in common. Going steady becomes a habit which is difficult to break.

CHECK YOURSELF   In the discussion immediately above on "Going Steady," underline as many phrases as seem to describe why people go steady. How many do you have? (There are 8 in all; see KEY for listing.)

★ KEY   Answers in order of their appearance in the text.

7 The couple love each other   8 Element of accident

4 Personal security   5 Symbol of achievement   6 To get to know each other

1 The only way to get around   2 To rate invitations   3 Social security

---

While there are valid and quite reasonable advantages in going steady, there are also factors worth looking into which indicate that it may be unwise to go steady too soon.

First, starting to go steady too soon lessens opportunities for exploring the field. After all, we spend much of our lifetime going steady with our one and only. The chance for knowing enough members of the other sex well enough to make a real choice of a life partner comes during the dating period. Shortening the period of exploring possibilities by settling prematurely on any one person may create a feeling of having missed something important.

Second, confining our entire interests to a single person during the time of social and emotional maturation limits the scope of our responses and self-understanding. We all respond differently to different people. By interacting with a wide variety of people, especially of the other sex, we discover facets of our own personality that otherwise might lie dormant only to be awakened after marriage, in some cases with distressing confusion. Specifically, a fellow should have had the emotional experience of being with a girl who made him feel tenderly protective, with another who gave him a pleasurable feeling of being mothered, with another whose hand he could clasp with a feeling of hearty comradeship, with another whose feminine appeal sent his blood to his face and his heart to his throat, with another who made him as comfortable and easy as a sister, and perhaps with still another who brought forth a pleasant combination of all these feelings in a satisfying mixture.

Third, one of the most uncomfortable problems to be worked out by steadies who start too soon and go on too long is that which arises when one takes the other seriously while the other is tired of the relationship. Breaking off may prove to be so difficult that the couple will remain together only because of the dread one has of hurting the other.

How to Break Off with a Steady

Our romantic compulsion to hold together has shut off frank discussion of how a relationship that is unpromising may be broken comfortably and with a minimum of pain. There are three practices in general use today: 1. The *love-'em-and-leave-'em* variety is characteristic of one method which is quick, easy, and effective. A relationship which was there yesterday just isn't today, because one of the couple just doesn't respond any more. He doesn't call her or drop around. She isn't in when he calls, if she is the one who is through. The difficulties of this method are that, although it is effective, hurts are inflicted both to the feelings of the one who has been so summarily jilted and to the conscience of the one who did the running away. 2. *Agonizing discussions* about how washed up we are; "if only you would do so-and-so we could go on still"; tormenting memories about how happy we once were; the break drags on uncomfortably, with hopes rising and falling sometimes for months. Grandpa had a point when he mused, "If you have to cut off the puppy's tail do it in one blow." Yet a certain amount of preparation and some explanation are usually helpful. 3. The *easing-off* type of break includes some understanding on the part of both members of the couple of what is happening, and an acceptance of the situation before the bond is completely severed. Some day people will be much wiser about these things. In the meantime we all can be more aware of both the need to sever certain relationships and the necessity of building the skills that will be most kind and effective.

Dating as Preparation for Marriage

Dating has a value as preparation for courtship, engagement, and marriage in addition to its value as recreation and play. The patterns and habits that are built up during the dating days are to some extent those which carry over into the courtship and engagement. A man bosses his wife very much as he did his fiancée in dating days, that is, if she acceded to that arrangement. Dating should be educational, but it may turn out to be miseducation.

Who makes the decisions on a date? Is it the boy who always decides where they will go, what they will do, how much they will eat? Or is it the girl who holds this balance of power in her skillful little fist? Can a date be democratic, each one contributing to and receiving from the relationship those things which he can and should? Does joint planning of activities spoil the fun? Can surprises be mutual? Does taking turns in running things help any in dating? Or does one person need to show who is boss and play that role down to the bitter end? These are basic problems too involved to be solved here, except to point out that role-taking begins in the dating period and sets the stage for later marriage and home management.

Money matters especially are often a problem. Why is it that boys always expect to pay a girl's way when they go out together? Even though a girl may be earning as much as or perhaps even more than the boy, why does he feel that he should "take" her? To realize how entrenched this custom is, just listen sometime to a group of young people discuss the pros and cons of sharing expenses on a date. The consensus almost always is that it just won't work . . . "the girl will feel funny," "the boy's ego can't take it," "the girl can make it up some other way," are the typical comments. Girls have been so conscious of having to wait until boys ask them for a date for which they will foot the bills, that recently girls have developed considerable skill in perfecting devices for asking men to functions where the girls carry the financial and social burden. Girls band together and put on a party to which they invite their own partners or a "bunch of boys," who are given all the courtesies of guests with none of the usual financial burdens assumed by men in mixed company. Inviting the boys out to the house for an evening, to come to supper, to share theater tickets that grandma just happened to have, to use "a pass to the ballgame dad gave me" are typical of the kinds of ruses now in common usage. The problem doesn't end there. It will pop up again early in marriage and become one of the areas for adjustment in establishing the new home. The whole problem of working wives is often not so much a matter of the wife's being out of the home for part of the day as it is a question of whose money it is that she earns. Do her earnings go into the family budget as do her husband's, or are they to be labeled as hers alone?

We conclude that dating in America is not a thing apart from the rest of life. It grows out of childhood friendships, out of customs, and merges into the involvements of courtship and engagement in a process which we will describe in later chapters.

Dating May Be Preparation but It Is Also Fun

The account of dating which you have just read emphasizes the values which come with learning the skills of boy and girl relations. You aren't born popular; you have to learn how to do the friendly things which will endear you to people. The speed with which you grow in competence depends on the encouragement given by your family, your eagerness to learn, and your rate of emotional maturation.

Just as there are all kinds of people, so there are many kinds of dates — informal old-friend dates, blind dates, formal dates, and so on. Each takes imagination and ingenuity to carry off right; each is a challenge to the growing person. Those who have read this chapter will see how many things there are to do on a date besides the same old stuff.

Dating has been explained as education in the discovery of emotions and their control. Sexual urges, unruly tempers, and needs for affection come to the fore out of the new experiences of dating relations. Participants come to find that gestures of affection enrich their relations if tied in with the discovery of common interests and goals. Out of dating, then, should come not only the ability to love and be loved, but also the alternatives to petting.

Finally, dating proves to have value in training young people in the art of democratic give and take. Girls are allowed more initiative in dating than they were in old-fashioned courting days and often stage events in which they assume the costs of the party. This equalitarian relationship carries over into later courtship, engagement, and marriage relations and makes for a more democratic marriage and family life.

Selected Readings

DUVALL, EVELYN MILLIS, *Facts of Life and Love* (New York: Association Press, 1950), chaps. 5–8.

——, *Family Living* (New York: Macmillan, 1950), chaps. 8–11.

KIRKENDALL, LESTER, AND OSBORNE, RUTH, *Dating Days* (Chicago: Science Research Associates, 1949), Pamphlet.

LANDIS, JUDSON T., AND LANDIS, MARY G., *Personal Adjustment, Marriage and Family Living* (New York: Prentice-Hall, 1950), chaps. 4, 5, 7.

MERRILL, FRANCIS, *Courtship and Marriage* (New York: Sloane, 1949), Chap. 4.

MOORE, BERNICE MILBURN, AND LEAHY, DOROTHY M., *You and Your Family* (Boston: Heath, 1948), Chap. 10.

WINCH, ROBERT F., *The Modern Family* (New York: Holt, 1952), Chap. 16 and Appendix, "Dating, Rating, and College Fraternities."

Technical References

CHRISTENSEN, HAROLD, "Dating Behavior as Evaluated by High School Students," *American Journal of Sociology* (May, 1952), LVII, No. 6, pp. 580–586.

CONNOR, RUTH, AND HALL, EDITH, "The Dating Behavior of College Freshmen and Sophomores," *Journal of Home Economics* (April, 1952), Vol. 44, No. 4, pp. 278–281.

KIRKPATRICK, CLIFFORD, AND CAPLOW, THEODORE, "Courtship in a Group of Minnesota Students," *American Journal of Sociology* (September, 1945), pp. 114–125.

KOLLER, MARVIN, "Some Changes in Courtship Behavior in Three Generations of Ohio Women," *American Sociological Review* (June, 1951), pp. 366–370.

LANDIS, PAUL, "Personality Differences of Girls from Farm, Town, and City," *Rural Sociology* (March, 1949), pp. 10–20.

LOWRIE, SAMUEL, "Dating Theories and Student Responses," *American Sociological Review* (June, 1951), pp. 334–340.

REMMERS, H. H., AND HACKETT, C. G., *Let's Listen to Youth* (Chicago: Science Research Associates, 1950), 49 pages.

ROCKWOOD, LEMO, AND FORD, MARY, *Youth, Marriage, and Parenthood* (New York: Wiley, 1945).

STONE, CAROL, "Sorority Status and Personality Adjustment," *American Sociological Review* (August, 1951), pp. 538–541.

WOLFORD, OPAL POWELL, "How Early Background Affects Dating Behavior," *Journal of Home Economics* (1948), No. 40, pp. 505–506.

CHAPTER FOUR

In Deeper than Ever

BECOMING INVOLVED: THE COURTSHIP PROCESS

How do you get in so deep?

Are lovers' quarrels normal?

Do friends push the couple even closer together?

Should girls be given more freedom in getting their man?

What about dating bureaus?

*T*HE COURTSHIP PROCESS TODAY REFLECTS THE INCREASING MUTUAL-ity of the man-woman status. At one time courtship referred to a process of persuading, or courting, during which the swain-in-love won the affections of his fair lady who was ostensibly not in love. Courtship today has been preceded by casual dating in which little or no commitment is expected, and consists less of a persuading period than a process of mutual involvement leading to a formal commitment in engagement.

Dating, courtship, and engagement are general terms used popularly to denote varying degrees of commitment in the sifting and sorting of the sexes into marrying couples. There is some appearance of orderliness in the stages from lesser to greater degrees of involvement.

Individuals may shift within these stages of involvement experiencing some of the stages and not others. Some are arrested at an intermediate stage and find it difficult to progress beyond that point. The wary bachelor and the uncoquettish spinster are examples.

Persons high on the popularity scale may keep several affairs going concurrently. Generally as the stage of involvement progresses the number of relationships maintained decreases sharply. Courtship, as we use the term in this chapter, begins with the stages of involvement in which the field has narrowed down, and one relationship has taken precedence over all others.

In the pages which follow, the social psychology of courtship involve-ment unfolds. Dating *activities* and *skills* constituted the focus of the last chapter. In this discussion we shift to the *relationships* and bonds of sentiment which grow up *between dating individuals*.

Several forces are at work to forge the bonds of sentiment which change the pair from a casual twosome to an engaged couple. Powerful

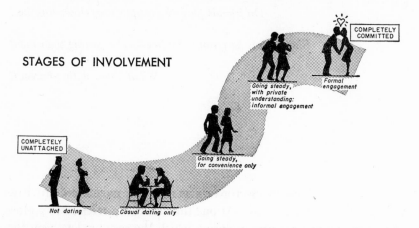

STAGES OF INVOLVEMENT

COMPLETELY COMMITTED

Going steady, with private understanding: informal engagement

Formal engagement

COMPLETELY UNATTACHED

Going steady, for convenience only

Not dating

Casual dating only

physical attractions are at work in heterosexual dating. Pride in having and holding are anticipatory of mutual ego-involvement. Finally, shared activities, whether recreation oriented or work oriented, create bonds of sentiment which are strangely strong. As these three processes support one another in the interactions of steady dating, courtship, a process of mutual involvement, ensues.

The Involvement Process [1]

The involvement process begins in dating, at which time there may be little serious intent, and ends in a climax of powerful emotional re-sponses which are most evident in the engagement and honeymoon

[1] We present the following discussion with acknowledgments to Willard Waller, who first developed the approach we are taking in his book, revised by Reuben Hill, *The Family: A Dynamic Interpretation* (New York: Dryden Press, 1951), pp. 176–190, and urge you to regard it as typical only of the middle class courtships in Amer-ica. No single courtship conforms in all details to the picture we shall present, but thousands approximate it in one or more ways.

periods. Human beings act upon one another emotionally when they are thrown into intimate relations. As emotions build up in one they are communicated contagiously to the other. Unless there is opportunity for release, the climax which is attained may reach great proportions. Here is the way it looks in the anger response: A mother may start the morning gay and relaxed, with a song on her lips, and may hardly notice the noise and bickering of the children. All too typically, frustrations pile up as the day gets under way. She finds the toaster doesn't work, the coffee cream is sour, her husband gets up late, is touchy and critical, and dashes off without kissing her good-by. The hot water faucet was left on all night and so there isn't any hot water for her dishes. She bears all this with patience and forbearance, but at 9:30, a half hour late already, the cleaning woman calls to say she's sorry but she guesses she won't be able to come today because Mrs. B. needs her to clean up after a party. The mother's forbearance cracks wide open, and a disproportionately heated anger response is unleashed. The cleaning woman doesn't understand it and is hurt. "She was such a nice lady all the other days, I wonder what's eating her?"

Courtship is a summatory process which builds up in much the same fashion, with many little experiences, some pleasant and some irritating, each affecting the other, and leaving the parties more involved than before. Each person becomes increasingly committed in his own eyes and in the eyes of the other. Once reaching a certain level of intensity, the process gets a movement of its own. It creates its own demands and needs, and each member finds himself more and more in need of the other to satisfy the new appetites which have been developed. The process tends to be irreversible after a certain momentum is reached, and the couple find they can't stop with being just good friends.[2] Some insightful couples have described the experience as not unlike an emotional build-up which occurs in a religious revival. The religious feelings mount as persons interact emotionally. The emotions of the more excitable in the congregation build up the slower, and, eventually, all experience conversion and the calm which comes with being sure they are right.

What are the specific components of the involvement process in this movement from casual dating to the emotional climax of engagement? When the brake is taken off a car on a hill, the car may start slowly

[2] *Ibid.,* p. 181.

enough at first, but there are the possibilities of excitement even at the
beginning. The components of the courtship process are present in
the dating period, but are kept in leash by powerful inhibitions until the
man, at least, is economically and psychologically ready to take the consequences of emotional involvement.

Coquetry. The involvement process begins with coquetry, behavior
which invites to amorous adventure. It is seen in the toning up of the
organism which occurs when boy and girl meet. The smile of the boy
when he sees a pretty girl is automatic, and he takes her in with a glance
which leaves nothing out. Her blush is evidence that she knows he sees
her, and her own coquetry is expressed in her sparkling eyes and flashing
smile. Both sense the coltish impulse to kick about with their feet,
which they suppress in favor of tossing the head, laughing, and giggling.

Coquetry is found in all cultures and has been described beautifully
in the literature of many peoples. Its tricks are legion. Small hints of
interest are given, and hints of erotic possibilities with alternate advance
and recession; great interest is followed by mock modesty, by teasing.
Teasing is one of the main techniques of coquetry by which tension is
stimulated in the other person to a higher level; the impulse is to chase
and be chased, but never quite to catch or be caught.

The Line. In America a familiar accompaniment and expression of
coquetry is "the line." The line is an exaggeration of our feelings, as if
the feelings we exhibit in coquetry were not enough. It is used by both
sexes and is called variously "handing her a line," or "laying it on";
among the Irish it is called "blarney." When you first meet a girl you
profess to be greatly impressed by her charms, and you hand her a line.
You don't expect to be taken too seriously or you will take flight. But
you want to be taken somewhat seriously, and so does she. Neither
knows how much is line and how much is sincerity.

The line was especially well developed by the lovemaking knights of
Arthur's mythical court. Much of our line is outright copying of these
lovers of old, and it is best done in parts of the South where, relatively
speaking, women still occupy a somewhat exalted position. The typical
gallant young Southerner at the slightest provocation can string a line of
sugared words and compliments which will delight any female listener.

The line covers up real emotional involvements by exaggeration.
Under the soft words may be conflict, because each has the uneasy feel-

ing that he is being tricked. Each avoids being caught by the loaded words of the other — each wishes, however, to dominate the fantasy of the other and to set him to dreaming.[3]

Each tends to become involved in his own line, which he comes to believe in part, but each worries because the other doesn't reveal the extent to which he is sincere. A sense of insecurity arises from not knowing just where they stand, and the lovers quarrel.

Lovers' Quarrels. The line finally becomes so burdensome that it has to be broken through, and the crisis comes in a good quarrel followed by crying and releasing of tension. Each reveals in the process how much he truly cares for the other, and the pair come to take themselves more seriously. The quarrel tends to redefine the situation upward.[4] The pair make up with a glorious sense of satisfaction and are more involved than before.

Common Interests. Quarrels leave the pair still using the line, but with more security and with a tenderness developing that wasn't there before. Each is surer of the other and both reach out to claim things which tie them together. Common interests further love involvements by giving the pair a common universe of discourse. The lovers can exclude the rest of the world, and they feel a sense of superiority as they talk on and on about things they understand better than anyone else in the world.

Increasing Intimacy. Coquetry enhanced by the mutual interchange of lines and the build-up of common interests brings the pair increasingly together. The line alone encourages physical intimacy, and love gestures confirm the sincerity of the verbal "I love you." The other person becomes a bona fide love object to be reckoned with — not just another date, but a person with feelings. Feelings of tenderness develop, and the lover finds himself more sincere than before, and impressed with his moral obligation to the other who believes in him so implicitly.

Idealization. Another component of love involvement, which owes some of its development to the line, is idealization. In the line all the desirable characteristics of the other are stressed to the exclusion of the annoying or disturbing characteristics, and it is not uncommon for young

[3] *Ibid.*, p. 185.
[4] Courtship quarrels are in contrast with divorce-directed quarrels which tend to define the situation downward. See our discussion of quarrels of alienation, pp. 284–291.

people to become so enamored of the love object that they come to believe their own line. The lover forgets his sweetheart's crooked teeth,
her so-so complexion, and her stringy hair, and remembers only her
lovely eyes and regal carriage. The greatest compliment a lover can be
paid is to be told, "You're different." Waller tells the story of a young
man who was very conscious of a wart on his chin and went to the expense of an operation to remove it. After it had healed, he presented
himself to his fiancée. "Notice anything different about my face?" The
moment was embarrassing; she had never noticed the wart in the first
place.

Idealization results in each replacing the other with an imaginary
person to whom he reacts. Separation for brief periods tends to accen-
tuate this process. Absence makes the heart grow fonder, because the
real person's presence gives way to the imaginary one. Each feels troubled that his own weaknesses are not seen, but doesn't try too hard to
expose them.[5]

Couple Unity. In the midst of this process couple unity develops.
Favored by the development of common interests which act to exclude
the public and to give the pair a feeling of superiority, the couple reach
out and seize upon evidences that they were meant for each other. One
couple in the course of their daily walk simultaneously focused their attention upon a certain mountain peak glittering in the sun and called it
"their mountain." They took every opportunity thereafter to admire
this symbol of their unity. Years later they returned to the exact spot
to get another view of the mountain which had come to mean so much
to them during their courtship period.

Early in the development of unity, rings or other articles will be exchanged to crystallize and render tangible that elusive "we feeling"
which they sense but can't describe. As each leaves the other, he carries away a reminder of their growing unity. It is as if the exchanged
articles could somehow summon the presence of the loved one, and the
separation is thereby made more bearable.

Another development in this process is the growth of a special lan-

---

[5] Unfortunately for later adjustments, the greater is the idealization, the greater is
the disillusionment which must follow in the marriage period. But couples should
remember it was their imagination which cheated them, not marriage! For a description of idealization among couples separated by war, see W. Edgar Gregory, "The
Idealization of the Absent," *American Journal of Sociology*, Vol. 50, No. 1 (July,
1944), pp. 53–54.

guage between the two, which they alone can understand. They develop their own idioms, pet names, and inflections which tend to alienate any third person and make him realize that two is company but three is a crowd. Left more and more together, the pair build up a shorthand language of symbols which obviates the necessity of completing sentences. Conversation is speeded up tremendously. Their language may look and sound to the outsider like a combination of nudges, knowing winks, and half-finished sentences, with poorly repressed mirth at things the outsider doesn't think funny at all. The jokes are hardest of all for the intruder to understand. They can be fully appreciated and understood only by the couple themselves. The jokes grow funnier the more frequently they are repeated, because they develop unseen nuances and are attached to other associations of a pleasant nature in the relationship. In summary, the process of developing pair unity is one of building a separate history and culture which the pair alone can understand. The relationship is stabilized in direct proportion to its success in throwing the pair on its own resources and in excluding, thereby, rivals and other members of the public.

Friends Encourage a Public Announcement. All of these activities of the couple have not escaped the eyes of friends, who play a very important role in furthering love involvements. Whenever a young man and young woman appear together, even in the casual dating stage, they risk being identified as a likely marriage pair by well-wishers. Friendly gossip — "We hear that Bob and Mary are getting serious" — gets back to the ears of the participants. Gossip columns of community and campus newspapers are widely read and further the public's identification of the pair. There is something about being identified by the public which changes the relationship. The sense of moral obligation on the part of the man, particularly, is a function partly of what the public thinks of his affair. Yesterday he might have been asked by a relative of the girl what his intentions were; today his conscience asks him the same question and is quite as effective in furthering his feeling of obligation to clarify things. The talk of people acts as further pressure to drop the exaggerations of the line and become more sincere in the relationship. "People are saying we are going steady but you haven't said a word about it. Margaret even asked me if we were engaged. The nerve. . . ." They quarrel, and in making up, many of the problems concerning their status which have given them the jitters are cleared up. The discussion and redefinition of the situation enables them to explain satisfactorily to themselves and to the public where they stand.

The public plays its part in clarifying the situation by treating the two as a unit, arranging for them to be together, inviting them to social affairs together. When a friend meets one member of the couple, he asks about the other member and expresses inferentially the hope that all is well between them. The pair come to feel that the public approves of the match and expects something to come of it. This sanctioning in itself has a pushing effect and changes the nature of the relationship subtly but effectively. Much of the exciting novelty of the relation is lost, but in its place comes a sense of responsibility and stability. If the pair are emotionally built up to a certain point, all it may take is a suggestion from a friend that they act as if they were engaged to crystallize the situation. It seems only natural and right to make a public announcement of their involvement, and a formal engagement takes place.

Variations from the Typical. As we have already warned, no single courtship will necessarily embody all of the components described, and many individual courtships will vary greatly from the pattern just presented. Young people who have come through courses in marriage and the family rarely take the line as seriously as described here, with the result that they build up fewer illusions about each other and indulge in relatively little idealization. Indeed, the courtship remains much more on the companionship level, and the emotions tend to be enjoyed on the spot rather than built up toward an explosive release at the honeymoon stage. These couples carry over into marriage fewer illusions about one another but nevertheless develop considerable fondness for each other as persons. They rarely build up ideas of the other as the incarnation of perfection so characteristic of those who have gone in for extreme idealization.

The courtship pattern followed by young people in isolated rural areas may also vary greatly from that of the middle class urban couple described in the foregoing pages. Rural courtships may conform more closely to those of the last generation and move more naturally and easily from keeping company to serious courtship to engagement and marriage. Each step in the process is well marked. Moreover, the couple have probably known one another for so long that there is little possibility of extreme idealization. The line is not likely to take such exaggerated form and would not be taken seriously if it did.

A third variation is seen in the courtships of war and postwar couples who have telescoped the dating and courtship and engagement periods in favor of immediate marriage.

These three variations from the patterns regarded as typical of the courtship process remind us of the range which exists in America. A more detailed consideration of the changes in courtship patterns which have occurred in the last three generations may give us the perspective we need to understand courtship today.

Changes in Courtship Patterns

The finding of a mate, and the details of arranging the betrothal, was until frontier days the prerogative of parents, and still is in many countries. Freedom of choice in this country dates from the days when all the eligible men and all the eligible women were known by the entire community. Young ladies knew from childhood the men who might come "a-courtin'." Rarely would a stranger be permitted to compete for the hand of a local belle. Freedom of choice was limited to the local eligibles and was therefore safe enough.

In the more settled towns of the Atlantic seaboard the problem was handled with prosaic formality. A formal introduction was followed by careful supervision of the relationship. A good girl refused to talk to any man who had not been first vouched for by a friend, and even then she consulted her parents for their approval. This system operated to limit the contacts of genteel young ladies to a relatively select group of eligible young men and discouraged social relations between ineligible women and men of good birth. Girls in those days had fewer opportunities to circulate, but the conditions under which they met men were conducive to the type of prolonged acquaintance necessary to judge men as potential marriage partners.

Today, there is less likelihood of marrying one's first love, and somewhat greater opportunity for exploring the field to find what one's preferences are.[6] Under the contemporary system, if there are years of

---

[6] A study which reveals clearly differences in courtship patterns in three generations is Marvin H. Koller's "Some Changes in Courtship Behavior in Three Generations of Ohio Women," *American Sociological Review*, Vol. 16, No. 3 (June, 1951),

professional training ahead, it is possible through dating to maintain contact with the opposite sex until marriage proves feasible.

A number of trends in courtship customs can be established from the contrasts between the beginning and the middle of the 20th century:

TEN RECENT TRENDS IN COURTSHIP CUSTOMS

1 Dating and courtship begin at earlier age
2 More frequent contact between the sexes
3 Dating and courtship last until later at night
4 More privacy for dating and courting pairs
5 Less supervision and chaperonage
6 More general acceptance of "going steady"
7 Wider range of patterns of intimacy and sex play
8 Many more discussable topics during dating and courtship
9 Higher readiness for education and guidance in courtship
10 Courtship culminates earlier in engagement and marriage

Difficulties in the Courtship System

Our somewhat unique pattern of freedom of choice has survived as an integral part of the courtship system today, but the community and neighborhood controls which helped it work in the colonial days have largely disappeared, particularly in cities. Blind dates are followed more often than not by regular dates without the slightest reference to the possibilities of parental approval or disapproval.

Another way of looking at courtship is as a device to sort out the compatible from the incompatible pairs of young people and provide the steps for leading the former to marriage and the latter back into circulation. If we had a courtship system which meshed well with the other parts of our changing culture, we should have fewer unhappy marriages and obviously many fewer divorces. The divorce rate is closely tied up with the number of poorly mated pairs who become engaged despite a minimum of common interests, and whose experiences in the engagement period are too superficial to reveal incompatibility. What

---

pp. 366–370. Koller studied 111 grandmothers averaging 78 years of age, 118 mothers averaging 48 years, and 140 married daughters averaging 23 years of age. The daughters reported over four times as many dates per week as their grandmothers. They circulated more widely and considered more men seriously as spouses before settling on the man they finally married. The earlier generations averaged longer engagements (11 months, 9 months, and 6 months respectively), but covered less territory in their premarital discussions and agreements.

has happened to our mate-finding machinery to break it down so completely?

Freedom of Choice Breaks Down. The courtship system of free choice has broken down as America has become urbanized. The conditions which produced the system of free choice have disappeared, and it is incumbent upon social engineers to devise new machinery or streamline the old. Sufficient research has been made regarding the situation to show the directions social planning for courtship should take. One authority lists four general needs: 1. the need for more initiative in courtship by girls; 2. the need for removing restraints upon the employment of women, such as the ban on married teachers, so that they would not be limited in their selection to men who could immediately provide full maintenance; 3. the need to increase opportunities for circulation of young people among several groups for a more varied experience and deeper companionship before a selection is made; and 4. the need for premarital counseling services to enable individuals to utilize the resources at their disposal.[7]

In frontier days men greatly outnumbered women, and the passive role of women did not seriously handicap them in obtaining desirable husbands. Today the sex ratio is reversed in many areas, and nowhere are there very many men to spare.[8] To meet this changed situation, the initiative in courtship should be taken more equally by both sexes. We grant the right of a woman to equal education and to equal freedom of choice of vocation and profession; at least the trend is in that direction. It is inconsistent, then, to continue the traditional courtship practice just because it is traditional. The newer findings of mental hygiene specialists indicate that the passive method by which women must lie in wait makes for greater frustration and more neurotic adjustments than the active program of pursuit permitted, as yet, for men only.[9]

---

[7] See Joseph K. Folsom's discussion of this problem in his book, *The Family and Democratic Society* (New York: Wiley, 1943), pp. 531–543.

[8] For a more detailed discussion of the sex ratio and its effects on the prospects for marriage, see pp. 155–156.

[9] In our discussion of the democratic date earlier, we discussed some of the feminine devices to arrange dates, initiate acquaintances, and assume a fair share of the burden of costs. Provocative discussions of the psychology of women are developed in: Karl Menninger, *Love against Hate* (New York: Harcourt, Brace, 1942); and Helene Deutsch, *Psychology of Women* (New York: Grune and Stratton, 1944). Further understanding of the cultural determination of femininity should be sought beyond these strictly psychiatric analyses.

Recommended Improvements

The proposal to increase greatly the opportunities for circulation of young people among several groups for a more varied experience and deeper companionship before making their selection strikes at the heart of the courtship problem. Gone are the limitations of the past, the barriers of formal introductions and parentally controlled courtships, but the facilities for bringing young people together in an atmosphere that is conducive to courtship have been slow to make their appearance. The need is particularly great in the larger cities where contacts between people are usually transitory and superficial. Letters such as the following are not uncommon in the collection of requests received by social agencies:

. . . I'm definitely disgusted with myself for not being able to go out and find romance as others do — but frankly, it's reached the point where I'm actually becoming morbid over my social deficiency — the more I try to fight it, the further back I seem to go. I don't know of anyone that can actually be of any constructive help, my friends are as much in the dark as I am when it comes to getting a girl friend. . . . When quitting time comes at the office, I hate to leave because it only means a lonely and empty evening. . . . Psychiatrists have told me, get married, it will give you a new set of social values. . . . Really that was just rubbing it in, because secretly that is what I've always wanted more than anything in life. . . . What I want isn't unreasonable — it's the very essence of society — it's no more than millions of couples since time immemorial have accepted as a matter of fact. . . . Chicago ought to have one of these [introduction services] for fellows like me.

There is a holdover of the romantic notion that the first meeting of two lovers must seem accidental and that their love must be confirmed by the evidence of fate having brought them together. There remains, therefore, a certain amount of resistance to the devices invented by more ingenious young people to widen their horizons, such as dating bureaus, dating exchanges, introduction services, and acquaintance bureaus. Dating bureaus on college campuses have sometimes failed because they attract mainly those most in need of an introduction service. Once students identify the bureaus as containing mainly the names of the socially inept, the project falls through, even though many may have been helped. Introduction services in large communities have usually fared better.[10] Established primarily to widen the circle of acquaintances rather than to arrange marriages, these services have succeeded where more formal arrangements have failed. The director of one such service described his clientele as composed of normal young people of fairly high education who, though able to find some companionship, were eager to be more selective in regard to tastes and interests. The conclusions and recommendations contained in his report in May, 1941, are distinctly quotable:

. . . they were an exceptionally fine type of young people, and their high average education, as well as conversations I had with them, indicate they approached the idea with a minimum of emotional resistance against the "stigma" of a dating bureau (which, after all, it was) and especially against a plan using a methodical, scientific approach to something which is not, under present social customs, ordinarily susceptible to anything but the usual haphazard, accidental, inspirational, romantic approach. In other words, these young people were better qualified than the average to perceive the breakdown of the older system and the necessity of something new and better.

As a result of the experience obtained from the experiment . . . I have come to the conclusion that the difficulties might be overcome fairly well. The *method*, consisting of tests, rating, references, and matching according to principles developed in recent researches (referring here to such tests as the Moss-Hunt-Omwake Social Intelligence Test, the Pressey Senior Classification test, and Bernreuter Personality Inventory furnished by the Psychological Corporation and to the researches of Dr. Kelley) is, I believe, fundamentally sound. If we are going to accept people as they are, and try to find the best combinations under those circumstances without trying to change people themselves, something of this very nature must eventually be adopted. . . .

The *procedure*, however, should be thoroughly revamped, in the light of current social customs. It appears to me that the principal emotional resistances are as follows: 1. the fear (often based on past experience) of getting "stuck" when on a "blind date," 2. the dislike of anything that approaches romance and luck from a "cold-and-calculating" angle, based (*a*) on the scientific methods employed and (*b*) on the fact that it was necessary to make a charge for the service, which was self-supporting.

Therefore, any new plan, if it is to succeed in numbers reached, must operate on a non-profit, unintentional basis. It occurs to me that this would be done best by adopting the program in some already existing organization

10 For a very optimistic account of a nonprofit introduction service in Newark, New Jersey, see Leigh Mitchell Hodges, "Introduction Please," *Reader's Digest*, September, 1942, pp. 15–18.

which is of such a nature that the interviews and tests can be given ostensibly for some regular purpose of the organization.[11]

The advantage of this social invention, which is no more incredible than the first television, is that it may be adapted with success by church groups, youth agencies, and counseling services as part of their youth service programs. These agencies are rapidly building up staffs of workers competent to carry out the procedure of a "friend-finding" bureau (interviewing, personality inventories, card indexing, and so on). The resistances to the procedure can be circumvented at first by the suggestions made above. The results should be a greatly improved courtship and mate-finding system for America.

Ideally, young people should have abundant opportunity to meet members of the opposite sex with a variety of interests and tastes and from a variety of economic and social backgrounds. They should, however, become sufficiently well acquainted with perhaps a dozen persons to determine whether there is a basis for marriage. Here, indeed, is another area in which social invention is needed: Many more boys are met than formerly, but girls know few of them on a basis adequate for judging their availability as husbands.

We will pick up in the next chapter the changes in the engagement as an institution, which need to be made to complete the process of sifting and choosing, which, we have shown, starts seriously in courtship. Dating and courtship may be the period of shuffling and pairing the players into what appear to be compatible twosomes, but the engagement period is the first official test of the pairing. When courtship is successful in bringing together congenial young people the engagement is likely to be less stormy. In any event, the engagement occupies the bottleneck position through which most marriages-to-be pass, and one of its assignments is to discourage mismatings. Our attention shifts at this point, then, to the engagement.

Selected Readings

BOWMAN, HENRY A., *Marriage for Moderns* (New York: McGraw-Hill, 1948), chaps. 6–8.

CHRISTENSEN, HAROLD T., *Marriage Analysis* (New York: Ronald Press, 1950).

[11] Report of Joseph Clawson of New York City in Joseph K. Folsom, *The Family and Democratic Society* (New York: Wiley, 1943), pp. 542–543.

DUVALL, EVELYN MILLIS, *Facts of Life and Love* (New York: Association Press, 1950), chaps. 9 and 14.

DUVALL, SYLVANUS, *Before You Marry* (New York: Association Press, 1949).

LANDIS, JUDSON T., AND LANDIS, MARY G., *Building a Successful Marriage* (New York: Prentice-Hall, 1948), Chap. 4.

MEAD, MARGARET, *Male and Female* (New York: Morrow, 1949), "Pre-Courtship Behavior and Adult Sex Standards," Chap. 14.

MERRILL, FRANCIS E., *Courtship and Marriage* (New York: Sloane, 1949), chaps. 4, 5.

SKIDMORE, REX A., AND CANNON, ANTHON S., *Building Your Marriage* (New York: Harper, 1951), Chap. 5.

WALLER, WILLARD, AND HILL, REUBEN, *The Family: A Dynamic Interpretation* (New York: Dryden Press, 1951), Chap. 10.

Technical References

BECKER, HOWARD, AND HILL, REUBEN, *Family, Marriage and Parenthood* (Boston: Heath, 1948), chaps. 7, 8.

BURGESS, ERNEST W., AND LOCKE, HARVEY, *The Family* (New York: American Book, 1945), Chap. 12.

BURGESS, ERNEST W., AND WALLIN, PAUL, *Engagement and Marriage* (Chicago: Lippincott, 1953).

FOLSOM, JOSEPH K., *The Family and Democratic Society* (New York: Wiley, 1943), Chap. 16.

KIRKPATRICK, CLIFFORD, AND CAPLOW, THEODORE, "Emotional Trends in the Courtship Experience of College Students," *American Sociological Review*, Vol. 10 (1945), pp. 619–626.

NIMKOFF, M. F., AND WOOD, A. L., "Courtship and Personality," *American Journal of Sociology*, Vol. 53 (1948), pp. 263–269.

WALLER, WILLARD, "The Rating-Dating Complex," *American Sociological Review*, Vol. 2 (1937), pp. 727–734.

WINCH, ROBERT F., *The Modern Family* (New York: Holt, 1952), Chap. 16.

CHAPTER FIVE

World's Fair, 2000

THE MEANING OF AN ENGAGEMENT

Are short engagements better than long ones?

Once you are engaged, what are your obligations?

What can an engaged couple do to prepare themselves for marriage?

What sorts of engagements ought to be broken?

Should engagement mean monopoly?

*T*HE MEANING OF BETROTHAL, THE INTERPRETATION OF ITS OBLIGA-
tions and duties, varies tremendously from couple to couple. For many
it is regarded as an end in itself, like a degree or a diploma, rather than
a period of preparation for greater responsibilities in marriage and family life. For many it is dominated by the thrills of novelty and new
experience rather than by the solving of problems and testing of personalities.

This chapter is designed to open the eyes of couples who regard engagement simply as a hurdle before marriage. We hope to show that
the betrothal has values of its own, and that time invested in a con-
scientious engagement returns dividends in more successful marriage
later on. It is a necessary bridge between the irresponsibility of youth
with its "single blessedness" and the married responsibility of adults.

The courting relationship to begin with is fairly casual, and there is
little pain involved if a rupture occurs in the relation. By engagement
time the couple has been caught up in a whole series of involvements
through the use of the line, occasional love gestures, idealizations, and
lovers' quarrels. Couple unity builds up out of common interests and
the growing feeling that they are meant for each other. Friends take

notice and encourage them to think of themselves as engaged. They are identified in the public's eyes henceforth as a potential married couple, and they are aware of the necessity of conforming to social expectations.

Engagement from a Man's Point of View

Engagement is commonly thought to be mainly of concern to women. According to the articulate male critic, engagement is a matter of putting up with a whim of the fiancée in order that she may have her quota of parties and showers, and that she may rate the society pages and may be duly congratulated and feted on her good fortune. She often supports him in this viewpoint by insisting that a girl gets married only once, and she has a right to all the attention and excitement she can get out of the preparations which attend the engagement period. Partly due to this attitude, many couples have married without bothering with engagement at all. Just what are the advantages of an engagement which a man should consider, for he is more frequently the offender in bypassing this period as needless ceremonial?

There are real advantages to the man of a full and complete engagement period, which hold in many instances for his fiancée as well:

1 The engagement may save a man from being dazzled by the supposed glamor of his fiancée, since it gives him opportunities to see her without make-up, over a period of time. It is the more enjoyable because it is conducted in everyday clothes instead of Sunday best.

2 The engagement may enable a man to become better acquainted with the thinking of the emancipated woman of the twentieth century. He may find that the present edition will not play the same submissive game his mother has and that she expects to be accepted as a person in her own right. If he wants a wife who will baby him as mother may have done, he may need to look elsewhere.

3 The engagement gives him an opportunity to get acquainted with his fiancée's family and to have his fiancée accepted by his family. In-laws are valuable assets, and their approval is most necessary. If they disapprove, they may act as a wedge to separate him from his wife when the first crisis develops.[1]

---

[1] Studies of marriage success list "approval of parents" as one of the important factors in marital happiness. See Ernest W. Burgess and Leonard S. Cottrell, Jr., *Predicting Success or Failure in Marriage* (New York: Prentice-Hall, 1939), pp. 168–

4 The engagement gives him time to arrange his financial affairs and to get ready for the economic burden of marriage.

5 The engagement may give him insight into the relative responsiveness of his fiancée. Even though there be a minimum of sex experimentation in the engagement, such deficiencies as frigidity, lack of capacity for demonstrating affection, and childhood fears will show up in the normal love play of the engagement.

6 The engagement gives the man a chance to see whether there is any possibility of sharing his business and professional interests with his wife-to-be. This is an important factor in the early years of marriage as both are struggling to attain a secure economic position.

7 The engagement gives the man who wants children the opportunity of noting in more detail his affianced's attitudes toward children and child rearing. (Not all women want children, you know.)

8 The engagement gives a man a chance to slip into his role of husband gradually and to learn some of the ropes while still in the engagement period. Nothing succeeds like success, and the engagement enables the novice to succeed by starting him out with premarriage problems and inducting him slowly into the complications of married life.

Woman's Point of View

The feminine reader will recognize here many values of an engagement which, when transposed, hold equally well for her. She should be aware also of the unusual opportunities the engagement offers for prolonged discussions of mutual interest. She can feel perfectly free, now that she is engaged, to express her desires and aspiration in marriage. She will want to find out the attitudes of her fiancé toward the role of the wife as homemaker or worker outside the home, his point of view on the issues of housing, extramarital friendships, handling of money, and so on. The initiative which a woman properly takes in this discussion is com-

---

170. In America we are inclined to dispose of the mother-in-law and other in-laws by a system of avoidance. Any story commiserating the victim of in-law interference is sure to get a laugh or a headline; see for example the following clipping from the *Detroit News:*

"Tom took his wife and two children out to spend a week with her parents in the country, while some repairs were being made on the house.

"At week-end the repair job wasn't finished and Tom telephoned to suggest that the missus extend her stay for a few days.

" 'I will not,' she hissed. 'You come right out and get me. I can't stand living with in-laws any longer.'

" 'What do you mean?' asked puzzled Tom. 'They're not my folks; they're yours.'

" 'Well,' said Mrs. Tom defensively, 'after you're married they're all in-laws.' "

ing to be recognized frankly. Since the engagement period has been characterized as the period during which the idea of marriage with this particular mate is being explored as a working hypothesis, such discussions are especially pertinent during this interval.[2]

A third reason for the engagement is to test the sincerity of the professions of affection which occur so frequently in the courtship period. The newly engaged want to be assured that the professing of love isn't part of the line, that this is really love. The girl wants to feel the tenderness of her affianced without the threat of rivals to disturb her. The members of an engaged pair inevitably bring from courtship certain resentments, memories of injustices and painful jealousy, as a result of the insecurity of the relation in competitive courtship days. Now is the time to bring out on the table the unresolved differences and conflicts which have heretofore plagued the relationship. Each can now speak his piece with more security. There are no longer rivals who might take immediate advantage of any temporary alienation. It is no longer necessary to jockey for position. The line, which was used originally to cover up the insecurity of the participants, can now be put aside. People leave the pair alone a lot more now, so they can be quite frank about themselves. The period can be one of personality testing and can also be one of exploration and experimentation.

Finally, the young woman knows that it is no longer primarily her parents' job, but hers, to investigate the background and future prospects of the man to whom she is engaged. Presumably she has made certain investigations during the courtship period, or she would not have become engaged. Within the privacy and intimacy of the new relationship the more detailed double checks on their reactions to each other are invaluable. It is incumbent on the pair to carry on this exploration in our crazy-quilt society, because there is no guarantee that our present mate-finding machinery has brought together individuals of similar backgrounds.

What, in summary, can the engagement do for our hypothetical courtship couple that warrants any further postponement of their marriage? The engagement has possibilities as a stage for getting better acquainted without the fear of rivals' cutting in, as an off-stage setting where the line, the wisecracking, and the kidding of the courtship may

[2] Hornell Hart and Ella B. Hart, *Personality and the Family* (rev. ed.; Boston: Heath, 1941), p. 178.

be exchanged for the more honest and earnest discussion. It has possibilities as a testing ground for the congeniality of personalities, as a school for solving differences and finding areas of agreement, as a waiting period for the doubting Thomases with their misgivings, and finally as a trial period with the public watching and judging. All the processes welding a couple together in courtship continue with greater force in engagement, but they operate with less uncertainty, because there is less danger that the relationship will be disrupted. The engagement period makes possible the continuation of these processes which make for solidarity to the point where the relationship can withstand the crises and the responsibilities of marriage.

Length of Engagement

How long should the engagement be? This is a frequent question in marriage classes. As we have pointed out earlier, each engaged couple is unique in experience and background, and each interprets engagement somewhat differently. To answer the question of length of engagement would require an intimate acquaintance with the history of the individual engagement pair. Much depends, for example, on the length of acquaintance before engagement and the degree to which the couple may have undertaken the personality testing and problem solving functions in the pre-engagement period. Many students who have read books or attended classes on marriage problems discuss during courtship questions which other couples less well oriented postpone for the engagement.

In both the Burgess-Cottrell and the Terman studies of marriage success already cited there appears to be a positive relationship between length of engagement and marital happiness.[3] The longer couples were engaged, the studies showed, the more satisfactory was their later marital adjustment. Actually, these statistics may reflect more than appears on the surface. There probably was a selection of the hardier couples of superior character who could survive a long engagement. We have no adjustment scores for those couples whose engagements were broken because they attempted to prolong the engagement beyond a sensible point.

[3] See Lewis M. Terman and associates, *Psychological Factors in Marital Happiness*, p. 198; and Burgess and Cottrell, *op. cit.*, p. 167.

The highest happiness scores in the Burgess study went to those married couples who had been engaged for two years or longer before marriage. Only 11 per cent of this group showed poor marital adjustment, while of those who had been engaged less than three months 50 per cent showed poor adjustment. The mean happiness scores of Terman's couples went up steadily in relation to length of engagement, reaching a peak among those who had been engaged five years or longer. One of these authors concludes from his findings that companionship rather than romantic love forms the best sustaining force for a mutually satisfying love relation. He apparently questions the lasting quality of a relation based primarily on romantic love, suggesting that there should be an opportunity for the relationship to mature over a considerable period of time before marriage.[4]

The case for fairly long engagements need not rest on these statistical studies of marriage success alone. There are obvious values in engagements which are long enough to prepare couples for marriage. Engagements need to be long enough to act as a screening device to alienate and separate incompatible couples who would otherwise marry, only to separate more painfully after some years of marriage. The answer to the question of length of engagement is given best, not as a definite number of months or years, but in terms of the indefinite "long enough." The engagement, then, should be *long enough* to perform the many functions of testing, discussing, learning, fighting, and loving which underlie successful marriage. If the student requires a more specific figure, it is probably safe to state that the engagement should rarely be shorter than six months and rarely longer than two years, depending on the length of previous acquaintance and the extent to which the engagement functions have already been started in the courtship period.

How long an engagement is too long? Henry Bowman has established rough criteria which may be helpful:

An engagement is too long if an excessive amount of nervous tension is generated; if the couple experience a sense of frustration; if they become more than usually tired of waiting; if they grow discouraged; if they become indifferent to each other; if they begin to accept the *status quo* as a substitute for marriage and lose interest in the latter; if the engagement constitutes more than a relatively small fraction of the total period from meeting to wedding. . . . We wish to counteract the opinion so commonly expressed

4 Burgess and Cottrell, *op. cit.*, p. 168.

among students to the effect that on the basis of a few months' courtship a couple may without risk enter upon an engagement of several years' duration.[5]

Engagements in the Face of Separation

An important variable to be considered in computing the length of the engagement period is that of distance, which all too frequently separates the engaged couple. The engagement of individuals parted for long periods of time because of war, employment, prolonged professional training, or other enforced absences is hardly to be compared with the engagement of young people actively pursuing the job of mutual exploration and problem solving day in and day out. Can the functions of engagement be satisfactorily carried on by correspondence?

In the ideal engagement, separation immediately after the announcement would hardly be contemplated. Rather, the announcement should normally be followed by a series of mutual investigations during more or less constant association. The pair needs time to win the approval of the families, relatives, and friends of both parties. This necessitates being seen in public together long enough for people to say, "I think they make a fine pair; they ought to hit it off nicely." The support of the public is not to be disregarded, even in these times, and it is hard to obtain public support of the marriage-to-be by correspondence. There are, however, several young couples who are working out their engagement duties quite conscientiously by correspondence. How are they doing it?

First, every effort is made to keep letters full of information about day-to-day experiences which tell about the changes in personality. The correspondents go in for frequent exchange of candid photographs and snapshots. These keep the couple up to date on physical appearance (new clothes, changes in weight, etc.) and give a visual picture of the places and people each is meeting. These tokens will later act as a source of common experience to tie the couple together.

Second, the couples find that some questions may be discussed more deeply and somewhat more objectively by correspondence than in face-to-face chats; for example, attitudes about children, money, religion, a wife's working, the use of leisure time, and the place of sex in marriage.

[5] Henry Bowman, *Marriage for Moderns* (New York: McGraw-Hill, 1948), p. 249.

Letters most certainly should not preclude many face-to-face talks on these subjects at some later date, but during the separation they do serve to clear up many questions.

A third device used by successful correspondents is to refer to particularly enjoyable books and newspaper and magazine articles as a means of getting the reaction of the other on questions of mutual interest. "I read an interesting article which you would enjoy. Remember your resistance to women working? Tell me what you think of it."

Finally, the correspondents should make relatively little effort to spare the other person the daily details of living. Realistic correspondence keeps the avenues of communication open frankly and honestly, and holds to a minimum the building of illusions of sweetness and light when things are actually going pretty poorly. This is an art which needs to be worked at — how to write what is happening without arousing anxiety, and yet not encourage illusory ideas by telling too little.[6]

Certain of the engagement functions will have to wait, to be worked out satisfactorily until the pair is reunited. The aspect of marriage preparations which has to do with living together in intimate association is an art and takes practice; the skills of getting along together must be learned. Engagement by correspondence prepares only for a marriage in which most contacts are by correspondence and might be good preparation for marriage with a traveling salesman. For normal, settled, married living, however, there is no substitute for daily association over a period of time to learn the art of resolving conflicts, of cooperative planning, of joint functioning, all of which are learned only by doing.

CHECK YOURSELF	Which of the following problems might lend themselves to effective discussion by correspondence?

      _____ 1 Problems of child spacing
      _____ 2 Choice of a place for the honeymoon
      _____ 3 The quick temper of one of the partners
      _____ 4 Source and stability of the man's income
      _____ 5 Changing of religion
      _____ 6 Handling a mother fixation problem

★ KEY   1, 2, 4, possibly part of 5.

---

[6] Confession of misdeeds, of past missteps, are quite another problem and will be discussed later in the chapter.

In brief, in the face of prolonged separation many of the functions of the engagement may be satisfactorily carried on by correspondence, but a period of association should be planned for before marriage to work out the problems of intimate relationships which remain.

Should Engagement Mean "No Stepping Out"?

Many of the questions which are raised about the engagement center around what is fair and just to expect of betrothed couples separated over long periods of time. Should engagement mean monopoly? Is it fair to date men other than the affianced? What are the risks of being misunderstood and perhaps having the engagement endangered thereby?

There should be no question about the engagement's being an amorous monopoly. Otherwise the relationship is no engagement and should be dissolved. There must be a recognition of the devotion each has for the other to the exclusion of rivals. Does that preclude dating others when the couples are to be separated indefinitely? This problem is one for each couple to work out in the light of their own attitudes and needs. Some couples will find it to their advantage to continue dating while separated, regarding it as recreation and as a valuable social experience. Couples who have doubts and mixed feelings may well decide to forego the experience of dating others until their own engagement is more firmly established emotionally.

In a survey of this problem at the University of Wisconsin, 65 per cent of the 608 students studied disapproved of stepping out, and only 14 per cent approved. The balance were undecided. The Wisconsin students were reacting, however, to a situation which differs greatly from wartime absences, where engaged couples are separated for long periods of time. Henry Bowman of Stephens College, in reviewing the problem of engaged college students dating if attending colleges in widely separated towns, concludes: "In general it may be said that, unless there are weighty considerations to the contrary, such students should date, even while they are engaged." [7]

Since a large proportion of social activities everywhere are organized around couples, it is important to have a partner in order to participate. To miss all these activities is to give up valuable social experience in understanding individuals of the opposite sex. After marriage the husband

[7] Bowman, op. cit., p. 253.

will not abstain from social contact, but will find himself constantly in association with persons of both sexes at parties and professional gatherings. Moreover, sooner or later he must learn to accept members of the opposite sex as persons rather than as potential marriage partners. He will want to be able to associate with them genuinely without the implication of amorous inclinations. If the engagement is sufficiently established to permit dating without fear of emotional competition, the individual couple being best equipped to judge, then dating may well be in order. Such dating, moreover, may help to relieve the strain of separation. Bowman adds, "It is also a good test of the couple's devotion, for if their love and trust cannot withstand a simple test like this, they are not ready to marry and their engagement is insubstantial." [8]

Several suggestions might well be made to make dating while engaged less hazardous and more enjoyable: 1. Dating should be for recreation or pleasure without amorous interest in the other person. 2. Dating should not be limited to one person exclusively. 3. Dating should be with the full understanding and approval of the affianced. 4. Dating should not be expected to come up to the standards of enjoyment of dating with the affianced, and unfavorable comparisons should not be made. The casual date is purely for recreation and convenience, whereas dating the affianced has the added lift of the love relationship which quite naturally increases the enjoyment.

Revealing the Past

Another question which frequently troubles young people entering upon an engagement is how much of the past should be revealed to the other. In the Wisconsin survey referred to previously more reluctance to reveal the past was found among women than among men; 29 per cent of the women disapproved and 33 per cent were undecided; 24 per cent of the men disapproved and 33 per cent were undecided. This gives some clue to the nature of the problem. Wisconsin women did not wish to reveal the past, which might reduce their chances of consummating a marriage, and many men felt the same way about themselves.

Frank discussion should be the order of the day during the engagement period; indeed, that is one of engagement's major functions. However, there is no obligation to rattle all the family skeletons in a

[8] Bowman, *op. cit.*, p. 254.

recital of past misdeeds and foolish indiscretions. These would be much better taken up with your marital counselor or minister or family physician or another trained specialist who will hear them out without becoming emotionally involved.

Whatever cards are put on the table should be laid down before the wedding. What items that might have a bearing on the couple's future should come out in the frank discussions of the engagement period? Certainly these: 1. a previous marriage and any financial obligations which that might entail; 2. hereditary or other defects which might involve reasons for not having children; 3. a history of tuberculosis, heart disease, venereal disease, mental breakdown, etc.; 4. an imprisonment record; 5. debts or similar obligations which might handicap the marriage.

How Much Intimacy during Engagement? [9]

One of the most difficult of all the questions of the engagement period is the one of the extent of physical intimacy. Some caressing and expressing of warm affection is normally desired and is definitely helpful in the processes of preparation for the intimacies of marriage. But while some lovemaking is desirable, full expression of the sex urge in premarital sex intercourse has hazards of guilt and shame which are extremely difficult for many couples to overcome. So the question inevitably comes up, "How far shall we go?" It is wise to have some kind of understanding on this matter so that each can notify the other of the proximity of the boundaries already set. Such understandings may naturally emerge out of the contacts themselves. If Jim laughingly whisks Mary off his lap with a gentle reminder that she is too much for him at the moment, Mary may understandingly accept both her attractiveness to her fiancé and his response to her. When recognized in time, such experiences need not be as frustrating and tantalizing as they are later on in the love play. One of the authors worked with a group of engaged couples in outlining the symptoms of "time to stop and do something else" that may be helpful to the student: 1. when either is flushed and uncomfortable; 2. when either senses an urgency to continue the petting; 3. when either finds himself or herself restless and sleepless for

[9] For other discussion of the issues of intimacy before marriage see the discussion of petting in the chapter on dating, pp. 59–62, and the chapter on sex morality, pp. 128–149.

extended periods after being together; 4. when the love play is an unpleasant memory with aspects of shame or guilt; 5. when being with the
loved one is fun only when there are physical contacts. The student will
be able to add his own guideposts to these general ones in setting up his
own boundaries for engagement conduct.

Every Engaged Couple Has Doubts

Engagement uncovers almost as many problems as it solves. Fortunate
indeed is the couple that does not end the probation period with many
doubts and mixed feelings. The disillusionment spoken of so frequently
as occurring during the first year of marriage may come before the wedding ceremony as a result of the questions raised in the engagement period. Still, it is probably better to face these realities all along the way
than to meet them unexpectedly in early marriage.

An engaged couple will do well to recognize at the outset that they
will have occasional misunderstandings and that these tiffs will be accompanied by mixed feelings and inner doubts. These differences need
not be a source of shock, however, if the couple expects them to occur
and concentrates on developing machinery for ironing them out, instead
of dwelling on the seriousness of the conflicts.

Engagement is entered into by most people in America during a
transition period in life between adolescence and adulthood, when most
young people face doubts and uncertainties. Those who are engaged
may make the mistake of ascribing these feelings of uneasiness to the
engagement and the new relationship. Realizing the fact that everyone
in this stage of life faces many problems may help relieve the situation
for some; part of the difficulty is just that of growing up.

One other source of doubt may be in the discrepancy between the
flesh-and-blood person and the dream the affianced has built up. Uneasiness that you are not as wonderful or competent as he or she thinks
you are is understandable. And, from another angle, many disturbances occur as one discovers in the engagement period the trick his imagination has played upon him. Bitter and painful quarrels may ensue
which are hard to resolve.

The fact that no couple faces marriage with absolute knowledge and
conviction of its ability to survive the crises ahead remains a source of

"How can we be mental companions if you're not ready
to eat when I am?"

insecurity throughout engagement; the jittery couple applying for a marriage license is an American stereotype. Anticipating difficulties built up from stories of trouble passed on from adults makes for mixed feelings about marriage itself, and the prospective bride and groom say, "We are all right now. Why can't it go on like this indefinitely?"

Elopement as an Escape. Some couples facing the usual doubts of engagement feel they may escape part of the responsibility by eloping. An elopement is just as much an impulsive escape from the realities of engagement and marriage as the hysterical breaking of an engagement on the eve of the wedding. Although conflict with parents is frequently the alleged cause, the desire to escape reality appears prominently. The elopement is usually carried off in haste, is inappropriate to the situation, and bodes poorly for marital happiness. Paul Popenoe studied a group of 738 elopements and found that they were divided among those who eloped because of parental objection to the marriage, those who eloped to avoid publicity, those who eloped to escape elaborate, expensive weddings, and those who eloped because of pregnancy. The marital adjustments of the eloped couples were observably poorer than those of couples married regularly. Apparently their escape from doubts and inner conflict was poorly conceived — they "jumped from the frying pan into the fire." [10]

As we can see from our previous analysis of engagement, there are objections to elopement quite apart from the escape element. The eloping couple are bypassing the testing and exploring functions of the engagement period, during which the gradual preparation for marriage occurs. Furthermore, they are alienating their in-laws and friends whose support they will need frequently in the days ahead.

Breaking the Engagement

There are two ways to *escape* from an engagement, one by an elopement and the other by a complete break. Both represent escapes from inner misgivings and doubts; they differ merely in the direction of the escape.

Yet one of the most important functions of the engagement as a social institution is to eliminate from marriage those matchings which cannot stand the experience of intimate association. Within our culture the only trial period before marriage is engagement, which is to say that there are many engagements contracted which should be broken before marriage. A high rate of broken engagements is preferable to a high rate of divorce and desertion.

The engagement should be entered into with the realization that it might be broken. If this possibility is recognized in the beginning, the break will be less severe for both persons. Even so, the habits of association are as difficult to cast off as any other bad habit, such as smok-

[10] See Paul Popenoe, *Modern Marriage* (New York: Macmillan, 1943), pp. 222–225.

ing or drinking, but a broken engagement is less painful than a separation after years of marriage.

What are reasons for breaking an engagement?   In general, any crisis which changes the basis on which the engagement was launched justifies a re-evaluation, with sufficient discussion to arrive at an agreement as to the proper course to follow.   This is good procedure in any pair relationship, whether it be engaged partners, marriage partners, business partners, or research collaborators.   All find it necessary to review their relationship whenever crises occur, in order to keep the partnership intact.   There is strong concensus that the following reasons justify re-evaluation of the engagement, with the possible agreement to sever the relationship: 1. recognition of fundamental feelings of alienation arising as a result of the more intimate relations of engagement; not just doubts and misgivings, but strong feelings of incompatibility; 2. recognition that the engagement was made originally under pressure from relatives or circumstances, and that the main reason for refraining from breaking the engagement is the fear of publicity; 3. recognition that either member of the pair is emotionally dependent on parents and too immature to stand the rigors of marriage; 4. changes in the economic future due to serious accident or health breakdown or similar disaster affecting ability to earn a living and carry on the functions of parenthood.

These reasons for breaking the engagement will be rejected in individual cases, but they should not be rejected because of fear of publicity, fear of admitting that one has made a mistake, fear of homicide or suicide threats, fear that the break will ruin the other's future.   "In the great majority of instances, suicide threats never get any further than the self-pity stage, and relatively few are ever carried out." [11]   Threats of vengeance or of suicide sprees exhibit a type of immaturity that would be highly undesirable in a marriage partner and are ample reasons in themselves for breaking the engagement.

There are two reasons for allowing the girl to announce the breaking of an engagement.   First, she needs to maintain face among her friends and loses status in terms of marriageability unless she is permitted to issue the announcement of the break.   Second, no breach-of-promise suit can be carried out successfully against any man if the woman has announced the dissolution of the engagement.   Established historically

[11] Bowman, *op. cit.*, p. 260.

as an indemnity for the woman whose opportunities for marriage were impaired by the broken vows, breach-of-promise suits still occur occasionally. The promise to marry is a legal contract, the breaking of which gives grounds for suit for damages; and as recently as 1929 a Michigan court awarded $450,000 in a breach-of-promise suit. One of the happy results of the improved status of women in our society is the growing feeling of disfavor toward breach-of-promise suits.

CHECK YOURSELF   Which of the following engagements should be re-evaluated with the possibility of a definite break?

_____ 1 John, engaged to Eunice, was in service and has been missing in action for almost two years.

_____ 2 Bob is Catholic, Jeanne is Protestant, and neither will change religion; they avoid the subject after three months of engagement.

_____ 3 Jim has returned from two years in the interior of Brazil, broken in health, quite possibly a permanent invalid — wishes to break his engagement of five years' standing with Eloise, since he will be unable to support her and a family in his condition.

_____ 4 Jack has broken three engagements and is on the verge of a breakup of the fourth with Georgene, of whom his doting mother disapproves.

_____ 5 A week before the marriage Susan meets quite accidentally the former wife of Frank, her fiancé, and learns details of his life he has never told her. His family assure her everything will be all right — Frank was only seventeen and infatuated — this time it will be different.

_____ 6 John swears he will commit suicide if Dorothy breaks their engagement; he waves a revolver to prove it.

★ KEY ·pǝʇɒnlɒʌǝ-ǝɹ ǝq plnoɥs llⱯ

Building the Engagement into a Marriage

The engaged couple expects to make a success of their marriage. All their plans are laid with that expectation in mind, and the public supports them in their resolutions. Some day there will be special orientation classes in every community in the country to which engaged couples will wend their way, to be introduced to marriage as the civilian is processed into army life and as the soldier is processed back into civilian life. Great industrial plants consider it important to give their new employees weeks of orientation into their policies and objectives, as well as into the ways of behavior in the organization, before entrusting them with free access to the plant. Marriage is worthy of even more careful attention. Some communities are now offering classes for engaged couples, and there are classes in over five hundred colleges and universities. In time young people everywhere will be able to receive such instruction. For Sally and Bill who have just announced their engagement, there are many helpful books and pamphlets available, as well as several tests and prediction scales, which are suggestive to the couple planning for a successful marriage.[12]

Premarriage Counseling and the Premarital Examination. In addition to study and testing, the engaged couple preparing for marriage will find available professional premarriage counseling services. Few people attempt to build a home without consulting an architect. Even where they have their own ideas about a house, sensible people consult an architect to have them checked carefully. The same point of view is rapidly becoming current with regard to marriage, which also is given design and symmetry only after careful planning and study. Premarriage counseling is becoming increasingly the source of architectural charts for the prospective bride and groom. Intelligent couples are saying, "Nothing's too good for our marriage," and the careful planning which their premarriage interviews stimulate gives them a head start on less careful students.

Premarital counseling often starts early in the courtship period and continues throughout the engagement. In addition to marriage prediction scales which test the similarity and compatibility of home and family backgrounds as well as certain social factors, the premarital guidance center will have available other personality tests which prove important in determining the emotional readiness of individuals for marriage.

Our earlier discussion of personality in marriage should have proved the necessity of understanding the nature of your own personality as well as the personality of the person you will marry. These tests in the hands of a skilled psychologist can be extremely revealing. Suppose they reveal emotional dependence and nervousness, with tendencies toward blues and depressions. The counselor may advise remedial attention just as the physician would advise a couple to postpone having a baby until a kidney infection cleared up. The couple will not want

---

[12] This book attempts to cover many of the questions Sally and Bill will raise. In addition, we have supplied a list of readings at the end of each chapter.

to take a chance on marrying immediately, but will recognize that the period in which these questions are best cleared up is during engagement, not after marriage.

Some counseling centers describe their premarital guidance as a "premarital examination." Actually the guidance program may take weeks and sometimes longer if problems are uncovered which deserve detailed attention. The premarital examination is a personal course of instruction, adapted to prepare young people for marriage by giving special attention to the individual background and specific needs of the couples concerned. In general, it includes: 1. a review of the personal and family backgrounds in an effort to locate the important factors that may influence marriage and avert avoidable mis-mating; 2. a study of the characteristics of the person, the temperament, disposition, and other emotional inclinations and attitudes, by means of interviews and tests; 3. specific sex instructions geared to clear up misconceptions, questions, and fears; 4. instruction in the healthiest approach to marriage, its problems and responsibilities as well as its possibilities for growth and development; 5. conferences and consultations with both members of the couple, and separately at the discretion of the counselor (group conferences after classes in marriage and family courses also provide helps to the engaged couple anticipating marriage); 6. a thorough physical examination and conference by the examining physician of the center. (See the details covered by the physician in his examination in Chapter Six, "Marriage and the Facts of Life.")

The premarital examination is one further means of objectively appraising the resources an individual couple brings to marriage.

Social and Legal Requirements for Marriage

There are certain minimum social requirements for marriage which the engaged couple will find enforced by public opinion today. Some of these are also legal requirements in many states, and include laws about age, race, mental and physical defects, previous marriages, and divorces.

In America there are fifty-one different jurisdictions with laws governing or limiting marriage, and the couple will do well to familiarize itself with the legal requirements in its state of residence. No two sets of state laws are exactly alike, although there are a few regulations that are general throughout the United States.

In most states the engaged couple would legally be denied a license if either party fell into any of the following categories: 1. already married; 2. first cousins; 3. insane or feeble-minded; 4. under age — generally under fourteen for girls, eighteen for boys; 5. having a venereal disease; 6. members of different races — white-Negro and white-Mongolian combinations prohibited regionally, determined by states.

CHECK YOURSELF   Which of the following conditions would result in the couple's being denied a license in most states?

_____1 Habitual drunkenness	_____ 6 Under twelve years of age
_____2 Already married	_____ 7 Tubercular
_____3 Epilepsy	_____ 8 Prison record
_____4 Feeble-minded	_____ 9 First cousins
_____5 Pauper	_____10 Venereally diseased

★ KEY 01 '6 '9 'ᔑ '乙

Most marriage legislation puts into written form regulations which have existed before in unwritten form as custom and public opinion. Bigamy, incest, child marriage, and miscegenation were under ban long before they became prohibited by law, and offenders were summarily dealt with for violating such social regulations by the effective controls of excommunication, ostracism, and "riding him out of town on a rail."

In addition to the legal requirements, which are for the most part stated in negative terms, we have social requirements more or less enforced which represent the desired levels at which marriage should take place.

SOCIAL REQUIREMENTS FOR MARRIAGE

Willingness and ability to carry out the matrimonial obligations of:

1 Sharing a common residence
2 Sexual access
3 Sexual fidelity
4 Conjugal kindness
5 Adult responsibility for homemaking
6 Financial support of dependents

What has been said about the engagement in this chapter which would bear repeating in quick summary?

1 The pattern in engagement is the best preview available premaritally of the marriage pattern for any given couple.

2 The optimum length of engagement is best stated as "long enough," — to perform the many functions of testing, discussing, learning, fighting, and loving which underlie successful marriage.

3 All the processes welding a couple together in courtship continue with greater force in engagement, but they operate with less uncertainty, because there is less danger that the relationship will be disrupted.

4 The engagement provides opportunity for maximum planning, learning how to make jointly choices which both parties can accept and support individually.

5 The engagement operates as a preventive of divorce since in breaking up those matchings which cannot stand the experience of intimate association, in effect it brings about a divorce before marriage itself.

Selected Readings

BOWMAN, HENRY A., *Marriage for Moderns* (New York: McGraw-Hill, 1948), Chap. 8.

CHRISTENSEN, HAROLD T., *Marriage Analysis* (New York: Ronald Press, 1950), Chap. 9.

HARPER, ROBERT A., *Marriage* (New York: Appleton-Century-Crofts, 1949), Chap. 6.

LANDIS, JUDSON T., AND LANDIS, MARY G., *Building a Successful Marriage*, (New York: Prentice-Hall, 1948), Chap. 8.

MACE, DAVID R., *Marriage* (New York: Doubleday, 1952), Chap. 2.

MAGOUN, F. ALEXANDER, *Love and Marriage* (New York: Harper, 1948), Chap. 7.

WALLER, WILLARD, AND HILL, REUBEN, *The Family: A Dynamic Interpretation* (New York: Dryden Press, 1951), Chap. 12.

Technical References

BURGESS, ERNEST W., AND COTTRELL, LEONARD S., JR., *Predicting Success or Failure in Marriage* (New York: Prentice-Hall, 1939), Chap. 10.

BURGESS, ERNEST W., AND WALLIN, PAUL, *Engagement and Marriage* (Chicago: Lippincott, 1953).

KUHN, MANFORD H., "The Engagement: Thinking about Marriage," in Howard Becker and Reuben Hill (eds.), *Family, Marriage, and Parenthood* (Boston: Heath, 1948).

TERMAN, LEWIS M., AND ASSOCIATES, *Psychological Factors in Marital Happiness* (New York: McGraw-Hill, 1938), pp. 197–201, 319–335.

WINCH, ROBERT F., *The Modern Family* (New York: Holt, 1952), pp. 434–467.

What are the sex differences between men and women?

How does conception take place?

When is it most likely?

What causes impotence?

How are venereal diseases contracted and why are they serious?

What should be checked in an adequate premarital examination?

SEX ADJUSTMENT COMES SHARPLY INTO FOCUS AS TWO PEOPLE marry and establish their right to live together as man and wife. Long before that, many questions about the nature of man and woman, their life together in marriage, and their preparation for it, are common among young people today. This chapter reviews the main areas of interest with a presentation of pertinent facts checked and rechecked with leading research workers and practicing physicians. The simplest medical terms: names of the sex organs, functions, and conditions are italicized when first used throughout the material, as an aid to adequate vocabulary, so often helpful especially in this area of life.

Sex Organs and How They Work in the Man

The male sex glands are two firm oval bodies about one and one half inches long which hang from the lower part of the front of the body between the thighs in a sac called the *scrotum.* They are called *testes* and have two very important roles to play. They produce a *hormone*

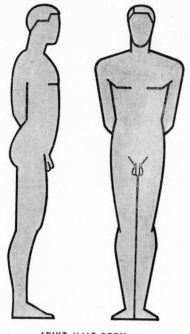

ADULT MALE BODY

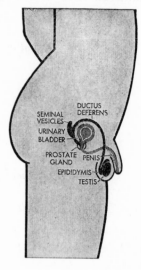

MALE UROGENITAL SYSTEM

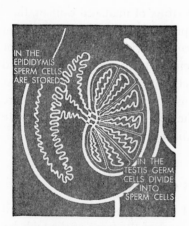

DETAILS OF TESTIS (Schematic)

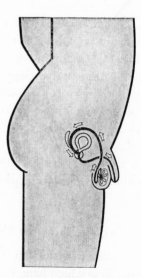

PATH OF SPERM CELLS

From *Life and Growth* by Alice V. Keliher (Appleton-Century)

(chemical substance) called *testosterone* which is largely responsible for the development of masculine characteristics, and they produce the male germ cells known as *sperm cells, spermatozoa,* or *male gametes,* by means of which a man is able to produce children.

Testosterone is absorbed directly into the blood stream and is carried to all parts of the body. Its presence produces the male type of body build, hair distribution, vocal range, and all other characteristics that go to make up the maleness of an individual.

Sperm cells are formed within tiny tubules in each testis. These empty into the *epididymis,* which leads into a slender tube, the *ductus deferens,* or *vas deferens.* A vas arises on either side and through it the spermatozoa travel slowly upward. Each vas runs upward from the scrotum into the lower part of the body, ending behind the bladder. Close by on either side, the *seminal vesicles* furnish the bulk of the fluid in which sperms are suspended. Surrounding the urethra in the region where the two *vasa deferentia* (plural of vas deferens) open into it, is a firm globular gland known as the *prostate.* This produces a secretion which nourishes and activates the sperm cells. Together the spermatozoa, the fluid from the seminal vesicles, and the prostate make up the *semen.*

The urethra runs through the *penis,* which in its relaxed position hangs just in front of the scrotum. At times of sexual excitement, the penis becomes engorged with blood and stands erect from the body. When ejaculation occurs sperms spurt out of the reservoirs through the ejaculatory ducts, through the prostate, and with the seminal and prostatic fluid are carried out of the body through the urethral opening in the penis. Hundreds of millions of sperm cells are present in the half-teaspoonful of semen that is released in the average ejaculate.

Semen is released during sexual intercourse, masturbation, or unconsciously during sleep. The latter process is known as a *nocturnal emission,* or "wet dream," and is nature's way of eliminating stored secretions when there has been no other more active form of expulsion. Such release occurs first at *puberty* (period of establishment of sexual maturity) and continues to take place with some degree of regularity during intervals of sexual *continence* (abstinence from intentional ejaculation of semen). It has been definitely established that a man may remain continent for long periods of time, or indeed for a lifetime, without injuring his health or destroying his masculinity.

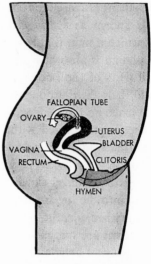

FEMALE UROGENITAL SYSTEM

ADULT FEMALE BODY

FEMALE GENITAL ORGANS

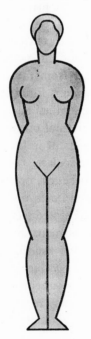

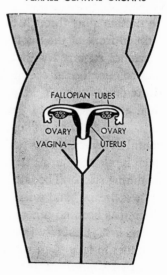

From *Life and Growth* by Alice V. Keliher (Appleton-Century)

Sex Organs and How They Work in the Woman

The sex glands in the female are about the size of those in the male, but they lie within the abdominal cavity, low on the right and left sides. They are called *ovaries* and, like the testes, have two important functions. They produce the hormones which control the femininity of the individual, the two most important of which are known as *estrin* (*estrogen*) and *progestin*, and they also produce the female germ cells which are known as *female gametes, ova,* or *eggs.*

Millions of sperm cells are formed daily during the active life of the male, but the female is born with all of the ova she ever possesses. From the time of puberty until the *menopause* (that period which marks the termination of the ability to bear children, commonly known as "the change of life") one ovum each month ripens and is expelled from the ovary. The production of hormones is related in large measure to the ripening of the ova. As an ovum begins to mature, estrin is produced and is carried by the blood stream from the ovary to the *uterus.* This stimulates the growth of the inner lining of the uterus and produces an initial preparation for pregnancy. When the ovum is mature it is expelled from the ovary (*ovulation*), and progestin is produced in the ovary. This hormone is also carried by the blood to the uterus and acts upon it to cause the final preparation for pregnancy. After the ovum is expelled from the ovary it enters the Fallopian tube where, if sperm are present, *fertilization* (entrance of the sperm into the egg) occurs, and subsequently the fertilized egg journeys into the uterus, where it becomes implanted into the already prepared wall. The secretion of progestin continues throughout pregnancy. If the ovum is not fertilized it dies within a few hours after its expulsion from the ovary. Despite this the uterus, under the influence of progestin, continues its preparation for pregnancy for ten or twelve days. By the end of this time the production of progestin ceases. The sudden cessation in the production of progestin affects the uterus and causes the vessels in the lining to bleed. This bleeding is the result of the fact that the body has prepared for pregnancy, but no pregnancy has taken place. This flow is called *menstruation* and consists of blood, mucus, and shreds of uterine lining. It lasts for three to five days. Before the menstrual flow stops, another ovum begins to mature; estrin is again formed and another period for preparation for pregnancy is on its way. This is what is called the menstrual cycle.

The female internal organs of reproduction other than the ovaries are the *Fallopian tubes, uterus* (*womb*), and *vagina*. The vagina forms the lowermost portion and is the canal into which semen is ejaculated from the penis during sexual intercourse. The uterus hangs above the vagina; it is a muscular, pear-shaped organ consisting of a lower small, cone-shaped or cylindrical portion known as the *cervix*, which extends into the vagina, and an upper large portion, in which the baby develops during pregnancy.

Extending up and out from each side of the upper portion of the uterus are the Fallopian tubes. The outer funnel-shaped ends of the tubes lie close to the ovaries so that when an ovum is liberated it is drawn into the open end of one of the tubes. Spermatozoa which may have been deposited in the vagina move upward through the opening of the cervix, into the main cavity of the uterus, and on into the Fallopian tubes. Fertilization normally takes place in one or the other of the tubes.

The lower end of the vagina has a puckered, crescent-shaped, pliable thin cuff of membrane called the *hymen*. In some virgins this is but a narrow rim of tissue; in others it forms a partial membrane which is easily stretched during cleansing procedures or at the time of first inter-

---

CHECK YOURSELF   Some aspects of the man's sex functioning correspond to that in the woman. Below, in section A, are lists of male and female parts.

A. Match the corresponding words in the male and female columns.

Male	Female
1 Sperm	1 Clitoris
2 Testes	2 Ovum
3 Penis	3 Estrin
4 Testosterone	4 Ovaries

B. Which organs are paired in the human anatomy (exist in twos)?

1 Penis	2 Testis	3 Uterus	4 Ovary
5 Scrotum	6 Seminal vesicle	7 Vagina	8 Fallopian tube

★ KEY   odd numbers not paired   A. Male 1, 2, 3, 4
          B. Even numbers paired;   Female 2, 4, 1, 3

course; and in others its thickness necessitates dilation or surgical nicking before sexual intercourse can take place.

The *external* *genitalia* (outer sex organs) include two hair-covered folds called the *labia* *majora* and two small inner folds known as *labia* *minora*. Between these lie the openings of the vagina and the urethra, and situated above the latter is a small structure called the *clitoris*, which is not unlike a rudimentary penis. This organ, located at the front meeting of the labia minora, is usually the seat of woman's early localized erotic (sex) response, and its manipulation usually leads to her sexual excitation.

How a Baby Gets Started

During intercourse semen is discharged from the penis into the upper end of the vagina. Many sperm pass through the opening in the cervix into the body of the uterus and out into the Fallopian tubes. Here fertilization takes place if an ovum is present.

STEPS IN FERTILIZATION

1 The ovum ripens in the ovary
2 The mature ovum escapes from the ovary into the tube
3 The ovum goes through the tube toward the uterus
4 Sperm cells deposited in the vagina travel up into the tubes
5 One sperm cell unites with the ovum in the tube
6 The fertilized ovum implants in the uterus

Immediately after the egg is fertilized it begins to divide rapidly into many cells, and by the time it has passed down through the tube and has reached its final point of attachment in the uterine lining, considerable development has taken place. Continued division and specialization of cells soon produce the *fetus* (baby within the uterine cavity), *surrounding* *membranes* enclosing fluid within which the fetus lies, and the *placenta,* a structure to which the fetus is attached by the *umbilical* *cord* and through which the fetus receives all of the oxygen and food material necessary for its development. There is no direct connection between the circulation of the mother and that of the fetus. Blood of both enter the placenta but always remain separated by vessel walls, and all exchange of food takes place across these membranes. Growth is very rapid, and at the end of nine months the fetus has increased in weight 800,000,000 times!

The baby is born through the birth canal (vagina) in a three-stage process known as *labor*. The first stage may last for fourteen hours or more for a first baby, and consists of muscular contractions which dilate the cervix sufficiently to allow the baby to pass through. The second stage of labor (one or more hours) is marked by intense bearing-down pains which expel the baby. Usually the head comes first. The final stage is the separation and expulsion of the *afterbirth*. (See the series of photographs and the fuller treatment of this section in Chapter Sixteen, "Where Babies Come From.")

Planning a Family

The healthy married couple may expect conception to occur a few months after marriage. Often the age of the mother and the readiness of the couple for children is such that an early pregnancy is highly desirable. Many couples, however, are better prepared for the arrival of children if they have had a period of several months in which to build a sound and satisfying marriage relationship before the onset of a pregnancy.

The normally fertile couple may expect one pregnancy to follow the previous one by intervals of a year or two more or less. Some women are physically able to take such frequent pregnancies without injuring their health or increasing the hazards for the newcomer. Many families, however, prefer to space the arrival of their children to provide adequately for the care of the children already in the home, the optimum well-being of the mother, and the readiness of the family for an additional member. For these reasons the normal healthy couple consider seriously the means by which they may limit the number and plan for the arrival of their babies. This usually means the use of some type of contraceptive device or technique. Abstaining from intercourse except for procreation is so extremely difficult for the normal couple living together that *continence* is rarely advocated. *Abortions* are so dangerous (see fuller discussion in Chapter Sixteen, "Where Babies Come From") that they are generally deplored as the most unfortunate means of limiting family size.

In wider use in the voluntary prevention of pregnancy are the efforts

HE. "I like children . . . How many do you want?"
SHE (dreamy-eyed). "Millions."

to prevent the sperm and the egg from meeting. This is called *birth control*, or more accurately, *contraception*. There are many procedures, devices, and materials, some of which the man may use, and others of which are the woman's responsibility. Of the methods now in use, no one is 100 per cent certain and all still leave something to be desired in simplicity, effectiveness, and personal acceptability.

One of the oldest attempts at contraception is *coitus interruptus*, in which the man withdraws the erect penis from the vagina before the ejaculation. This abrupt interruption of the full sex act robs the couple of complete fulfillment, and is rarely acceptable to a well-mated pair.

The *rhythm method* is dependent upon an accurate plotting of supposedly reliable regular periods of fertility and sterility in the monthly cycle of the woman. The fertile period occurs roughly midway between menstrual periods, leaving the days just preceding and immediately following the menstrual flow as "safe" periods. Fluctuations in length of the cycle and variations in the time of ovulation make an accurate plotting of the occurrence of ovulation difficult.

Doctors and birth control clinics prescribe mechanical devices and chemical preparations to prevent conception. These are fitted to the needs of the particular couple and have become widely accepted. Moreover the religious, social, and medical needs of the couples are respected and taken into full consideration by expert marriage counselors in the premarital conference discussed later in this chapter.

In case of the chronic illness (such as severe heart disease, active tuberculosis, etc.) of the wife, and for other serious reasons where having children would be dangerous, permanent prevention of pregnancy may be accomplished by *sterilization*. This procedure in no way interferes with menstruation, or with the normal sex life of either the man or the woman. Tying the tubes of the woman to permanently prevent the meeting of sperm and egg is a major operation. But the tying of the vasa deferentia of the man is a simple procedure and in no way affects the masculinity of the husband or interferes with normal sex desires and intercourse.

Venereal Diseases

Gonorrhea is one of the venereal diseases which is contracted by sexual contact. Both syphilis and gonorrhea have serious effects on the human body, and where untreated are costly in their toll of health and fertility.

Gonorrheal infection in the woman has its start in an infection of the urethra and cervix. If not treated skillfully it may move up from the vagina, through the cervix, and the uterus, into the tubes, and even on into the abdominal cavity, where it may cause peritonitis. The tubes frequently close as a result of the infection, causing sterility thereafter, since the sperm can no longer get through to meet the egg.

The progress of gonorrhea in the man is somewhat similar. Starting at the point of contact, it may progress up through the entire genital tract, leaving blockages in its wake. It is the most frequent cause of male sterility, since it produces closure of the tubes of the epididymis.

The early symptoms of gonorrhea are frequent, burning, and painful urination, and a lemon-yellow discharge from the site of infection. Prompt, effective medical treatment is imperative. The use of sulfa or penicillin has greatly increased speedy and complete recovery especially if treatment is started at the outset of infection.

It is of utmost importance to understand that the germ of gonorrhea can easily be carried (by means of towels, hands, etc.) from infected and discharging parts to the eyes of the person having the disease. This may result in a severe infection of the eye which, unless promptly and properly treated, may result in blindness. Blindness in the newborn has been almost entirely eliminated by the use of silver nitrate in the eyes of the baby at birth. This drug kills the gonococci (germs of gonorrhea) that may have been present in the mother and could infect the baby's eyes in its passage through the vagina.

Syphilis is caused by a minute corkscrewlike organism called a *spirochete* ("ch" as "k"). This germ is caught from the infected person at the point of contact — usually the genitalia and rarely the lips or mouth. A few days after the infection a hard sore called a *chancre*, teeming with spirochetes, appears at the point of infection. The second stage of skin rash and patches on the mucous membranes follows. The disease may then become latent for months or years, after which severe damage to the central nervous system (brain and spinal cord), to the heart and blood vessels, or to other vital organs may cause insanity, paralysis, and death. Because of its many different manifestations, syphilis is frequently called "the great masquerader." It is one disease which cannot be self-treated. A reliable physician or clinic should be sought as soon as possible after infection may have taken place, and the treatment must be continued until the patient is completely cured and officially released.

Treatment of the syphilitic mother greatly reduces the likelihood of *congenital syphilis* in infancy, especially when treatment is begun before the fifth month of the pregnancy. For that reason routine tests for syphilis (Wassermann or Kahn) are given expectant mothers so that if the disease is present treatment may be started while there is still time to protect the baby.

The man may protect himself from infection by the use of a protective sheath or other prophylactic materials with immediate resort to physician or prophylactic station following contact. No similar prophylactic measures are available to the female because of the more generalized nature of her sexual contact.

So-called "innocent infections" through nonsexual contact have been reduced through the wide use of paper drinking cups, paper towels, and the general acceptance of hygiene. Venereal infection of the adult through nonsexual contact is rare.

Laws have been passed in most states requiring the examination of both men and women before marriage for presence of venereal infection. Syphilis is diagnosed by Wassermann or Kahn blood tests, and gonorrhea by the microscopic examination of a smear from the cervix and urethra. Infected persons are allowed to marry only when treatment has reduced the disease to a noninfectious stage.

CHECK YOURSELF   You are to check the courses of action most advisable for the person who finds that he has been exposed to one of the venereal diseases.

_____ 1 Wait a few months and see what develops.
_____ 2 Ask at the nearest drug store for a cure.
_____ 3 Find out what your best friend suggests.
_____ 4 Laugh it off. It's probably nothing to worry about.
_____ 5 Go immediately for medical attention.

★ KEY   The only acceptable answer to this question is 5.

Sex Adjustment in Marriage

The couple approaching marriage should understand what happens in coitus, how the sex reponses of man and woman differ, and how to acquire the skill necessary for mutual satisfaction. Though women respond more slowly than men, a sexually awakened woman may be aroused to a high and sustained pitch that is exquisitely desirable. Woman's response is not localized to the same degree as man's and usually takes more time to arouse either with tenderness or in the love _foreplay_, or both, that precedes the actual introduction of the penis into the vagina. Caressing, fondling, and assurance of endearing love are as much a part of the sex act as the more highly dramatic climax that is to follow, and they must be given enough time to bring both of the partners to a readiness for the next step.

Orgasm in the man is noticeably marked by the ejaculation of semen. The woman's climax is marked by rapid breathing and a series of spasmodic sensations which release her tension. Orgasm in both man and woman is followed soon by supreme feelings of satisfaction and tenderness. Occasionally a woman is capable of and desires a multiple orgasm. When the man is not able to accomplish another erection immediately, his manual manipulation of her clitoris and vulva may be satisfactory. Any activity or position in coitus is normal and acceptable if it brings satisfaction to the couple. The duration of the sex act varies from a few minutes in its basic biological component to an hour or more where the foreplay and afterplay are extended. The frequency of intercourse differs widely. During the first few weeks of marriage it may take place nightly. Later in the marriage it may take place one, two, or three times a week. Crests in the woman's desire may make for more frequency at certain times of the month. A great deal of variation is normal so long as the partners themselves find the arrangement satisfactory.

Simultaneous satisfaction is not always achieved in every coitus. Most couples find that it occurs more frequently as their skills improve and as they experience more and more a feeling of unity in their entire relationship. Conditions which are conducive to a satisfying sex experience are often ignored in poorly planned marriages. Personal hygiene as well as a feeling of absolute privacy, and of quiet surroundings that are clean and attractive, are important for success.

Sex Response

Some people do not respond sexually to their lovers. The inability to have an erection on the part of the man is called *impotence*, and is likely to be humiliating and difficult for both the man and his wife. This inability to perform the sex act in a desirable manner results usually from deep-seated psychological fears and feelings of guilt that yield best to psychiatric attention rather than to any localized or purely physical treatment. Quacks have exploited men for years with promises of quick return of full sex functioning.

Lack of sex response in the woman is even more frequent and is the cause of much distress in married living. *Frigidity* in the woman may be expressed in absence of sensation, with an inability to experience orgasm or to get release in intercourse, or in an active dislike of the whole experience, with accompanying pain, nervousness, and feelings of revulsion. This condition frequently results from one of the following causes: 1. inadequate early sex education, 2. a feeling that sex is shameful, 3. resentment at being a woman, 4. hostility toward the husband, or 5. fear of being hurt or of becoming pregnant. Any of these is sufficient to make the woman unable to enter eagerly into the relationship. Temporary withholding of sex relationships because of anger is not infrequent even among fairly well-adjusted women, and is a mild manifestation of chronic frigidity.

Few women enter marriage sexually awakened and ready for complete response in the sex act. Many American girls are brought up to be "nice," to repulse the advances of men, and to refrain from any genital stimulation. Marriage demands a completely different pattern of behavior, and it is extremely difficult to remake oneself overnight. To overcome the conditioning of a lifetime and replace it by the attitude of mature marital cooperation takes time. An understanding husband and/or professional help before an unsatisfactory pattern becomes too well established prove helpful in correcting this condition in many women.

Physicians are often able to speed up the woman's response by preparing her more fully for marriage, teaching her to dilate the hymen, and by freeing the clitoris from the folds that may cover it. The husband who makes full use of the excitability of the *erogenous zones* (sexually excitable areas), such as the breasts, thighs, vulva, and especially the clitoris, in fondling that is gentle and directed toward the arousal of his spouse often finds that her response grows with his increasing skill in kindling it. Loving understanding, patience, and practice are all that are usually needed to make for sexual compatibility of two normal people. The so-called *sexual incompatibility* of the divorce courts is rarely a physical problem, but rather one which has emerged through the lack of knowledges, skills, and appreciations necessary to build mutual compatibility. Sex satisfaction or dissatisfaction reflects the whole husband-wife relationship.

The Premarital Examination

The physical examination of couples about to marry has been a boon to many couples in detecting and clearing up all kinds of difficulties and in offering an opportunity to ask questions and obtain the information necessary to inaugurate a successful marriage. This is not to be confused with *premarriage counseling* in which the many personality, family, economic, religious, and legal factors are explored (see pp. 103–104).

What may be expected in the premarital examination depends upon both the physician and the couple. Here are some of the things a well-trained doctor and an alert couple keep in mind to be included.

PREMARITAL PHYSICAL EXAMINATION

1 Medical history including the previous sex history of both the man and the woman, possible hereditary problems in either line, and the menstrual history of the woman.

2 Clarification of any item or questions one or both members of the couple bring in, along with any that arise during the consultation. Selected books may be recommended as helpful.

3 Brief review of the anatomy and physiology of both male and female genital systems in the human (with charts or films if desired).

4 General physical examination including blood and urine studies, heart, lung, and pelvic conditions, and search for any possible pathologies in both the man and the woman.

5 Pelvic examination of the woman with especial attention to the condition of the vaginal orifice and the adequacy of the vagina for sexual intercourse.

6 Possible instruction in a program of hymen dilation, where indicated and compatible with the attitudes of the couple.

7 Examination of the clitoris, and plan for freeing the clitoris as indicated.

8 Laboratory study of cultures from vagina and cervix with especial concern for the presence of gonorrheal infection, with immediate program of treatment if tests are positive.

9 Examination of the male genitalia with laboratory tests and a program of treatment for possible infection. (Sperm count and motility may be included if desired.)

10 Blood tests for the detection of syphilis in both individuals. Positive findings are followed at once by adequate treatment. No evidence of the disease is the clean bill of health required in most states before the license is issued.

11 Discussion of plans for contraception, as requested, with particular reference to the initial period of the marriage, and the religious factors that may be pertinent: a) plan for plotting the "safe period" if rhythm method is to be used, or b) fitting a diaphragm if religious and personal factors allow it.

12 Specific advice on vaginal lubricants and coital procedures as requested and indicated.

Obviously such a program of premarital consultation cannot be carried out effectively in one brief office call. It is usually wise for the couple to go for their first premarital consultation as soon as the definite date has been set for the wedding (see Chapter Nine, "Wedding

Plans"). At that time, the general exploration of common factors included in items one through three above may be covered, and appointments made for more detailed physical examinations of both man and woman at separate times (and possibly by different physicians). It is important that the pelvic examination of the female be done some time before the marriage where possible so that a program of dilation of the hymen and correction of any remediable conditions be effected well before the actual marriage date. It is not uncommon for the girl to take her mother or some close woman friend with her for this first pelvic examination, although it is not essential to do so. The blood tests required in most states proving the members of the pair to be free from communicable syphilis must be taken within the time limit set in the state of residence, usually within the fortnight preceding the marriage.

Premarital counseling includes not only the physical examination discussed here, but also the exploration of the personality, social, cultural, family, economic, and religious factors that are important for the building of a marriage (see Chapter Five, "The Meaning of an Engagement").

The Fact Is . . .

The establishment of a satisfying sexual adjustment is often not accomplished immediately. It may take the couple many weeks or months to mutually adjust sexually.[1] The week-end furlough honeymoon of wartime with its haste and sense of urgency is hardly conducive to the establishment of a mutually satisfying relationship. This is especially true if the bride is not fully ready for the consummation of the marriage. Such factors as a tough and resistant hymen, or the slight spasm of the muscles of the opening of the vagina, may be painful and may add to the fear and resistance of the bride.

Failure to synchronize the response of man and woman is another frequent cause of dissatisfaction in intercourse early in marriage that may be lessened by adequate marriage preparation. As the man gains in experience with his bride he is able to slow down his response, and by gentle, skillful caresses to arouse his wife to the place where both reach the climax at approximately the same time, with mutually shared

[1] Judson T. Landis, "Adjustments after Marriage," *Marriage and Family Living*, IX, May 1947, pp. 32–34.

exhilaration and release which is important to both for complete fulfillment.

Happiness in marriage is dependent not alone on perfecting the physical sex act to the point of mutual fulfillment. As studies and clinical evidence have richly indicated, it lies more within the personality adjustment of each member of the couple and in their larger relationships as two whole persons than in any physical tricks or techniques. True married living revolves around such interchange as is found in planning for the children, spending the family money, making plans for vacations and holidays, rejoicing over personal advances, and comforting one another in times of illness or disappointment. It is these day-by-day experiences in common that set the stage for the fullness of sexual response which, for most couples, symbolizes their unity and is far more satisfying than the purely physical release involved.

Selected Readings

BECKER, HOWARD, AND HILL, REUBEN, EDS., *Family, Marriage, and Parenthood* (Boston: Heath, 1948), Chap. 10.

BROWN, FRED, AND KEMPTON, RUDOLF, *Sex Questions and Answers* (New York: McGraw-Hill, 1950).

BUTTERFIELD, OLIVER, *Marriage and Sexual Harmony* (New York: Emerson Books, 1946).

CHESSER, EUSTACE, *Love without Fear* (New York: Signet Books, 1949).

CLARK, LE MON, *Sex and You* (New York: Bobbs-Merrill, 1949).

DUVALL, EVELYN, *Facts of Life and Love* (New York: Association Press, 1950).

ELLIS, ALBERT, *The Folklore of Sex* (New York: Boni, 1951).

FISHBEIN, MORRIS, AND BURGESS, ERNEST, EDS., *Successful Marriage* (Garden City: Doubleday, 1947), Part I, chaps. 5, 6; Part II, chaps. 1–3, 5.

GROVES, ERNEST; GROVES, GLADYS; AND GROVES, CATHERINE, *Sex Fulfillment in Marriage* (New York: Emerson Books, 1942).

HIMES, NORMAN, *Your Marriage: A Guide to Happiness* (New York: Rinehart, 1940).

KLING, SAMUEL, AND KLING, ESTHER, EDS., *The Marriage Reader* (New York: Vanguard, 1947), Part Seven.

LANDIS, JUDSON, AND LANDIS, MARY, *Building a Successful Marriage* (New York: Prentice-Hall, 1948), Chap. 11.

MAGOUN, F. ALEXANDER, *Love and Marriage* (New York: Harper, 1948), Chap. 9.

ROCK, JOHN, AND LOTH, DAVID, *Voluntary Parenthood* (New York: Random House, 1949).

STOKES, WALTER, *Modern Pattern for Marriage* (New York: Rinehart, 1948), chaps. 3–6.

STONE, HANNAH, AND STONE, ABRAHAM, *A Marriage Manual* (New York: Simon & Schuster, 1952, revised).

VAN DE VELDE, T. H., *Ideal Marriage: Its Physiology and Technique* (New York: Covici Friede, 1937).

Technical References

DICKINSON, ROBERT, *Atlas of Human Sex Anatomy* (New York: Williams and Wilkins, 1949).

FORD, CLELLAN, AND BEACH, FRANK, *Patterns of Sexual Behavior* (New York: Harper, 1951).

KINSEY, ALFRED; POMEROY, WARDELL; AND MARTIN, CLYDE, *Sexual Behavior in the Human Male* (Philadelphia: Saunders, 1948).

LANDIS, CARNEY, AND OTHERS, *Sex in Development* (New York: Paul Hoeber, 1940).

MENNINGER, WILLIAM, "Sexual Aspects of Marriage," in *Program Notes Third Annual Scientific Assembly*, American Academy of General Practice, 406 West 34th St., Kansas City, Mo. (T. E. Rardin, M.D., ed., 1951), pp. 9–13.

POTTER, EDITH, *Fundamentals of Human Reproduction* (New York: McGraw-Hill, 1948).

CHAPTER SEVEN

"Everything that's fun is either illegal, immoral, or fattening!"

DOES MORALITY MAKE SENSE?

Are your love affairs anyone's business but your own?

What is conscience?

Why are there so many rules about sex relations?

Can you have fun if you are good?

$\mathcal{D}$OROTHY IS A LOVELY BRUNETTE OF NINETEEN, AND BILL IS a medical student in his second year of medicine. They have been engaged for four months, and Dorothy wants to get married right away. She claims she will be no financial liability to Bill because her job at the hospital will continue whether she is married or not. The major obstacle in the way is the adamant objection of Bill's parents. They are convinced that Dorothy and Bill are too young and have refused flatly to continue any further support to Bill in his medical school education if he marries now.

Bill somehow can't see the need for marriage right now, not for what they want anyway. His arguments have become so plausible that he is beginning to believe in them himself — there are other medical students in the same boat, and they have managed to wink at the sex codes without being struck down. Dorothy and Bill are coming to a crossroads for which they are unprepared.

Many of Dorothy's friends in their heated discussions claim that the world has changed and that people have to change to fit the new life. When your friends, people who should know, people who are up to date in their thinking, talk that way it makes you wonder. One of the most telling arguments is that no one would know. In a big city you can gain anonymity in a matter of five minutes' walk from your home, and your behavior is strictly a private affair.

Dorothy has been taught all her life that sex intercourse is best saved for marriage, because it is so much more enjoyable then. Her quandary is very real, and she resolves to write her brother who is in graduate school. He has always listened to her without blame whenever she has done anything shocking. He will give her problem an unbiased appraisal even though he is her brother. She poses four provocative questions for him to answer:

1 People in other countries aren't so strict; why should I be?
2 I've crossed the line and recrossed it in my thoughts; why should it be any worse to do it with my person?
3 It's my life, and if I choose to be unhappy, isn't that my own business?
4 How can you tell anything's good or bad without trying it?

We quote with permission excerpts from the brother's response:

You know, my dear, that you've hit upon a very important and complicated problem there, a problem on which I certainly do not feel myself competent to make any definite pronouncements, but one which must be decided eventually by yourself, in the solitude and perhaps loneliness of your own mind. . . .

I think that probably the most important point against any such course of action as you apparently contemplate is one which you yourself mentioned when you wrote that it's probably fear of having to live with yourself afterward that's holding you back. I can't stress too much how important that is. Whatever we might like to see our society become, the fact remains that as it is today, it makes no provision for sex relationships outside of marriage. "Well," you'll probably say, "that's an old-fashioned idea, and to heck with it!" That's all very well, but when you kick that overboard, you also dismiss many other things which you very likely can't get along very well without. You at one stroke alienate yourself from the larger group, from your past training, from your ideals and values as they used to be, from your parents, and often from your friends. You say that the line is so slender that you wonder that you haven't crossed and recrossed it many times, but you miss the important point, that that is one line which crossed can never be recrossed.

It's true that your friends may never know, that your parents may continue in blissful ignorance, that the group may never discover you; but the truth of the matter is that it's really impossible to separate yourself from the group, because from one standpoint you are the group, and the group is you. All the past training that you've had all your life has been dictated in large measure by the standards of the group; your mind to a large extent contains, not things you have thought up by yourself, but things that the group has thought up for you, and made part of your very being. On the other hand, it is you and the many others like you that uphold and continue the traditions of the society and make social life possible. However, just because you are, in a sense, society, you cannot feel free to break loose from it, for you are not all of society. . . . What I mean here is that it's not necessary for your actions to be made public in order for them to be made unpleasant. It's the rare person (if, indeed, there can ever be such a person) who is able to tear himself away from social standards so entirely that he is able to avoid punishing himself when he breaks a social rule.

That is what would happen to you. With reasonable care you would probably not be found out — anyhow, not for some time. By the exercise of reasonable precautions, you would probably not become pregnant — though even the best contraceptives are far from being perfect. But — you would find yourself out, and you would find that you were worrying quite a bit about becoming pregnant, if not this time, then the next. The main thing, however, is that you yourself would know what you were doing, and would feel very guilty about the whole thing. You would punish yourself with the fear of discovery, and with the realization that, in our society, you were doing something that, rightly or wrongly, is considered wrong. You might not analyze the situation in this manner, but you would have a vague, ever present, gnawing feeling of guilt, and you would most certainly not be happy.

There are two things you might answer to this. One is, Why should this be so, when in other societies such premarital relations are permitted? Another is that after all it's your life, and if you choose to be unhappy for awhile, well, nobody's the loser but yourself.

The first is the fallacy of moral relativism, and it's really another way of putting what I've been saying all along. It's all right to do such things in other societies because they're organized along those lines. No social sanctions are attached to such behavior; provision is often made for any children which may result, and the whole matter is aboveboard and recognized. Moreover, even in such a sexual paradise as the Marquesas Islands, the people have found it necessary to make promiscuity a condition of a compensating factor — the absence of romance. In these islands, where almost complete freedom is the rule, the children are brought up from the cradle with the idea that to form permanent and very personal attachments is wrong. These people have found it necessary to frown on exclusiveness and jealousy as much as we frown on philandering. It's almost like action and reaction, force and distance, in physics. It's a seesaw. If you get one thing, you have to sacrifice something else.

The second idea, that you're not hurting anybody but yourself, is just not so. It's true that you're over eighteen, and that therefore, by our somewhat peculiar laws, your body is your own to bestow on whom you wish, but the assumption behind this custom is that by the age of eighteen the social patterns are so deeply ingrained in your mind that you will act in accord with society's expectations. And if you try to fool society by not acting as it expects, the repercussions will affect not only you, but all those about you, and not only the you of the present, but quite possibly the you of the future. For after all, if you begin to worry and to feel guilty your family will notice it, and they will worry. They will ask embarrassing questions which you will be unable to answer, so you will evade them or else lie, and the evasion will make you worry more, and the lie will make you feel even more guilty. And not only your family, but your friends will notice your nervousness and your short temper and your little jumps and starts at inconsequential things, and they will wonder about you and worry also, and everything they do or say will make you wonder whether maybe they haven't found out, so you will begin to avoid them, and become even more unhappy, as they will too.

Moreover, an unpleasant experience of this sort will leave its psychological mark on you for the rest of your life. The sex act is one of the most personal and intimate acts which a man and woman can share together, and if it is done in secret and in haste, it is very likely, for that very reason, to be unpleasant, to lack its full meaning, and to make the whole business of sex a source of fear and disgust. This sort of attitude could very easily carry over into your married life and make it, too, unpleasant and repugnant, and prevent you from truly enjoying what you have every right to expect. . . . There are some things in life that it's too dangerous to try, just for the sake of experience, and sex intercourse before marriage is one of them.

Don't get me wrong, dear, I realize that sex is fun — up to a point — but I feel that when it comes to intercourse, the possible consequences are too dangerous to be played with in a lighthearted manner.

There Are No Immoral Societies

One of the most frequently heard justifications for premarital sex activity today by the set who describe themselves as "emancipated" is that our customs are unduly restrictive, and that since other people are not so strict there is no good reason for our own standards of chastity. Stories of the bliss of the South Sea Islanders still sell well, and the movies continue to exploit the selfsame fiction. The popularity of the movies of the South Seas is probably derived from the life of irresponsibility and of minimum regulation which they picture, a dream world which corresponds in part with the average man's inner fantasies. These pictures are highly inaccurate portrayals of life among the primitives, whose regulations and taboos often outnumber our own.

In every society sex conduct is regulated as part of the total system of family behavior. None have yet been studied in which absolute promiscuity is encouraged and supported by the moral codes. All human groups have regularized the relationships between men and women and have placed some limits to the sex conduct of their members.

Those who talk about the sexual paradise of the primitives are usually persons with little or no knowledge of the total culture in question. Unless one has had the actual experience of living in another society with the serious intention of learning its intricacies, it is difficult to appreciate the extent to which the sex mores are woven into the warp and woof of the culture. The particular ideals of what constitutes correct sex behavior are part of a design for living within a particular society.[1]

The relative rigidity and laxity of control with respect to premarital sex conduct make sense in terms of the history of the group and the way other aspects of life are regulated. Where extramarital relations are condoned there is provision for the offspring of these unions, an arrangement we don't have in our society. The unmarried mother has status, and her child is not discriminated against because of his mother's extramarital conduct.

What Does It Mean to Go Primitive?

Most of us do not have the alternative of spending the rest of our lives among peoples known as primitives. We can, however, utilize the findings of anthropologists to place our own society in the mosaic made by all societies. Ours is a restrictive society with regard to sex conduct, but we are by no means the only society to place bans on promiscuous sex expression. In a recent sampling of the several hundred societies which dot the world, literate and nonliterate, ancient and modern, George Murdock tabulated from the files of the Cross-Cultural Index of Yale University one expression of restrictiveness and permissiveness; namely, the normative patterns regarding premarital relations. He reports that nonincestuous premarital relations are fully permitted in 50 per cent of the societies, conditionally approved in 20 per cent, and forbidden in about 30 per cent. Many of the most populous societies fall in the "forbidding" category.[2]

There are actually many societies which are stricter than our own

[1] Scudder Mekeel, "Preliterate Family Patterns," in Howard Becker and Reuben Hill, eds., *Marriage and the Family* (Boston: Heath, 1942), p. 55.
[2] George P. Murdock, *Social Structure* (New York: Macmillan, 1949), p. 265.

with regard to sex conduct. Relatively speaking, present-day Americans enjoy considerable sex freedom. Viewing our position from the perspective given by history, we see that there have been societies antecedent to our own which were much more restrictive, i.e., Puritan New England or, more recently, the Victorian era in England and in America.

How can we account for the apparent permissiveness among some societies? What appears to be illicit behavior from our standpoint is regarded as perfectly correct conduct by the members of these societies. Nevertheless there are regulations which control premarital relations. There are rules of etiquette governing the proper times and places, and means of negotiation. But the purpose of these institutionalized rules governing courtship is not to restrict sexual access so much as to regularize it. Take, for example, the Marquesas Islands, which some observers have termed the sexual paradise of the South Seas. On these enchanting isles it has been necessary, in order to prevent open strife among promiscuous males, to repress all feelings of tenderness and overt jealousy. Otherwise the society would break up from the violence of competition and conflict for women. From birth, the Marquesan child is never once allowed to experience feelings of tenderness, of belonging to someone who is dear to him. Children are weaned as early as possible. Food is thrust into their mouths without the loving and fondling that is characteristic in our society. Children are never picked up and kissed, and as a result, when they mature no tenderness seems to be expected or given in adult love relations. In such a society there is little manifestation of jealousy even in the face of frequent sharing of partners. The price of institutionalized premarital relationships in the Marquesas Islands is the absence of romance, exclusiveness, and the privilege of jealously protecting one's beloved from alien seducers.

In America we live in a restrictive culture which maximizes companionship of the sexes socially and intellectually but restricts sexual intimacies to married couples. Jealousy and strife are minimized by insisting upon continence before marriage and marital fidelity to one partner after marriage. This enables us to maintain tenderness as an integral part of our love life and makes possible possessiveness among lovers. It is important to us in America to have and to hold, exclusively, some one person. Our heights of romantic ardor are built out of the obstacles placed in our way by the restrictions of the sex codes. We have been reared to expect tenderness and romance in our love life and are unprepared for sex relations without genuine intimacy. Over the years a moral code meeting these specifications has been formulated and has proved relatively workable. That code is monogamous marriage — one man for one woman — at a time.

How Conscience Develops

Conscience develops out of childhood learnings from parents, playmates, and other teachers. Because these builders of conscience were limited to our society in their own childhood, we too are taught only the right ways of this same society. Any person with any bringing up at all has been so effectively taught the characteristic do's and don't's of his group that he is unable to experiment with any complacency with the customs of another society. To do so would violate his own conscience. Let's see why.

Conscience is built during the most impressionable years. The teachings which make up conscience are imposed upon the child when he is powerless and helpless to object, at a stage in his development when he is most plastic and receptive and before he can verbalize his thoughts into rational form. Conscience is rooted into the nonverbal, feeling layers of personality. The result is that he accepts the doctrines without argument, and they remain with him into adulthood to guide him when he deviates from the paths described as desirable in childhood. He learns that he can't argue with his conscience. He has strong feelings that some things ought to be done and strong feelings that some things ought not to be done, and that's all there is to it.

Why should the child become set so soon about moral questions? In the first place, parents react more strongly about moral than secular questions because they too have consciences with which they can't argue. Parents are after all children older grown, and they communicate their negative feelings to their own offspring whenever the little rascals violate one of the social conventions. In the second place, there is more likelihood that punishment and unpleasantness will accompany violation of the moral codes. The child comes to recognize that the all-wise parents feel especially negative about moral indiscretions. Finally, the child may connect the moral learnings with the satisfaction of his basic needs of hunger, thirst, affection, and security. Powerless as he is, he must accept what he hears, or so he imagines, lest he risk the loss of these vital satisfactions. This threat is enough to bring the most recalcitrant into line.

The genius of the conscience is that, once it is established in a child, the immediate presence of the parent is no longer necessary to control him. Inhibitions are built up to such an extent that uneasiness may accompany violation of parental teachings, even if the act is not detected. Knowledge that the act is condemned and that the individual may be brought to task at some time is sufficient to support the ideal of correct conduct.

It is in the many informal family situations that we see the process of conscience formation most clearly at work. Drop in on any family meal for a picture of moral training in action. Questions are asked, answered, or evaded in turn. Significant for all are the topics meticulously avoided, as well as those assiduously discussed. Bossard's study of family table talk shows the effectiveness of the family in moral instruction:

Helen, aged twelve, tells of a neighbor's child, that proverbial and perennial scapegoat. Father, who is envious of the neighboring father's business success, expresses himself freely concerning the conduct of his daughter. Mother, who dislikes the neighboring mother, is equally heated. Helen, without understanding the motives involved, is quite impressed. The neighboring girl's conduct *was* reprehensible. . . .

. . . many of the lessons of the family meal . . . are unplanned and spontaneous. "Katie kissed John," pipes up the well-known little brother, and in the wake of his disclosure may follow either an eloquent silence, or a colorful discussion concerning kissing, John's intentions, John's job, Katie's prospects, and mother's attitude toward early marriages. These are . . . common grist in the family round-the-table mill, as it grinds, now slowly, now rapidly, but always exceedingly fine.[3]

The conscience is built largely out of these experiences in informal living. The family is the first society in which the child is taught to live, and it in turn fulfills the obligation of inducting him into the larger group. The development of conscience is the family's device for ensuring the child's preparation for full-fledged participation in society.

As the child enters adolescence, the peer culture becomes more and more important in modifying conscience and determining approved behavior. The do's and don'ts of childhood are devalued as "corny" and good enough for children but unsuitable for grown-up young people.

[3] James H. S. Bossard, "Family Table Talk — An Area for Sociological Study," *American Sociological Review* (June, 1943), p. 299.

Keeping clean, paying attention to manners, and watching language are not as important to companions as to parents. Telling dirty jokes and painting washroom pictures are ways of defying elders. The most striking characteristic of this peer culture in adolescence is the approval given to the members who take risks, who flout conventions, who defy parents and teachers and other authorities. The conscience of the child wrestles with the prodding of the peers who see in the flouting of conscience evidence of their new-found independence.

In most cases the conscience wins the battle, because the peer culture of the next older set is more approving of moral behavior. The members of that set have found that they don't necessarily have to flout the conventions to be accepted as adults. On the contrary, they perceive that one of the differences which distinguish them from adolescents is their more ready acceptance of the societal codes. With some pride this older set, now readying itself for marriage, incorporates some of the values and vested interests of the larger adult culture. Thereafter the sets in which the maturing person travels become increasingly conservative, and the members support and pass on the moral codes to others as their parents have before them.

How Conscience Works

How does conscience work and how can you tell whether yours is well developed? Take the case of Jim R. who was reared in a good family in the Middle West. He has been produced in a certain mold and is not entirely free, therefore, to make his own choice with regard to sex conduct. One evening on a dare he violated the code of decency by appearing at a formal dancing party clad only in swimming trunks and dress shoes. As he approached the dance floor from his car he sensed the pounding of his pulses, the increased heartbeat, and the tingling of his skin. Physiologically his condition was one of greatly increased circulation. Psychologically he displayed agitation, mortification, and self-consciousness as the full import of his actions flashed before him. He spent very little time on the dance floor, because he sensed that everyone was looking his way; and he was so hot and uncomfortable that he thought he would suffocate. He finally fled from the place to escape what proved to be an intolerable situation. Conscience supported by societal disapproval proved his undoing.

In many ways Jim's attitudes toward what is right and wrong with regard to marriage are also so deeply ingrained by the time he gets to the marrying age that he cannot violate them without painful emotional reactions. However strongly he may feel intellectually about a "freer" sex life, he can do little about this conscience of his. He is unable to go safely far beyond his emotional reactions of guilt, which are visible in his bodily manifestations in the form of blushing, headaches, nervousness, sleeplessness, indigestion, nausea, and similar expressions of malaise. Parents, teachers, ministers, and now his associates have done their work so well that Jim cannot violate their teachings even in their absence. The codes have now become a part of his thinking, and very shortly he will be a party to indoctrinating his own children with similar convictions as he takes on the responsibilities of parent and adult.

Of such stuff is conscience made. You may start with an untamed, undomesticated potential rebel at birth, but if he lives long enough and the conditioning is effective enough he will turn out to be a conservative conformist like Jim R. To Jim, morality will increasingly make sense, because it is the only comfortable alternative open to him.

Ethical Judgment

Our discussion so far tends to give us a wholesome respect for the moral codes of our society and for the vehicle which carries those codes in us, namely, conscience. Is it sufficient to have a good working knowledge of the moral codes and a well-developed conscience? Are these sufficient bases for conduct? The teaching of ethics would be greatly simplified if these questions could be answered in the affirmative.

Conscience works well when faced with familiar problems, but given new and complex situations it is frequently ineffective in providing the answers. And in a rapidly changing society the average individual is constantly meeting new situations for which the conscience provides no ready-made solutions. Moreover, reference to the moral codes is useless, because unique cases are not covered there. In addition to a working knowledge of the moral codes and a well-developed conscience, then, ethical judgment is needed, the ability to size up the new situation and perceive which of the available alternatives is least bad. This decision needs to be based on the recognition of the consequences which would follow the proposed behaviors. The individual employs reflection to follow out in his mind the results of each course of action. He attempts to answer the question, Which of the proposed courses of action will least hurt the parties concerned?

The appeal merely to the conscience is not likely to be permanently satisfactory, therefore, because the conscience is based more on childhood indoctrinations than on adult experiences. Emotionally trained to approve some actions and to disapprove others, we are unable to learn through conscience why the action is ethical and right. The desire to do the right thing is no guarantee of understanding about what is right.[4]

Moreover, life in shifting, changing America is so complex that we are frequently faced with the choice of alternatives no single one of which is altogether satisfactory from the standpoint of conscience. Ethical judgment must be added to conscience to select the alternative action which is least bad and most ethical. For example, is it right to steal a revolver from a friend who would otherwise commit suicide with it?

Until recently young people in our society needed only conscience to tell them what was correct behavior, at least in the area of sex relations. Today many young people are entering adulthood with the necessity of answering for themselves whether they will remain continent until marriage or include sexual experimentation in their premarital learnings. No longer can one's guide be conscience alone. Added to it must go insight into the consequences of premarital experimentation, into its effects upon personality and on the future of the relationship. The responsibility for these decisions is too great to place on young people until they are thoroughly informed. Young people acquire insight by learning the consequences of deviant behavior, the results of promiscuous relations, and the need for permanency to achieve a satisfying relation. Happily, one of the helpful outcomes of the relaxation of the sex mores has been the lifting of the ban on discussion of sex and sex problems. Frank discussion of moral problems and enrollment in marriage education courses can provide young people with a picture of the

[4] Harold H. Titus, *Ethics for Today* (New York: American Book Company, 1936), pp. 18–20.

consequences of behavior which, on the rational level, can supplement the conscience, which is on the emotional level, as an important guide to conduct.

A famous physician, wise in the ways of sexually disturbed people, recently pointed out the principles of sex morality in a question-answer session with several hundred students in a marriage class. He had been asked the question: "Is it all right to pet if you think you are in love?" His answer appeared directed toward the boys of the class: "I would say you should be able to answer the following questions: Is it genuine, this affection? Is it fair to the girl in the long run? Are you hurting yourselves emotionally by building up appetites you can satisfy only in marriage? I find that patients who come to me for help are disproportionately drawn from individuals who were promiscuous before marriage. An act is right if it makes for the development of personality and human welfare; an act is wrong if it leads to the destruction of human personality. Sex is powerful, but neutral, neither good nor bad; how it is used makes it right or wrong. With this start I feel you should be able to construct the type of situations in which petting would be all right and the situations in which it would be wrong."

Emancipation: Freedom to Grow

One of the great values of our society is freedom, but all too frequently it has been construed as freedom from tyranny, from regulation, from restrictive covenants, rather than freedom to do creative work, to achieve new goals. Are the moral codes too restrictive? Do they "keep love in fetters"?

Our thesis is that self-realization and freedom to grow lie in the direction of moral living, that the person in our society who enjoys the greatest freedom is one who knows the demands of the social order and uses them to free himself for creative activity.

First, it is an accepted fact that habit is the great conservator of human energy. Deviation from the norms of morality, for example, is a departure from routine and exposes the person to increasing nervous strain: he has new decisions to make and an uncharted course. Conscience, moreover, acts as a guide to warn whether such and such behavior is acceptable or reprehensible in the eyes of other people. It is not designed to shackle but to guide behavior, to enable a person to maintain his status, his reputation, and his friends. To lack conscience or to ignore it almost inevitably results in loss of freedom, for officers of the law, or lesser authorities fully as powerful, such as employers, teachers, or neighbors, enforce the regulations of our social order. Whether it is right or wrong so to restrict an individual's behavior is not an idle question. In order to preserve a measure of social harmony, society does restrict him.[5]

Freedom for the individual comes through conformity to the traffic rules of life's highway. Violation of these rules does not establish the fact that our rebel is free: he just loses his driver's license through his indiscretion and has to walk thereafter. Violation of the sex taboos increases the restrictions on his freedom. Henceforth he will be even more limited in the girls he may date, and he may eventually lose his position in the rating scale which enables him to rate a desirable marriage partner.

We are all on probation, so to speak: if we violate the rules which society has established to ensure social harmony, we risk losing the privileges of the free run of society. We win our freedom to love and work and play by demonstrating our ability to operate "within the grooves" without a guardian to keep us in line.

Responsive Integrity

Another aspect of freedom is the winning of unqualified acceptance of other persons. Once an individual recognizes within himself the capacity to work with others as persons rather than as potential sex objects, he frees himself for much wider and more varied relationships with members of the opposite sex. He sees the possibilities in exploring personality, in sharing points of view and collaborating in creative work, all of which possibilities are closed to the person hampered by the feeling that every friend must be fondled and caressed to be enjoyed.

The "wolf" (male or female) whose aims are sex-directed, in contact with any member of the other sex, is often not so much sex-starved as he is in need of ego-bolstering. The girl who leads a man on to prove to herself that she can, is often so insecure as a woman that she must constantly prove to herself as well as to others that she is desirable. The

---

[5] We have already shown that the sex codes of premarital continence in our society serve to minimize jealousy and strife, pp. 133–134.

heart-hunter usually collects conquests because he or she needs evidence of personal power. When satisfactions outside of sex become possible, a girl does not need to measure her success by whether she got "him" to kiss her or not; the man no longer requires physical submission as proof of his acceptance.

More fortunate are those persons who are free to know and enjoy and to love a wide variety of fine people of both sexes in a variety of situations, for theirs is the love that frees them for further growth of personality. As such emotional growth takes place, mate love is enhanced rather than challenged, since the sex channeling of affection remains exclusive while the emotional responses grow richly inclusive. Such persons have what is called *responsive integrity*.

Responsive integrity is the ability to respond to another person honestly and as a whole person without having to block off or deny basic aspects of the self. If we are honest we must admit that we find all sorts of people attractive and lovable. The desire to attract and be attracted to others does not cease with marriage. Conscience tells us that we belong exclusively to one mate; so the tendency to feel guilt, shame, and a denial of our real feelings dams up the out-going responses. As long as this repression is successful we cannot allow ourselves to respond honestly to others. If, on the other hand, the emotional currents become so strong that they overflow the limits set by the conscience, they may set up a whole sequence of unacceptable behavior. Neither alternative is wholesome, since both prevent us from responding as a whole; either we must deny our feelings of affection, or we must break with our own ideals of right and wrong. Responsive integrity enters in when we accept our feelings for others, when we learn how to channel them in ways that are acceptable, and to enjoy wholesomely and freely the emotional satisfactions of our relations with others. Refusing to admit our dislike or our love for another does not lessen the potency of the feeling. Repression only masks the emotion, which somehow, someway, must burst forth eventually with accumulated force and vigor.

But responsive integrity does not mean going around with emotions unbuttoned, letting feelings spill over as they will without control. Necessarily involved is a great deal of self-imposed restraint and control to keep expressions of feelings within the bounds of the particular relationship. The gushy girl who fusses around her brother does not share as much of him as does the sister who expresses her affection in more acceptable, sisterly ways. The touchy person who flies off the handle shares fewer confidences than the poised, unshockable one with whom people feel safe. Self-control for the sake of the recognized values of the relationship allows more freedom of access to others than is granted the less disciplined, who find themselves in emotional hot water much of the time.

Take Sue and Emma, for instance. They both admire and work closely with an attractive married man in their office. Emma flashes her lashes and maneuvers for compliments and opportunities to be close to him. She goes to great lengths to let him know that he touches off her affectional responses. Yet she cannot win. If he responds to her advances, he will either be turned away from her by his own feelings of guilt, or he will take advantage of her availability without the loyalty and permanence most girls need to make sex satisfying. Or by completely succumbing to her seduction, he faces the possibility of the breaking up of his home, which would inevitably be fraught with guilt, some ostracism, and pangs of conscience. More likely he will find her advances uncomfortable and take steps to remove himself as far as possible from her silly, one-sided flirtation.

Sue, on the other hand, just as honestly admits her interest in her colleague. But she lets her affection stimulate her productivity in the job they are doing together. She throws herself wholeheartedly into doing the kind of work that he will admire and that will do credit to them both. She expresses her admiration for his achievements in this way and so spurs him on to greater creativity. Theirs can be a growing relationship with a depth and breadth of permanence, because neither threatens the other with demands that are not intrinsically a part of their own working relationship.

Responsive integrity, then, means wholehearted response to others through the avenues provided by the particular relationship. Responsive integrity is established when a person, accepting both his impulses and his conscience, exerts the self-controls that allow him freely to channel the full power of his feelings. It is one important aspect of emancipation, of freedom to grow, because it opens up to him opportunities for friendships and working relationships with men and women which might otherwise have to cease with marriage's traditional exclusiveness. Persons with responsive integrity can frankly recognize that real affection is a source of motivation in working with other people and that the enjoyment of work and play with others need not be followed by sexual contact.

Consequences of Immorality Harmful to Personality [6]

We should give some credit to our forefathers who were sensitive enough to understand the sheer power of sex and place it under rigid controls. They were mistaken, however, in thinking they could run away from it by banning the discussion of sex problems: we can't play ostrich and act as if the sex drive weren't there. We too recognize the wisdom of carefully controlling sex; it is not to be treated flippantly. Within marriage sex often presents problems. Outside of marriage it is difficult to gain permanent satisfaction from sex experiences. Psychiatrists and marriage counselors daily observe the explosive and destructive power of this phenomenon in wrecking the lives of hitherto well-adjusted people.

Sex Is Personal. With most animals sex appears to be purely biological, a releasing of physical tensions. A female dog or cat in heat will accept one male after another without the slightest compunction, and with no concern as to who sired previous litters. Among humans in whom the response to persons as persons is so important, the situation is not simple. The mature individual can never be satisfied with a merely physical experience. He needs also affection and sympathy and tenderness. The physical experience alone leaves him hungry and unsatisfied. "All or nothing at all" is more than a once popular song. It can be sung with meaning by members of both sexes. Although the boy may prize the sensory gratifications more than the unawakened girl, he needs, nevertheless, the personal meanings to achieve any permanent satisfactions from the relationship.

The average girl is unable to obtain physical gratification without abundant affection and attention. Sexual gratification for her is not a simple affair. She needs a basic personal security to achieve it. She needs understanding, tenderness, and constancy. There is clinical evidence that she needs a series of experiences, rather than single isolated experiences, and it is important that they be with the same person. Time and experience in becoming accustomed to each other are neces-

[6] We acknowledge help in this section from Dr. S. M. Duvall, *Men, Women, and Morals* (New York: Association Press, 1952).

sary to achieve complete satisfaction. Short-run, surreptitious affairs lack both of these requisites. Because sex is personal in addition to being biological, it is unlikely that promiscuity can produce the desired satisfactions.

Emotional Involvement. If an unmarried couple decide to have sex relations, they must be assured of more than a casual, fly-by-night affair in order to achieve any degree of satisfaction. They will want to assure for their relation sufficient permanence to attain within its duration a mature sexual union. There are some who claim to have achieved this goal. Such permanence is rare, yet it is the prerequisite for satisfying sex relations.

Unfortunately the history of couples who establish full sex relationships outside of marriage is not encouraging to read. Even engaged couples who have agreed on marriage plans find full sex relations bring unanticipated consequences. The pangs of conscience are something they expect and know how to handle because they expect to be married soon. They put up with these in order to experience the presumed satisfactions of complete intimacy. The experimenting couple, however, expect their love to be strengthened by their increased physical intimacy. But there are many indications that their idealized images of one another may be shattered thereby, that the sense of mystery, the aura of holiness, will vanish. Interest in the other wanes at the end of the chase, and the tensions of unrequited sex lose their titillating power as they are released, and the couple realize that they have "gone the limit." These ingredients of the romantic complex are lost simultaneously with the recurrence of guilt feelings. Because we are conditioned to expect romantic love as a necessary prerequisite to marriage, its lessening is interpreted as meaning that we were really not meant for each other, that the engagement should be broken off so that we may hunt for someone else.

As we shall learn in later chapters, much the same transformation of emotional relationships takes place within marriage and partly for the same reasons. When romance wanes after marriage, however, it is not so hazardous. By then the ties have been formally sanctioned through the wedding ceremony, the couple has established a common household with its many satisfactions and interlocking functions.

If the experimenting couple is not engaged, and has no plans for marriage, the emotional involvement may be fully as complicated. Once a couple attains a state of satisfactory sexual union, either the boy or (more usually) the girl begins to wish for something more permanent. If the relationship is satisfying, one or the other tends to become involved emotionally and begins to press for marriage. The member who is postponing marriage is thereupon frightened, and a bitter quarrel may ensue. The break at that point may prove disastrous to them both. But such is the nature of the sex relationship. If it is satisfying there will inevitably result profound emotional involvements that are not counted on. There is no halfway house; it is all or nothing at all.

Sex can be safe and satisfying, only under circumstances which make possible the full and rich development of its emotional involvements. If the physical aspects were all, those who know how to guard against physical dangers of disease and pregnancy might safely have as free a sex life as an alley cat. But they are not. Because of the psychological aspect, the temporary affair is almost all risk and little promise. Sex requires for its satisfaction a complete response of the whole personality. As a general policy, this means marriage. Biologically, people can go the limit, psychologically, only within the security of a sound and permanent marriage relationship.[7]

But Many Cross the Line

The Ten Commandments are violated by people who would not deny their ethical soundness. The sex codes are no exception. Estimates of deviation from the single standard of sex morality, are at best approximations; from 20 to 80 per cent of unmarried males by the age of twenty-five have had premarital intercourse, depending on the study you cite. From 10 to 50 per cent of all married males have intercourse with women other than their wives, at some time while they are married. Even the estimates of Alfred C. Kinsey and his associates, the highest reported to date, indicate that extramarital intercourse accounts for only from 5 to 10 per cent of their total sex outlets.[8]

Deviation from the code of premarital continence and marital fidelity is the only instance in our society where one instance of nonconformity places a person in the category of being a deviant permanently. Stealing, lying, and cruelty to persons are not uncommon among young

[7] S. M. Duvall, *op. cit.*
[8] Alfred C. Kinsey, and associates, *Sexual Behavior in the Human Male* (Philadelphia: Saunders, 1948), p. 588.

people, and even among oldsters, yet if the person is honest, truthful, and kindly 90 per cent of the time, we tend to regard his behavior as conforming. With regard to sex, however, there is a tendency to divide young people into two camps, those who are virginal, that is, have never experienced sex union, and those who are nonvirginal, which groups together all who have experienced intercourse one or more times. In concluding this discussion of sex morality we distinguish between categories of deviants, and suggest that those who have had premarital intercourse only once or twice in the past conceive of themselves as conforming to the moral code.[9]

Morality Does Make Sense

The case for conformity to the moral code has constituted the content of this chapter. This particular code applies to old as well as to the young, to men as well as women. It involves a single standard of morality. Our case has placed relatively little stress on the dangers of pregnancy, of disease, and of social ostracism which are included in the negative approach to this problem. Ours is a positive approach. Conformity to a single standard pays dividends in emotional stability, creativity, and integrity. Nonconformity for most socialized Americans brings a certain quantum of guilt, dangers of involvement to the point of personality distortion to both parties, and possible probationary status in one's peer group. Morality makes sense because:

1 **Our society is organized around moral behavior as the norm.**
A moral code has grown up through years of experimentation with man-woman relationships which minimizes the strife of men fighting over their woman. Our monogamous marriage form is our solution of that problem, and to support it we insist that there be no sexual intercourse before marriage and that intercourse after marriage be restricted to marriage pairs.

2 **Conscience needs to be reckoned with. It's more comfortable to be moral.**
We feel so strongly about the necessity of preserving what has proved to be a satisfying form of marriage and family life that we impose these ideas

---

[9] For the discussion of ethical implications of the many varied situations covered by the sex code read especially Section III, "Sex Morality in Specific Situations," dealing with the morality of adultery, fornication, prostitution, and sexual intercourse in marriage in S. M. Duvall, *Men, Women, and Morals* (New York: Association Press, 1952), pp. 123–237.

on our children during the most impressionable period of life. Moreover, children, through observation in informal family situations, internalize the do's and don'ts associated with sexual behavior and make them a part of themselves in what we have termed conscience. So effective is this indoctrination that the matured adult feels completely secure only when he is behaving in accordance with the patterns prescribed by his parents, teachers, and friends.

3 **Ethical judgment rests on an understanding of the social order.**
Ethical judgment into the best solutions to unique situations depends partly on the understanding and acceptance of the moral code and partly on a knowledge of the consequences of behavior. On both counts the moral person has advantages over the morally illiterate.

4 **Social approval of friends is important to personal security, and the older we get the more conservative our friends become on moral issues.**
Status and reputation in the adult world rest upon the proof that a person behaves as his peers feel he should. During a short period in adolescence the adolescent peers encourage types of behavior forbidden by conscience, but thereafter the successively older sets he joins approve and support the moral codes. To obtain unqualified approval in his world it becomes important to exemplify in his behavior the standards of correct sex conduct.

5 **Self-realization, freedom to grow, and freedom to work with others lie in the direction of moral living.**
The person in our society who enjoys the greatest freedom and has the greatest social access is one who knows the demands of the social order and uses them to free himself for creative activity.

6 **The consequences of immorality are harmful to personality and to members of society.**
Behavior, in the final analysis, must be judged by its effects on people. An act is right if it makes for the development of personality and human welfare; an act is wrong if it leads to the destruction of human personality. Because of the psychological aspects, the temporary affair is almost all risk and little promise. To live morally is simply the best way of living under existing conditions.

Selected Readings

BECKER, HOWARD, AND HILL, REUBEN, EDS., *Family, Marriage, and Parenthood* (Boston: Heath, 1948), especially discussion of petting, pp. 241–243, and 319–321.

DUVALL, SYLVANUS M., *Men, Women, and Morals* (New York: Association Press, 1952).

GLUECK, ELEANOR, *Moral Goals for Modern Youth* (New York: Social Action, 1943).

LEUBA, CLARENCE, *Ethics in Sex Conduct* (New York: Association Press, 1948).

MEAD, MARGARET, *Male and Female* (New York: Morrow, 1951).

MERRILL, FRANCIS E., *Courtship and Marriage* (New York: Sloane, 1949), Chap. 3.

TITUS, HAROLD H., *Ethics for Today* (New York: American Book, 1936).

Technical References

BLOOD, ROBERT O., JR., "Romance and Premarital Intercourse — Incompatibles?" *Marriage and Family Living* (May, 1952).

BOWMAN, CLAUDE C., "Cultural Ideology and Heterosexual Reality: A Preface to Sociological Research," *American Sociological Review*, Vol. XIV, No. 5 (October, 1949).

——, "Social Factors Opposed to the Extension of Heterosexuality," *American Journal of Psychiatry*, Vol. 106, No. 6 (December, 1949).

ELLIS, ALBERT, *The Folklore of Sex* (New York: Boni, 1951).

KINSEY, ALFRED C., AND ASSOCIATES, *Sexual Behavior in the Human Male* (Philadelphia: Saunders, 1948).

MacMURRAY, JOHN, *Reason and Emotion* (New York: Appleton-Century, 1937), especially pp. 93–144.

MURDOCK, GEORGE P., *Social Structure* (New York: Macmillan, 1949).

PLANT, JAMES, *Personality and the Cultural Pattern* (New York: Commonwealth Fund, 1937).

PORTERFIELD, AUSTIN L., AND SALLEY, H. ELLISON, "Current Folkways of Sexual Behavior," *The American Journal of Sociology*, Vol. LII, No. 3 (November, 1946).

QUEEN, STUART A., AND ADAMS, JOHN B., *The Family in Various Cultures* (Philadelphia: Lippincott, 1952).

CHAPTER EIGHT

"She had a successful career ahead of her.
Thank goodness she saved herself in time!"

WHO GETS MARRIED?

Why do some people never marry?

Is it true that opposites attract each other into marriage?

Do remarriages work out?

Do people marry for different reasons?

Does who you are influence whom you marry?

Who marry most happily?

*A*MERICA IS ONE OF THE MOST MARRIED NATIONS IN THE world; indeed, it can be said without fear of contradiction that marriage is our favorite institution. Ninety-one per cent of the population who live to age fifty-five marry. With these facts in mind, this chapter has been designed to answer: 1. why marriage is so popular in America; 2. why people get married; 3. why some people never marry; and 4. why some who marry are happier than others.

Why People Marry

Ask the man on the street why he gets married, and he will probably tell you that he does it because he loves the girl. His friends may recognize other motives as they observe that the girl has money, and that she has obtained for him a soft berth in her father's business. In other countries it isn't necessary to mask all motivations under the label of love. Marriages of convenience are recognized and given status. We Americans find it difficult to admit any other reason for marrying except love. But there are many, many other reasons.

First of all, the average person develops needs in his parental family for affection and emotional security which can only be satisfied in the intimacy of a home. As he grows up it becomes necessary for him to find the satisfaction of these deepest needs and wishes away from the parental home. It is most natural that he will feel impelled to establish his own family to meet these needs.

Some word should be said for social pressure as a reason for marrying in America. Parents, relatives, employers, and married friends offer advice and point to the joys of wedded life to everyone who reaches marriageable age. There are places you can't go without a partner, and you find yourself excluded from pleasant associations with former friends now married. Social living becomes awkward, particularly in small communities; restaurant food is often inferior and quarters are unsatisfactory. Almost everyone will point out that the single pattern of living is abnormal, that marriage is the good life!

The table below is an attempt to list the major needs for which young people anticipate satisfaction in marrying. These are only general reasons for getting married. The list would lengthen if you were to add your own highly individual reasons.

MAJOR REASONS FOR MARRYING IN AMERICA

Companionship and Love

Need for intimate response, for understanding, for belonging to someone exclusively.

Home and Children

Desire to have a home and children of one's own to symbolize adult status.

Adventure and Romance

Falling in love with love; arises as hunger in those whose lives seem drab or filled with boredom.

Escape

Desire to escape an unhappy situation, difficult job, small town, or poverty, marriage promising a way out. (Often a jump from the frying pan . . .)

Consolation for Failure

Rebound. (Show the world by marrying the rescuer; may marry anyone who sympathizes, mistaking need of sympathy for love.)

Join the Bandwagon

Marrying in wartime because everybody's doing it.

Conquest

Desire to obtain a person who rates, who is badly wanted by others. (Rhett Butler married Scarlet O'Hara in *Gone with the Wind* to conquer her.)

Social Expectation

Pressure of friends and parents to settle down and marry. (Girl marries a man she doesn't love to escape stigma of being an old maid.)

Sex Attraction

Response toward any attractive person of opposite sex. Important reason for initial contacts but second to companionship and understanding in marriage. (Like the flavoring in the cake; cake would be tasteless without it, but flavoring alone would be no cake!)

Social Status and Security

Social acceptance. (Life in America organized for married people both socially and economically; promotions, advancements, opportunities go to married men.)

Why Some People Never Marry

If all that has been said is true, why should anyone remain unmarried? There are many factors which limit marriageability today, some highly impersonal, such as the maldistribution of marriageable men, geographically and occupationally, and the increasing surplus of women of marrying age in the general population. Other factors which are much more personal are unhappy childhood experiences, emotional immaturity, mother and father fixations, standards of beauty and glamor, and perfectionist standards. Ten out of every hundred mature American men remain bachelors through choice or individual circumstances. Approximately 8 per cent of American women also remain unmarried. An analysis of their reasons for remaining celibates is in order.

Some few people really don't want to marry for the reason that their early experiences in the home were unhappy. They carry over bitter attitudes toward marriage and family life and would probably make poor marriage partners. Some prefer the freedom of single blessedness to married responsibility. They may wish to avoid the obligations involved in living intimately with another adult. From a purely habit standpoint, it is much simpler to continue with the routines of unmarried living. Sometimes a man is so tied to his mother, or a girl to her father, that no other person can ever take the place of the beloved parent. There are some people who have had distortions in their love development which make it difficult for them to love a person of the op-

MARRIEDNESS VS. UNMARRIEDNESS, 1890–1951

U.S. Bureau of the Census, *Current Population Reports*, Series P 20, No. 35, Table 2: "Marital Status of Persons 14 Years Old and Over, by Sex, for the United States": "Civilian Population, 1947 to 1951, and Total Population, 1890 to 1940."

posite sex. A sense of shame or of unworthiness that has come from painful childhood experiences may keep one from forming the deep attachments that lead to marriage. It is probably best that these latter do not marry too. When they do marry the results are often tragic.

More frequently, a person who wants to get married cannot find someone who is desirable and equally desirous of marriage. Impossibly romantic ideals of the perfect mate may keep the available choices from seeming suitable. The physically handicapped, for example, are often disappointed in their search for a desirable mate. Certain physical characteristics tend to be rejected out of all proportion to their significance in a marriage partner. Hair on the lip of a woman, or lack of it on the scalp of a man, lessens the attractiveness of the person in our society. Extreme height in the woman or shortness in the man diminishes choices of dating partners and of mates. Birthmarks and other superficial disfigurements may operate almost as strongly in eliminating a person from the competitive struggle for a mate as many more basic handicaps. The attitude of the person toward his handicaps is usually more important than the mere fact that he has them. If shame, inadequacy, and avoidance of people are his predominant attitudes, the handicap may seriously affect his chances of marriage. On the other hand, attitudes of acceptance, of friendliness, and objectivity toward oneself increase the possibility of rich friendships and satisfactory marital choices.

Too Few Marriageable Men. For years Sweden and France and other European countries have experienced a severe husband shortage. The man scarcity has recently spread to include America, much to the dismay of the millions of girls now coming into the marrying age. In 1950 the potentially marriageable female population which includes the single, divorced, and widowed, outnumbered the marriageable males by two million. Only in the youngest age groups are there boys enough, and most of these are not economically ready to marry.

The deficit of men in the marrying ages is due to a number of factors. There is first of all a higher death rate among males through greater biological weakness and greater exposure to industrial hazards. Man is not the stronger sex! Second, we have used up the very convenient surplus of males who arrived through immigration, and there are no prospects of any more coming to replace them. Third, more men than women are to be found in the unmarriageable categories of convicts, psychotics, invalids, hobos, professional soldiers, and so on. Finally, the war casualties and war marriages of younger men to older women tend to decrease even further the supply of eligible men.

For girls who want to do something constructive about getting a husband in the face of the present shortage, the figures show that there are still some sections of the country where men outnumber women. Detroit and Sacramento have 110 and 113 men per hundred women respectively. The New England states average only 96 men for each hundred women, compared with 111.4 in Idaho, 114.1 in Wyoming, and

113.1 in Nevada. Girls who take their statistics seriously should consider Alaska, where men outnumber women 145.7 to a hundred. It makes a difference too whether a girl is in an occupation which throws her constantly into contact with men. Schoolteachers and librarians have low marriage rates, whereas dining-room hostesses marry in relatively great numbers.

Careers and Education Discourage Marriage. Professional training for men and for women results in postponed marriages, sometimes indefinitely postponed. The pattern of getting established and earning for a few years before marrying means that young men in professional schools are not good marriage prospects and won't be for some time to come.[1] Young women, therefore, face the fact that many of the young men they have known in college are not ready to marry, and that when they do marry they will take girls of a younger age group. To complicate matters further, college women plan to marry someone at least as educated, as intelligent, and of as high social status as themselves. The more training a woman obtains, the narrower becomes the field from which she can choose a husband who will meet her educational qualifications.

Standards Too High. Holding out for a standard of living that is unattainable keeps still others from marriage. With the emphasis on getting ahead in the world, some young people postpone marriage until they can maintain the standard of living to which they have been accustomed in their parental homes. Advertisements of model homes with automatic dishwashers, TV sets, tiled baths, and built-in conveniences are all too often accepted as the current attainable standard. As a matter of fact, a very small percentage of American families live under such conditions. Few new families can hope to start out as well equipped as the *"Ladies' Home Journal* brides," complete with sterling-silver table service, white satin bridal gown, and so on. To some ambitious young people it seems important to delay marriage until the physical setting resembles the romantic picture of what the advertisers

[1] Paul Glick and Emanuel Landau found age at marriage to average 29.5 and 31.5 years for husbands whose incomes were respectively in the $5,000–5,900 and $6,000 and over brackets as compared with ages at marriage of 23–24 years for husbands in the $1,000–2,999 bracket. Occupational groups also varied in average age at marriage. See "Age as a Factor in Marriage," *American Sociological Review*, Vol. 15, No. 4 (August, 1950), pp. 517–529.

say every young couple should have. The trouble is that the postponement all too often becomes permanent!

Even so, millions yearly testify to the popularity of marriage as an
institution by getting married. The proportion married in America increased from 60 per cent of the population 14 years of age and over to
67 per cent from 1940 to 1950. Even the widowed and divorced don't
remain unmarried for any length of time. To be in the married status
is regarded universally as highly desirable. An analysis of this marrying
population appears in order. Who gets married, and to whom? Do
likes marry opposites or people like themselves?

Who Marries Whom?

We tend to love and eventually to marry people like ourselves. It isn't
an accident that doctors marry nurses and farm girls marry farmers.
The more a boy and a girl have in common, the more likely they are to
meet. Once they have met, the more traits they have in common, the
more apt they are to marry. This tendency to marry someone who has
social traits similar to one's own is called *homogamy*. Recent studies
have shown that homogamy is overwhelmingly predominant over heterogamy (the marriage of dissimilar people). Two investigators [2] studying the social characteristics in a thousand engaged couples found that
all but six of fifty characteristics showed more resemblance than dis-
similarity. The factors studied included religious affiliation and behavior, family background, courtship behavior, conceptions of marriage, social participation, and family relationships.

The table on page 158 provides a listing of the factors found most frequently to be more similar than dissimilar among the thousand engaged
couples studied.

A recent novel clearly describes how parents of a couple react to differences in religious and social background. The daughter of a socially
prominent family is attracted to a young lawyer of another religious
faith. A scene with her father and mother ensues, in which the parents
try to tell their daughter why they object to her choice:

"Why?" he repeated, looking at her. "All right, I'll tell you why. I
don't want my daughter to go through life neither flesh, fowl nor good red

[2] Ernest W. Burgess and Paul Wallin, "Homogamy in Social Characteristics,"
American Journal of Sociology (September, 1943), pp. 109–124.

FACTORS SHOWING GREATEST SIMILARITY AMONG ENGAGED COUPLES [3]

Courtship Characteristics

Age at beginning of courtship
Number of going steady experiences
Number of persons consulted about engagement

Conceptions of Marriage Held

Attitude toward married women working
Attitude toward having children
Number of children desired
Attitude toward divorce

Family Attachments

Happiness of parents' marriage
Attachment to father
Attachment to siblings

Religious Behavior

Religious affiliation
Church attendance
Active membership

Social Habits and Participation

Drinking habits
Smoking habits
Leisure time preferences
Extent of participation in organizations

herring, living in a kind of no man's land where half the people you know will never accept him, and half the people he knows will never accept you. I don't want a son-in-law who'll be an embarrassment to my friends, a son-in-law who can't be put up at my club and who can't go with us to places where we've gone all our lives. I don't want a son-in-law whom I'll have to apologize for and explain and have to hear insulted indirectly, unless I can remember to warn people off first."

"We want you to marry someone — someone like us. Someone who'll fit in and whom we can" — Margaret Drake caught her breath, then managed to say — "can all be proud of," and suddenly shoving back her chair, she got up and left the room.[4]

Similar reactions are found among young people themselves. There is no denying that marital choice is affected by the similarity in attitudes

[3] Drawn from research study by Burgess and Wallin, *op. cit.*, tables 1–6, pp. 113–122.

[4] Selection from Gwethalyn Graham Erickson Brown, *Earth and High Heaven* (Philadelphia: Lippincott, 1944).

and backgrounds. As has been shown in a previous chapter, pair unity develops with the formation of a common language and common goals. It is the couple's excuse for excluding the rest of the world and is possible only where the members start out with many things in common.

Do Opposites Also Attract? According to current folklore, the secret of mating is to select someone who will be exotically different in make-up. Accordingly, if you are a spendthrift you need a wife who will pinch the pennies, or if you are hyperactive you need a wife who is slow and easy going. The tales go even further in that they point out that opposites have a fatal attraction for one another, that brilliant men marry the beautiful but dumb, that brunets seem drawn to blondes. To date, research proves these generalizations to be fallacious. They may be based more on the visibility of the exceptions than on an accurate counting of the total marrying public. Correlations of some magnitude are found between couples as to height, age, weight, intelligence, ethnic and occupational background, and geographical area of residence. The correlations with regard to temperament [5] are not so marked; indeed the findings are often conflicting. If opposites do attract each other it is only a temporary attraction; opposites don't marry in significant numbers.

However, at least one author argues for keeping the question of homogamy and heterogamy open for further investigation. Robert F. Winch points out that little evidence has been offered that persons with similar need patterns tend to marry. He poses the proposition that homogamy operates to establish a field of eligible persons from whom marriage partners are selected, but that within the field of eligibles individuals tend to mate with those whose need patterns generally complement their own rather than with those whose need patterns are similar to their own.[6] This is entirely consistent with our later discussion of "meeting of needs" as a major cohesive factor in marriage.[7]

Intermarriage by Servicemen Overseas. As a special case of heterogamous marriage in which opposites do marry, the unions of American

[5] Ernest W. Burgess and Paul Wallin are among those who find homogamy in temperament. They report a slight but statistically significant trend for like to mate with like with respect to 14 of 42 items from the Thurstone Neurotic Inventory and 9 of 23 self-ratings on traits; see "Homogamy in Personality Characteristics," *Journal of Abnormal and Social Psychology*, Vol. 39 (1944), pp. 475–81.
[6] Robert F. Winch, *The Modern Family* (New York: Holt, 1952), p. 403.
[7] See Chap. 15, "What Holds a Marriage Together."

servicemen and foreign women merit attention. Charles Fritz made an analysis of the 92,465 foreign war brides who entered the United States, 1945–1948, to join their American husbands under Public Law 271 (War Brides Act).[8] He found trends toward homogamy even among these international marriages. For example, over one half of the foreign brides were from English-speaking countries. Moreover, the majority of men marrying foreign war brides were themselves children of foreign-born or were of mixed nativity. There was a distinct tendency toward homogamy in ethnic backgrounds of the husbands and the foreign war brides. Indeed, Eastern and Southern European brides tended to migrate to residence areas of their own nationality.

No definitive information is yet available concerning the success of international marriages resulting from World War II and the subsequent occupation of Germany and Asiatic countries. From data on international marriages of earlier date it is apparent that intermarriage of people with different family backgrounds proves hazardous because neither party completely understands the values cherished by the other. Fully accepted by the members of neither society, the intermarried pair usually finds itself excommunicated from contacts with many people and is usually forced to join other atypical couples for purposes of social intercourse.

Most of the research on intermarriage has been centered on interracial marriages in this country.[9] Without exception the findings from this research argue against intermarriage. The situation may be even more aggravated in cases where the marriage takes place in far-away lands. Intermarriage of a Negro and a white person in South Side Chicago may actually be fraught with fewer difficulties than the mythical intermarriage of Sergeant Hagen of Murdo, South Dakota, with the daughter of a Nigerian chief in far-away Africa. Students of the problem consider the differences in the ways of life of the participants in such a marriage to be more divisive than the differences in skin color or facial features.

Where opposites do marry, interests which they have in common

[8] "A Study of World War II International Marriages," Master's Thesis, University of Chicago (March, 1950).

[9] For a summary of the studies of intermarriage see two publications by Milton L. Barron, *People Who Intermarry* (Syracuse, N. Y.: Syracuse University Press, 1946), and "Research on Intermarriage: A Survey of Accomplishments and Prospects," *American Journal of Sociology*, Vol. LVII, No. 3 (November, 1951), pp. 249–256.

usually outnumber the highly visible characteristics in which they differ. Successful intermarriages are possible if the parties first make sure that in every other area the essentials for a happy adjustment are present. They should be certain that they share similar attitudes toward work, play, children, and religion, and that they are temperamentally compatible. Such a test eliminates, it is true, most marriage possibilities in foreign lands — the differences in upbringing disqualifying most couples.

Remarriages

Almost a fourth of the marriages in recent years have not been first marriages. Most divorced persons remarry, and except in the ages after forty-five most widows and widowers do too. In fact, the chances of remarriage are much higher for both divorced and widowed, age for age, than for single persons. The advantage of the divorced person is so great over the single and widowed, however, that even increasing age doesn't greatly reduce the likelihood of marriage. For example, a spinster of thirty has approximately a fifty-fifty chance of marriage; the widow of thirty has a sixty-forty chance; but the divorcée of the same age has 94 chances out of a hundred of remarrying. Not until the divorcée is forty-five do her chances drop to the fifty-fifty level of the thirty-year-old single woman.[10]

Most remarriage after divorce occurs within five years, and by fourteen years all but one seventh of the divorced have remarried.[11] The remarriages of widowed are much slower. About one third of the men and two thirds of the women had not remarried after fourteen years. There is a selective tendency for widowed or divorced women with children to remarry quickly or not at all.

The evidence concerning the relative success of remarriages is conflicting. Women appear to be poorer risks in second and subsequent marriages than men.[12] One worker calculates that second marriages in general are about 50 per cent more risky than first marriages.[13]

Second and subsequent marriages are less well off economically than

[10] Paul H. Landis, "Sequential Marriage," *Journal of Home Economics*, Vol. 42 (October, 1950), pp. 625–628.
[11] Paul C. Glick, "First Marriages and Remarriages," *American Sociological Review*, Vol. 14 (December, 1949), pp. 726–734.
[12] Landis, *op. cit.*, p. 627.
[13] *Ibid.*, p. 627.

CHANCES IN 100 OF MARRIAGE FOR SINGLE WOMEN AND OF REMARRIAGE FOR DIVORCED AND WIDOWED WOMEN *

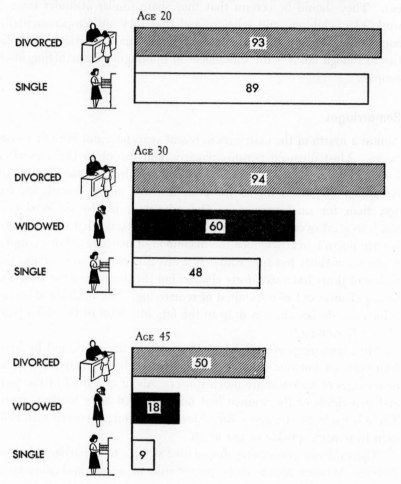

* From Landis, *op. cit.*, p. 625, based on calculations from records of twenty-two states and the District of Columbia.

first marriages. This is true, not only in terms of money income of the remarried men, but also from the standpoint of improved occupational level. A general pattern of improvement in occupational level is discernible for men during their initial ten years of married life, but no such pattern is discernible for the first ten years of remarried life.[14]

What Type of Couple Marries Most Happily?

Many novels end with the implied statement, "and they lived happily ever after." Few mature persons will be taken in by such a poorly couched generalization, but until recently there were no studies to show how couples whose marriages remained happy differed in make-up from those who became chronically unhappy after marriage. Scattered studies in the nineteen twenties paved the way for two research groups early in the 1930's working quite independently, one in Illinois[15] and the other in California.[16] Their task was to test the factors making for happiness in marriage. Although the two studies used different criteria of marital success, the first using "marital adjustment" and the second "marital happiness," the factors most highly associated with marital success corroborated each other in both studies at many significant points.[17] Because these studies were limited to regionally restricted populations, conducted primarily with urban white couples, it was important that comparative investigations be launched to test these authors' findings in other settings. Comparable studies have now been completed in Min-

---

[14] Glick, op. cit., p. 734.

[15] Ernest W. Burgess and Leonard S. Cottrell, Jr., Predicting Success or Failure in Marriage (New York: Prentice-Hall, 1939).

[16] Lewis M. Terman and associates, Psychological Factors in Marital Happiness (New York: McGraw-Hill, 1938).

[17] Most of the research studies to date have employed either the yardstick of "happiness" in marriage or "adjustment," depending heavily on self-ratings and friends' ratings on happiness for ranking the couples studied. The happiness concept involves such difficulties as person-to-person differences concerning the nature of happiness, the possibility that happiness may be determined to a considerable degree by factors external to the marriage, and the chance that happiness is a temperamental characteristic of the person rather than a property of the marriage. Adjustment as a concept puts high priority on agreements between husband and wife on the major issues of marriage without specifying at what cost these agreements are achieved; namely, by wife giving in, having no ideas of her own, and so on. Adjustment may be rated high simply because there is absence of marital conflict. Actually some conflict in marriage may be necessary for growth. For a more detailed critique see, Waller and Hill, The Family: A Dynamic Interpretation (N. Y.: Dryden, 1951), pp. 342–370.

BACKGROUND FACTORS IN MARITAL SUCCESS*

Favorable	Unfavorable	Unrelated
PERSONALITY CHARACTERISTICS		
Permissive and considerate attitudes — *both*	Lacks self-confidence — *husband*	Extraversion — intraversion
Cooperative attitudes — *both*	Combinations where man day dreams and woman does not	Friendliness or offishness
Compatibility of temperament	Combinations where man feels inferior and woman does not	
Combinations where neither is neurotic	Combinations where woman makes friends easily and man does not	
Combinations where both are intellectually superior	Prone to argue points — *wife*	
	Determination to get own way — *wife*	
	Unhappy temperament, pessimistic — *both*	
	Variability in moods — *both*	
	Feelings easily hurt — *both*	
	Self-sufficiency in facing troubles alone — *both*	
CULTURAL AND FAMILY BACKGROUNDS		
Similarity of cultural backgrounds	Dissimilarity in cultural and family backgrounds	Number of siblings
Similar educational achievements	Wife's cultural background higher than husband's	Birth order in family
Father of high occupational level — *both*	Residence in the city during childhood	Differences in educational achievements of parents
Firm but not harsh home training — *both*		Modernist or fundamentalist religious beliefs
Happiness of parents' marriage — *both* (Not true for Negro couples)		Economic circumstances at marriage
Happiness of childhood — *both*		
Conservative home backgrounds		

SOCIALITY FACTORS		
Frequency of attendance at church and Sunday school (Not true for Swedish couples)	Unconventionality with respect to religion, sexual ethics, drinking	Number of persons with whom one has "kept company"
Number of friends — *both sexes*	Religiously inactive	
Residence in single-family dwellings		
Socially conservative		

RESPONSE PATTERNS		
Love based on companionship	Romantic infatuation as basis of love	Amount of "petting" before marriage
Length of acquaintance before marriage	Disapproval of marriage by parents — *especially husband*	Fear of pregnancy
Similarity between parent of opposite sex and affianced — *both*	Conflict with father — *both*	
Strong attachment to father — *both*		
Self and mate enjoy engaging in many activities together		

SEX FACTORS		
Sex information received from parents first — *both*	Premarital intercourse by either or both (low but negative relationship to subsequent marital adjustment except in case of Negro and Swedish couples)	Sex techniques used
Frank and encouraging attitudes of parents toward child's curiosity about sex — *important for husband*	Prudishness and excessive modesty — *wife*	Frequency and duration of intercourse
Similarity in sex desires	Fear of sex — *wife*	Degree of pain experienced by wife at first intercourse
Orgasm capacity in wife	Husband-wife differences in strength of sex drive	Methods of contraception used
Amount of pleasure wife experienced at first intercourse — *wife*		

* (Drawn primarily from studies cited in technical references, p. 169)

nesota, Michigan, New York, Indiana, North Carolina, Sweden, and China, by Kirkpatrick and Taves, Landis, Williams, Locke, King, Karlsson, and Smythe, respectively.[18] In addition, Williams has studied rural couples, King has studied Negro couples, and Karlsson and Smythe have investigated couples in other societies. The findings of these investigations converge at a number of points in spite of the multiversity of the populations studied.

A summary of the factors on which the studies are most frequently in agreement has been prepared on pp. 164–165 under five major headings: "Personality Characteristics," "Cultural and Family Backgrounds," "Sociability Factors," "Response Patterns," and "Sex Factors." For ease and convenience in reading, these five areas are broken down into attributes which are favorable, unfavorable, or unrelated to marital success. These findings cannot be applied successfully to individual cases. At best they are statistical averages derived from the study of many hundreds of cases. It is important to realize that for every finding reflected in this table there are numerous marriages which are happy even though they do not possess the quality listed.

To the extent that the factors in the preceding table can be measured before marriage, the general matrimonial risk of a person may be calculated much as the life insurance companies compute the life chances of an individual applicant for insurance from actuarial tables. Of greater import to young people about to marry would be data which would enable them to calculate their own matrimonial risk in combination with a particular person. Research has not yet progressed to this point in the field of marriage prediction. It is our considered judgment that the present factors need further testing before any combined applications may be made safely.

Personality and Temperament. Terman has found that marital happiness is largely determined by one's all-round happiness of temperament.[19] Happiness of temperament is not to be confused either with Pollyannish or sugary attitudes or with the happy-go-lucky disposition, but refers to the items listed under personality characteristics in the table just described. Non-neurotic, permissive, adaptable, cooperative individuals can live comfortably with any but the most disagreeable mate.

[18] For publication data on these studies see the list of technical references at the end of the chapter, p. 169.
[19] L. M. Terman and M. Oden, *The Gifted Child Grows Up; Twenty-Five Years Followup of a Superior Group* (Palo Alto: Stanford University Press, 1947), Chap. 18.

Certain types of personalities would find almost any marriage unbearable, and their attributes are listed in the unfavorable column of the same table. Marriage brings with it situations which are frustrating, perplexing, and burdensome. Personalities which thrive under stress are said to have high aptitude for marriage.

Cultural and Family Backgrounds. Cultural homogeneity of backgrounds simplifies the forging of workable family routines, facilitates the arrival at mutually acceptable solutions to problems, and increases the likelihood of quick and open communication when one's needs are not met. Childhood background, including the happiness of parents' marriage, the history of happiness in childhood, and the disciplinary policies of parents, all appear significant in later marital happiness. One's apprenticeship in the intimacies of family living starts in the parental home. If it has been inadequate, or unhappy, or distorted, it is usually necessary to obtain the training for a happy marriage elsewhere: in the homes of friends, relatives, or from counseling and formal schooling. Young people whose home experiences have been unhappy are not infrequently highly motivated to avoid similar mistakes in their own marriages and make great strides under proper guidance.

Sociability and Conventionality. Sociability, or the tendency to join with friends of both sexes for companionship, is highly associated with marital adjustment. It is linked in our list of factors with conventionality of social behavior: attendance at church, and conservative political leanings. In America there is apparently some stability obtained from conforming to the expectations of the community, having the marriage ceremony performed by a minister or priest, and maintaining affiliation with a church.

Response Patterns. The capacity to give and receive affection, as measured by replies to questions on demonstration of affection, is associated with success in marriage. Love based on companionship and a community of interests and activities appeared in happy contrast with love relationships based on romantic infatuation and highly individualized interests. Companionship based marriages were usually of longer acquaintance before marriage. The response patterns appear to be derived partly from parental family experiences and partly from the history of one's past pair relationships in dating, going steady, and engagements. Strong attachment to the father, some similarity between parent of opposite sex and the affianced, and approval of the marriage by the parents reflect the pleasurable history of parental relationships antecedent to marriage. The capacity to give and receive affection probably stems directly from this series of attachments.

Attitudes toward Sex. Sexual adjustment in marriage depends much more upon psychological than upon physical factors. Marriages are therefore more likely to be satisfying in this realm where the first sex information has been received from parents rather than acquired on the street. Parental frankness in answering the questions of children about sex and in giving them adequate information tends to develop healthy attitudes toward the sexual experiences of marriage. These in turn are undoubtedly related to achieving similarity of sex desires, developing orgasm capacity in the wife, and other tasks of sex adjustment in marriage.

In brief summary this chapter has pointed up the popularity of marriage in America. It is without doubt our favorite institution. Nine out of ten Americans marry at least once during their lifetime. The reasons for marriage rank companionship, home and children, and security high. Marriages for convenience are not only rare but rationalized as based on love where they occur.

Failure to marry can be attributed to impersonal factors such as maldistribution of marriageable men geographically and occupationally, and to personal factors having to do with unhappy childhood experiences, mother and father dependence, ineligibility because of American standards of beauty and glamor, and perfectionism in mate choice. Higher education tends to narrow the field from which a woman may choose a husband, but once married her chance of success in marriage increases.

The evidence is overwhelming that homogamy operates in mate selection. If opposites in background and attitudes attract each other it is apparently only temporary because they don't marry in significant numbers. Exceptions may be found in the area of need patterns where opposites with complementary need patterns may possibly mate profitably.

Finally, we found that couples were more likely to marry happily who brought happiness of temperament to marriage, who were from culturally similar backgrounds, conventional in their outlook on religion and other issues, and whose capacity to give and receive affection was unimpaired at marriage.

Selected Readings

BOWMAN, HENRY A., *Marriage for Moderns* (New York: McGraw-Hill, 1948), chaps. 2, 3.

LANDIS, JUDSON T., AND LANDIS, MARY G., *Building a Successful Marriage* (New York: Prentice-Hall, 1948), Chap. 3.

LANDIS, PAUL H., "Sequential Marriage," *Journal of Home Economics,* Vol. 42 (October, 1950), pp. 625–628.

SCHEINFELD, AMRAM, *Women and Men* (New York: Harcourt, Brace, 1944), Chap. 16.

WALLER, WILLARD, AND HILL, REUBEN, *The Family: A Dynamic Interpretation* (New York: Dryden, 1951), Chap. 11.

Technical References

BARRON, MILTON L., *People Who Intermarry* (Syracuse: Syracuse University Press, 1946).

BURGESS, E. W., AND COTTRELL, LEONARD S., JR., *Predicting Success or Failure in Marriage* (New York: Prentice-Hall, 1939).

BURGESS, E. W., AND WALLIN, PAUL, *Engagement and Marriage* (Chicago: Lippincott, 1953).

CENTERS, RICHARD, "Marital Selection and Occupational Strata," *American Journal of Sociology,* Vol. 54 (May, 1949), pp. 530–536.

ELLIS, ALBERT, "The Value of Marriage Prediction Tests," *American Sociological Review,* Vol. 13 (December, 1948), pp. 710–718.

GREENBERG, JOSEPH H., *Numerical Sex Disproportion* (Boulder, Colorado: University of Colorado Press, 1950).

KARLSSON, GEORG, *Adaptability and Communication in Marriage* (Upsala, Sweden: Upsala Sociological Institute, 1951).

KIRKPATRICK, CLIFFORD, *What Science Says about Happiness in Marriage* (Minneapolis: Burgess Publishing Company, 1947).

KOLB, WILLIAM L., "Sociologically Established Family Norms and Democratic Values," *Social Forces,* Vol. 28 (May, 1948), pp. 451–456.

LANDIS, JUDSON T., "Length of Time Required to Achieve Adjustment in Marriage," *American Sociological Review,* Vol. 11 (December, 1946), pp. 666–677.

LOCKE, HARVEY J., *Predicting Adjustment in Marriage* (New York: Holt, 1951).

TAVES, MARVIN J., "A Direct vs. an Indirect Approach in Measuring Marital Adjustment," *American Sociological Review,* Vol. 13 (October, 1948), pp. 538–541.

TERMAN, L. M., AND OTHERS, *Psychological Factors in Marital Happiness* (New York: McGraw-Hill, 1938).

WALLER, WILLARD, AND HILL, REUBEN, *The Family: A Dynamic Interpretation* (New York: Dryden, 1951), Chap. 17.

WINCH, ROBERT F., *The Modern Family* (New York: Holt, 1952), Chap. 15.

CHAPTER NINE

"Please, Miss Larve, just say 'I do'."

WEDDING PLANS

How formal does a wedding have to be to be right?

How do you decide whom to invite to your wedding?

What do you do first in getting ready for a wedding?

Who pays for what?

Just how flexible can you be and still have a nice wedding?

*U*NLESS YOU WANT TO BE MARRIED IN THE CITY HALL, OR BY A Justice of the Peace with all the haste and impersonality involved in such a marriage, you will need to make some wedding plans. Most girls look forward to some kind of wedding. However, many girls and most men do not want a very large formal type of wedding. You do not need to elope to avoid such a wedding. There are simple, inexpensive weddings that are satisfying at the moment and that will bring warm memories long afterwards. But of whatever type, a wedding has to be planned to be effective.

When you marry, you may not have much choice about the kind of wedding yours will be. In some circles, the bride's mother takes over almost completely and manages everything from the first invitation to the last detail with only occasional reference to the preferences of bride and groom. Your wedding may have to conform to the expectations of your father's friends and associates or be according to rigidly pre-scribed forms. Or, you may find yourself being married in the chapel of a military post, either with strict formality and full military honors, or in the stark simplicity of a ceremony arranged at a moment's notice.

Setting the Wedding Date

The date of your wedding may have to be set at the time of a military leave or a long-awaited vacation from work. Then all your plans and arrangements are made around those dates as soon as they are fairly definite. If there is some flexibility, the bride usually sets the date that will come at a time when she is not menstruating, and allows time to get her clothes ready, and wedding arrangements completed. She talks over possible dates with her fiancé and together they choose a wedding time that will be most convenient to them both.

As soon as the couple has selected a tentative date for their wedding, it is wise for them to clear it with both immediate families, to rule out the possibility of a conflicting date of importance, and to reserve the date definitely in family plans. This is not too early to contact the church, chapel, or club to make sure that it may be reserved for the hour of the wedding, unless of course this is to be a home wedding. Which brings us to the question, what kind of wedding is it to be?

Types of Weddings

The type of wedding you have depends upon many factors: 1. your own hopes and dreams through the years; 2. the amount of money you want to spend; 3. the families you both come from, their wishes and interests and social standing; 4. your location with particular reference to the kinds of places suitable for a wedding; 5. the number of friends and relatives you want to invite; and 6. the amount of time you have to plan ahead for the wedding.

Weddings range all the way from simple informal affairs to large formal pageants. You may choose the type of wedding that best fits your situation from any of the following general patterns with whatever modifications make the occasion most meaningful to you.

1 *Small home wedding* with only members of the immediate families present, and whatever decorations, music, and refreshments seem suitable. Such a wedding is the least expensive in time and money, and can follow the individual wishes of the couple more freely than other types.

2 *Informal chapel wedding* to which only immediate relatives and close friends are invited, with the couple receiving their guests in the foyer

following the ceremony. Although there may be no reception as such, the immediate wedding party may go somewhere for a wedding breakfast afterwards if they wish. This type of wedding can be easily arranged, kept as simple as the couple desires, is inexpensive, and can be quite lovely. One modification of this is for the wedding to take place following a regular service in the bride's church, to which the guests come as soon as the previous service is over. This is convenient for organist, minister, and many guests. The altar is already decorated, and extra arrangements are kept to a minimum.

3 *Small wedding in church, home, or club* to which members of the two families and friends are invited, followed by a reception, that may include a longer guest list, if desired. The reception may take place in the church parlors, in the home, the club, or in some other suitable place nearby. The longer guest list may be for the ceremony itself with only a few chosen friends and family members invited to the reception that follows in another place. When the reception is held at the place of the ceremony, all those attending the ceremony are invited to the reception as well.

4 *The home, garden, or club wedding and reception* for everyone in the same location. In this type of wedding there is a flow from the ceremony to the receiving line to the refreshment tables with all guests participating. This may be an elaborate affair of *The Father of the Bride* variety, or it may be a simple ceremony under the trees in the yard or at an altar improvised inside. A sit-down wedding breakfast, a buffet supper, or simple refreshments of the stand-up sort, around whatever menu is appropriate, is chosen depending upon the number of guests, the accommodations, personnel to serve, and of course the budget.

5 *Formal, or semiformal church wedding,* followed by a small home or club reception to which only a few friends and the two families are asked. Here the pomp and splendor are in the ceremony, with the secondary interest in the reception. This can be as elaborate or as simple as the bride and her family may desire. The formal ceremony itself demands both time and money to be in accordance with traditional form. A wedding consultant to advise on the costuming of the wedding party, decorations, wedding processional, the recessional, and all such details, can be a great help in the formal wedding, which to be proper must conform to convention.

6 *Large, formal church, cathedral, or synagogue wedding,* followed by home, hotel, or country club reception to which all wedding guests are invited. Here, money is no object, and the bills may total many thousands of dollars. This may represent not only the family's investment in the couple, but as is often the case, is one way of attaining or maintaining social position and/or cementing business interests. Such a wedding lies outside the scope of this writing. Professional wedding services are in the business of arranging large formal weddings down to the last detail, under contract for a suitable fee.

Whom to Invite and How

It is usual for the family of the bride to invite the guests to the wedding. As soon as the decision has been made as to the type of wedding it will be, the bride and her family, in consultation with the groom and his parents, make out the list of persons to be invited. If the wedding is to be a small home affair, with only members of the immediate families present, the matter is a simple one except in problems of close relatives by blood or marriage who have been cut off from the family by distance, divorce, or estrangement. It is wise to invite all such family members as is at all possible. To exclude them from such an important occasion is often to widen the breach and to make for feelings of guilt and uneasiness among those present. Whether or not they are included, the decision should be the joint responsibility of all the family members planning the wedding.

Members of the immediate family and close friends may be invited to the small home, or informal chapel wedding, personally by the bride or her mother, by word of mouth, telephone, telegraph, or informal note, whichever is most convenient. In this case, announcements of the wedding are sent to all other relatives and friends as soon as the ceremony has been performed.

Guests to formal or semi-formal weddings are always invited by engraved wedding invitations according to prescribed forms available at the engravers. These are mailed from three to four weeks in advance of the ceremony. The order should be placed with the engraver about six weeks before the mailing date. Outside envelopes in the quantity decided upon may be secured from the engraver at the time the order is placed, so that addressing may be done in pen and ink at home while the engraving is being completed. If the list is very long, it is well to alphabetize it and check for duplicates and omissions before addressing the envelopes.

The engraved invitation may be used also in informal weddings to which a considerable number of guests are being invited. If engraving is too costly an item in the wedding budget, there is a form of raised printing that is frequently used instead of engraving that is much less expensive. The same general forms, dates for mailing and other customs are followed.

On the outside envelopes go the full names and addresses of the guests. Both husband and wife are invited as a Mr. and Mrs. unit, except in a case like the following. When the entire office force goes as a group to a wedding of one of its members at or close to office hours, it is not expected that the husbands and wives of members of the office staff will be invited.

If there is some question about the correct address of the guest, the return address of the sender may be included on the outside envelope; otherwise it is not necessary.

Names of members of the family not specifically indicated on the outside envelope may be written on the inside envelope of the wedding invitation, so that it may be clear just who it is that is being invited. In the case of a couple with two children, for instance, the names of each one of the four would be listed one under the other on the inside envelope. It is not necessary to invite the children to the wedding, but if one is invited, the other(s) should be included except for some important reason. Names of other relatives (brothers, sisters, mothers, etc.) living in the same residence may similarly be included in the listing of names on the inside envelope, or, somewhat more properly, they may receive separate invitations. It is usual for family members at different addresses and for members of an engaged couple to receive separate invitations.

Unless you put R.S.V.P. on the invitations to your wedding and reception, your guests are under no obligation to reply. So, if you need to know the number of guests to be expected, be sure to indicate on the invitation that a reply is expected, including the address to which the reply is to be sent, if there is apt to be some question about it. Replies to formal invitations are usually written in the third person and mailed first class. Informal invitations may be acknowledged by a simple note, or verbally by telephone, or by person to person.

If you have a considerable number of acceptances and regrets to keep track of, you will need some kind of system that will give you an accurate count. One bride-to-be simply set two boxes, one marked "YES" and the other "NO," on a convenient table. As replies came in the mail, or were given members of her family, they were dropped into the "YES" box if they were acceptances, and the "NO" box if regrets. Her tallies of each gave her a basis for an estimate for the caterer, and a final figure of total response. *Tip:* Always plan for a few extras; you never can tell!

Announcements

Engraved (or raised printing for economy's sake) announcements of the marriage are sent to all relatives and friends who did not receive an invitation to the wedding. Announcements follow a slightly different form than invitations, examples of which are available to serve as models at any stationer's or engraver's office. Lists of persons to receive announcements are collected from both bride and groom and their families, compiled and checked for duplicates as is done for invitations. Envelopes are personally addressed in pen and ink at home while awaiting delivery of the announcements and the inside envelopes. These may be prepared ahead. But, they are not mailed until after the ceremony, usually by some member of the bride's family. An "at home" card giving the address of the newly married couple and the date by which they will be settled may be enclosed with the announcement, or included in it, for the convenience of those who may wish to call, or send wedding gifts to the couple.

As with the invitations, the bride's parents' names are the first named on the announcement. In cases of death or divorce, the remaining parent's name alone is correct. When the bride is a mature woman long out of her parental home, she may announce her own marriage quite properly according to forms already developed and available as models.

If, for some reason, the formal announcement is not desired, either the bride or some senior member of her family may write to relatives and friends not present at her marriage, telling them about it, and thus announcing it informally. Likewise, the groom or one of his parents writes members of his family and friends about the wedding as soon as convenient.

Wedding Gifts

As soon as invitations are out, wedding gifts begin to arrive. Each one should be personally acknowledged by the bride just as soon as possible. With all the other things she has to do as the wedding date approaches, some sort of system will help. It is wise to plan ahead on where gifts will be kept and how they will be displayed. As each gift arrives, it is labeled with a number corresponding to that which the bride writes for it in her gift record along the following headings:

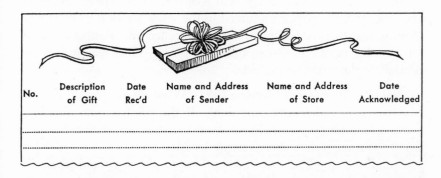

No.	Description of Gift	Date Rec'd	Name and Address of Sender	Name and Address of Store	Date Acknowledged

Such gift records appear in the back of wedding books given brides by some stores, or she may make her own in any way that seems most convenient for her to keep her gift record straight.

When a gift arrives, the bride may wait until her fiancé drops by before opening it, if they enjoy opening gifts together. Or, she may open it and enter it into her record at once, carefully preserving the card, and perhaps the packing slip from the store from which it was sent. (WARNING! Many gifts are multiple, so wrappings should be searched carefully before they are discarded.) If she keeps close by the spot where she unwraps her gifts such items as pen, note paper, stamps, and her address book, she will find that it does not take too long to immediately acknowledge each gift as it arrives. It is gracious of her to specifically mention the gift and express her warm appreciation for it and tell how she plans to use and enjoy it.

Returning Wedding Gifts. It sometimes happens that a couple will have no use for a gift that has been sent them. One couple received seventeen sugars and creamers, only a few of which could be expected to be used. In such a case, and in all other cases where the gift does not fit into the plans of the couple, it may be returned to the store from which it was sent and exchanged for something more suitable. It is therefore wise for the bride to save the packing slips and the inner box in which the gift comes, for use in case it is to be exchanged. In a situation like this, the bride may acknowledge the gift as usual, being careful not to say anything to offend or hurt the sender at the same time that she avoids telling a falsehood. She can always express her gratitude for being remembered without mention of the possible inappropriateness of a gift.

In the event that the engagement is broken, after wedding gifts have been received, the gifts are returned to the senders with a little note indicating that the wedding plans have been cancelled. Postponement of the wedding in case of illness, death, or for any other reason does not necessitate the return of the gifts.

Broken or Undelivered Wedding Gifts. What should you do if a gift is delivered in a damaged condition? If the gift has been sent by a store, it is quite proper to call or write the store saying that the item sent to you on such a date as a gift by Mrs. So-and-So has arrived in such and such condition, and asking them to pick it up and replace it. If the package was wrapped and sent from home, it is best to say nothing about its condition when acknowledging the gift. If the giver asks you specifically about the gift, of course you will have to tell her.

The undelivered gift is another cause for frequent embarrassment. Aunt Mary told Jane that she was sending her an electric toaster for a wedding gift. The wedding is long since over, and still no toaster, nor further word from Aunt Mary. Jane needs a toaster, but hesitates to buy one when Aunt Mary still might send it as she volunteered. What should Jane do? One real possibility is that Aunt Mary ordered the toaster to be sent as a gift, and the store failed to fill the order. Jane might operate on this assumption and, writing a pleasant note to Aunt Mary, mention her anticipation of receiving the toaster that Aunt Mary said she was sending. If Aunt Mary wonders why no acknowledgment of her gift has come, she can either have the store check its records, or she may tactfully ask Jane if the item has been delivered. Such a follow-up on either the giver's or the receiver's part is a kindness when carefully managed.

Suggestions for Wedding Gift Selections. Many stores offer prospective brides a service, in which the bride goes over the stock and selects those things that she would like to have. The store then lists these, including her choice of silver pattern, household china and glassware, color schemes, etc., so that those who wish to send some suitable gift may choose from the list of possibilities registered with the store. This assures the sender of giving something that will be appropriate, and the bride and groom of receiving things that they want and can use.

Friends and family members often ask either the bride or her mother what would be acceptable as a wedding gift. It is quite all right to reply specifically if it is done in such a way that the sender is given some latitude for the cost of the item. For instance, if the giver indicates that she would like to send silver, the name of the pattern selected may be given her so that she may add a piece or as many pieces as fit her budget. Or, a list of several items of varying costs may be suggested. In answer to the direct question about the acceptability of some specific item: "Would you like an electric iron?" the reply may be frank appreciation or rejection of the suggestion; e.g., "Oh, we'd love one, thank you," or "Thank you, it's a grand idea, but Ted's mother has already sent us one."

In answer to the question, "Is money an acceptable wedding gift?" Emily Post says "No," listing as her reason the fact that the money is spent and the couple has nothing definite to remember the sender by. However, many couples who marry today find money a highly acceptable gift in many instances. Some couples are not able to establish a household of their own for some time. For them the problem of storing wedding gifts may be a difficult one. Other couples go to housekeeping in limited quarters where there will be no place to put many of the things that they get for their wedding. Most young couples start out with limited finances that must be stretched as far as dollars can go and, knowing just what they need and what they can do without for a while, can possibly more wisely spend the gift allotment than could all but their closest associates.

One possible compromise between Emily Post and modern expediency is the giving of a United States Government Bond, which may be turned in for cash at once if needed, or "salted away" as a gift of security from the sender until it matures, or until it can be used to purchase some much needed item for the new household.

Clothes for the Wedding

Your wedding clothes and those of your guests will be in keeping with the type of wedding yours is to be. Procedure for the formal wedding rigidly prescribes the clothing worn by bride, groom, and all members of the wedding party. More simple weddings allow considerable latitude within certain general conventions. Wedding clothes do not need to be expensive to be appropriate and effective. They may be as elaborate as the bride and her family may choose.

What the Bride Wears. The bride chooses her wedding outfit as the keynote theme of her wedding. If the wedding is formal, her dress will be in traditional white or near-white in some suitable fabric, with a train from three to seven yards in length over which falls the wedding veil from the bridal headpiece of fabric, flowers, or jewels in keeping with the period and style of the gown. Depending upon its elaborateness the formal wedding gown may cost anywhere from several hundred to several thousands of dollars. To be right, it must be carefully fitted.

Any bride-for-the-first-time may wear a traditional white wedding gown no matter what the type of her wedding. For the informal wedding, the bride's outfit may be a simple floor length model and either no train or one of a yard or so in length, with a veil that is finger tip length caught in a simple fabric headpiece, or a garland of flowers. She may wear the wedding dress that she has inherited from her mother or grandmother, carefully fitted to her figure. She may buy her gown and veil, or have it made for her, or as some gifted girls do, she may make it herself. The cost may be as low as a few dollars and her time; or it may mount up depending upon the quality of the material, the professional fitting needed, and "the name" of the designer.

The bride may choose to wear a ballet length gown in white or pastel color. Or she may wear a street length gown in some soft becoming color and fabric. Or, she may select a well-cut suit and blouse with which she would wear hat and gloves. Shoes and other accessories are chosen in keeping with the rest of her outfit.

Outfits for the Bride's Attendants. There are just two rules for what bridesmaids should wear: 1. bridesmaids' costumes are in the same period as the bride's, and fit into the wedding theme that she has set. 2. bridesmaids' costumes are alike, except possibly in color. Fabric, styling, and accessories harmonize with the costumes worn by the bride and her attendant.

The matron of honor, or the maid of honor (if unmarried) is the personal attendant of the bride and chooses her costume to complement that of the bride. She may or may not wear a hat or headpiece depending upon the nature of the costume. When gloves are worn they are long with a short-sleeved dress or short with a long-sleeved dress. Her flowers may be in any harmonious color and style. Her outfit is usually slightly different from that of the bridesmaids' but harmonizes in color and styling.

The flower girl, usually a child of the family or close friends, wears a dress like that of the bridesmaids or one that is of the same general type, with suitable accessories.

The Groom and His Attendants Dress Alike. Whatever the type of wedding, the men of the party dress alike. At the formal evening wedding, the groom, his best man, and the ushers all wear full dress suits: "White tie and tails." For the formal daytime wedding, cutaway coats and dark gray striped trousers, gray tie and gloves are prescribed. A simple wedding calls for dark blue suits, white shirts, plain ties, and no gloves for the men of the wedding party. In summertime, informal white jackets and dark blue trousers are sometimes worn at informal weddings.

Only the men's boutonnières are different. The groom's lapel blossom is usually white, while those of the groom's attendants may be in color. The groom's boutonnière may be somewhat more elaborate than the best man's and the ushers'; some little distinction marks the groom as "the man of the day" apart from his attendants.

In some circles suits of the same material for bride and groom have been popular. The color usually is some shade of blue, although there is no reason why some other color becoming to both could not be chosen. Black is rarely worn at weddings because of its association with mourning. Brown and gray suits for men are not usual at weddings, but there is no absolute rule that forbids them. In general, although there are conventions about what is proper to wear, the choice is up to the bride and groom whose wedding it is!

Calendar
OF THINGS TO DO
The Wedding Planned Well in Advance

THREE TO FOUR MONTHS BEFORE THE WEDDING

• Set the wedding date (in consultation with members of both families in so far as is possible).

• Consider possible types of weddings suitable to your situation and choose the kind of wedding you both and your families can agree would be best.

• Select the place for the wedding and reserve it for your date.

• Consult your minister, priest, or rabbi about your marriage and wedding plans.

• Make arrangements for the reception, reserving the date, determining in general the kind of food, who will prepare and serve it, and the number of guests in round numbers.

• Choose your wedding attendants and invite them, specifying the definite date and the type of wedding.

• Select the color scheme and general motif of the entire wedding, keeping in mind the season of the year, the type of wedding chosen, the budget, and your own preferences.

• Plan bride's wedding gown and accessories, and those for bridal attendants in keeping with your type of wedding, your over-all scheme, your budget, and whether the gowns will be handmade or purchased.

• Start a master list of persons to be invited to the wedding, including those suggested by you both and your families. Make a plan for thinning if the list becomes too long to be accommodated. Develop a system for checking duplicates.

TWO TO THREE MONTHS BEFORE THE WEDDING

• Order invitations from your stationer or engraver according to the model and the script desired. Order in round numbers in lots of fifty or one hundred, allowing more than the total of lists compiled to date. Calculate the percentage of acceptances you can reasonably expect, and so estimate the number of invitations it will be feasible to send.

• Arrange for announcements (to those not being invited to the wedding) according to the same plan of estimating numbers as for invitations.

• Order informals for acknowledging your wedding gifts at this time if you prefer these to other simple suitable note paper. The number should approximate that of the size of the invitation list.

• Explore possibilities for where you will live, making whatever tentative arrangements are possible. If you are fortunate in having a definite place into which you will move, it is not too soon to plan for its furnishing and to start getting it in order.

ONE TO TWO MONTHS BEFORE THE WEDDING

• Bride goes to a good gynecologist for her premarital examination according to the suggestions outlined in Chapter Six. She follows through on his (or her) recommendations before the wedding, including a return for routine blood tests a week or two preceding the wedding date.

• Groom gets his complete premarital examination, making appointment for blood tests.

• Address the invitations in preparation for mailing three to four weeks before the wedding. The outside envelopes may be picked up before the engraving is finished if you wish. The envelopes are addressed in pen and ink in a legible hand by the bride with whatever help is offered by members of her family, the groom and perhaps members of his family. One bride made a party of it with both families gathered around the dining room table, address books at hand, following a pleasant informal meal in joint-family style.

• Decide on your honeymoon plans considering the special interests of you both and the function of the honeymoon (see Chapter Ten). Make advance reservations for accommodations and travel.

• Select "going away" outfits and trousseau, including appropriate accessories.

• Check your luggage needs.

• Express interest in what both mothers will wear to the wedding, giving what suggestions and help seem to be indicated.

THREE TO FOUR WEEKS BEFORE THE WEDDING

• Mail the wedding invitations (*not* the announcements, yet). First class postage is expected. Air mail is indicated only for relatives and friends in far distant places.

• Order the wedding cake and make final arrangements for the wedding breakfast and/or the reception. Estimate the number to be served with final figure promised as replies come in, just before the wedding (two or three days to a week is usual).

• Select the photographer and discuss with him what kinds of pictures you will want, and make definite appointments with him.

• Check on the legal requirements for marriage in your state.

• Arrange for out-of-town guests.

- Bride gets a·permanent if she needs one, and makes appointments ahead for the day before the wedding, or at a time that seems best.

- Select and order your flowers for the wedding.

- Arrange for decorations needed for the wedding, the wedding breakfast, and the reception.

- Register your preferences at the wedding bureau of the store where your friends and family will most likely shop for your gifts.

- Plan for the way in which you will acknowledge your gifts as they arrive, and how they will be displayed.

THE WEEK OR TWO BEFORE THE WEDDING

- Final check with your doctors, routine blood tests preliminary to getting the license.

- Go together for your marriage license.

- Arrange transportation for the wedding party.

- Make final preparations for the rehearsal and for presenting gifts to the wedding party. The rehearsal is usually the day before the wedding. A simple party in connection with the rehearsal is an acceptable time for bestowing gifts upon members of the wedding party. Caution: Do not attempt too elaborate an affair the night before the wedding. You'll want to be rested and fresh then.

- Groom gets hair cut; bride gets hair done and whatever else that will make her feel lovely.

- Allow plenty of time for dressing and last minute details on your wedding day.

The Wedding Planned on Short Notice

- Set the date and decide the type of wedding, clearing the time with the minister and both families.

- See your doctor(s) for a complete premarital examination and the blood tests required in your state.

- Make arrangements for what you both and the other members of the wedding party will wear.

- Write invitation notes and order announcements.

- Arrange for wedding cake, refreshments, flowers, and photographer.

- Get your marriage license.

- Keep calm, share the responsibilities, enjoy every minute of it . . . it's your wedding!

Wedding Costs

Wedding costs fluctuate with the times. When prices are generally high, then everything used for the wedding costs more than when price levels are low. But even then, wedding costs vary tremendously. Your wedding may be as economical or as expensive as you make it. One study made by Professor B. F. Timmons [1] in 1937–38, when prices were generally low, reported the following actual wedding costs incurred by 154 couples:

COSTS	$1.00–250.	251.–500.	501.–750.	751.–1000.	1000. and up
CASES	63	51	22	6	12

Even when price levels are high, a wedding does not need to be an extravagant item in your budget. The items that tend to make the wedding expensive are largely those having to do with "show." By choosing simple wedding costumes and decorations and keeping refreshments within line, a wedding may be very lovely and still of moderate cost. Or, if money is no object, an elaborate wedding can cost many thousands of dollars.

According to convention wedding costs are assumed by both the bride and her family and the groom and his in the manner outlined below.

Although this listing represents the general custom in the United States, it need not be interpreted rigidly. As in other aspects of wedding procedure it is well to know the traditional conventions so that you may know from what you depart when you plan your own wedding.

HOW CUSTOM DIVIDES WEDDING COSTS

The Bride or Her Family Pays for . . .

$ Wedding gown and veil
$ Bride's personal trousseau
$ Wedding reception, breakfast, or dinner
$ Transportation to church and reception
$ Wedding decorations and music
$ Invitations and announcements
$ Gifts for the groom and the bride's attendants

[1] B. F. Timmons, "The Cost of Weddings," *American Sociological Review* (April, 1939), pp. 224–233.

$ Bride's bouquet and mothers' flowers
$ Bride's "going away" corsage
$ Wedding trip
$ Wedding ring
$ Minister's fee
$ Marriage license
$ Gifts for the bride, best man, and ushers

The Marriage Ceremony

Virtually all groups, primitive and civilized alike, have a special ceremony marking the transition from the courtship to married life. In our own history we had for hundreds of years two ceremonies: the betrothal, which was a business arrangement between the families to take care of property arrangements, and the wedding ceremony, which came somewhat later and carried the mark of finality.

The wedding ceremony was originally performed by the father among the Hebrews, the Greeks, and the Romans; but as the early Christian church became powerful, the priest's blessing was added to the ceremony. As the church concerned itself more and more with marriage, witnesses were added, and all marriages were performed by the clergy. With the Reformation the Protestants came to regard marriage as a civil contract, and the state undertook the responsibility of supervising the ceremony in Protestant countries. In Europe today it is not uncommon to be married by a civil court and then to repeat the ceremony at a church wedding. In America we have delegated to the clergy the civil authority to perform marriages, giving them thereby both civil and religious sanction over marriage.

The functions of the marriage ceremony today are:

1 To impress on the couple and all relatives and friends the changed status of the pair, both legally and psychologically.
2 To announce the new status; to give public support and stability to the relation emphasized by the titles *Mr.* and *Mrs.* and by the assumption of the husband's family name by the wife.
3 To give legal protection to the wife and to the children born of the union: to place the responsibility for their care and support with the pair and not with the state.
4 To glorify and sanctify the relation (religious marriage), giving it divine blessing and approval — God approves.

Wedding Services. Weddings in the many churches of the various faiths differ widely. Not only the procedures prescribed by the particular church but the training and beliefs of the individual minister and the preferences of the couple play a part in determining the nature of the wedding ceremony. An occasional couple write a part of their own ceremony, incorporating their own convictions and commitment with the traditional vows. Some ministers have developed their own introductory statements that precede the usual vows in the wedding ceremony. The following is used by permission as illustrative.

WEDDING CEREMONY
Address to the Congregation

There is an ancient story which contains a profound insight: It is not good for man to be alone. We rightly approach a wedding ceremony with reverence and with awe. For marriage has welled up out of the depths of personal and social need. In it the fundamental impulses of the individual and the race, biological, personal and social, come to an overt focus. The ceremony itself is the public avowal of a new relationship, the most basic which can exist among men. It signifies that two people stand at one point along the unending stream of human development, a point at which countless others have stood before and countless more will stand in ages which are to come. Yet it is for the human race, as for them, unique in the totality of timeless aeons. The centuries of the past have looked forward to this occasion. Those of the future should have good cause to regard it with respect and gratitude.

It is meet and proper that so awe-inspiring an occasion, when Eternity emerges as a visible point in the present, should be celebrated with dignity and solemnity. All races, tribes and cultures, from the most primitive to the most advanced, have made of this step an occasion for rejoicing and an expression through ceremony and rite of profound social concern. So today, society expresses its legitimate and inescapable interest. For a wedding is more than the joining of two persons to each other. It is the closing of a link in the endless chain of human relationships, a link which binds the present to the past and out of which the future can most advantageously emerge.

The wedding is properly a religious ceremony. For in marriage, basic forces which determine human destiny find their richest and most creative expression. The noblest sentiments and highest ideals of the human soul stand by in expectant concern for their future. The God who sustains all which is, ultimately presides.

Address to the Couple

For you, this ceremony will mean entrance into new relationships which will affect many aspects of your lives. Your legal status will be altered in important respects. The merger of names will symbolize an extensive change in your social status and relationships. Changed personal relationships, some of which may prove onerous, will remind you that things are no longer as they were.

It will mean for you a new security in your personal lives. For marriage is an oasis of refreshment and renewal in an often arid world, a point of stability amid the bewildering and often alarming changes of a rapidly shifting social scene. Your marriage will mean that each of you will have one whom you know and can respond to as a whole personality. In all the welter of mass humanity and whirling shifts of friendships, you can find stability. Marriage will mean for you that intimacy which is necessary for the best satisfaction of the deepest needs of your souls. You will find a new security in acceptance, a security which is freely yours without the need for pretense and dissimulation. For you there will always be one situation in which you can be as you really are, without risk of rejection. Marriage means in part, the weaving of a rope of relationships upon which each of you can put the full strain of your own worst, without fear that it will break.

You will find a new security and richness of love. Among the greatest needs of all is a two-way flow of affection. Marriage will increase and enrich this for you, unimpeded by conventions and unspoiled by fear of its loss. Such married love is above and beyond all other forms of human love. In it alone are intermingled the depth, intimacy, and permanence essential for your greatest satisfaction and growth.

Your wedding means a recognition and acceptance of new social obligations. To marry is to enter into partnership in a building enterprise. It means the construction of a social relationship which inevitably involves others. To marry is not only to establish a center of emotional security for yourselves. It is to create a basic unit of society. And in so doing you find your own greatest fulfillment.

The vows which you are about to take pledge you to fidelity, one to the other. This does not merely mean fidelity to taboos, or even to a person. The man and woman who live together secure in each other's love are being faithful to far more than each other. They are being faithful to a social situation which can produce people who can live without fear, who are sufficiently mature emotionally as neither to seek nor to need dictatorship and aggression. They are being faithful to the basic foundations of the social structure in which all are formed and nourished. They are being faithful to the provisions which society makes for the protection and the development of the deepest needs of persons. When you marry you do far more than to take unto yourself a spouse. You take a piece of the social future into your hands.

Then follow the usual vows and prayers.

THE WEDDING PARTY IN ORDER OF APPEARANCE
AT 3 PHASES OF THE WEDDING

Processional Usher escorts groom's parents to front pew right of center aisle
(Just before) THEN
Bride's mother is seated by usher at left of center aisle (signal for the wedding march to begin)
NOW THE PROCESSION
Ushers two by two
Bridesmaids two by two
Maid or matron of honor
Ring bearer — *if any* [2]
Flower girl — *if any* [2]
Bride on her father's right arm
(Groom, best man, and minister stand at the altar, facing the processional)

Recessional Bride on groom's right arm
Flower girl alone or with the ring bearer
Maid or matron of honor alone or with the best man [3]
Bridesmaids two by two or paired with ushers
Ushers two by two or with the bridesmaids
As soon as the wedding party has gone out, two ushers return at once for mothers of the bride and groom
The guests then depart

Receiving Line Bride's mother
(Left to right) Groom's father [4]
Groom's mother
Bride's father
Bride
Groom
Maid or matron of honor
Bridesmaids (if preferred they may mingle with the guests, as the ushers and the best man do)

[2] If children are in the wedding party, they should be rehearsed carefully once or twice before the ceremony, at the place of the wedding.
[3] The best man may go directly to the vestry for the groom's hat and coat, and his own, joining the wedding party at the door, if this seems more convenient in what comes next.
[4] The bride's father may stand beside his wife, then the groom's mother and father, then the bride and groom. This more modern form keeps the principal couples together and is sometimes more pleasant and graceful for the receiving line.

Special Cases

There are many special situations in which the usual forms and rules do not seem to apply. Let us consider just a few of them.

Two Faiths — Two Ceremonies. When members of two faiths marry, their wedding has to be worked out to meet the requirements of their respective churches as well as their personal preferences. If a Catholic is to have his or her marriage recognized by the Roman Catholic church, it must be performed by a Catholic priest according to the rules of the church. Some faithful Jews feel married only when it has been done by the rabbi.

One Baptist bride called her pastor on the evening of her wedding day and begged him to "marry us again, for I just don't feel right being married only by his rabbi." This minister replied that it was hardly necessary to be married again, since they were already married, but that he would be willing to *reaffirm* their marriage and give it his blessing as a Christian clergyman. This pleased the bride, was satisfactory to the groom, and violated nothing in either's religion.

Some couples marrying across religious faiths, plan for such a dual-wedding service in which all members of both families as well as the dictates of both churches will be satisfied. It seems hardly necessary to remind you that such things are best discussed and agreed upon early in the relationship, with plans laid well in advance so that all concerned know what to expect.

Double Weddings. Two couples (usually sisters or brothers) may marry without other attendants, each serving as the other's witnesses. Or the double wedding may have all the pomp and splendor of the huge church wedding, *times two!* In the latter case, the older bride and her attendants enter first, then the younger bride and her attendants, with the recessional in the same formation with each couple leading its own bridal party. If the brides are sisters, one invitation may be issued for their double wedding, in which case the older sister's name appears first.

Divorce, a Complicating Factor. If the bride's parents are divorced, the invitations may be issued by her mother, with her present husband as host, if she has remarried. In this case, the bride's father may give her away if she wishes, after which he steps back to the pew behind her mother. Whether or not he remains for the reception is best decided by discussion well ahead of time. Except in most unusual cases, the absent parent is invited to the wedding, and members of the family behave without bitterness toward each other.

The mature bride whose parents are divorced may issue her own invitations and announcements and walk down the aisle either alone, or on the arm of a favorite uncle or other older male relative.

Similarly, if the bride is herself a divorcée, she may issue her own invitations, and the couple may announce their own marriage. If the bride is a very young divorcée, her parents may announce her marriage as usual. The remarriage of a divorced woman is usually not formal, or in a white gown and veil. It may be held in a chapel, home, or garden, with one attendant (not a child by a former marriage).

Orphaned and Widowed Brides. The bride who is an orphan may have a formal wedding if she wishes, by asking some older woman to be her sponsor, and walking down the aisle on the arm of some favorite older male relative or close family friend.

The remarriage of a widow is usually simple and informal, and not in white wedding gown and veil, which is the symbol of first marriage. Her own children may attend her if she wishes. She may write personal notes as invitations and announcements, using her full name.

Sickness and Death in Wedding Plans. An invalid mother, grandmother, or sister may attend even a formal church wedding in a wheel chair, or the wedding may be planned at home where she is. Bride, groom, or any of the bridal attendants may participate in any wedding in a wheel chair or on crutches if need be. In the case of a close member of the family being suddenly stricken ill just before the wedding, the ceremony may be postponed by notifying the guests by wire, phone, or note.

When one of the parents of bride or groom dies suddenly, the wedding usually is postponed with some such wording as this: "Owing to the sudden death of Mrs. John James Jones, the marriage of her daughter Janice to Gerald Raymond Brown has been indefinitely postponed." This notice may be sent to the local papers, and to all guests already invited to the wedding. The marriage may proceed on the date planned but then it is a simple quiet wedding with only members of the immediate family present.

Broken Engagements. It is not only in Hollywood that something breaks up a couple before the wedding date; it happens in real life too. In such a case, there are two things to do at once: 1. cancel the wedding; and 2. return to the senders all wedding gifts. Guests already invited to the wedding must be notified that the wedding plans have been cancelled, whether or not they have sent gifts to the bride. Couples feeling embarrassed about cancelling their wedding should remember that it is far better to call off an unpromising marriage before it gets started than it is to carry each other into the anguish of an unhappy union. One of the functions of the engagement period is to sort out incompatible pairs.[5] It may take the wise guidance of a competent counselor to help the couple discover whether the break originates from something simple and superficial, or whether it stands for something basically wrong in the match.

Moving up the Date. In these days when so many things may happen to change things, it is sometimes necessary to advance the date of the wedding. A military leave is granted earlier than expected, a vacation date is advanced, an opportunity opens up, all sorts of things may call for an earlier date than the one originally planned. The procedure for meeting this type of case is simply to contact the guests and tell them where and when the rearranged wedding is to be. A simple wedding can be arranged at the last minute in the chapel at the military post, in the bride's home, in a club or garden, or even after one of the regular services of the church, if the couple are flexible in their planning. Indeed, this might serve as a motto for wedding plans generally: "Be Prepared for the Unexpected."

To be useful wedding plans should be based upon the values of those being married. If you realize that tradition has been upset many times, and that conventions serve but as guides, you can plan your wedding in ways that will be most meaningful to you and to those whom you love and want close to you on this your day of days.

[5] See Chapter Five, "The Meaning of an Engagement."

Selected Readings

BENTLEY, MARGUERITE, *Wedding Etiquette Complete* (Philadelphia: Winston).

BOSSARD, JAMES H. S., AND BOLL, ELEANOR S., *Ritual in Family Living* (Philadelphia: University of Pennsylvania Press, 1950).

BOWMAN, HENRY A., *Marriage for Moderns* (New York: Whittlesey House, 1948), Chap. 9.

BRIDE'S MAGAZINE, *The Bride's Book of Etiquette*

EMBASSY PUBLISHING COMPANY, *Wedding Embassy Year Book*

FENWICK, MILLICENT, *Vogue's Book of Etiquette* (New York: Simon and Schuster, 1948).

GROVES, ERNEST R., *Marriage* (New York: Holt, revised, 1948), Chap. 11.

LEACH, WILLIAM H., ED., *The Cokesbury Marriage Manual* (Nashville, Tennessee: Abingdon-Cokesbury Press, 1939).

MARSHALL FIELD AND COMPANY, *The Bride's Book* (Chicago: Marshall Field, 1950).

MCLEOD, EDYTH THORNTON, *The Bride's Book* (New York: Archway Press, 1947).

Modern Bride, magazine published by Ziff-Davis Company, 185 North Wabash Ave., Chicago 1, Ill.

POST, EMILY, *Emily Post's Etiquette* (New York: Funk and Wagnalls, recent revision).

TIMMONS, B. F., "The Cost of Weddings," *American Sociological Review* (April, 1939), pp. 224–233.

Vogue, "Invitation to the Wedding," Vol. LXXIX, No. 9, p. 84.

WOODS, MARJORIE BINFORD, *Your Wedding: How to Plan and Enjoy It* (New York: Bobbs-Merrill, new revised edition, 1949).

WRIGHT, JEANNE, *The Wedding Book* (New York: Rinehart, 1947).

PART 2

WHAT IT MEANS TO BE MARRIED

CHAPTER TEN

For Better, for Worse . . .

What type of honeymoon is best?

Are all the honeymoon intimacies easy to take?

Why do people talk about "settling down" as if it were so important?

Does marriage really make you different?

Is it true that unless you watch out love dies soon after you get married?

*T*HE WEDDING IS OVER. THE UNITY WHICH HAS BEEN BUILT UP DURing courtship and engagement has now been publicly recognized and ceremonialized. Now at last the roles of *husband* and *wife* which have been played in fantasy many times may be tried out. Once married, the man and the woman start on a journey from which it is difficult to turn back. In the chapters which follow our discussion will throw some light on the situations couples face in marriage, the skills and abilities needed, and the normality of trouble and frustration as a new family is launched into operation. Key ideas which merit attention include the following:

1 Marriage is a more complex way of living than single life and therefore is likely to aggravate rather than cure symptoms of immaturity such as restiveness, uncertainty, and unhappiness.

2 A key need of early marriage is to settle down and work out the routines of daily living.

3 As romantic love is replaced by conjugal love, the marriage becomes stabilized.

4 Conflict in marriage is normal and may be used constructively to hold the partnership together.

5 Happily married couples, in adult terms, are not necessarily couples who never quarrel but are those who have learned the techniques of resolving conflicts which arise.

6 Keeping the channels of communication clear is important for marriage solidarity.

The Honeymoon

In the early weeks of marriage young people are perhaps more impressionable than at any other time in their lives. Hope and expectation are keyed to concert pitch. Idealism is at its height. The newly married individuals continue the pattern of the engagement in ever increasing tempo, the pattern of widening the range of their mutual exploration of one another's personalities. These processes parallel, some will say overlay, deep anxieties about the undefined future and the realization that this relationship which is so precious has the capacity to hurt. All these conditions can bring about a delicately balanced state of the emotions in which small embarrassments are capable of having a devastating effect.

David Mace [1] expresses the situation well:

From one point of view, getting married could be represented as a rather terrifying experience. For something like a third of their life span two people have lived independent of each other — probably without even knowing of each other's existence. They have formed their own personal habits and learned to live their own private lives. Now, after a comparatively short acquaintance, they come together in the closest human intimacy, living together, sleeping together, yielding themselves up to each other. At the time, they don't think of this as an invasion of their privacy. Their strong desire for each other draws them together and they make their surrender eagerly. But for all that, the mutual unveiling of their bodies and minds can sometimes have profoundly disturbing and quite unexpected consequences. . . . To make these early adjustments as easy as possible we have wisely provided the institution of the honeymoon.

Full of excitement, thrills, and anticipation of delightful intimacies, the honeymoon is a continuation of the period of bliss characteristic of the engagement period. Two sources of emotion flow over in most marriages during the first weeks, the growing pleasures of the sex experi-

[1] David R. Mace, *Marriage: The Art of Lasting Love* (New York: Doubleday, 1952), pp. 46–47.

ences and the fears of the unknown and undefined future of the marriage. These are major components of romantic love. Indeed, the honeymoon marks the crest of the feelings identified as romantic love feelings. Thereafter the fear element, which has its source in the apprehension of the unknown and unpredictable problems of marriage, subsides unless activated by extramarital thrill-seeking or a new love affair. Romantic love feeds on the new and the unknown. As marriage settles down to a walking gait, romantic love is normally exchanged for a less exciting but more permanent combination of love feelings based on companionship and mutual interdependence, identified elsewhere as conjugal love.[2]

Conjugal love first appears in the companionable phase of the engagement relation and develops greatly during the early months of marriage. During the honeymoon the couple pick up souvenirs and buy furniture, which are quickly given a sentimental value. The snapshots of the honeymoon trip and the trails taken together are often reviewed. Thus the memories of the honeymoon make up some of the first tangible evidences of the conjugal love on which enduring marriages are based.

Planning the Honeymoon. The wedding journey is designed to meet specific needs and should not be postponed for several weeks or months until, for example, the bridegroom gets his vacation. The value of the honeymoon lies in the opportunities it gives the newlyweds to meet the first experiences of marriage away from people who know them, thus providing them a little time to get over the self-consciousness which comes with playing new and untried roles. Point number one in planning, then, is to set the wedding date at a time when a honeymoon is possible.

Although the plans for the honeymoon are for the most part jointly laid, the exact dates for the wedding and wedding journey are rightly set by the bride. The timing of the menstrual period and the irregularities which often accompany emotional stress are factors which need to receive attention in launching the marriage.

The engaged couple can add enjoyment to their first days of marriage if they depart from the trite honeymoon tours to Niagara Falls and Washington in favor of a trip which characterizes the individuality of

[2] See Chap. 15, "What Holds a Marriage Together."

their relationship. One couple who had met in Europe on a hosteling tour planned a similar tour by bicycle through New England. Another made their common passion for bird life the center of their plans for a week's outing at a bird sanctuary neither had visited before. A third couple spent most of their time in New York attending plays and operas when they weren't catching up on their sleep at a bohemian apartment off Washington Square. In this business of planning, the couple needs to realize that one man's meat may be another man's poison. A trout stream in the Rockies is no place for a couple of tenderfeet, the advertisement of the travel associations to the contrary. Life on a dude ranch can be very irritating if the couple doesn't know its cattle ponies. Point number two is to plan to do something on the honeymoon which both enjoy and can do reasonably well. There will be other occasions for the new and unusual when both parties are surer of themselves and are under less emotional tension.

The hazards to be avoided by the honeymooners are excessive costs and overfatigue. If the engagement has been one of planning and discussion, the honeymoon costs will have been worked out along with the budget of the first year's expenses. Placed in juxtaposition to the other costs of the year, the honeymoon will usually be estimated at a reasonable figure. Some estimate of the number of miles to be traveled and the number of things to be seen and done needs to be made. Trying to do too much in too little time will result in overfatigue and set the stage for quarrels when the couple is least able to cope with them.

Suppose we list a few do's and don'ts which might be reviewed by the couple anticipating marriage and a satisfying honeymoon:

1 Select a place where you can be completely alone and away from people who know you, and where privacy is assured.
2 Plan your trip to obviate overfatigue as much as possible.
3 Arrange for hotel or room reservations in advance.
4 Plan for time to loaf and sleep — newly married couples go to bed early and get up late.
5 Carry on with the planning and exploration talks of the engagement, discussing points on which you aren't able to find a basis for agreement as well as those on which you are.

Excitement of the Wedding Journey. The honeymoon customarily lasts a week or two and for obvious economic reasons rarely extends beyond a month. The wedding journey is an excellent introduction into marriage, providing as it does for a release of the tension which has piled up in the days before the wedding and for the maximum expression of idealism. The honeymoon also provides a point at which realities are allowed to intrude, as the pair prepares to return to familiar surroundings and mundane responsibilities. Fortunately the period of ecstasy does not continue long, for moving from one thrill and discovery to another is exhausting.

The adjustment in the first years is sometimes most difficult for those couples who have restricted their love activities too prudishly in the courtship and engagement period. They find themselves suddenly in marriage with all the barriers down and with all too little preparation for the expression of the excitement and attraction which arise in the intimacies. It is not uncommon for one or both parties to experience feelings of guilt or revulsion, to the mutual distress of both parties. For other couples who have anticipated great thrills in the first sex relations, there is sometimes disappointment — reality doesn't live up to the expectations. Said one such couple, "We were surprised that that was all there was to it; somehow we had expected more." The girl felt cheated, and the boy was hurt and worried that his wife wasn't thrilled. Both needed to realize that enjoyable sex response is a matter of learning, and that it grows with the years. They failed to grasp the fact that early sex relations are necessarily awkward, both because of their newness and because of the anxiety both feel toward the unknown. Where fear is present sex response is inhibited, and only after the couple have become thoroughly secure in their new role of husband and wife, of Mr. and Mrs., can they expect to attain the heights which the uninformed honeymooners feel is their right the first night.[3]

The honeymoon intimacies are taken almost as a matter of course by the couples who are able to recognize the sexual urges and expressions for what they are. They have studied what to expect, and after a certain amount of normal love play in the engagement period, the honeymoon presents to them an extended period of easily assimilated new ex-

---

[3] See Chap. 15, "What Holds a Marriage Together." In Stanley Brav's intriguing study of honeymoons nearly half of his respondents reported that they failed to achieve complete sexual harmony during their honeymoon, yet the majority considered their honeymoon a complete success. Sexual harmony was not considered essential to honeymoon success. See Stanley Brav, "Note on Honeymoons," *Marriage and Family Living*, Vol. 9 (Summer, 1947), p. 60.

periences. They are able to recognize and understand their own urges and make the most of them.

A fourth group of young people "make the most" of the honeymoon experiences, because they feel that the intoxication of early marriage is the most desirable part of marriage, that marriage should be one continual courtship in which love is kept aglow with constant thrills. This is the school which reflects most closely the Hollywood pattern of perpetual romance and which judges a marriage by the continuation of the burning thrills of love. If the love-light dies, a divorce ensues; and the light burns again only as new love appears, followed by another honeymoon, another trip to Reno, another honeymoon, and so on. These people take their fiction and movies too seriously and apparently know little or nothing about the studies of happily married men and women. Although the great majority settle down in time to more or less routine married living, there is usually an intervening period of disillusionment before they hit a normal stride. For these young people the psychiatrists would list coming to terms with reality as the most important single accomplishment of the first year of marriage.

Establishing an Etiquette of Intimacy

Still another area of interpersonal adjustment which the honeymoon makes possible involves the intimacies of personal hygiene. The early days of marriage could be greatly eased if young couples received more help about these matters, at least as much as about the intimacies of sex. They would be spared a good deal of distress if, as well as preparing themselves for sexual union, they recognized also the fact that in close intimacy of marriage men and women must learn a warm tender consideration for the little details of bodily hygiene which are part of the business of living. David Mace has pointed out that in the course of married life there are many lowly services which husband and wife must perform for each other. One of the important adjustments which must be made in the early weeks together is to get over any false modesty which the couple may feel about their own or each other's bodies.[4]

Why should couples, in this day and age of frankness and freedom of inhibitions about sex, find the intimacies of sensory details connected

[4] David Mace, *op. cit.*, p. 50.

with other bodily functions fraught with embarrassment and disgust reactions? The answer may not be obvious.

In America, the land of locked bathrooms and fully clothed people, of private bedrooms and dressing quarters, the child is often reared to adulthood carefully protected from the sensory details of the bodily functions of others. He is taught to disguise his intention of going to the toilet by asking if he may wash his hands. Girl children particularly are protected from vulgarity, as Americans define it. Added to and accentuating the problem is the universal tendency in the courtship and engagement period to idealize the other person, to endow the person with qualities of saintliness, and to shrink from the thought that the other person carries on the same bodily functions as common folk. While still holding these ideas, the carefully protected boy and girl marry and face for the first time the details of married living, with the doors of privacy torn off. The imaginary picture of the other person was nobler and kinder. The sensory details overwhelm the sensitive, sheltered girl and all too often produce reactions of disgust and revulsion.

Too much intimacy, too little privacy, in too short a period! Because of the way we have been reared, we must preserve some of the illusions for a time, at least. A minimum of privacy will need to be maintained indefinitely, just because Americans react to bodily functions of urination and excretion the way they do. This is difficult in overcrowded apartments with no private dressing quarters and with shared bathrooms, but every effort should be made to ease the transition gracefully from the more spacious parental home with its privacy to the more restricted accompaniments of married life. The informed couple will meet the challenge.[5]

Disillusionment and Settling Down

Disillusionment sounds like an ugly word, but it means, simply, "facing realities." G. V. Hamilton's study of two hundred married persons, *A Research in Marriage*, showed the illusions of the engagement and honeymoon period to have lasted well into the second year of marriage for most of his cases. Twenty-nine per cent stated that they had settled

---

[5] A searching analysis of the reactions of Americans to lack of privacy is given in Markoosha Fisher's *My Lives in Russia* (New York: Harper, 1944), pp. 59–76.

down to facing realities after one year, and 20 per cent after two years.
The balance didn't know how long it took them to complete the process
of disillusionment. Many couples claim to have had no difficulty in
settling down after returning from the honeymoon, stating variously,
"The process developed naturally," "We didn't expect marriage to be so
very different and it wasn't," "It was a relief to find marriage so livable
after all the ghastly accounts of divorce and separation," "We just kept
on being good pals instead of going dramatic during the honeymoon,
and we couldn't see anything to be disillusioned about." These couples
started their period of disillusionment by facing realities in the courtship and engagement period, as their statements reveal, and made the
transition into marriage with a minimum of anxiety.

Walking is the best gait for most people, but most honeymooners
hit a tempo more akin to a gallop in the series of thrills sought and experienced. The change of pace which must come is called "settling
down," and is a phase of disillusionment. Disillusionment includes not
only the removal of blinders which have kept the lover from seeing the
wart on the chin of the loved one, but also the mutual discovery that
marriage doesn't change personalities. "We are still our old familiar,
boring selves, and we thought we would be different when married. It
looked as if we could change when we were engaged and on the honeymoon, but now. . . ."

Disillusionment is partly due to the discrepancy between what we
have imagined marriage to be like, or been told it was like, or read it
was like, and what we find it to be. Notice the discrepancy between the
following stereotyped picture of the couple who lived happily ever after
and the facts. It is the case of Mary Jane and Jim who were married
and settled down in a cute little house with checked curtains at the
windows. They are supposed to have had three years of happy married
life, writes our ad writer for marriage:

Mary Jane, in a crisp house dress kept spotless and unfaded by Lux, has
laid out breakfast — everything Beechnut but the eggs. Jim Junior is busily
eating up his cereal for the fun of finding the Mickey Mouse at the bottom
of the dish, thoughtfully supplied by the makers of Cream of Wheat. Jim
Senior, spruce in an Arrow collar and fortified by a perfect night's rest under
the auspices of the Simmons Bedding Company, is about to make his way
to the office to earn the thirty-five dollars a week which somehow are to pay
for the hundred-dollar radio, the Monel metal kitchen, the dapper little car,
and the self-satisfied look that comes to those who have provided nicely for

retirement at fifty-five. This intimate view of American home life is familiar to us all through the kindness of advertising mediums of every variety and haunting ubiquity. We are fortunate because without their aid we should never see such a pretty picture.

Let us peek in again without the rosy spectacles supplied by the nationally advertised brands. Mary Jane's frock for mornings at home looks a little frayed and faded. Her apron has definitely seen neither Lux nor a harsh washing soap for several days. She scrapes dispiritedly at the breakfast plates, slightly repulsive with congealed egg yolk and slimy cold bacon grease. For the fourteenth time she exhorts Junior to stop dawdling and eat his cereal. She is not, at the moment, enjoying her marriage very much. Why should she? Washing dishes day in and day out is not the same thing as canoeing in the moonlight with your heart's beloved. . . . Mary Jane is remembering five o'clock with Jim waiting at the corner, of dinner with dancing, of going to the movies, or a concert, or the theatre, or just a long ferry-boat ride. Of the difficult good-night kiss and the ecstatic knowledge that soon she would have Jim all the time for always. She is thinking rather wryly of how entrancing, how full of promise, this battered dishpan looked when it first emerged from pink tissue paper at the shower the girls gave her. She may even think, a little cynically, as she surveys the grey grease pocked surface of her dishwater, of the foaming pans of eternally virgin suds she expected from her perusal of the advertisements. Well, she's married now. She has her own house, her own dishpan, her husband, and her baby. All the time and for always. She doesn't even go to the movies any more because there is no one to stay with Junior. She speaks so crossly to the child now that his tears fall into the objectionable cereal. Why on earth won't Jim let her get Mrs. Oldacre in to stay evenings? He'll be earning more soon; Mr. Bayswater practically told him he would be put in charge of the branch office as soon as old Fuzzy retired. Five dollars a week savings — much good that does anyway. Mary Jane's thoughts about her husband become quite uncharitable. "If he only had the least understanding of the kind of life I have, but all he notices is Junior's shoes are scuffed out and he would not even try that Bavarian cream I fixed yesterday. It's all very well for him to think Jimmy Junior's cute when he sneaks out of bed — he doesn't have him all day and all night and nothing but Jimmy Junior."

Thus Mary Jane at nine o'clock of a Monday morning. At three P.M. the sight of Junior tugging a large packing box about the yard suddenly makes her heart turn over with delight and pride. What a duck he is. . . . She smiles all to herself with pleasure at the sunlight falling through the peach curtains on the blues and browns of her livingroom furniture. That recipe for apple pan dowdy — she'll try that for supper. Jim will be home in two hours and a half, home for a whole lovely evening. And Monday is Philadelphia orchestra night on the radio. For no reason at all life is abruptly good, very good.

Jim, meantime, is having his own problems, big and little. Mary Jane is a frequent pain in the neck to him. He likes his eggs with the whites firm and the yolks runny. Mary Jane gets them wrong every time — sometimes leathery, sometimes slimy. Why does she have to be so cranky with Junior, and why can't she keep him quiet mornings? She should know a man needs all the rest he can get. He has to give his best to the job — marriage is too expensive to loaf or to be tired. Mary doesn't understand that at all. He gave up his big chance in the Texas branch just for her, didn't he. But does she appreciate it? And yet Jim, too, has his hours of excitement and delight, of deep satisfaction in his wife and his son and his home and himself in the role of father in the family.[6]

How do you react to this latter view of marriage? It is more accurate than the version thrust upon us by the advertisers, but it is still only the top layer, the part we see, the common-sense interpretation of satisfactions and discords in the lives of Mary Jane and Jim. The roots of conflict lie much deeper in the personalities of sparring partners.

If the discrepancy between what you imagined marriage would be like and what it is in reality is as great as that presented above, don't feel marriage has cheated you. The first step toward permanent and satisfying marriage is disillusionment, the willingness to accept one's self and one's partner on the level of everyday living, to take the worse along with the better.

It should be pointed out that well-adjusted couples will recognize moments of rapture and the moments of disappointment, as well as the strong undercurrent of partnership in the run-of-the-mine emotions of daily life. The role of moods is important, some days we're up, some days down, some days romantic and some days realistic. Disillusionment, although primarily concerned with facing realities, includes finding a place for the delightful moments of the happier mood.

Setting up Housekeeping

In a play of recent years called 3 Is a Family, the young mother breaks down and weeps after her exasperated husband has criticized her inefficiency and mistakes in keeping the house straightened up, and her failures with the baby. "You must have patience with me; I know I'm inefficient, but you see, I've never been a mother before." The job was too big for her to handle all at once. She knew she was in a mess but

---

[6] Reprinted from *The Happy Family* by John Levy and Ruth Munroe, by permission of and special arrangement with Alfred A. Knopf, Inc.

"Remember! You said you loved me . . ."

was powerless to climb out of it. New jobs are like that, and marriage
with its new household tasks takes some experience and planning.

Or take the poor bride in the cartoon on this page. Obviously, she
did not manage her time correctly. She probably slept too late, took
too long to get the groceries, left the chicken too long while she went
to the store. She is counting on love to get her by! "If he loves me he
will forgive and forget." If he is impatient and cross, she will claim he
doesn't love her. But in a marriage based on companionship and conjugal love, the girl might say, "How would you like to pitch in and help
me clean up? This job of being a wife is more difficult than I thought
— and kiss me, dear, first!"

Both parties in a new marriage face adjustments to a level of living
less well ordered and substantial than existed in the parental family.
After all, it took their parents twenty to thirty years to provide their
home with all its facilities and to organize their routines so faultlessly.
The new husband may obtain an understanding of his wife's problems
if he pitches in to help with the meal, setting the table and washing up
the dishes afterward — as well he should. The new wife needs to realize
she can't follow the same budget for her personal expenditures that she
could under her father's high salary, and she should thank her lucky

stars she has a wardrobe built up which will hold her over the first few years. These are only a few of the adjustments which occur in the shift from parental family living to the life of newlyweds.

Out of the clinical studies by psychiatrists of hundreds of housewives come these findings of value for new husbands: Personalities which require order, which require that a house be neat and spotless, that every chair have a special place and all clothes be put away, in other words, personalities which make wonderful housekeepers rarely make adaptable, understanding, patient wives. Rarely can a wife be both a perfect housekeeper and an understanding, flexible companion. The husband may get a not-so-good housekeeper who won't worry and fuss about him and the children. But the compulsion to keep order which makes for perfection in household management is incompatible with normal rough and tumble married living. Take your choice! A man may enjoy keeping things "shipshape" while on duty, but at home who wants to live under the eagle eye of an inspecting admiral?

Major Accomplishments of the First Year of Marriage

Courtship, engagement, and marriage can merge imperceptibly without jarring adjustments. A student's letter to one of the authors shows how normally and easily he and his wife achieved this merger:

> I didn't learn much about family in my first month of marriage, but I did learn a great deal about marriage. We moved into our own house, budgeted our time and expenditures; we consulted a physician about birth control methods and got a very good start on our adjustment to the new roles we had assumed. Nobody told us a great deal about how to manage our affairs and it seemed to come natural to us. . . . I am very happily married; I have a wonderful wife and mother for my children and two of the swellest, healthiest, most perfect kids that anybody could ask for.

If all marriages developed as naturally and normally as Bob's and Myrtle's above, there would be much less justification for formal education in marriage and family life. These young people changed the company they were frequenting and took on the roles and responsibilities of the new relation, just as they might shift tempo and dance steps on the dance floor. Ordinarily a person has to learn the steps in a new dance, but if he has watched carefully and is supple enough he can imitate the new step satisfactorily. In more stable communities young people have known each other since school days, and at maturity may slip quickly into the more intensified relationships of courtship and engagement with a pretty clear idea of the reactions they may expect from each other. They assume the responsibilities of marriage relatively easily because the examples of successfully married people are constantly before them. Married people, moreover, are available to check with as the marriage progresses.

In our discussion in this chapter we have blazed a trail for couples who do not have models of marriage so clearly accessible. The story tells of certain minimum expectations for couples in the first year of marriage. They have carried over into the honeymoon and first months of marriage the fascinating pattern of exploration and experimentation started in the engagement. They have learned how to live intimately together and may have achieved a satisfying sexual relationship. They have come to accept the realities of marriage with its routines and schedules and unromantic regularity. Romantic thrills are giving way to more companionable sentiments.

Our newlyweds have come to think of themselves as belonging to the married set and now feel comfortable in the roles of husband and wife, both at home and elsewhere. They are winning a status in the community as married folk and will soon be inducted into the circles of gardeners, marketing specialists, and canning artists. Some people may already have begun talking about the advantages of "having your babies while you are young."

Although there have been many quarrels and conflicts during the first year, the differences are being ironed out, and the friction has worn smooth the edges which seemed so easily irritated the first few months. The pair still has its differences but has come to know that quarreling is no longer any threat to its relationship, which in itself is a major accomplishment. Our new husband and wife have come to accept married life with its ups and downs and are prepared now to take the worse along with the better. The first year of marriage has been stimulating and satisfying. For the couple who worried about the pitfalls of marriage it is reassuring to know that marriage is sometimes full of fun!

Selected Readings

CHRISTENSEN, HAROLD T., *Marriage Analysis* (New York: Ronald Press, 1950), Chap. 10, "Mate Adjustment."

HIMES, NORMAN S., *Your Marriage: A Guide to Happiness* (New York: Farrar and Rinehart, 1940), Chap. 11, "The Wedding and the Honeymoon."

LANDIS, JUDSON T., AND LANDIS, MARY, *Building a Successful Marriage* (New York: Prentice-Hall, 1948), Chap. 10, "Achieving Adjustment in Marriage."

LEVY, JOHN, AND MUNROE, RUTH, *The Happy Family* (New York: Knopf, 1938), Chap. 2, "Settling Down to Marriage."

MACE, DAVID, *For Those Who Wear the Altar-Halter* (New York: *Woman's Home Companion*, 1949), essay on the early weeks of marriage.

MAGOUN, F. ALEXANDER, *Love and Marriage* (New York: Harper, 1948), Chap. 2, "The Nature of Marriage."

MERRILL, FRANCIS E., *Courtship and Marriage* (New York: Sloane, 1949), chaps. 7, 13.

SKIDMORE, REX A., AND CANNON, ANTHON S., *Building Your Marriage* (New York: Harper, 1951), Chap. 13, "The Wedding and the Honeymoon."

TRAVIS, LEE E., AND BARUCH, DOROTHY W., *Personal Problems of Everyday Life* (New York: Appleton-Century, 1941), Chap. 9.

WALLER, WILLARD, AND HILL, REUBEN, *The Family: A Dynamic Interpretation* (New York: Dryden Press, 1951), Chap. 13, "Married-Pair Living."

Technical References

BRAV, STANLEY, "Note on Honeymoons," *Marriage and Family Living,* Vol. 9 (Summer, 1947), p. 60.

COTTRELL, LEONARD S., JR., "Roles and Marital Adjustment," *Publications of the American Sociological Society,* Vol. 27 (1933), pp. 107–115.

SLATER, ELIOT, AND WOODSIDE, MOYA, *Patterns of Marriage: A Study of Marriage Relationships in the Urban Working Classes* (London: Cassell and Company, 1951), Chap. 9.

TRUXAL, ANDREW G., AND MERRILL, FRANCIS E., *The Family in American Culture* (New York: Prentice-Hall, 1947), Chap. 21.

WINCH, ROBERT F., *The Modern Family* (New York: Holt, 1952), chaps. 15, 16.

CHAPTER ELEVEN

Where Does the Money Go?

MONEY MATTERS IN MARRIAGE

How much money does it take to get married?

Do budgets have to cramp your style?

How about wives working?

Is insurance a must?

Does it take brains to shop?

Is it easy to borrow money?

How can you keep out of debt?

$\mathcal{M}$ANY HONEST, RESPONSIBLE, HARD WORKING PEOPLE WHO have good incomes, cannot manage their personal finances successfully. Joe Bank who was earning $100 a week can hardly be regarded as a charity case. Neither was he dishonest. Yet he was in serious financial difficulties. He owed over $1000 and was getting deeper into debt all the time; yet he had had no unusual expenses, such as operations or illnesses. He was not now borrowing from a loan company. He had borrowed several times before, only to find his troubles increased. In desperation he admitted his own inability to get out by himself, and had gone for help to a company whose job it was to help people get out on their own power. There are many thousands like him: people who earn enough to live comfortably and well, but somehow cannot seem to make ends meet. The purpose of this chapter is to help, not only those in financial difficulties, but all who would like to live better on the incomes they have.

Can We Afford to Marry?

What income should we have before we marry? How much should we have in the bank? If we marry, will we be able to afford it? The only proper answer to this is that it depends upon how much you demand. The 1950 census tells us what families actually did have to live on as of 1949. Almost a fourth of all American families (22.9%) had incomes of less than $1000 a year. Less than half (43.2%) had as much as $3000. About 16 per cent had as much as $5000, 6 per cent had over $7000 and 2.4 per cent over $10,000.[1] Rising costs, as indicated in the chart below, add still further to the economic difficulties of families. Obviously most families will never have anything like the incomes which some people regard as necessary to support a family.

The question "Can we afford to marry?" then, must depend largely upon the prospective bride and groom for its answer. A discussion of the following questions may help in providing such an answer: How much income are you both accustomed to? Could you get along happily on less if necessary? What are your present and immediate respon-

POST-WAR LIVING COSTS ARE THE HIGHEST EVER
In 1949, $1.00 bought only as much as 59 cents in 1939

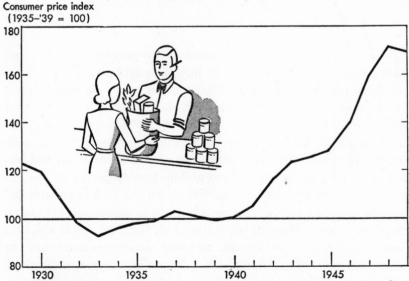

Consumer price index
(1935–'39 = 100)

From *Children and Youth at the Midcentury — A Chart Book*, Health Publications Institute, Inc., Raleigh, North Carolina.

[1] U.S. Bureau of the Census, 1950.

sibilities for the support of relatives? (Do not include the support which you may later be called upon to give to parents who may remain self-supporting for many years.)

In estimating your probable costs after marriage, figure that two can live as cheaply as *two*. What is it now costing both of you to live? If the prospective wife is living with her parents, estimate the money value of what she is now receiving from her family, such as room, board, medical and dental service, and perhaps an allowance, all of which she may lose after marriage. In confronting your financial problems, do not expect to start in where your parents are now, either.

About That Budget

Does the word "budget" scare you? A budget is only a plan to get the most from your income. Can you afford this or that? How do you know unless your income is budgeted? Do you find it hard to make ends meet to pay all the bills? Do you wonder "where it has all gone"? Before you plan your budget, here are some facts you should bear in mind.

Expenses for various items will not be the same for each month or each year. In winter the fuel costs will run high, in spring and fall the clothing bills. Some years there will be extra expenses, such as a new car or a baby. Professor Bigelow points out that there is usually a family cost cycle which rises steadily through the years to a peak, and then declines sharply after the children have become self-supporting.[2] Changes in the financial condition of the country at large also profoundly affect family financial planning. Families vary also in their interests and desires. Some wish to spend more for one item, and some for another. In view of all these factors, then, it is hardly sound to say that a family should spend a certain proportion of its income for food, rent, clothing, or any other particular item. Each family must work out its own budget in the light of its income and desires. The following suggestions may prove of help in working out the budget:

1 List your monthly income.
2 List all *items of regular expense* which are predictable, such as rent, gas, light, telephone, installment payments, and insurance. Include groceries if you can estimate their cost with reasonable accuracy.

   2 See his chapter "Financing the Marriage" in Howard Becker and Reuben Hill, eds., *Family, Marriage, and Parenthood* (Boston: Heath, 1948).

3 List your probable expenses for other essentials, such as clothing, carfare, and laundry.

4 Allocate a personal allowance for each member of the family, including children old enough to spend money. (Such expenditures should be the private business of each individual, accountable to no one.) List each name with the amount of the allowance beside it.

5 Add all the above expenses together, and subtract the total from the monthly income. How much do you have left? Circle it in pencil. If you don't have a balance, your plane of living is too high!

6 Now comes the fun. Forget about how much you have left. Make a list of everything you want which you might conceivably afford. Spread yourselves. Include new furniture, dishes, silverware, washing machine, sporting goods, books, an exciting vacation, or anything within reason. Most of these you may not be able to get, but it is fun to write them down.

7 Go over this list carefully and arrange the items in order of preference. Yes, this is a good time for family squabbles, for differences of opinion and taste, but these might just as well come right out into the open. If you are not yet married and the girl friend cannot be present, arrange the items for yourself, with a family situation in mind.

8 Now go back over your so-called fixed necessities and see if they are as essential as you thought. You may decide to go without so much beer, cigarettes, or candy, and spend the money saved for a better vacation next summer, or for linoleum for the floor, or for a new suit. Cutting down on movies and entertainment might enable your wife to get the silver fox scarf she has always wanted, or you to get the fine tennis racket or set of golf clubs you have set your heart on. You will be surprised how many things which you thought you could not afford now become possible. Driblets added together often make a sizable sum. List in one column what you might leave out and in a second column what may now be included.

9 Now go back to point five. How much did you have left over after providing for the running expenses of the household? Add to it what you have saved from your driblets. Then take about three fourths of this total and plan to buy as many things on your list under point seven as you have money for.

10 Keep careful accounts, but do not be a fanatic on the subject. If you cannot remember where that dime went, forget it and go to the movies as you had planned.

11 Oh, yes, what about that other fourth of what you had left (point 9) after deducting all usual running expenses and buying what you wished? Save it. For what? For emergencies, such as sickness and hospital bills; for the education of the children; to give yourself a start on a home of your own; or just to start a bank account. But do not save it all.

For before next pay day you may run into something which you very much want but which is not in the budget. If you can, get it. For if your budget is too tight it will prove so uncomfortable that you may become disgusted and chuck the whole thing. Leave a little room for moving about.

So you see, the budget is not a Demon Chaperon always keeping you from having what you want. It is a way of showing you how to get what you want most, instead of losing much of your income in little expenditures which leave you nothing to show for them. Almost any family will find in a really sound budget a faithful servant. Do not let it throw you. If you treat it well, it will give you a real raise in pay, and after all, that is what budgets are for.

When You Have to Borrow

Many young couples find that unexpected illness, responsibilities for parental families, new babies, and a host of other costly items have a tendency to pile up so quickly that borrowing money becomes necessary to meet the bills. Spending beyond one's income just for routine living is a complicating factor in family finances. This common experience is a result of many factors: 1. the bombardment of advertising; 2. the attempt to keep up with the Joneses or to live up to the standard set by the vocational or social or neighborhood group with which the new family is identified; 3. the realignment of a standard of living that is involved when young people step out of homes that have been going concerns for twenty years or more into a new household that doesn't include even an eggbeater. So getting some kind of financial help from outside is sometimes imperative.

It is almost as difficult to borrow money wisely as it is to earn it. What are the possibilities?

1 **Friends.** If you suddenly find yourself without carfare or money to pay the dinner check, borrowing from friends may be essential, but as a general practice avoid it like the plague. In the first place, you probably will not be able to borrow enough to do much good in any real crisis; and secondly, you are very likely to lose your friends, because of your own embarrassment if for no other reason.

2 **Relatives.** Accepting a loan from members of the family is a matter so dependent upon the nature of the relationship between borrower and

lender that no generalization is safe. Some young people do not feel comfortable in having to depend upon the family after they are on their own. Others approve of the various forms of family subsidy that are the modern equivalents of a dowry — showers, new home, bonds, allowances, etc.

3 **Advance on salary and wages.** This borrowing technique may help out if the crisis is temporary; otherwise it merely postpones the inevitable.

4 **Loan sharks.** These financiers make loans easy but may charge several hundred per cent interest before they are through with you. Never borrow from a loan company which asks you to pay a rate of interest several times as high as that of a legitimate loan company. If you get into the clutches of a loan shark, seek legal advice at once. If his interest rates are beyond the legal rate he cannot collect.

5 **Legitimate loan companies.** Available in most cities are loan companies which do not try to use tricky devices. Partly because of the high cost of collection, however, they charge about 2.5 to 3 per cent interest a month, or 30 to 36 per cent a year. Without in any way casting reflection upon such companies, we must recognize that this is a much higher rate of interest than most borrowers can afford to pay, or need to pay.

6 **Banks.** These institutions are designed primarily to loan to business enterprises, not to individuals for personal expenses. Usually they loan relatively small sums to individuals, and only if bonds or similar collateral is deposited with the bank in sufficient quantity to cover the loan. If you own bonds which you do not wish to sell, the bank may be the very best place to secure a loan at a relatively small rate of interest. If you do not own such securities, you may find that you will be unable to secure the loan.

7 **Credit unions.** There are now credit unions operating on a membership basis through labor unions, industries, and fraternal orders. The usual rate is 1 per cent a month, or 12 per cent a year, far lower than you are likely to pay elsewhere. By all means, before you borrow elsewhere, find out if there is a credit union connected with your place of employment or some other group to which you belong. If you must borrow, the credit union is best designed to meet your temporary need.

Giving Yourself a Raise in Pay

Obviously many people have serious money problems just because they do not earn enough. However, the financial difficulties of many middle class people arise mainly because they do not spend wisely the money which they receive. Some families are constantly bemoaning their poverty and longing for a raise in pay. But when the raise in pay does come, they find to their consternation that they are farther behind than they were before. The reason is that for every dollar of additional income they get, they raise their expenditures two dollars. No amount of additional income which they can ever hope to get can solve their problem. They must solve it themselves on the expenses end. Let us consider some suggestions for so doing.

Don't Throw Money out the Window. Here are some of the more common wasteful expenditures:

1 *Participating in confidence games and frauds.* You may never have bought fake oil stocks, but what about the panhandler on the corner whose take averages $30 a day? What about the numerous fake charities which abound? Did you pay a registration fee to that so-called employment agency? Or fall for the "free lot won with a lucky ticket" gag? Poor families which can ill afford the loss are annually mulcted of sums which run into millions. Approximately $200 per family is lost annually in such deals. Two hundred dollars would really help your budget.

2 *Gambling.* There is little bona fide gambling in the United States. Most of what is called gambling is really the donation of suckers to swindlers. Slot machines pay off from five to thirty cents on the dollar. Pools and bookie bets often give odds no better.

3 *Buying worthless products, especially drugs.* Do you pay good money for stuff in bottles guaranteed to take your unpleasant breath away, massacre bacteria, prevent colds, and warm up cold love affairs? Know, then, that most of these mouth washes, antiseptics, and patent medicines in general are essentially frauds. If your weight reducer potion is only a fraud, you are lucky. If it were effective, it would be highly dangerous. One way of helping your budget is by looking in your medicine cabinet.

4 *Buying things you don't want.* We all see things in stores which attract us. But when we get them home we wonder why we ever bought them. Anyone who goes through the stuff which he has bought but never used or cared about will get the idea. These white elephants, herds of them, cost money, lots of it. Cut them out and you can increase your income, considerably.

Get More and Better Goods for Less Money. You can, you know. Many products can be purchased for less money than the general public pays. Consider, for example, the following instance. Two little wives went to market. Mrs. Squander and Mrs. Canny went to the same shopping district on the same day. Each bought the articles and paid the prices indicated in the accompanying table.

No, you are wrong. Mrs. Squander did not get better goods. The last five items which each bought are identical in quality. In the sheets Mrs. Canny got the best buy, with a tensile strength of 71 and 72 pounds for warp and fill respectively. Those bought by Mrs. Squander had a tensile strength of 62 and 67. And tensile strength is probably the best indicator of wearing quality.

	MRS. SQUANDER PAID		MRS. CANNY PAID	
6 muslin sheets, 81″ × 108″	@ $4.09	$24.54	@ $3.00	$18.00
2 men's broadcloth shirts, 2 & 2 ply		14.00		8.00
2 nylon jersey slips		15.90		11.90
6 pairs of nylon hose, 30 denier, 51 gauge	@ $1.90	11.40	@ $1.35	8.10
1 bottle, 100 5 gr. aspirin tablets, usp		.50		.19
1 fld. oz. bottle, make-up base		1.80		1.20
		$68.14		$47.39

With the remainder of her money, Mrs. Canny was able to get in addition:

1 chenille bedspread, good quality	$7.95
1 slip cover for chair	9.00
1 roll aluminum foil	1.69
1 sponge mop	1.37
2 magazines at 35¢ each	.70
Grand Total	$68.10

Contrary to popular opinion, the best is *not* always the most expensive. Thousands of tests have shown that some products will last much longer than others which cost more. The less expensive articles are often the nicest, as well as the most durable. Price tells little about quality. Getting more and better goods for less money is one of the simplest ways of giving yourself a raise in pay. But, you say, how can I buy for less? How can I be Mrs. Canny in my shopping?

1 *Judge products on the basis of scientific tests, rather than sales or advertising claims.* The government does not buy jeeps on the basis of the pictures of pretty girls in advertisements. Neither do railroads buy rails because Betta Harake says they are the smoothest she ever rode on, or because a luscious radio voice describes them as "bright, shining, smooth steel ribbons." Nor does the printer of popular magazines buy

his paper on such a basis. They all depend upon specifications and tests. So should you. Since the consumer can hardly maintain his own testing laboratory, he must depend upon some such service as Consumers Union or Consumer's Research.[3] Like clocks, their counsel is not always accurate, but taking their advice is far better than guessing. On the basis of such reports it becomes possible to buy with confidence nonadvertised brands which often sell at considerably lower prices than nationally advertised products. For example, a half-pound of a certain kind of baking chocolate selling for fifteen cents is the same quality as a nationally advertised brand selling for twenty-three cents. Not only soap flakes and similar products, but electric refrigerators, washing machines, radios, trailers, and tires could often be bought from chain stores or mail order houses for as much as 25 per cent less than nationally advertised brands of comparable quality and size. And the companies stand behind them, too.

2 *Purchase where you can secure good quality at a low price.* It may cost as much as seventy-five cents to assemble and deliver an order of groceries. Credit is expensive in both bookkeeping and losses. Such costs must necessarily be reflected in the prices charged for goods. The "name" of the store and personal service may also cause a further increase in prices, and consequently the mark-up of one store may be twice that of another. It is significant that the O.P.A. specifically permitted certain classes of grocery stores to charge higher ceiling prices than others. So if you want to give yourself a raise in pay, trade where the mark-up is low. The difference may be considerable.

3 *Take advantage of sales, especially seasonal sales.* Some supposed sales are frauds, but reputable houses do have bona fide sales at which goods, especially furniture and clothing, are offered at considerable discount. Saturday specials at chain stores often offer attractive opportunities for saving.

4 *Save money by paying cash.* With many products, especially radios and electrical equipment, some shops and stores will give a sizable discount to any cash customer who demands it. Regarding some merchandise it has been said that "only saps pay retail prices." It is usually cheaper to buy anything for cash. Bookkeeping and bad accounts are costly. The store which charges the same price for either cash or

[3] For addresses of these services, see p. 235.

credit really charges a higher price. If you do not have the cash, either borrow it or wait until you do have it.

5 *Consider buying secondhand items.* With some products, such as furniture, radios, or refrigerators, secondhand or discontinued models can sometimes be secured for half price. Perhaps you are prejudiced against secondhand goods. Remember, however, that new goods become secondhand after they have been in your house for only a few days. With products which have motors or mechanical equipment which will wear out, there is more risk. In any case, with a large purchase it may pay you to have some expert appraise the product for you, even if you must pay him a sizable fee. This precaution is especially important if you buy a house, new or old.

6 *Let the family become experts too.* Have each member of the family specialize in certain types of buying by reading up on the product and doing all the purchasing in that area. When contemplating a large investment, such as furniture, a refrigerator, or a car, special study should be given before buying.

7 *Keep what you have in good repair.* A stitch in time saves not only nine; it may save the whole garment. A little glue, a screw properly placed, may save the whole table or chair. Shiftlessness is by no means the only cause of poverty, but it is often a contributing factor. If you do not know how to make minor repairs, it will pay you to learn. Here again, specialization by each member of the family may prove economical.

Be Discriminating Regarding Luxuries. Many families of modest income could raise their standard of living considerably simply by eliminating one or more of the luxuries which consume so large a proportion of their earnings. Let us consider some of the more dispensable luxuries of the average couple.

1 *Entertaining and dining out.* Couples naturally want to do some entertaining. If this involves expensive food or liquor, the cost will run up. One couple dared to substitute simple sandwiches and carefully planned games for drinks, and got away with it. The saving may easily mean the difference between going into debt or keeping ahead of the game and being able to get something you have always wanted. Meals eaten out may cost a couple several dollars a week more than meals eaten in. It's all right if you want to spend your money that way. On

the other hand, don't complain about not being able to afford that new pair of shoes or that tennis racket which a very few weeks of economy at this point would make possible.

2 *Expensive apartments.* In most cities it is possible to secure commodious, comfortable apartments at a price considerably less than that charged for those with a swanky address. One couple who moved from their expensive place found that with the difference in rent they were able in the course of a single year to buy a good watch, an electric sewing machine, an extra radio, a fur scarf, two really good pieces of furniture, and a serviceable secondhand typewriter. What a simple way to raise your standard of living!

3 *The car.* A car is a desirable thing to own; it is a convenience, and sometimes a necessity. But for most people it is a luxury, since they could get along quite well with public transportation. If you are a mechanic, you may be able to operate a car at relatively small expense. Otherwise it can easily add several hundred dollars a year to your expenses. To determine its actual costs include gas and oil, licenses, insurance, depreciation, and interest on the investment of car and the garage. If you do not have a car, you will have a surprising sum available for other things.

4 *Proving you are better than the Joneses.* This is the most expensive luxury of all. Most people either feel inferior to others or wish to feel superior. It is too much work actually to become superior, or people may not have what it takes. So they try to compensate by paying more for what they buy. There are a few connoisseurs who really appreciate choice things and are willing to pay for them, but most people who pay high prices do so in order to make themselves feel important. A lady was considering two sets of dishes, one of which cost $100, and the other $150. She ordered the more expensive set without hesitation. She wanted the best, she said. After the dishes were delivered the store owner called up in distress. The clerk had made a mistake and mixed the price tags. Her dishes were the $100 set. Instead of getting her $50 back, she at once ordered the set which she had previously rejected. She was buying, not primarily dishes, but a feeling of personal importance.

This is a game at which you cannot win, for as soon as you find yourself able to outbuy everyone in your set, you move up the economic scale where the competition is keener, and you are right back where you were. If you doubled your income you would live and associate with people on a still more expensive level, and still could not keep up. Some people who get $3000 a month complain that they cannot live on their incomes. For most people there is and can be only one solution to their economic problems: learn to enjoy life in simple and inexpensive ways and stop trying to impress yourself and others by the prices which you pay. Many would find that if they learned to depend for their enjoyment upon themselves as family members who can have fun together rather than upon the things that money can buy, most of their economic problems would automatically be solved.

Production in the Home

Many people today do not include production within the home as part of their real income, nor do they consider how such income can be employed most effectively. Much production centers around the preparation and serving of food, and it is questionable whether this pays as such. We pointed out earlier that it might cost several times as much to eat out as to eat in, but this is true only if the family is already paying most of the preparation costs anyway. For example, if a five-room apartment renting for $100 a month includes a dining room and kitchen, the rental costs of preparing and serving food alone will amount to about $40. In addition, there is all the investment in equipment, including the refrigerator, stove, dining room and kitchen furniture, and dishes, plus the cost of gas and electricity used for food preparation and preservation. It is fair to say that the cost of serving food in the home must be estimated at about $2.00 a day, not including the cost of the food itself. Most of these costs go on whether food is served or not.

This is not, however, a complete picture, for the couple or family which lives in a room or two with no kitchen or dining facilities does not enjoy the same conveniences. The dining room, for example, is not merely a place for eating but also a work room, and makes the home more spacious. Furthermore, providing food in one's home brings satisfactions which eating out all the time cannot give. Thus, much of the overhead of the apartment which includes dining room, kitchen, and necessary equipment can be counted as necessary costs of satisfactory family living, just as you now regard the costs of the living room and its furnishings. Furthermore, the effort involved in the serving of meals is not necessarily unrewarding labor. Some people enjoy preparing food and decorating a table, just as they do dancing or playing tennis.

The preparation of food is not the only productive activity commonly carried on within the family. The making of clothing may in some families be considerable, and the repairing of furniture, clothing, or other equipment may have high economic value. Cleaning is another service of real value, as you will quickly discover if you pay to have it done. Since most women have more time in the home than men do, much of the responsibility for its productive activities falls upon them. If both husband and wife work outside the home, however, there is no reason why women should be expected to do more than their share. Women do not naturally cook and sew any better than men. Some of our best chefs and tailors are men. Conversely, the war has shown that women can become excellent mechanics. Any difference is due to the particular individual, not to the sex, and even individual differences are often due to past learnings and experiences. In this connection it should be noted that children can and should assume many productive tasks around the home, not only to make the household tasks less burdensome for others, but to develop the children as well and ready them to assume the responsibilities of a family when they marry.

Should Wives Continue to Work after Marriage?

Here is something to argue about. Before we line up in battle formation, let us objectively examine a few relevant facts. How did the issue come about in the first place? Years ago the productive tasks of the home were much greater than they are today. With childbearing and the lack of modern aids and conveniences, the work of most wives was probably greater than that of their husbands. Of them it was said, "Man works from sun to sun, but woman's work is never done." Gradually, however, the family bought more and more of the things which women used to make in the home: soap, clothes, and later bread and canned goods. Women bore fewer children and had more and more conveniences, such as vacuum cleaners and electrical kitchen equipment, to aid them. Since these purchases were made with the money earned by men, the burden on the husband became increasingly greater. He had to do what he did not have to do before: earn enough for two, as well as enough for the children. The woman's burden became increasingly lighter, and for some almost reached the vanishing point. In the earlier days, marriage was essentially an economic partnership. Neither husband nor wife supported the other, and even the children were supported only during the first few years. As time went on, however, and wives and children bought more and produced less, the increased burden on the husband became accepted as the normal and proper situation. In the middle and upper income groups, wives often became merely expensive luxuries. The extent of the support of a wife came for many men to be a test of their abilities. Far from resenting this situation, men often assumed the cost proudly as evidence of their earning power. Many came to resent violently the idea of their wives' working outside the home as a reflection upon their ability to provide support. This attitude is now changing, despite the anguished cries of those who cherish it. The idea that a man should support his wife, which is hardly more than a generation old, seems rapidly passing out. With this preliminary discussion, then, let us look at the situation as it seems to shape up today.

1 Some women are temperamentally so built that if they do not have a job of their own they either "blow up" or constantly meddle in the affairs of their husbands, and possibly those of other husbands as well. With them a real job outside the family meets a vital psychological need.

2 A few women have special talents and skills which ought not to be wasted. In this class belong some of our more talented teachers, authors, artists, and executives. Such women may take time out for children, but will and should remain employed for most of their productive years.

3 Wives of certain professional men, such as ministers, governmental officials, or big business executives, may find their full-time employment as helpers and hostesses for their husbands.

4 Wives of farmers usually have a full-time job where they are.

5 Many women are really employed extensively outside their homes, but are not so regarded because they are not paid. They are prominent in church work, P.T.A.'s, and various civic and community organizations and enterprises. A woman is not unemployed because she is not paid for her work.

6 Most wives have neither the strength nor the ability to carry on a very big job outside the home while their children still need careful supervision. Most wives in cities could carry on a real job, at least part time, before their children come and after they are grown.

7 Some women are so lacking in talents and interests that housekeeping, even without children, taxes their capacities to the utmost.

The wives of today who are employed, then, are doing essentially the same things their great-grandmothers did, except that now they are doing their jobs outside the home. During the first year or so of marriage the earning power of the husband is relatively low, while the expenses are relatively high. Usually all the furniture has to be bought, and the couple need to save up enough money for the first baby. During this period an increasing proportion of wives will insist upon carrying their share of the economic load. If the earnings of both husband and wife are used up for current living expenses, however, they face a real problem. A baby will mean that their expenses are considerably increased at the same time that their income may be cut almost in half. Many couples guard against this difficulty by living on the husband's income only and saving all that the wife earns. Putting some of the latter into home furnishings is one form of saving; the rest is banked. Then when the baby comes, their income for ordinary use remains the same, and they have a nest egg to take care of the extra expenses.

Some Hints on Insurance

Insurance is like marriage — no family should be without it. Yet to most people it is somewhat of a mystery. They may believe in insurance. But they have little understanding of *what* it is, *when* they should take it out, *how much* and *what kind* they should have, and *with whom* they should take it. Let us first consider the purpose of life insurance.

The primary purpose of life insurance is the protection of those who are financially dependent in some way upon the insured. We usually think of dependents as wife and children. The "dependent" may also be a creditor who has insured the life of a debtor so that in case of sudden death he can get his money back. A company may find its manager so valuable that they insure his life for a huge sum to protect themselves against a sudden deprivation of his direction. In any case, you do not take out life insurance because *you* need it, but because your dependents (of whatever type) need it.

When Should Life Insurance Be Taken Out? When you have dependents who need it, and not before. You would not take out automobile liability insurance before you have a car, or fire insurance on your "Dream Home" not yet built. Then do not take out life insurance before you have dependents, except in the case of G.I. insurance. This is so much cheaper than ordinary insurance that you should take it out while you can still get it, and hang on to it. Otherwise, wait until you have dependents. Don't be so silly as to think that if you take it out at a younger age, it will be cheaper. The rate will be lower, but you will be paying for more years, so the total cost will be greater. No insurance company can insure you for extra years, even the younger years, without additional cost.

The more dependents you have, the more insurance protection they need. Here we face a problem. As a man's family increases, so does their need for insurance. But as the children grow up and become independent, this need will decline. How can a family get high protection while the children are young, without saddling itself with a huge burden which will later be unnecessary? The answer is simple. Get the kind of insurance which gives you the greatest protection at the least cost, and automatically terminates when you no longer need it. This is term insurance. With some companies you can get this renewed each year without further examination, at an increasing rate. Or you can get it for a specific period, five, ten, or twenty years for the same rate each year the policy is in force.

The best family plan would be for the husband and wife to each take out a policy to protect each other, the husband taking out the larger amount. They should expect these policies to continue until death. In order to keep the payments equal, ordinary life seems the best. The children, however, do not need protection until the death of the father would normally occur. They need protection until they are old enough to take care of themselves. Therefore with each pregnancy the father would take out another twenty year term policy on himself. For the same money he can give his children twice the protection he could with ordinary life. Furthermore, when this protection is no longer needed, his costs will decline.

Should we insure the children themselves? If they have dependents, yes. If not, no. If you want to build up a fund to put them through college, buy government bonds. They will have a better chance to go to college if you insure yourself, not them.

How Much Insurance Should Be Carried? Statistics show that many families take out far more insurance than they can or will keep up.[4] On the surface the lapse and surrender rate may not seem excessive. For ordinary life it ranged from a low of 2.2 per cent in 1944 to a high of 11.9 per cent in 1932. Industrial insurance rates were 6.8 per cent in 1944 to 27.9 per cent in 1932. But these rates are for all policies in force, *and for one year only.* We can get a truer picture if we compare the amount given up each year with the amount bought each year. During the low years, people gave up more than they bought, not including normal maturing. In the best year, 1944, they gave up a third as much as they bought of the ordinary life, and more than half as much as they bought of the industrial policies. One study made in New York State covering ten years showed that over half of all ordinary life policies taken out were given up, and three fourths of all industrial insurance policies. So don't let an agent talk you into overloading. Better take a smaller amount and hang on to it. How much you should take will depend largely upon such considerations as:

1 The size of the family and the ages of the children.
2 The standard of living which the protected family expects.
3 What the wife could earn. A woman who is a permanent invalid needs more protection than one who is strong and healthy. The wife who has some training or skill, like nursing, stenography or a license to teach, needs less protection than one who would face widowhood without abilities or skills.
4 Other economic resources. In time, savings or the gradual accumulation of property may lessen the need for insurance protection. Include also any forms of social security, governmental or private, by which the family is protected.

What about Insurance as an Investment? This book is not written for wealthy people who may need huge policies in order to get cash with which to pay heavy inheritance taxes. For the ordinary family, the investments in insurance are for two purposes: to "level off" payments and to invest savings. The first kind is seen in the whole life policy. As people become older, their insurance costs rise. If the payments are

---

[4] The figures here quoted were compiled mainly from the *Life Insurance Fact Book* (1951), published by the Institute of Life Insurance, 60 East 40th Street, New York City.

to remain the same throughout life, the company must "overcharge" people while they are young, so that they can "undercharge" them when they become old. The excess paid in the early years is saved by the insurance company and appears as the loan or cash surrender value of the policy. The interest on this saving is used to help pay the total costs of the policy. On the average the savings will be enough to pay off the entire policy by the time of death. This investment is actually a type of convenience to the policy holder, making it possible for him to meet the payments of later years without payments being prohibitively high.

Savings may be invested through the endowment policy. This is really a form of term insurance at about four times the cost. The excess is saved and invested by the company. If the person outlives the term of the policy its face value (say, $1000) is returned in a lump sum. But if he dies before the policy expires his beneficiaries get only the same amount they would have received from a term policy. The company keeps the excess. If he had bought a term policy and saved the difference in cost, in case of prior death the beneficiaries would have received the thousand plus all the additional savings. These could amount to over $900. Endowment insurance is a "tails I lose" "heads I break even" proposition; not an intelligent proposition, even if you will probably live. It has one defense. Some people seem unable to save anything, even when their earnings are high. If they have to make payments on an endowment policy they may end up with savings which otherwise they would have squandered.

Apart from such compulsory saving, there are at least two possibilities for investment for the ordinary individual which are better than insurance. Government bonds are both more secure and more fluid. And if you want to guard against inflation, there are sound investment companies which will invest your money with as much care and skill as an insurance company.

Finally, remember that insurance agents are human beings. Most of them are not dishonest; neither are they saints. Their incomes depend upon the amount of insurance they sell. Don't expect them to recommend policies of other companies, even if they are cheaper and better for your needs. Expect of them what you would of any salesmen; that they will do their best to sell their products. When they sell protection they are often rendering a valuable service. When they try to sell their banking and investment services, their efforts are more questionable.

What Type of Policy is Best? For those who can get it, G.I. insurance is the best insurance available. But most people will have to buy through regular companies. Some of these are ingenious at developing all kinds of "special" policies. But if you understand a few basic principles, you can easily reduce them to a few major types. For example, one policy provides for low payments during the first five years (when your earnings are presumably low) and substantial increase after that. This is likely to be a term policy which automatically becomes converted to whole life after five years.

Industrial insurance is not really a different kind of insurance, but rather a way of paying for insurance. Instead of making monthly or annual payments, you pay a collector who stops in each week to collect. Because of the costs of such collection, this is the most expensive type of insurance and should be avoided. Likewise, the limited payment policy is not a different kind of insurance, but merely a way of paying for whole-life insurance more rapidly, so that at the end of a specified period the interest on your reserve takes care of all future insurance costs, and you need pay no more in yourself. Group insurance is cheap, and valuable for those who, because of physical disabilities, cannot get any other kind. A group, such as the employees of a certain company, are insured as a whole. When you leave the employ of the company, your protection automatically ceases. In other words, it is term insurance, the term being the length of time you remain with the same firm.

We have suggested that insurance be used for protection only, and not for investment. There is one exception, the annuity policy. This is a type of social security operated by the insurance company instead of the government. If your retirement pension is not already adequately provided for, and you wish to be assured of an income for your old age, the annuity policies of insurance companies should be given serious consideration. The plan is for you to pay a certain amount each year into the fund. When you reach the retirement age as stated on the policy, the company either pays you a flat sum or a stipulated income for the rest of your life. If you die before the policy becomes due, the amount already accumulated is paid to your estate.

With Whom Should You Take Your Insurance? Some unscrupulous or uninformed people may try to tell you that in insurance you get just what you pay for, and that therefore it makes no difference with which company you take out your policy. This is simply not true. A comparison of ten large companies showed that the annual net cost per $1000 of ordinary life taken out at the age of eighteen varied from $4.90 to $7.50. Over a period of years such differences may amount to many hundreds of dollars, depending upon the amount of insurance taken out and the type of policy. In some states, including New York, savings banks sell certain types of policies at a cost much below the usual rate. Teachers and similar groups can often secure insurance from companies specially organized to serve them. All such possibilities should be carefully considered. Those who plan to take out any large amount of insurance might save considerably by going to an insurance advisory service (which has no insurance to sell) and paying a fee for competent guidance and advice.

Life insurance for most people is one of the most important and least understood expenditures a family makes. A well-rounded program of protection will, however, include such other types as health and accident insurance, whether or not there are dependents. Every family should have hospitalization insurance to cover every member, including the children. If a policy which also includes medical care is available, so much the better. Anyone who owns property which might burn, such as a house or furnishings in a home, should have adequate fire insurance protection. A car owner should have liability insurance, and probably fire and theft insurance. Since for these forms of insurance also the costs of reliable companies vary extensively, careful investigations should be made. The policies of mail-order houses and cooperatives often offer especially attractive buys.

Fitting Money Matters into the Total Picture

To the unmarried, sex may seem to be the really important factor in marriage. To those who have been married for some time and face a monthly array of bills, money may appear to be the really crucial issue. Actually the real significance of any individual factor like money is its relationship to the total picture. Money matters are related to all aspects of family life — they affect family life and it affects them.

"I told Charlie we'd have a perfect marriage
if we never mention money."

Obviously, any home worry affects the way a man does his job. If he leaves his home angry and resentful, his attitude will almost inevitably be reflected in his relations with his coworkers, the customers, or the boss. The man whose home is breaking up, or who fears that it may break up, cannot keep his mind on his work to the best advantage, all of which will ultimately affect his chances of promotion or even of keeping the job he has. On the other hand, a sense of happiness and security at home may considerably augment his earning power. It may well give him a goal for effort. He wants to show the little woman that when she married him she made no mistake. A new baby may call forth not only cigars but additional exertion. If at home he has found happiness and support, if his home experiences build him up psychologically, he actually is a better man and can earn more.

The effect of income on marital success is more involved than the effect of happiness on income. Certainly extreme destitution is poor soil in which to grow the fragrant flowers of marital happiness. The home of the simple Scotch peasant which Burns depicts in his "Cotter's Saturday Night" is stable, but one would hardly describe it as happy. The moral of the story, however, is sound: the most important consideration is not the amount of income, but the family attitude toward the total situation. This attitude is affected profoundly by two considerations: the security of the income, and the social standards by which it is measured. The cotter did not have much, but he was relatively secure in what he had. No world-wide economic forces threatened to move his economic earth, or cast the mountains of his livelihood into the midst of the sea of depression. Come what might, pestilence or famine, he would always have a job, an opportunity of directing his efforts in productive channels. He would never have to tramp the streets, day after day, looking for work which was not to be found, nor would he have to mope around the house or the tavern in hopeless despair. Furthermore, his standard of living, while low, was not lower than that of his neighbors, save that of the Laird, to which he did not even aspire.

Studies show that stability of income is far more important than amount of income. People need enough money to provide for basic physical necessities, but they can get along on very little provided they can be reasonably sure of that little. When they are never sure what they can depend upon from one year to the next, their morale is undermined, and their economic insecurity is reflected in greater marital unhappiness and conflict.

Another factor is personal and social expectation. A family with a $6000 income which insists on associating with a $12,000 income crowd will always feel poor and pinched. The wife may feel that she should have married better and the husband that he has failed. This situation may easily give rise to serious marital conflict. If, on the other hand, they are members of a $3000 crowd, the situation may be the reverse.

Money matters, then, can and do affect marriage profoundly. Their effects, however, depend primarily upon the intelligence with which they are understood and handled. No matter how large the income, money problems can become pegs upon which other difficulties and conflicts are hung and carefully preserved. On the other hand, a wise and ethical adjustment in other matters will reflect itself in greater money income and security, and sound financial relationships can make even small incomes strong enough to bear the load.

Selected Readings

BIGELOW, HOWARD F., *Family Finance* (Philadelphia: Lippincott, revised, 1953).

BONDE, RUTH, *Management in Daily Living* (New York: Macmillan, 1944), Chap. 7.

CAMPBELL, P. C., *Consumer Interest* (New York: Harper, 1949).

CANOYER, H. G., AND VAILE, R. S., *Economics of Income and Consumption* (New York: Ronald Press, 1951).

FOSTER, LEBARON, *Credit for Consumers* (New York: Public Affairs Committee, 1945), Pamphlet #5, revised edition.

HIMES, NORMAN E., *Your Marriage: A Guide to Happiness* (New York: Farrar and Rinehart, 1940), chaps. 12–18.

How Families Use Their Incomes, U.S. Department of Agriculture, Publication No. 653, 1948.

JORDAN, DAVID F., AND WILLETT, EDWARD F., *Managing Personal Finances* (New York: Prentice-Hall, revised, 1945), chaps. 1, 2, 6.

McFADDEN, FRANCES, "I Can't Afford My Wife's Job," *Harpers Magazine*, September, 1952, pp. 62–65.

NICKELL, PAULENA, AND DORSEY, JEAN M., *Management in Family Living* (New York: Wiley, revised, 1950), chaps. 15–20.

RADELL, NINA H., *Financial Planning for the Individual and Family* (New York: Crofts, 1947).

REID, MARGARET S., *Consumers in the Market* (New York: Crofts, revised, 1942).

TAYLOR, JAY, "Going Broke on $10,000 a Year," *Harpers Magazine*, July, 1952, pp. 60–65.

Consumers Services

CONSUMER'S RESEARCH, Washington, New Jersey.

CONSUMERS UNION, 38 East 1st Street, New York City 3.

HOUSEHOLD FINANCE CORPORATION, 919 N. Michigan Avenue, Chicago, Illinois. *Better Buymanship* pamphlets on specific products, and other inexpensive pamphlet material for consumers.

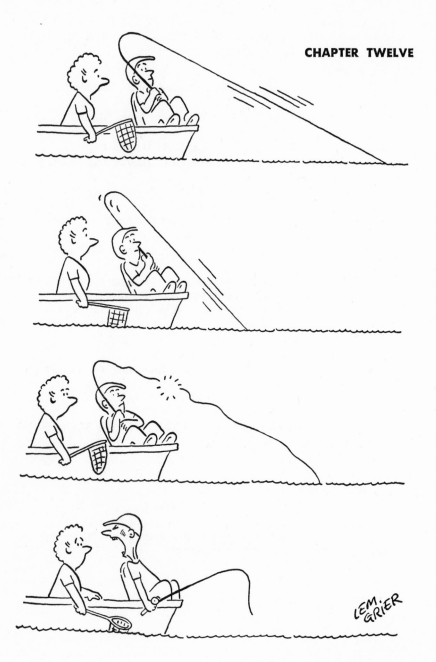

COMMON CONFLICTS IN MARRIAGE

Is it true that the way to hold marriage together is to bear and forbear?

Shouldn't the course of true love run smooth?

Can fighting be fun?

How can unpleasant fighting be stopped?

What kind of help is there for the discordant?

*H*AD ROMEO AND JULIET LIVED TOGETHER LONG ENOUGH, THEY probably would have had their disagreements like everyone else. Whenever two individuals undertake a close and continuous association, inevitable occasions arise when there is a clash of wills. The closer the association and the freer the personalities, the more vigorous this clash may be. Since marriage is the most intimate and the most demanding of all adult human relationships, this element of conflict is an inescapable part of its nature.

Conflict is Normal

Two tasks that are productive of conflict face the newly-wed. The first is concerned with establishing a common set of workable routines, a mutually acceptable way of living, and a new set of family policies out of the two systems carried over from the parental families of the betrothed. The second task involves two egos struggling for individual survival as the marriage moves to bring about incorporation of both in a common joint personality. Conflict serves a useful function in setting the optimum distance and nearness personalities can take in a new marriage. Much of the "fussing" at one another which occurs in the first years reflects these two processes of accommodation of ways of living and a healthy resistance to self-destruction.

Every marital union is, to a certain degree, a mixed marriage. The two parties bring from their parental families different wants and variant ideas of what's funny and what's important. Every time a decision is reached in a young marriage, some of these differences are likely to come to light. Only by grinding the gears a bit at the start is it possible to learn how to mesh them correctly. Consensus of opinion can only follow exchange of differing views.

Susan and Jim are a couple whose conflicts should have occurred early in marriage rather than late for the good health of the relationship. They were seventeen and nineteen respectively when they married, just out of high school. Susan was especially eager to make the marriage a success.

Jim and his four brothers had been reared by his widowed father without experience in the needs and wants of women in a family. He was never exposed to the orderliness, neatness, and regularity of housekeeping procedures so prized by the good housewife. He professed ignorance of the costs of permanents, sheer stockings, and household articles. To complicate matters even more, Jim had been reared to feel that the man should be the head of the house and control the purse strings.

Susan appears to have overlooked these differences between them during the engagement, and early marriage found her ill prepared to cope with the situation. Instead of forthrightly battling out the issues when Jim came late for meals or sometimes didn't eat at all, as had been his pattern in parental home, Susan adapted herself to her husband's unorthodox behavior. After the children arrived, it became increasingly difficult to manage financially with what Jim gave her.

Susan made no moves to battle for joint handling of the family finances. She held back the angry words with the intention of preserving harmony. Tensions built up in the financial area and, as so often happens, spilled over into the recreational area, and finally affected their sexual relations which heretofore had been mutually enjoyable.

Jim now admits to Susan's pastor, to whom she has appealed for help, that his marriage has gone sour. Yet he is baffled by it all: they have had only one or two serious squabbles after six years of marriage.

Six years is too long to go without a quarrel. There were basic differences here that begged attention before settling down to the routines of living. A good fight might have cleared the air, defined the issues, and ventilated the house of some of the unresolved tensions before they cracked the relationship. Conflict has a dual function: the solution of issues and the release of the resentment and tensions which arise in every relationship.

Withholding Circumscribes the Relationship

Consistently repressed tensions are hard on the relationship. They tend to circumscribe and narrow the topics of conversation in a marriage, and to delimit the areas of activity together. In the case of Jim and Susan, family entertainment, family finances, and sex relationships were rarely discussed because of the strain both felt when these matters came up. Tensions disturb the normal functioning of the family because they accumulate and spread and become associated with other areas of living.

The second area of married life in which conflict serves a useful purpose is in setting the boundaries of ego protection and ego involvement. There is a marked tendency in the ecstasy of the honeymoon and early months of marriage to establish a closeness of association which becomes burdensome, especially when erotic discoveries have ceased to suffuse the relationship with pleasure. Quarrels destroy these burdensome patterns and bring into being more tolerable customs. Where the early intimacy of marriage is not relaxed, it produces strain upon both and it rewards neither correspondingly — it is a sort of tax which makes everyone poor and enriches no one proportionately — and the conflicts which redefine this situation are therefore highly useful.

Married couples seek by experience to find the optimum nearness that they can tolerate. Like porcupines who approach one another for warmth yet are repelled by the other's barbs, the married couple must achieve that distance which is optimum for warmth without being too ego involving. Clearly this can be achieved only through conflict of a sort. Ultimately the couple must feel for themselves the reality of each other's emotional resistances and take the measure of each other's capacity for mutual accommodation.

Sometimes restrained discussion is advocated as a better alternative to quarreling. But the danger is that cold discussion arrives only at

"That's all I have to say on the subject, my dear.
The argument is closed."

an *intellectual* solution which fails to do justice to the *emotional* elements in the conflict.   If research and clinical evidence are valid, it is best that these emotional elements be expressed.   Marriage partners can come to terms on a basis of reality only when they have *felt* the heat of each other's hostile feelings.   A marriage should be organized to include the expression of both positive and negative emotions if it is to be a communicating and satisfying relationship.

Changing Feelings about Marital Conflict

In Chapter Twenty, "Marriage Isn't What It Used to Be," you will find discussed the liberation of the wife and child from the traditions of the patriarchal family and the transformation of the father from a dominating figure to a companionable partner in family life. Many of these remarkable changes have occurred in the past generation, but most people are not sufficiently out of the woods of transition with respect to freedom of discussion to accept discord and disharmony in marriage as evidence of growth. As participants in the transition we are uncertain about the desirability of quarreling, and many of us will feel conscience-stricken after "indulging," as we call it, in a marital spat. Let's draw the lines clearly between the two schools of thought and see the direction in which we seem to be heading.

First, let us look at the school of marriage whose traditions linger with us yet, the patriarchal system of thought which flowered in Puritan New England. Out of this period came our hundreds of maxims glorifying marital bliss, family harmony at all costs, and so on. It was an adult-centered world, in which children were to be seen and not heard, where the wife and mother was passive, patient, benign, and long-suffering. Peace and quiet in the home were evidence of the power and absolute authority of the father. Quarreling of any variety was evidence, on the other hand, of the breakdown of patriarchal authority and was to be quelled without delay. Writers and public speakers of the period supported the father in his position by repeating platitudes for the edification of children and their mothers. We use some of them today: "Forgive and forget," "Bear and forbear," "Let bygones be bygones," "Speak when spoken to," "God bless our happy home," "Home, sweet home," "Turn the other cheek," "A soft answer turneth away wrath."

The harmony of the patriarchal household was purchased at a high price in frustration and dulled sensibilities. Actually there existed much of what might be called covert conflict, deep resentment at the high-handedness of the authority which enforced harmony at such cost. It is probably safe to say that there has been less increase in marital conflict since Puritan days than one would suppose. The conflict has merely changed from covert, undercover resentment and discord to open conflict. Families in those days couldn't afford to waste their energies, they thought, fighting among themselves, and they attempted to bury the differences which cropped up within the family rather than air and settle them once and for all. It was important to preserve front both within the family and without. Indeed it was a matter of family pride and a mark of class to preserve harmony in the home.

We are burdened today with the vestiges of the self-righteous, sweetness-and-light mode of thinking. The hundreds of couples who come to marital guidance clinics regularly to gain relief from guilty feelings of unworthiness because they quarrel at home are living proof of this assertion. Moreover, the emergence of a democratic, person-centered family with its accent on the sacredness of personality has not cleared away the debris of broken patriarchal traditions. It will take a little time. Meantime, children in democratic homes will be given assurance that quarreling is not something to fear or condemn, but something to understand. Some of the guilt and unworthiness may be made to disappear with our generation!

The Mental Hygiene of Conflict

Mental hygiene, which was ushered in with the democratic, personality-oriented family, accepts a certain amount of overt conflict as normal. Much of the conflict merely indicates the presence of differences which occur as a couple explore new areas or attempt new tasks. Gradually the friction wears the protruding parts smooth, and a consensus is reached. Thereafter conflict is less likely to occur in that specific area, but it may and should bob up again and again as long as the family continues to meet new and different problems.

The modern couple will expect that in marriage they have a place of security and intimacy where they are free to behave like human beings with the normal variety of emotions. The workaday world, organized as it is, does not permit the frank expression of resentment, vanity, jealousy, and selfish ambition along with tenderness and love, all of which exist in the normal person. The individual must control his annoyances and his affections, he must often act like something more than human to get along in our complex industrial society. If he flies off the handle at his boss he may lose his job. There needs to be some place, however, where the individual can give vent to his annoyances and be himself, and that place seems to be in marriage. If there is that kind of cantankerousness in a marriage, the couple should chalk it down as proof that their marriage is performing one of its main functions — providing a place to let off steam and re-establish emotional balance. If a marriage is so fragile that it must be maintained by the same kind of artificial manners that keeps an office force functioning, it is pretty precariously based. One insightful authority has stated in positive terms,

"One of the functions of marriage is to weave a rope of relationship strong enough to hold each person at his worst."

As a couple enter marriage they face a number of adjustments, some of which are painful in the sense that it is painful to learn to ride a horse, to play a piano, or to develop any other complex skill. But new adjustments of marriage are more than learning new tasks: they also involve unlearning and revising old habits.

Many of the quarrels in marriage are helpful devices to dispel tensions engendered by unlearning of old habits and learning of new ones. Some arise out of the frustrations which the discipline of marriage exacts, and others arise quite naturally out of the unprepared-for intimacies of marriage. Much of conflict merely reflects the growing edges of a new relationship. It denotes growth and change rather than a passive acceptance of the new tasks on the part of either party. In the early stages much of the conflict consists of defining the issues and finding where the other stands on the many new problems they are facing.

Productive and Destructive Quarreling

Having taken the position that much of the conflict in marriage is normal and desirable, we must still distinguish between productive and destructive conflict. Destructive quarrels, to take one form of destructive conflict, are those which leave fewer assets in the relationship than it had before. Destructive quarreling is directed at the person and succeeds in destroying the illusions and fictions by which the person lives. It is a type of conflict which concentrates on the other's ego. It is of the belittling and punishing variety. Destructive quarrels lead to alienation as the love object is transformed into a hate object, and separation is thereby made possible. Destructive quarrels have at least one value. They succeed in sufficiently alienating incompatible couples so that engagements are broken, or if marriage has occurred, so that early divorce follows.

Productive quarrels may be differentiated by the fact that the marriage is made stronger through a redefinition of the situation causing the conflict. Productive quarreling is limited and directed at an issue, and it leads to a new and more complete understanding. Issues, problems, and conditions rather than the person himself tend to be the object of productive quarrels. Ideally, the quarrels tend to become fewer and less violent as the marriage progresses and basic routines and solutions to problems are established. The quarrel tends to become a discussion progressively delimited in the areas it covers.[1] Gradually the couple learn the techniques for handling conflict, so that for problem solving purposes at least it is not so violent nor so painful.

Another type of productive quarrel of the early years of marriage is that which relaxes the strain which builds up out of the unprepared-for intimacies of marriage. It gives the couple an opportunity and an excuse to desist from the intense honeymoon attachments and get a breath of air. Quarrels in the honeymoon and first year, moreover, serve to bring the parties face to face with the realities of their marriage. Some conflict helps to remove the blinders from their eyes and enables them to appreciate one another as persons rather than as imaginary incarnations of perfection. The reaction, "But you seemed so different, so much taller and romantic, when we were engaged . . . ," may bring pain of disillusionment but is a healthy experience. If romantic illusions have been built up it is a productive quarrel which brings the newlyweds down to earth. A husband can't live long in a rosy haze with an imaginary wife and remain mentally healthy.

One of the benefits of productive quarrels is that they reveal to the married couple how strong their relationship really is. Some men and women, deluded by the romantic notion that love must have left when monotony comes in, are surprised at the force of the love emotions which arise as a result of a quarrel. Quarreling thus helps to stabilize the marriage by reminding the couple, as they kiss and make up, of the depth of their love.

Dynamics of Conflict

What are the alternatives open to the couple who find themselves becoming panicky because of the frequency of their blow-ups? The more severe and deep-seated conflicts will require the attention of a competent psychiatrist. Quarreling which has departed from issues to concentrate on the person, which we have termed destructive conflict, becomes progressively severe after a few brutal truth sessions, and may be halted only by recourse to a highly skilled third party. Marital guid-

[1] Willard Waller and Reuben Hill, *The Family: A Dynamic Interpretation* (New York: Dryden Press, 1951), p. 310.

ance clinics accept just such cases, helping the couple accomplish, with the aid of the consultant, that which unaided they are unable to do for themselves.

CHECK YOURSELF   Which of the following excerpts from quarrels suggest destructive and which productive quarreling?

Destructive   Productive

_____   _____   1 "You aren't fit to be a mother, leaving the baby all week with strangers."

_____   _____   2 "Why didn't someone tell me marriage would be like this, cooking and ironing and scrubbing all day?"

_____   _____   3 "You will never amount to anything and neither will we as long as we depend on you to support us, you loafer."

_____   _____   4 "This is the last time I'm waiting for you for supper; after this you'll get your own or come on time."

_____   _____   5 "You aren't the man I married. What did I ever see in you? Oh, I could just die. . . ."

_____   _____   6 "You sit home all day reading or go out to some catty dames' bridge club and leave the house like a pig pen."

_____   _____   7 "Get a cookbook, sister, get a book and start studying. This is the last lousy meal I'm eating here, understand?"

_____   _____   8 "Darling, you must put on your rubbers. You aren't so young as you were."

★ KEY   7 '9 'ᔭ '乙 :ǝʌᴉʇɔnpoɹԀ   8 'ϛ 'Ɛ 'Ɩ :ǝʌᴉʇɔnɹʇsǝᗡ ★

Fortunately, not too many couples are burdened with conflicts which get so far out of hand. So much of conflict is normal and a part of living that it need not be the occasion for panic. The informed couple learn to recognize the source of their differences early and to relay to one another the message that excitement is brewing, without spoiling the fun by appearing too much in control of the situation. Let's look at the process a bit more in detail.

Most conflict situations find one party the aggressor and one the defendant. Married people need to know how to play both roles well to get the most out of the quarrel. They may have to change roles right in the middle to keep things moving to a satisfying climax in which tensions are fully released. There is sometimes what appears to be a bit of perverse interdependence, the aggressor needing the defendant, and after a while the defendant needing the aggressor, to carry the fight on. Both would feel cheated and disappointed if either party retired from the fray too soon.

The privilege of initiating the conflict is available to the party who develops the irritability first. He or she has a chip on the shoulder and is looking for trouble. The aggressor role includes, therefore, the insight to recognize in oneself feelings of malaise, uneasiness, or frustration and the willingness to do something about it. It includes the skill of identifying and forthrightly relaying to the partner the sore spots in one's make-up as they are touched in the sparring — "Ouch, that hurts." Obviously, it should also include the willingness to kiss and make up when the inner tension has subsided. Often the tension subsides without solving the problem which occasioned the outburst. But there is no hurry; the immediate need is to relieve the tension under which the aggressor seems to be operating. The original problem may lend itself to solution the next morning when things look rosier.

The marital sparring partner who plays the defendant role has a special responsibility. If the irritability of the aggressor seems due to hunger, sickness, fatigue, pregnancy, menstrual blues, or tensions aggravated by other physiological disfunction, the situation may call for listening it out, for reassurance and sympathy rather than active opposition. The person who has been emotionally wounded in his workaday contacts may need the same understanding and sympathy. Humiliations and personal defeats may be offset by the understanding interest of the partner. The partner needs to be sure of his ground, for there is nothing more infuriating to the person out to pick a fight than failure on the part of the defendant to respond to his aggressions. The need for response is all the keener in the person on an emotional spree.

In interpersonal relations much depends on the ability of the participants to anticipate the responses of the other. So much behavior consists of anticipated reactions that the skillful sparring partner must learn what the other expects and say, "He's asking for it; I'll give it to him." The sore spots alluded to above may sometimes be painful, and the partner may need to work around them in his verbal punching. For the wife to jeer at her husband's inability to make more money or to become president of the firm would be for most men a blow below the

belt, because she aims at the area over which he has least control. Likewise for a man to taunt his wife about her inability to have children
may be such a cruel jab that she will never quite recover. In time the
sparring partner learns to anticipate the hidden weaknesses and finds
where to aim his blows to get the maximum release of tension with a
minimum damage to the personality. This discussion may sound far-
fetched to the student who has had no occasion to think it through,
but every couple in conflict experience some of these reactions in some
degree. Some participants become very skillful in their battling and
recognize conflict for what it is, a tension-dispelling experience of real
value.

Stages of Conflict. Unless the newly married have had a background
of conflict in their respective parental families, they may be devastated
by their first quarrels. In time they will come to recognize that conflict
has a pattern and runs a course which is predictable. At least three
stages are discernible.

1 At the beginning of the battle, the first stage, there is often petulant irritability and jittery nagging on the part of the wife, if she is the aggressor.
If the husband is the aggressor, the symptoms of tension express themselves in emotionally toned growling, griping, and overcritical comments
on the sloppy house, the overdone steak, or the bill from the hairdresser.
The aggressor is readying himself to take out his accumulated frustrations
on the partner, who takes it just so long and then begins to fight back.
2 The second stage is often the battle royal itself. It consists of laying the
cards on the table, meeting accusation with accusation, arguing, cajoling,
wisecracking. The second stage may be relatively short, a matter of minutes in fact, and again it may last in relatively nonviolent form for hours
into the night, depending on the issues and the nature of the tensions
which occasioned the conflict originally.
3 The third stage begins as the aggressor recognizes a let-up in his inner tensions and as he communicates that fact to the other by offers of concilia-
tion and peace. The defendant may by this time have built up tensions
himself and may be unwilling to kiss and make up, which may prolong
the battle until both are relatively more relaxed. The participants often
find this stage the most difficult to bring about. Pride, hurt feelings, and
resentment hold over in unfinished conflicts, and although the battle may
be over the war never really ends. Covert conflict all too frequently continues after the overt battling has subsided. More skilled couples prefer
the third stage to any other, because it brings the release of tension and a
glorious feeling that the world is right and marriage is "swell." For these

couples conflict is not something to fear, but something to utilize in order to strengthen their relationship when tensions and misunderstandings arise.

Ways of Handling Conflict

Opposition in marriage is universal and normal, but skillful handling of marital conflict must be learned. The channels of communication between husband and wife can be kept open during conflict only if they each use gestures of acceptance of the other as they differ. In the old West there was a saying, "Smile when you say that, pardner; them's fighting words!" In marriage, opposition is less likely to arouse animosity if the partner prefaces his assertions with a family gesture of acceptance. Heat in an argument, and animosity directed against the person are joined in some conflicts, but they need not be threatening if the combatant is secure, knows he is loved, and that the love is not conditional, dependent upon his agreeing with the spouse.

There is real danger for those who have studied a little psychology, or a little psychiatry, and who attempt to apply the psychiatric labels to the partner under stress. It is rarely helpful, for instance, to say in the heat of the battle, "You are being hostile," or, "You are acting paranoid," or, "You are being regressive," and so on.

An obvious requirement for successfully handling conflicts in marriage is previous experience with conflict in one's parental family or with one's peers. There needs to be a deep held conviction that problems can be solved and that consensus is possible. A happy by-product of observation of successful quarreling in one's parental family is the absence of fear when conflict looms in later marriage. People who are afraid of combat are often the first to get hurt.

Proud should be the family which has reared its children to be tough-minded, invulnerable to the glancing blows of inept opponents. Thin-skinned, sensitive people find it difficult to focus on the problem, tend to take opposition personally so that it is difficult to carry through a productive conflict which sticks to issues.

There are still other ways of handling tensions than the forthright methods described above. In the film, *Who's Boss*, the husband warns his wife upon arrival that he has had a hard day and may prove irritable during the evening by *twirling his hat*, and his wife has a signal just as voiceless; she *wears her apron astern*. With this advance notice, the partner less fatigued can take some responsibility for providing a sounding board for the day's tensions. The wife may decide to "feed the beast" at least a snack, if supper is going to be late, knowing that hunger complicates any tensions which may have arisen. The husband may whisk the children out from under foot, knowing that preparing a hot meal requires supercoordination that demanding children can upset.

Some married partners who perceive conflict ahead attempt to battle out their tensions first on the wood pile, or with a golf club, or bowling. The wife may scrub the floors or pound Sibelius out on the piano. When they return to face each other the original conflict is probably still unresolved but they are better prepared to deal with it, now that the feelings of unpleasantness have subsided. This is a species of running away, to fight another day. But the problem is ultimately tackled!

Some individuals are teamed in marriage with partners unable to play any of these combatant roles. They are conflict shy, avoid trouble at all costs, and resort to substitutive activity to keep their marriage on an even keel. Daydreaming, rationalization, deprecation, martyrdom, illness, and idealization are some of the mechanisms employed to escape from the reality of the marriage. The conflict is handled by avoiding it, by the wife or husband becoming too ill to face it. Martyrdom is closely allied to illness as a way out of facing the conflict. The martyred partner glories in the hurts and troubles which afflict her (it may be the husband) and thus avoids the real basis for conflict. Not uncommon in workaday America is the man (or woman) who escapes the pain of discordant marriage by plunging into work and spending all his time at it. The daydreamer manages, on the other hand, to forget marriage entirely, or sufficiently so not to be bothered about real life situations. In fantasy she creates a substitute husband who is kinder and more romantic than the real one. Rationalization, deprecation, and idealization are all mental mechanisms which enable the person to make the best of an unsatisfactory situation without really facing it squarely. We say, "Other people are worse off than we," or "I don't think I deserve anything better; after all I'm just a working man," or "She's a good mother for the children." [2] The obvious difficulty with these substitutive adjustments is that they tend to mask the real issues. Even though

[2] One of the most exhaustive treatises of marital conflict and the mechanisms used to displace conflict is Harriet R. Mowrer, *Personality Adjustment and Domestic Discord* (New York: American Book Company, 1935).

they start as temporary expedients in the trial and error adjustments of early marriage, the marriage structure may be based permanently on a substitutive basis.

Marital Counseling as a Means of Meeting Progressive Conflict

Marital counseling services are available in a number of large cities for couples whose marriage conflicts prove too much for them. The case of Charles and Edna demonstrates the possibilities of professional counseling services for cases of progressive domestic discord.

Charlie is a young physician just getting a good start in building up a practice in a small Midwestern city. Three years ago he married Edna, who sang in the choir of the Methodist church. In their courtship and engagement period they did all the things young lovers do, from discussing the kind of furniture they liked to the number of children they would have. Their marriage has been a happy one on the whole. Their year-and-a-half-old son is a darling whom they both adore. The practice is building up so well that they are making regular payments on a little bungalow at the edge of town. Everything should be wonderful. They love each other, have their little home, their baby, and the promise of the kind of future they both have looked forward to all their lives. The one problem that has disturbed them both greatly has been their frequent and heated quarreling. Spats seemed to start up over nothing. But once they were started Edna found herself getting so mad she just couldn't contain herself, while Charlie shut up like a clam, and after he had stood just so much slammed out of the door, not to return for several hours. Edna felt that if Charlie loved her, he would be willing to stay and talk it out and make some rules so that they wouldn't fight over the same thing again. He felt that she was being unreasonable most of the time and that she should be able to control her temper better. The situation became so acute that several months ago they went to see their minister about it. He was an up-and-coming young pastor with a good training in helping people out of trouble, and after listening to both sides of the case, suggested that they go to the not too distant city and visit the marriage and family counseling agency here. He told the couple what they might expect from such a service and said that he was suggesting that they go to such a center in much the same way as he would recommend a good hospital or doctor if some troublesome physical difficulty didn't respond to home remedies.

Two week ends later the couple were found chatting pleasantly with the counselor. She assured them that she wasn't going to pry into anything that either of them didn't want to tell her, but that sometimes it helped to talk out bothersome problems with a person who was not tied up emotionally in the situation. She helped them both to see that she was not a Mrs. Ellery Queen who could unravel human mysteries in the first twenty minutes, but that her training might help her to suggest to both of them just where to look for the real reasons for their trouble. The counselor indicated that by working together, some suggestions for meeting the situation might emerge. The couple seemed relieved to find that the counselor was not assuming a know-it-all attitude and that she seemed to be the sort of friendly person who could be trusted to like you, whatever you told her. She looked as if she would hear your story without being shocked or making too much of it.

Each described the situation as he saw it. The wife got so excited as she relived the last quarrel that she started to cry. Then feeling better, she leaned toward the counselor, saying earnestly, "You see how much this matters to me. If only we could get to the bottom of it all, I'd be the happiest girl alive." She was encouraged by the counselor's reflection that it was just that motivation to do something about it that was the most important step toward an effective solution.

After several individual interviews and a simple personality study of each, the couple came in again for a joint conference. At that time they were each helped to share with the other the insights they had gained concerning their problems and to look at them together. It was slow going the first time, a new way of approaching the problem for both of them. By the third and fourth session with the counselor they were much more at ease, and had begun to talk in terms of what they would do now that they were returning home.

Within three months they were both more comfortable with the whole idea of their quarreling, and neither of them became panicky when one started. As time went on, the quarrels grew less frequent and lasted for shorter periods. Each developed some understanding of what it was in their early experiences which made them feel so differently when a conflict situation emerged. Both began to develop some skill in handling themselves and in understanding the other when the fur

"Oh, it's nothing to worry about. Every marriage requires
an adjustment period."

began to bristle. Of course they still squabble, and they probably always will. But they can take it now, and are comforted by the recognition that there is less of it to have to take.

The baby sister who recently arrived has added to their sense of being a family, and to the growing satisfactions of their life together. As young Doc put it himself, "No one could have told me a year ago that marriage could be like this. Why, with all the education I had, I never had the foggiest idea that you could be as scientific about your feelings as you can about a tonsillectomy. I want some books to read. This has all been an eye opener to me."

Yes, it's an eye opener to many folks. Listening to the Mr. Agonys on the radio and reading the lovelorn columns in the daily papers give many people the idea that asking for help on a personal or family tangle is childish. Many are afraid that the problem will be taken out of their hands and that they will be told what to do without having a part in the decision. Others are skeptical about the type of person who acts as a counselor. Still others hesitate to tell their personal problems to a stranger who may not keep their confidences. All of these fears and reluctances are perfectly justified. There is a certain sanctity about our emotional and married lives; we don't want things spread all over town. It is this respect for the persons and for their confidences that is characteristic of a good counseling service and of a well-trained counselor. This is the big difference between the shoddy quackery that we are all afraid of and the reliable, modest, helpful counseling service which is becoming more widely available.

Criteria for judging a good counseling service are fairly simple to enumerate. Briefly summarized they are as follows:

A GOOD MARRIAGE COUNSELING SERVICE

1 Doesn't promise quick results or make snap judgments.
2 Doesn't diagnose until after a careful study has been made.
3 Keeps all information confidential.
4 May charge nominal fees which are frankly discussed.
5 May call in other trained specialists to help.
6 Uses only trained professional workers from reputable colleges specializing in such fields as social work, human development, psychiatry, and related areas. (At least a master's degree in the specialized area is the usual professional standard.)
7 Is affiliated with such reliable bodies as local councils of social agencies, and nationally with such professional organizations as the National Conference of Social Work, and the National Council on Family Relations.
8 Does not advertise or try to drum up business, relying instead on slowly building up a clientele of satisfied users through referrals from other agencies and professional persons.
9 May have a membership and a board of directors of reliable citizens who take the responsibility for supporting and interpreting the program to the community.

What, then, have we said about marital conflict? First, much conflict is normal. It performs a valuable function in maintaining emotional balance through the release of tensions accumulated in a workaday world. Second, much of conflict in early marriage is understandable as the outcome of merging two different sets of family habits into a new pattern — a painful process which is speeded up by overt conflict and definition of the issues. This type of conflict tends to be progressively delimiting in the area it covers as the marriage continues and

serves a valuable problem solving function. Third, in distinguishing between productive and destructive quarreling, the former was shown to
be limited, and directed at issues, problems, and conditions rather than
at the person. Destructive quarreling concentrates on the ego of the
participants and destroys the fundamentals on which the marriage is
based.

In line with the newer thinking concerning the nature of personality
needs, this chapter has advocated more honesty in the husband and
wife relationship. This involves facing issues squarely and mastering the arts of conflict in rough and tumble discussion. It is not so much
the conflict in marriage which is to be deplored as the inability to face
the issues and battle them through. Conflict has a dual function: the
solution of issues, and the release of the resentment and tensions which
arise in every relationship.

Every couple needs to learn the techniques of handling conflict situations. Thousands of informed, mature married couples are reporting
the feasibility of the approaches to conflict described in this chapter.
To aid others less fortunately endowed, the inexperienced, the immature, and the progressively discordant couples who are unable to handle
the complexities of normal conflict in marriage, there are fortunately an
increasing number of reputable marital counseling agencies close at
hand.

Selected Readings

DEARDORF, NEVA R., "A Puzzle in Cross Words," *Survey*, Vol. 49, pp. 288–
    290.
FOLSOM, JOSEPH K., *The Family in Democratic Society* (New York: Wiley,
    1943), Chap. 13, "Marriage Interaction."
HILL, REUBEN, "Quarreling Comes into Its Own." *Parents' Magazine* (Sep-
    tember, 1946), pp. 24 ff.
LEVY, JOHN, AND MUNROE, RUTH, *The Happy Family* (New York: Knopf,
    1938), Chap. 5, "Living Together."
MAGOUN, F. ALEXANDER, *Love and Marriage* (New York: Harper, 1948),
    Chap. 10, "Emotional Adjustment."
MOWRER, HARRIET, "Discords in Marriage," in Becker, Howard, and Hill,
    Reuben, eds., *Family, Marriage, and Parenthood* (Boston: Heath, 1948),
    Chap. 12.
NIMKOFF, MEYER, *Marriage and the Family* (Boston: Houghton Mifflin,
    1947), Chap. 15, "Marital Adjustment."
TRAVIS, LEE E., AND BARUCH, DOROTHY W., *Personal Problems of Everyday
    Life* (New York: Appleton-Century, 1941), chaps. 13–14.

WALLER, WILLARD, AND HILL, REUBEN, *The Family: A Dynamic Interpretation* (New York: Dryden Press, 1951), chaps. 14–15.

Technical References

BERKOWITZ, SIDNEY J., "An Approach to the Treatment of Marital Discord," *Journal of Social Casework*, Vol. 29 (November, 1948), pp. 355 ff.

BURGESS, ERNEST W., AND LOCKE, HARVEY J., *The Family: From Institution to Companionship* (New York: American Book, 1945), Chap. 18.

CUBER, JOHN F., *Marriage Counseling Practice* (New York: Appleton, 1948).

FRAZIER, E. FRANKLIN, "Certain Aspects of Conflict in the Negro Family," *Social Forces*, Vol. 10, pp. 76–84.

GLUECK, BERNARD, "Some of the Sources of Marital Discontent," *The Family*, Vol. 16 (March, 1935), pp. 3 ff.

HOLLIS, FLORENCE, *Women in Marital Conflict* (New York: Family Service Association of America, 1949).

JUNG, MOSES, *Modern Marriage* (New York: Crofts, 1940), Chap. 4.

KARLSSON, GEORG, *Adaptability and Communication in Marriage* (Upsala, Sweden: Upsala Sociological Institute, 1951).

KEYSERLING, HERMANN, "The Correct Statement of the Marriage Problem," *The Book of Marriage* (New York: Harcourt, Brace, 1926).

KIRKPATRICK, CLIFFORD, "Techniques of Marital Adjustment," *The Annals* (March, 1932), pp. 179 ff.

KRUEGER, E. T., "A Study of Marriage Incompatibility," *Family*, Vol. 9 (1928), pp. 53–60.

MUDD, EMILY H., *The Practice of Marriage Counseling* (New York: Association Press, 1951).

CHAPTER THIRTEEN

"I've got some money saved from my
newspaper route we can use, Dad."

WHEN CRISES COME

Does sudden poverty make or break a family?

Is desertion a poor man's divorce?

What is meant by "death education"?

What is the immediate reaction to death of a loved one?

How can you handle the case of the "other woman"?

What are the marks of recovery from a family crisis?

*T*O FIND YOURSELF BROKE WITH A FAMILY TO SUPPORT AND NO JOB in sight is tough; to take the death of a family member in stride is more difficult still; to adjust to the faithlessness of husband or wife requires insight and understanding; and to face possible desertion or divorce is beyond the powers of most young people. Yet these are the crises virtually all families face at some time. Death, the crisis least talked about of all, will normally hit the average family not once but several times. Sudden poverty hovers constantly over all but the wealthiest of families under an industrial economy which has produced cycles of inflation, depressions, and widespread unemployment every five years since 1790. These are hard blows to take but they are part of living — families must be prepared not so much to avoid them as to regard them as challenges. Indeed, there is no avoiding trouble if you want to have the satisfactions of living in a real world. The question which should be raised is not, "How can I avoid family crises?" but, "How can I learn to take them?"

The first step in learning to take trouble in stride is to realize that other people the world over are facing similar problems — not, "Why does all this have to happen to us?" but, "I guess we're having our turn now." Another step in learning to take it is to recognize the normality of problems and conflict. Much of the anguish which follows a crisis arises from the shock of the unexpected and the fear that no recovery is possible. The shock of the blow is easier to absorb if one is relaxed and unafraid of the pain which is bound to follow. Some families are so well prepared for trouble they grow under it. Their preparation for crises began back in courtship and early marriage, and even before.

In the early years of marriage the husband-wife relation stabilizes, with each taking roles with prescribed duties, many of which continue after children arrive. Later, with the children, the family heads work out solutions to the problems of daily living. Members learn the answers to most questions, and they express it neatly — "This is the way we do it at our house," or, "I was brought up to think this way." Conflicts are settled and decisions made regarding vacations, birthday parties, and school difficulties. Well-organized families have the resources for meeting these problems without too much distress and readjustment.

When the family meets a situation for which there is no ready solution from past experience and no immediate answer forthcoming from family members, then the family is said to face a *crisis*. Sudden poverty, infidelity, divorce, desertion, and bereavement are good examples of disruptions which throw most families into temporary confusion. Some families may be permanently disabled, particularly if the remaining members are unable to absorb the duties of the persons incapacitated by the crisis. Other families are drawn closer together by the threat to their unity and survive the crisis stronger than ever.[1]

We have selected for discussion in this chapter crises that produce both demoralization (loss of morale and family unity) and dismemberment (loss of family member): sudden impoverishment, infidelity, desertion, and bereavement. Divorce will be discussed in some detail in the next chapter. The variety of family breakdowns is large and worthy of our attention as we enter the discussion of family crises.

What conditions must a family maintain to withstand the buffeting of circumstances in this turbulent country of ours? The family mem-

---

[1] It appears that middle-class families may have more troubles but weather them more successfully than working class families according to Earl L. Koos, "Class Differences in Family Reactions to Crises," *Marriage and Family Living* (Summer, 1950), pp. 77–78.

A CLASSIFICATION OF FAMILY BREAKDOWNS [2]

Dismemberment only	Loss of child
	Loss of spouse
	Orphanhood
	Hospitalization
	War separation
Demoralization only	Nonsupport
	Progressive dissension
	Infidelity
	Sense of disgrace — reputation loss
Accession only	Unwanted pregnancy
	Deserter returns
	Stepmother, stepfather additions
	Some war reunions
	Some adoptions
Demoralization plus	Illegitimacy
dismemberment or	Runaway situations
accession	Desertion
	Divorce
	Imprisonment
	Suicide or homicide

bers must be physically fit and healthy; they must have adequate mental resources to cope with complexities and unpredictables; they must be adaptable and flexible; they must have achieved a workable adjustment to one another as members of a group and must be proud of their family membership; and they need to have an income from some source adequate to maintain a normal standard of living. In addition, to remain healthy, the family needs the support of neighbors and friends and of community agencies like the church and the school. Lacking any of these attributes, a family may muddle through for a period of years without breaking up. But in the face of a crippling crisis such a family will become badly disorganized, and dismemberment or demoralization will take place.

[2] Expanded by Reuben Hill in *Families under Stress* (New York: Harper, 1949), p. 10, from a classification originally suggested by Thomas D. Eliot, "Handling Family Strains and Shocks," in Howard Becker and Reuben Hill (eds.), *Family, Marriage, and Parenthood* (Boston: Heath, 1948), p. 617, n.

Down on Your Luck

Sudden impoverishment is one of the crises which has been studied most completely, and there is considerable agreement concerning its effects on the family. One of the surprising findings from the depression of 1929–36 was the ability of many families to absorb the shock of impoverishment without demoralization or great personal disorganization.[3] The reactions of the family when the breadwinner is laid off and the income ceases must be seen against the backdrop of associations within the family and the family's earlier reactions to crises. As children are added to the family, methods of adjustment develop and become habitual. Father traditionally earns the money and spends most of his day away from home. Mother runs the domestic end of the household, supplying services and supervision of the children, who are primarily consumers with minimum responsibilities and who are accustomed to depend on parents for the satisfaction of their major wants. There comes a crash on the market — people are thrown out of work. The loss of father's job and the subsequent loss of income disrupt this habitual arrangement. It leaves father with time on his hands at home, exercising unaccustomed supervision of children, and it places other members of the family in situations for which they have no accustomed responses.

One of the best descriptions of the nature of the crisis of impoverishment is drawn from a study of one hundred Chicago families:

The development of a crisis often involves disorganization, that is, a breakdown in the organization of the family or person. The depression, as a crisis, may effect wide-spread disorganization, for the influence of the economic aspect of the family is so pervasive that lowered income may affect every realm of family life. The family may have to abandon certain objectives, such as buying a home or educating the children: it may be unable to conform to certain social and community standards in which it has always taken pride, such as the prompt payment of rent and bills or the maintenance of a certain type of home: it may be disturbed by the shifting of the dominant role, perhaps from the father to the mother or to a son or daughter. Not only is the family organization shaken, but the members of the family most affected also may become personally disorganized over the loss of accustomed activities, a lowering of status, or a failure to meet responsi-

[3] Ruth S. Cavan and Katherine H. Ranck, *The Family and the Depression* (Chicago: University of Chicago Press, 1938), pp. viii–ix.

bilities. This disorganization may be evidenced by worry, nervous break-downs, excessive fears, or demoralization.

A crisis and the disorganization that accompanies it are highly charged with emotion, a reaction to be expected when habits become ineffective and new modes of response must be found and adopted. In the case of the depression the emotion tends to be fear — fear of loss of status, of loss of money reserves, of failure to have needed food and clothing, of the necessity to go on relief. When re-employment is not found, worry, discouragement, and depression follow. Some people become resentful or angry, but most of them are simply afraid of a moneyless existence for which they have no habitual conduct and no philosophy. For many people the condition of unemployment continues over many months, even over several years. It is almost impossible, however, for a highly charged emotional state to continue over a long period of time. Therefore, the period of unemployment cannot be considered as a static period. The situation, as it appears during the first shock of unemployment, is not the situation as it would be described six months or a year later. The unemployment may still exist, the income may still be low: but the experience of a person who has been unemployed for a year is not the experience of a person who has just been told that he has no job. At some point the disorganization reaches a climax and the extreme tension lessens. This turning point is psychological; it may not coincide with the time at which employment is lost. Self-confidence and financial resources may postpone the peak of the crisis until an indefinite number of months after the time when unemployment begins. Perhaps the disorganization may be said to culminate when the family accepts the fact that it can no longer continue its old mode of life, when it admits that it can no longer control the situation by its old procedures. Such a realization usually brings with it severe emotional reactions which have perhaps been manifesting themselves in minor form during the period when the disorganization was developing. This period of acute emotional stress is usually terminated either by an adjustment to the situation or by the development of pathological reactions. If an adjustment to the new circumstances occurs, new roles are assigned, new functions defined, a new status accepted. This adjustment may take the same form as the old family organization, so that after the period of disorganization the old roles, functions, and status are readily resumed; or the adjustment may involve roles of a lower status, curtailed functions, and lowered community status. In the case of a break or failure to adjust, the family may disintegrate through separation of its members or the person may escape through mental illness or suicide. In any case, there is a tendency for the period of extreme disorganization to reach an end, either through reorganization or disintegration of the group or personality.

. . . another factor must be considered: the habitual ways in which families and members of families have met earlier changes and crises. A crisis, because it sweeps away the customary ways of living, tends to expose the resources or deficiencies of the family or person. The family that, in the past, has faced a difficult situation squarely, evaluated it, and made adjustments to it may be expected to react in this way to the depression, even though there may be an initial period of disorganization. The family that, in the past, has refused to face issues or has evaded difficult situations may be expected to evade facing the changes in family life brought by unemployment or decreased income. It seems clear from the present study that only rarely did the crisis cause the development of any totally new reactions. Rather, the crisis caused an exaggeration of previously existing family and personal habits. The man who occasionally drank began to drink to excess. The family that was harmoniously organized became more unified and the members more loyal. Reactions to the depression therefore cannot be stated categorically; the depression as a family and personal crisis must be viewed in the light of previous methods of meeting difficulties used by the family or its members.[4]

Although no studies have yet been published on the subject, it would not be surprising to find that the impact of rapid fluctuations of income upward in war-boom prosperity days was fully as disorganizing for some families as the sudden impoverishment experienced by millions in the depression of 1929–36. In both instances the family is faced with a disruptive occurrence in which the old customs of the group and the old attitudes and habits of the family members are no longer consistent with the new situation brought about by the crisis.

Desertion: A Breather from Marriage

Closely allied with impoverishment and internal dissension is the crisis of desertion, which afflicts approximately 300,000 families a year.[5] It has been sometimes called the "poor man's divorce," because it occurs so frequently among the economically impoverished. As a forerunner of divorce, desertion is also relatively common in the upper classes. Still it is not divorce, because it has no legal status whatsoever. "It is the ruthless and lawless evasion of responsibilities, whereas divorce is at

[4] Cavan and Ranck, op. cit., pp. 5–8.
[5] Jacob T. Zukerman estimates one million women and children are today the victims of family desertion; see his discussion, "A Socio-Legal Approach to Family Desertion," Marriage and Family Living (Summer, 1950), p. 83. As of June, 1949, roughly 50 per cent of the 536,714 families receiving federal-state support under the Aid to Dependent Children program were those in which father was absent from the home and not supporting the children.

least legal and recourse to it is playing the game in the open, by the rules."[6] It differs from separation in that the latter includes some arrangement, voluntary or compulsory, for support of the deserted.

Of all the crises, desertion is the most devastating on the morale of the family because of the difficulty in bringing about any program of stabilization. Reorganization of the family around the remaining members may be postponed indefinitely pending the return of the deserter. Realistic solutions are rejected in favor of wishful hope or cowering fear, depending on the attitudes toward the absent one. Moreover, if the deserter does return there is always the fear, or hope, that he may abandon the family again in the face of difficulty. Desertion represents an escape of a sort, not unlike drinking or neurotic illness, which is conveniently used by the offender both as a club or power device to control the family and as a means of release when family responsibilities become too confining.

Men desert in significantly larger numbers than women. It is considered socially much more criminal for mothers to desert their children than for fathers to do so. The desertion in many cases appears to be timed to avoid the economic responsibilities which pyramid as new dependents are added to the family. Social agencies report periodic desertion of husbands just before the birth of a new baby. The men sometimes return when the agency has paid the bills and the economic situation is stabilized. It is rare that a case can be so simply explained. Indeed, in most cases there exist in the family before desertion bitter dissension and deep emotional tensions.[7] The immediate economic pressures aggravate a situation which is already tense and which may precipitate action causing the man to flee. Because the deserter so often returns, desertion has been called a vacation from marriage, a "breather," during which each party has the chance to think the matter over.[8]

Although desertion may be the solution to a personal problem for the deserter, it leaves all the complications of a family crisis in its wake. The family members, after the first desertion at least, are unable to find

[6] Ray E. Baber, *Marriage and the Family* (New York: McGraw-Hill, 1939), p. 481.
[7] Almost 70 per cent of desertions studied in 1949 by Zuckerman occurred in the first ten years of marriage, *op. cit.*, p. 84.
[8] Ruth S. Cavan, *The Family* (New York: Crowell, 1942), p. 287.

any ready-made solution to their difficulties. Added to the economic embarrassment occasioned by loss of support is the threat to family pride and to family integrity. The children feel a psychological let-down and will interpret the father's departure as rejection, particularly if they loved him. The mother may rightly interpret it as a reflection on her personal attractiveness. The seeds for demoralization are sown with every member of the family. The deserted family is ripe for disorganization, and is often unable to bring about a reorganization because of the refusal to admit that the situation is permanent. Thousands eke out a living at a submarginal level for several weeks or months or years before reporting to a welfare agency, hoping against hope that a reunion will be possible to restore things as they were.

Infidelity

One of the least understood yet most discussed crises in family life is marital infidelity. Like desertion it represents a solution of a personal problem for one member while creating a family crisis for the others.

Few crises are filled with more insecurity and sense of loss in a marriage than that involved when "the other woman" or her male counterpart breaks the sense of unity so important to marital solidarity. The fear of faithlessness haunts many married people and is especially understandable when the members of a pair are separated for long periods of time. The triangle rarely fits into a family circle. Even when popular opinion tended to be lenient in allowing a man to sow his wild oats, to have his fling, to go gaily through his dangerous forties and his treacherous fifties, his "poor little wife" was pitied as deeply as though she had been bereaved. Friends and neighbors watched to see how she was taking it. Her loss was accentuated by a keen sense of inadequacy and shame, for hadn't she failed to hold her man?

With the explosion of the myth that "men are built that way," constancy has tended to be more widely expected of husbands. But the emancipation of women has been misinterpreted by some wives as license and has made infidelity a double-edged sword that cuts both ways. Acceptance of woman's new freedom requires a whole new definition of our sex mores so that free interchange between people of both sexes may be possible socially, industrially, professionally, politically, intellectually, and financially without threatening the unique emotional sphere of the marriage relationship. This transition involves redefining what is "right" and what is "wrong" in many areas of common experience.

The check test below will enable you to test the findings discussed in Chapter Seven, "Does Morality Make Sense?" Grandfather would

---

CHECK YOURSELF   Try out your own feelings about the following situations by checking *all right, it depends, questionable,* or *wrong* the conduct of the key person in the situation.

ALL   IT
RIGHT   DEPENDS

——— ———

QUES-
TIONABLE   WRONG

——— ———

1 A *married secretary* works late to get out some important letters for her boss. He sends out for sandwiches which they eat together at her desk. No one else is in the office at the time except the cleaning woman.

ALL   IT
RIGHT   DEPENDS

——— ———

QUES-
TIONABLE   WRONG

——— ———

2 A *married woman doctor* spends one night a week at a clinic in a poor section of town. It has been customary for some time for one of her colleagues (a married man physician) to drive her home when they are both through at the clinic.

ALL   IT
RIGHT   DEPENDS

——— ———

QUES-
TIONABLE   WRONG

——— ———

3 A *woman* whose husband spends weeks at a time in Washington on business has taken in an older man war worker as a roomer. No one else lives in the home except her year-old child.

ALL   IT
RIGHT   DEPENDS

——— ———

QUES-
TIONABLE   WRONG

——— ———

4 A *married enlisted man* who hasn't been home in over a year is stationed near an urban servicemen's center. He has become acquainted with a hostess there, whose apartment he visited for dinner recently.

ALL   IT
RIGHT   DEPENDS

——— ———

QUES-
TIONABLE   WRONG

——— ———

5 A *woman* whose husband is overseas met one of his old friends recently while lunching downtown. He accepted her invitation to stay and have lunch with her as they talked of her husband's work and interest. As he left her at the conclusion of the luncheon, he invited her to come out and see his family soon.

ALL RIGHT	IT DEPENDS
QUES-TIONABLE	WRONG

6 A *man and a woman* (both married but not to each other) have jobs as inspectors that involve their traveling together a great deal by car. Frequently they are gone from home for days at a time. When away from home, they stay in hotels near the plant they are visiting. She registers under her own married name and occupies a separate room.

ALL RIGHT	IT DEPENDS
QUES-TIONABLE	WRONG

7 A *singer* whose home is in Connecticut must spend two or three nights a week in town at her work. It is often necessary for her to work with her agent (a married man) and her accompanist (an attractive young bachelor) at her New York apartment in the evening. It is not always possible for her husband to be present on the nights she must remain in town.

ALL RIGHT	IT DEPENDS
QUES-TIONABLE	WRONG

8 A *farmer's wife* is alone with the hired man in the house every Saturday night while her husband takes stock to market (an all night job).

ALL RIGHT	IT DEPENDS
QUES-TIONABLE	WRONG

9 An unusually talented nurse is unable to continue her professional work now that she is married because *her husband* does not trust her with "all those good-looking young doctors."

ALL RIGHT	IT DEPENDS
QUES-TIONABLE	WRONG

10 A *woman* whose husband handles legal cases for a large feminine clientele insists that there always be a third person present when her husband is on a case. She threatens to divorce him if she ever finds that he has been with a woman alone anywhere at any time.

---

undoubtedly check more of the situations as "questionable" or "wrong" than would members of our generation. The customs on which our codes of morality are based require a liberal use of insight into the consequences of behavior before applying them to specific situations like those above. Loyalty and fidelity are unusually hard to define in a world of changing values. Using the aids already given in the aforementioned chapter, however, one should be able to work out satisfactory answers to questions of marital fidelity.

If we interpret fidelity narrowly, as many people do, to make the appearance of evil equivalent to the thing itself, any situation which looks as though it might be compromising would be interpreted as infidelity. Chaperons were provided to supply complete surveillance in the dim past when infidelity was suspected in any situation in which extramarital sex experience might take place. Again, if we were to brand as evidence of infidelity all expressions of affection for anyone other than the spouse, we should also run into a dilemma. The normal person becomes genuinely fond of a great many friends and associates of both sexes. Is a person faithless who feels genuine affection for many fine people?

When we interpret loyalty, however, as mutual trust in each other and as faith in the marriage itself, neither the detective role called forth by the first definition nor the uncertainty inspired by the second is involved. The blow falls only if we find that our faith and trust have not been justified. It is only then that a crisis is said to occur. There is no crisis if there is no problem, or if the family members are equipped to meet whatever problem arises with their present resources.

Why, Then, Faithlessness? Infidelity may almost always be seen as a symptom of unmet affectional need. The nature of the unmet need varies from couple to couple. Infidelity on the part of the husband may be an attempt to prove his manliness, or it may be a revolt against his conscience,[9] or again a method of working out little-understood impulses stemming from childhood experiences. The other woman may represent a refuge from an overprotecting wife, or she may be a means of attacking the wife. Extramarital affairs grow out of the same attraction a forbidden piece of candy has for a hungry, undisciplined child — further proof of the importance of emotional maturity in marriage. Monogamous marriage requires that the participants be sufficiently mature to find in their relationship the satisfaction of their basic needs.

The Crisis of Infidelity. The act of infidelity by itself may be relatively unimportant to the stability of the marriage. It is the interpretation of the infidelity which the couple make that introduces panic into the relation; what the participants see as the motive behind the defection is

9 See the discussion of "How Conscience Develops," pp. 135–137.

more important than the act itself. To some couples the slightest flirtation may prove calamitous, because it symbolizes much more than that to them. Others may tolerate without anxiety considerable swapping of partners and promiscuity in relations. A complicating factor in the interpretation of flirtations and unorthodox behavior with others is the health of the spouse. When he is bedridden, a man eyes his wife's recreational activities much more narrowly than when he is on his feet. Pregnant women are frequently suspectible to jealousy and read infidelity into situations where none exists. Jealousy is the product of insecurity and fear — the anxiety produced when one senses the possible loss of a love object. Unfortunately for the aggrieved person, jealousy may drive the mate into acts of infidelity which originally he may not have intended.

What to Do? Meeting the crisis of infidelity with the necessary understanding leads couples so threatened to marriage counselors and similar professional advisers. A good counselor can relieve the pain of the moment and can often deal with the underlying causes of the infidelity, the unmet needs and frustrations of the couple. Seeing infidelity as a symptom needing treatment is a more scientific answer to the question of what shall be done about it than has heretofore been given. Such a patient platitude as "give and forgive," or the self-righteous assumption that evidence of infidelity should always be promptly punished with separation and divorce, fails to meet the issues and introduces no satisfactory readjustment or reorganization to the marriage. Even when the other affair has gone so far that the salvage of the marriage is impossible, the abandoned mate may be helped by counseling to understand what has happened so that his or her resources may be mobilized for building life stronger from then on.

Death as a Family Crisis

As it must come to every man. . . .

Of all the crises which afflict a family none is more sure to occur and none receives less advance preparation than death. Its discussion is discouraged in our society, and anyone who mentions seriously the possibility of death entering his family is shunned as a bit morbid. Death as a subject of conversation is almost as taboo today as was sex fifty years ago. Today we prepare our children for the shock of the birth of a brother or sister, for the newness of the first day at school, and, in the case of a girl, for her first menstruation, but to prepare children for death in the family is almost unheard of. There is no program of death education to cushion the shock of this universal crisis. Not only children, but adults as well, are shielded from the realities — mothers are not told when their children are dying — patients afflicted fatally are not prepared for the event that is a certainty.[10] Until recently it was bad taste for picture magazines to show pictures of actual battle dead. In sum, there is virtually no preparation for the emotional shock that accompanies the death of a dear one. For that reason death is frequently a personal as well as a family crisis.

The importance of death as a personal crisis lies not primarily in the fact of dying or ceasing to exist biologically, but in the emotional shock which follows the break in the unity of the family. Two things happen to the member who is closely identified with his family: 1. he senses that the circle is broken and that the family is threatened with dissolution (What will ever happen to us, now that mother has gone?); 2. he senses that a part of himself as a person has been cut off, amputated, so to speak. The closer the identification with the deceased, the more distressing is the sense of personal loss.

The Shock Varies. The situation is eased considerably for family members who have left the parental home and have established families of their own. The emotional dependence which existed before their departure from their childhood home has been replaced by relative independence, and the sense of loss is diminished accordingly. The passing away of relatives, even brothers and sisters, brings less grief than the loss of parents with whom one is emotionally more closely identified. To make one further comparison, it might be safe to say that the mature independent adult normally senses greater pangs of grief at the loss of husband or wife or child than at the loss of a parent from whom he has won independence.

In general, death following a long-drawn-out illness brings less shock than sudden death for which no preparation can be made. Much of the mourning occurs in the period of illness as the relatives vacillate between acceptance of the loss of the loved one and wishful thinking that a cure can be found. Gradually, as the medical evidence piles up, the

10 Cavan, *The Family*, p. 317.

negative prognosis is accepted, and the parties assimilate the idea of permanently losing the afflicted one. As accommodation to the idea of losing part of one's self takes place, the afflicted one becomes an object of pity rather than a symbol of personal loss. It is at that point that the expression may be heard, "I hope his suffering will soon be over."

In time of war, bereavement is lightened to some extent by the public recognition achieved and by the realization that others face equal or worse crises. Although the hole that any one person leaves can never be completely filled, there is less of a break in family unity, because the other members have already made some adjustment to the absence of the member at the time he entered the armed services. The shock is lessened by the presence of neighbors and friends who offer understanding and genuine comfort. Moreover, death in wartime is given purpose and made meaningful both at home and in the war zones. In their adjustment, family members plunge into the common task with renewed determination to bring to fulfillment the goals for which *he* died.

On the other hand, bereavement in time of war is the less bearable because the victims are taken in the prime of life. The uncertainty of death in a "missing in action" notice leads family members to disbelieve later notices of death. For some people, only the rites of death serve as corroborators of fact, and the overseas death is hard to realize. When the body is not in evidence, it is easier to convert grief into disbelief.[11]

To the person away from home who loses a member of his family the bereavement may be very difficult. He may feel for a time that the bottom has fallen out of life. He will miss the relief which comes in joining with relatives and friends in mourning. He finds that a part of himself as a person may no longer be responded to and that there is all too little help in healing the wound. Every opportunity should be taken to talk about the loved one with ministers, counselors, and others who are professionally trained to listen and understand. Letters home can draw off the overflow of emotions if one can express himself on paper and has the courage to let himself cry during the process whenever he feels like it. Weeping has already been mentioned as an effective tension-dispelling device. A person in mourning should allow himself the same privileges in the interest of recovery.

11 Thomas D. Eliot, " — of the Shadow of Death," *The Annals of the American Academy of Political and Social Science*, Vol. 229 (September, 1943), p. 94.

First Reactions. Even when anticipated, the actual death of a beloved person comes as a shock, and the first reaction is usually one of disbelief. A numbness comes over the bereaved and acts as a buffer to protect him from a shock that is too devastating to absorb all at once. It is quite common for persons to feel that the entire experience is a dream, unreal, and that they will awake to find things as they were.

The apparent calmness of the bereaved mourners immediately after receipt of the news is often a detachment cultivated to protect the self from the total reality. It may represent a repression of the news into the nether depths of the mind, where conflict may rage at great emotional expense to the individual. As realization intrudes upon consciousness, periods of uncontrolled abandon may appear, with weeping, cursing, self-blame, even self-injury. Accompanying these reactions is the longing for that part of the self which has been amputated: the beloved, now irrevocably departed, is relinquished with the greatest reluctance. The mind will play strange tricks on the bereaved — he will hear the voice of the departed, sense the presence of the other, and dream that they are together again. Clothing, mementos, locks of hair of the deceased, will be preserved as symbols to summon the presence of the departed. In extremity, the mourner may in his despondence be impelled to commit suicide to rejoin the other. These are first reactions which carry on after the rites of the funeral period are over. The routines of the mortuary, of funeral and burial, serve to dispel the illusions of disbelief and to channelize the emotions into approved lines. The rituals of funeral and burial are performed by professionals who take the responsibilities off the hands of the bereaved, yet give them the maximum opportunity for undisturbed grief.

In contrast to the well-defined routines of the funeral is the lack of definition for readjustment afterward. The professional undertaker retires from the scene, and no other professional person enters to aid the members of the family in the next phase of their readjustment. Each family is left more or less to shift for itself, with occasional help and advice from well-meaning relatives and friends. The family members are urged to resume normal activities as soon as possible — no time is allowed in our society for unnecessary show of grief, although it is not considered good taste for a widow or widower to remarry in less than a year's time after the funeral. Three days' sick leave are allowed the worker in civil service positions for funeral and mourning. He is expected back at work after that. Life must go on!

Trial and Error Adjustments. The first reactions to death are largely protective, designed to save the personality from serious damage. Eventually the bereaved seeks to assimilate the realities and makes trial and error attempts to pick up the threads of normal living. There are alternate periods of plunging into work and activity and of lassitude and depression. As time passes, periods of activity become longer and the periods of depression become shorter and less frequent. During the person's attempts to arrive at some pattern of stabilized behavior, he finds it necessary to force himself to respond to people, to children, and to his work. He resumes his duties with great effort at first, but gradually the routines are assumed and he rejoins the workaday world. There are also during this period frequent attempts to secure attention through wearing mourning symbols — the desire to tell of troubles to others is evident. There is much sharing of fate with children and friends.

Back in Life's Channel. As a reward for the many trial and error attempts at resuming normal activities, a new life organization will develop, and the bereaved will achieve the permanence and stability of settled living. The bereaved has accepted the death of the beloved and has made the experience a part of his personality, instead of walling it off and struggling against it. He is now able to resume relationships with others and may even substitute these relationships for those he had with the deceased. Religion is often a major source of support at this time, as we shall show in Chapter Nineteen.

One of the characteristics of the recovery is the emphasis upon participation in activities, upon entering into community services and other socially approved endeavors. If the deceased was active in any of these there is often an identification by the mourner in carrying on the work the other had started.[12]

Successful recovery from bereavement means gradual relaxation of its tensions and frustrations in favor of some more satisfactory or at least tolerable patterns of behavior. The bereaved find someone else through whom

---

[12] Adapted from David Martin Fulcomer, "The Adjustive Behavior of Some Recently Bereaved Spouses" (doctoral dissertation, ms., Northwestern University, 1942), quoted in Eliot, " — of the Shadow of Death," pp. 88–92.

they can satisfy their affectional needs: or they find religious beliefs which fully reconcile them; or they reabsorb their energies and redevote their affections in some life work as an alternate channel; or they assume the role of the deceased or project his personality by some conspicuous service in his name, or through creation of some appropriate and constructive memorial. Even gradual relaxing through forgetting . . . may produce successful recovery. . . .

. . . One may never feel a decision to take up life again: it is, in a sense, life which takes one up again. Mourning may never be absolutely finished, but it gradually approaches zero as a limit.[13]

CHECK YOURSELF When condolences cease to arrive and the world moves on, there is apt to be a slump in the adjustment process. Which of the following are evidences of successful and which of unsuccessful recovery from bereavement?

Successful   Unsuccessful

_____   _____   1 Grief comes to be enjoyed for the attention it brings.
_____   _____   2 Energies and affections are reabsorbed in some life work.
_____   _____   3 The goals of the deceased are assumed in part by the bereaved.
_____   _____   4 Religion is abandoned because of failure to bring comfort.
_____   _____   5 Gradual relaxing occurs through forgetting.
_____   _____   6 Place at the table is set for the return of the deceased.
_____   _____   7 Ability is developed to talk about the deceased with warmth and appreciation unmixed with pain and self-pity.

★ KEY   Successful: 2, 3, 5, 7   Unsuccessful: 1, 4, 6

Ways of Meeting Family Crises

The family may be said to face a crisis when it meets a situation for which there is neither a ready solution from past experience nor an immediate answer forthcoming from family members. Individual families face the crises of sudden poverty, infidelity, desertion, and bereavement in many ways. By way of summary we show next, in greatly telescoped form, the steps which family members take in the tedious process of adjustment to any one of the major crises we have discussed: [14]

[13] Thomas D. Eliot, "Bereavement: Inevitable but Not Insurmountable," in Becker and Hill (eds.), op. cit., p. 664.
[14] Modified and adapted from a chart developed by Eliot, "Handling Family Strains and Shocks," Becker and Hill (eds.), op. cit., pp. 637–638.

First, comes the news of the event, followed by:

Second, prompt recognition of the facts or refusal to believe its actuality, failure to face facts, and

Third, prompt, realistic action in the emergency or escape mechanisms such as fainting, suicide, running away, drinking, tantrums, or violence;

Fourth, a period of rationalization, of fixing the blame, of clearing the self of responsibility, after the immediate situation has been met in some way, to protect the ego.

Fifth, a struggle to attain a livable balance, a trial and error search for solutions; depending on the previous ways of meeting crises the person will follow one or another of the major patterns of readjustment below:
   a. Escape: e.g., desertion, divorce, suicide, enlistment, dependency, delusions, drink, drugs, distractions, vice.
   b. Submission or defense: e.g., apathy, resignation, religion.
   c. Compensatory efforts within the existing and accessible resources of the family's members:
      1 Redoubled work.
      2 Substitution of new channels of income, affection, energy.
      3 Persuasion.
      4 Appeal to others for help: relatives, church, charity, clinics, relief, etc.

Sixth, attainment of a final adjustment and solution of problems by the intelligent use of new resources and the renewal of routines consistent with the new situation, enabling a new life organization to emerge — a reestablishment of stable habits, self-control, reorganized economic life, and normal social life — for those who do not find permanent adjustment in one of the phases of stage five.

Selected Readings

CAVAN, RUTH, *The Family* (New York: Crowell, 1942), Part III.

DUVALL, EVELYN MILLIS, *Facts of Life and Love* (New York: Association Press, 1950), Chap. 13, "Love Out of Bounds."

DUVALL, SYLVANUS M., *Men, Women, and Morals* (New York: Association Press, 1952), chaps. 7 and 8.

HARKNESS, MARJORY GANE, "Notes on Being a Widow," *Atlantic Monthly* (November, 1935), Vol. 156, No. 5.

KOOS, E. L., *Families in Trouble* (New York: King's Crown Press, 1946).

LEVY, JOHN, AND MUNROE, RUTH, *The Happy Family* (New York: Knopf, 1938), Chap. 3.

WALLER, WILLARD, AND HILL, REUBEN, *The Family: A Dynamic Interpretation* (New York: Dryden Press, 1951), Part VI.

Technical References

ANGELL, ROBERT C., *The Family Encounters the Depression* (New York: Scribner, 1936).

BAKKE, E. WRIGHT, *The Unemployed Worker* (New Haven: Yale University Press, 1940).

BECKER, HOWARD, "The Sorrow of Bereavement," *Journal of Abnormal and Social Psychology* (January–March, 1933), Vol. 27, pp. 391–410.

BECKER, HOWARD, AND HILL, REUBEN (EDS.), *Family, Marriage, and Parenthood* (Boston: Heath, 1948), especially chaps. 21–22.

CAVAN, RUTH, AND RANCK, KATHERINE, *The Family and the Depression* (Chicago: University of Chicago, 1938).

ELIOT, THOMAS D., "War Bereavements and Their Recovery," *Marriage and Family Living* (February, 1946), Vol. 8, pp. 1–6.

FRITZ, M. A., "A Study of Widowhood," *Sociology and Social Research* (July–August, 1930), Vol. 14, pp. 553–559.

HILL, REUBEN, *Families under Stress* (New York: Harper, 1949).

KOMAROVSKY, MIRRA, *The Unemployed Man and His Family* (New York: Dryden, 1940).

SHAND, ALEXANDER, *The Foundations of Character* (London: Macmillan, 1914), pp. 301–369.

CHAPTER FOURTEEN

The Mention of the Possibility of Divorce

FACTS AND FEELINGS ABOUT DIVORCE

Why do people who talk so much about getting a divorce take so long to

make up their minds?

Is it true that you have to make a pretense of fighting a divorce in court even

if you both want it?

Do people who get a divorce live happily ever after?

*S*O, YOU SEE I HAVE DECIDED TO LET HIM HAVE A DIVORCE." THIS
was the concluding sentence in Jane Black's letter to her brother John
about her marital difficulties.

John Barton leaned back in his chair and puffed away at his pipe.
What had there been in this marriage of Jane's which was so different
from the marital felicity of his other sisters? The union had been
teetering from the start but, because of the five children, had lasted
twenty-two quarrelsome years.

Now it looks as if divorce is a certainty. "Eric comes home and
switches on the radio, then quick switches it off loudly to remind me
that I objected six months ago to a certain program — he has never
since listened to the radio in my presence. He used to make cracks at
me for listening to the radio serials and claimed the announcers sounded
like oafish clucks. Then for about two years he would leave the radio
on all the time himself, day and night — no discrimination whatsoever.
I can't seem to please him and I swear I'm not going to try any longer.
He has fixed it so I only get $500 insurance if he dies; the rest goes to
the children. The other day he said his brother had the right idea, he
got rid of his first wife. And I told him his brother also got rid of his

second and third and wasn't happy yet. He glared at me and swore he wouldn't live with me the rest of his life; life was too short. I told him I would be happier if he started his lawyer at work on the divorce right away but he wouldn't get the children, if I had to carry the case to the Supreme Court. He shut up like a clam and hasn't spoken to me since and that was three weeks ago."

John's difficulty in diagnosing his sister's troubles is understandable. Marriages which end in divorce are not greatly different from some which persist until death. There are marriages which never see a divorce court but in which the atmosphere is much more hostile than in homes about to be broken. Conflict is not unique to unhappy marriages but is present in all homes. Much of the contention is normal and understandable, indeed almost inevitable, if marriage is to function as a release from tensions. Only perfectionists would consider the bickering of family members resulting from the inevitable collision of wishes as evidence of intolerably unhappy marriage.

Many divorces occur between ostensibly congenial couples who may only have needed help at one point to work out misunderstandings which they were emotionally incapable of handling alone. (Remember the case of the doctor and his wife who profited so greatly from marital counseling, p. 250.) Another reason for the similarity between marriages which persist and those which end in divorce is the fact that many marriages which are chronically unhappy don't break up. These produce psychologically if not legally broken homes, which are quite as devastating on the personality of children. There are, therefore, marriages which might better be dissolved by divorce, and there are marriages which have been broken by divorce but might have been salvaged by a marital counselor.

Causes of Divorce

The search for causes of divorce has been a popular quest, and the conclusions vary from the simple theory of temptation by the Evil One to the complex theories of the sociologists and psychiatrists.

The most popular explanation of divorce by the general public is the moralistic one. The marriage has been solemnized and sanctified and the couple are living in blessed righteousness, when one of the mates commits an unpardonable sin against the marriage. The moralists say that he chooses to do it because of a depraved will. No other reason is necessary. The unpardonable sin is, of course, adultery, which is the only bona fide ground for divorce among deeply moralistic folk.[1]

Economic Factors and Divorce. A series of studies have established the close relationship between low income and high divorce rates. Divorces are disproportionately found in areas of high mobility, dense population, low home ownership, high delinquency, and high proportion on relief, which are also areas of low income.[2] Similarly divorce varies sharply by occupational groupings. "Proneness to divorce" increases from an index of 67.7 for professional and semiprofessional groups to 180.3 for nonfarm laborers and 254.7 for service workers, according to a sample survey of the Census Bureau in April, 1949.[3] Very much the same pattern was found true of a random sample of divorced couples in Detroit by Goode in which the unskilled are reported to have had divorce rates roughly three times those of the professional and proprietary classes.

The relationship between economic factors and divorce is more subtle than the juxtaposition of income and divorce rates can possibly depict. In a society in which the living is not *made* by family members working together, but is *earned* by the breadwinner, the symbolic character of income is magnified. Conflict rages on the economic front when the interpersonal relations in other areas of life are strained. The "theme of complaints" from research on family difficulties places "money matters" in the top position in Terman's list of husband-wife complaints.[4] Economic strain is possibly greater in the lower strata and more likely to be expressed in noneconomic situations such as sex and repudiation of marital responsibilities. Whereas the wife may withdraw sexual favors and affectional response, the husband withdraws eco-

1 A major shortcoming of the moralistic theory is that very few divorces occur as a result of adultery. Kinsey's reports on extramarital intercourse for American males places adultery in the vicinity of 50 per cent of married men interviewed, whereas the reporting of adultery as grounds for divorce in 1948 was only 2.6 per cent of all divorces reported in the twelve states making up the area reporting divorce statistics to the National Office of Vital Statistics. See *Divorce and Annulment Statistics: Specified States*, 1948 (Washington: Federal Security Agency, August 7, 1950), Vol. 35, No. 12.
2 See summary of studies by Bossard, Shroeder, Weeks, and Glick in the article by William J. Goode, "Economic Factors and Marital Stability," *American Sociological Review* (December, 1951), Vol. 16, No. 6, pp. 803–812.
3 *Ibid.*, p. 805.
4 Lewis M. Terman, *Psychological Factors in Marital Happiness* (New York: McGraw-Hill, 1938), p. 105, cited in Goode, *op. cit.*, p. 807.

nomic support as the spiral of interpersonal conflict reaches a climax. Goode points out that this withdrawal of economic support is laden with less guilt at the lower-class levels because one of the components of the attitudinal complex of the lower-class father toward his children is a tendency to think of them as belonging more to the mother than to himself. They are primarily her task and responsibility, and her waning loyalty relieves him of at least some of his guilt concerning the children. If she no longer "deserves" his support, then neither do they.[5] These generalizations provide ample evidence of the complexities of the interrelationships of economic factors and the phenomenon of divorce. Closely related to the economic as a theory of divorce causation is the explanation provided by social changes as they affect family instability. It bears close appraisal at this point.

Social Change. A theory of the cause of divorce is that it has increased with the growing stresses and strains on the family. The strains to which the larger social structure has been subjected have been registered on the family, which is the smallest social unit. Wherever the family finds itself cut off from the props of social control and social pressure, divorce increases. The shifting of population from the influences of stable, controlled rural life to the anonymity of the city accounts in part for the weakening of millions of family groupings in America.

One expression of social change has been the improved opportunities for women both in education and in employment. Marriage for the educated woman capable of earning her living ceases to involve merely a meal ticket and becomes a more companionable, although a more precarious, arrangement. Women today are economically more independent and enjoy increased equality in the courts. These factors explain in part the greater ease with which they obtain divorces in our time.

One way to test the theory that divorce is a function of social change is to observe the divorce rate during periods such as war or revolution, when social change reaches its zenith. Inventions pour in, new ways of life are devised and accepted, populations are on the move, expediency is the watchword.

A glance at the figure will show that there was a 40 per cent increase

---

[5] Goode, *op. cit.*, p. 809.

in divorce rates immediately following World War I. In the period of prosperity in preparing for World War II (1938–40) the number of divorces reached a high of one divorce for every five marriages. It reached the peak of one divorce for every two and one half marriages in 1946 and in some boom communities more divorces were recorded during this period than there were marriage licenses issued.

The social change theory explains why there are more frequent divorces than there used to be but not why particular marriages are broken. The breakdown of neighborhood controls, the declining size of the family, the decline in the number of hours spent together, and the increasing mobility of people have operated to make individual families more susceptible to disorganization, but these changes operate on most American marriages without producing equally divisive effects. We must turn elsewhere for the balance of the explanation.

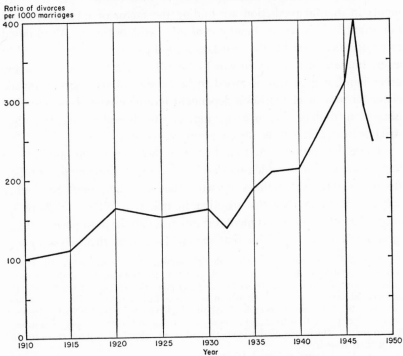

RATIO OF DIVORCES IN EACH YEAR TO AVERAGE ANNUAL MARRIAGES
IN PRECEDING 10 YEAR PERIOD FOR THE U.S.

Metropolitan Life Insurance Company *Statistical Bulletin*, Vol. 30 (April, 1949).

Incompatible Personalities. Another explanation which gives us some clue to prediction is offered by the marriage counselors, the psychoanalysts, and kindred psychotherapists. In the early childhood experiences in the parental family preferences are formed which make it easier to get along with some persons than with others. In a happy marriage the partner must meet some of the preferred childhood specifications, which often include resemblance to the father, the mother, or in individual cases, the favorite brother or sister.

Unfortunately we not only form preferences in childhood but we also develop pet hates — for Jim Mallory who struck you when you cut across his lawn, or that old witch Cissy Perkins who peevishly threw sticks at your pup! The childhood memories do not lose their power to influence us as adults, although we may come to forget the source of our hates. Marriage to an otherwise charming person who faintly reminds one of a pet hate may soon, for no other reason, prove intolerable.[6]

Patterns of dependence and aggression also appear to be important in achieving cohesion in marriage. Burgess and Wallin in their experiments in marital prediction are finding the factor of interdependence important.[7] Certain combinations of roles work out well. A girl raised to be dependent on her father makes a good partner for a man raised to assert himself in a family in which the father was dominant. On the other hand, a man who is raised to be dependent on a strong female character may, if he marries a dependent feminine type of woman, find himself in trouble. The marriage may eventually end in divorce as they struggle over who is to be dependent upon whom.

These illustrations may sound extreme, but they reveal quite clearly the personality twists which make one person bad company for another. Because certain personalities are what they are, there must be conflict between them as they live together in marriage. The irritations go deeper than the conscious mental states and date back to patterns fixed in early childhood, and for that reason don't lend themselves to self-

---

[6] In order to identify himself with the problem, the reader should think back over his experiences since childhood and see what situations produced the following feelings, common to the members of a divorcing pair: (1) feelings of revulsion in the presence of another person with whom you were forced to associate continuously; (2) desire to escape an intolerable situation which you were unable to handle with the resources you had at hand; (3) impulses to argue with certain types of personalities no matter which side of the fence they were on, impulses to show them up and reveal their stupidities.

[7] E. W. Burgess and Paul Wallin, *Engagement and Marriage* (Philadelphia: Lippincott, 1953).

doctoring. The quarrels are of the sort which never become resolved and never stop, because they are due to blockings or repressions out of the control of the conscious mind. They concern little things which the couple have insufficiently talked out but which have become so much a part of them that they can no longer stop quarreling long enough to talk them out.

Escape and Run.[8] What are the differences between couples whose quarrels are chronic and couples whose quarrels become progressively more bitter and destructive? The latter furnish a great number of our cases of divorce and separation, and an examination of their make-up may give us a clue to the causes of individual divorces.

One difference is the presence in one partner of the desire to escape, a desire strong enough to involve willingness to pay the penalties of divorce. This desire to escape may be traced to infantile techniques of handling situations by running away, but is more often the result of the shifting of love from the spouse back upon himself. From a normal heterosexual attachment a narcistic self-love is produced in which the spouse becomes a source of bitterness, a thwarting agent from which escape is imperative. The whole marriage comes to be looked upon as a frustration. The desire to escape becomes even stronger if another more suitable love object comes into view. The love will be transferred to the new object in what is known as "a rebound," and the desire to escape from the original marriage is accelerated. He is falling out of love with one as he falls in love with another! The desire to escape, then, is one of the observable differences between couples who are fighting in order to separate and those who fight but don't separate.

To answer the question of why one marriage ends in divorce and another persists requires investigation of the individual marriage. Aside from the social changes which have made marriage precarious for all couples, the following are helpful explanations of divorce in individual marriages: the unfortunate combination of personalities, the carry-over of childhood infantilisms, and the presence in one of the partners of the desire to escape. All these factors seem to explain in individual cases the progressive conflict and alienation which precede separation and divorce.

[8] We are indebted to Willard Waller for many of the ideas expressed in this and the next subsection. See *The Family: A Dynamic Interpretation* (New York: Dryden Press, 1951), pp. 509–527.

A glance at the happier side of the picture reveals positive reasons for the high cohesiveness of certain marriages in the face of social change and challenging crises. Combinations of personalities which are good for one another, the presence of interdependence, emotional maturity and the ability to take crises as they come, the presence of resources to meet crises, and the habit of happiness and happy relationships with parents and brothers and sisters, all seem to characterize stable and permanent marriages.[9]

Alienation: Courtship Reversed

The transition from single to married life is relatively easy because all our previous training leads to marriage, and our own inner motivations prompt us to accept it. The whole procedure is not unlike canoeing downstream with well-wishers on shore waving us along. Our progress is accomplished more or less without effort because it all seems natural and right.

In the stages preceding the actual divorce many of the events of the courtship are experienced with reverse emphasis. The differences lie in the reluctance with which each step is taken and the regret apparent as the inevitable separation approaches. Neither partner likes to admit he has failed in this life project which started with so much promise and expectation of success. Even after the divorce, marriage exerts a strong back-pull, and the number of reconciliations of divorced couples attests to the strength of the desire to make marriage a success.

In our discussion of courtship we showed how each step in the process was a further commitment and how obligations were built up until a summatory effect was produced. The process by which the couple became permanently involved developed a movement of its own which carried the couple along. Alienation too is a similar development, which moves step by step from married life to separation and readjustment to life without the partner.

The accompanying table shows the typical stages of both processes. Alienation, like courtship involvement, proceeds to its conclusion in a series of commitments which are not easily renounced. Each response leads to the next in line, and the motive for each new step is furnished

[9] For more details, see Chapter Fifteen, "What Holds a Marriage Together," pp. 302–318.

by the experiences up to that point — alienation cannot easily be arrested. After each crisis the relationship is redefined on a level of greater alienation. The destructive quarrels which are so characteristic of the marriages ending in divorce are often followed by intervals of comparative peace in which the couple make a determined attempt to adjust to life with each other. The conflict picks up again, however, around another sore point and continues until the couple can bear the pain of separation more comfortably than continued opposition. This concept of alienation will be clearer as we describe the critical points in the movement from early marriage to separation.

TYPICAL CRITICAL POINTS IN COURTSHIP INVOLVEMENT COMPARED WITH ALIENATION CRISES LEADING TO DIVORCE

Boy meets girl	First mutually destructive
•	
Going together	quarrel
•	•
Eye-opener quarrel	Affectional responses withheld
•	•
Going steady	Mention possibility of divorce
•	•
Public begins talking	Others find out
•	•
Mutual understanding	Move into separate bedrooms
•	•
Mention possibility of engagement	Break up housekeeping
•	•
Engagement announcement	Divorce agreed upon
▼	▼
MARRIAGE	DIVORCE

Alienation Crises

Quarrels occur in any marriage, as we have shown in the chapter on conflict. It is the mutually destructive type of quarrel which is most difficult to handle and which characterizes the progressive alienation of couples heading for divorce. If the process can be said to begin anywhere, it probably starts with the first brutal truth session in which both partners frankly expose their real feelings about the other. We have defined quarrels of this type as destructive because they concentrate on the person rather than on issues or conditions. They leave the relation with fewer assets than it had before. They attack the ego and reduce the self-respect by which persons live. Constructive quarrels, in contrast, make the marriage stronger through a redefinition of the situation causing the conflict. The destructive quarrels are progressive and succeed eventually in alienating couples to the point where separation is inevitable.

Affectional Responses Withheld. Disturbance shows up relatively early in the affectional response area. "Don't come near me until you're ready to say you're sorry," was Jane's response to Jim after their first explosive upset. The withholding of affectional response quite naturally broadens to include the sex life of the couple, in which antagonism is quickly reflected. There could well have been excellent sex adjustment to begin with, but through loss of understanding neither feels right about continuing intimate relations. Some people withhold affection to punish the mate just as they do to punish a child. Withholding of affection in marriage always evokes insecurity and anxiety, particularly for those individuals who have identified the good marriage entirely with continuous love intimacies. The familiar Hollywood pattern of early divorce is the only remedy that the over-romantic have devised to meet this situation. For most marriages the withholding of affection and sex intimacies is merely a first symptom of difficulty, to be followed by many more severe crises before divorce takes place.

Mention of the Possibility of Divorce. In the course of conflict there comes a great moment when mention is made of the possibility of divorce, the stage roughly equivalent to the declaration of love in the courtship process. Each member of the pair has thought of separation but neither has mentioned it, not knowing what the response would be.[10] One should differentiate between the banter of husband and wife in which the threat of divorce is used playfully and the more critical use of the threat among couples in serious conflict. The blow falls hardest on the one who is told. He is the one who must take the role of opposing the divorce and usually holds that role to the end. But there is an interdependence, which may seem to some perverted, each needing the other to continue the conflict, to work out the hostility. Both persons are really alienated, but one presses the fighting and one opposes the divorce. Each requires the continued participation of the other; indeed, each would be disappointed if the other stopped struggling. The

[10] Waller, *The Family*, p. 514.

passive one suffers more intensely, but has the virtuous feeling of being right, while unconsciously desiring to break the relation.[11] The immediate effect of the mention of the possibility of divorce, then, is one of restraint from strife, but when the hostilities begin again the couple have become used to the idea of divorce, and definite steps are taken in that direction.

Others Find Out. At some point the fiction of solidarity is broken as the public is let in on the couple's troubles. The relationship changes, goes on a different basis. The expectation of success which was so important in holding the marriage together originally is replaced with the admission of failure. For many sensitive couples this is the master symptom of alienation: "People are talking about us." The couple have lost face and are no longer a pair in the eyes of the public. Invitations which include them both will decrease as friends refuse to take the risk of a row.

The public divides into two camps, friends who are for the wife and friends who are for the husband. They act as a wedge to divide the two. The more sympathy expressed to members of the pair separately, the more committed the couple becomes to separation. Take the following case:

> I was first conscious of the fact that I did not want to go back to my wife, or that a part of me did not want to go back about two months after our break. I analyzed this, and thought that traced to the fact that I had introduced myself into this new community on a single-man basis, and people had sort of come to think of me as a separate individual, rather than as a married man. Then later I had talked to several people and I had wondered what they would think if I went back to this woman who had caused me so much trouble. They sympathized, of course, and that made it all the harder. Then later, people insinuated to me that I was such a fine fellow that it must have been my wife's fault. In telling the story of our break I had always been careful not to say anything against my wife, for two reasons: one that she is really a very nice person and the other that she might come to this new place and I didn't want people prejudiced against her when she did. But the very fact that I tried to be fair with her and take the blame myself made my friends all the more certain that whatever had happened had been her fault rather than mine.[12]

[11] *Ibid.*, p. 520.
[12] Willard Waller, *The Old Love and the New: Divorce and Readjustment* (New York: Liveright, 1930), pp. 131–132.

This case exemplifies well the role of the public in bringing about commitment to a permanent separation. The man's failure to identify himself as a married man further complicated the situation and accelerated the movement toward a complete break.

Breaking Up Housekeeping. The crisis of separation is one of the most severe because of the associations tied up with the home. Every piece of furniture symbolizes something, every piece brings back memories of common experiences. These belongings which must now be parcelled out and divided are reminders of days when. . . . The phase of separation which is probably most poignant is that of leaving the home to take up separate quarters. This act seems to signify more than anything else the lengths to which alienation has gone.

The severance of such a meaningful relationship is usually extremely painful. Although quarrels and conflict are useful in bringing out a decision that will stick, the couple should be able to say they tried hard to make their marriage go and to live up to the expectations of friends and well-wishers. Reconciliations which fail show the uselessness of continued compromises and force the conclusion that the marriage won't work and can't be made to work. The separation which comes with taking up separate quarters is a signal to friends and the public that the rift is serious. Usually both parties become committed permanently to the break, and they finally agree to divorce. The interval between separation and divorce is sometimes short, sometimes long, depending on the readiness and preparation of the parties.

Divorce. Divorce is a final severance, for which some preparation has to be made. It may take months before the actual work of reconstructing one's life can begin. The decree doesn't close the case, however; one doesn't divorce and live happily ever after. Indeed, the divorce court experience is described by some participants as being the most trying shock of the entire alienation process. Both members of the couple suffer through the procedure, with a feeling of numbness, of unreality, as if they were not really themselves but someone else looking on at the crazy scene.

After the divorce there is a period of mental conflict in which the individual attempts to reconstruct his world, often a period of depression, melancholia, and even suicidal attempts. Tensions build up which can be handled only with careful and skilled guidance. The divorced person should be watched for any evidence of depression and encouraged to seek counseling if symptoms appear.

Postdivorce Adjustments. Already during the alienation period preceding the divorce, personality adjustments are taking place. The many habits which hold marriages together, sex habits, response habits, food habits, work habits, all of these have to be broken and reoriented for the parties to face single life healthily. Everyone who has tried breaking a habit knows how painful the process is and how easy it is to fall back into the old routine again. Those who have gone on diets to keep a certain weight remember how insistently appetites cry out for foods to which they have become accustomed. The divorcing person faces the frustration of not one but several fundamental habits, and the separation is doubly painful if he must make that adjustment quickly. The habits of married living are much more fundamental than dancing or smoking or eating, and as they are broken, living loses its savor.

As the person is forced to turn within himself for satisfaction, the results are often curious. He becomes capable, or so he thinks, of doing grandiose things. A man revives dreams of boyhood and believes that in a short period he will become a great banker or writer. A woman after thirty years of being hemmed in by housewifely duties sees possibilities of attaining startling personal success. Now that the routines of married life no longer exist as hampering bonds, the person sees no bounds to his possible accomplishments.

Sour-grapes rationalizations [13] work overtime to convince the person he has done the right thing. Pleasant memories are repressed, and the illusions which supported the marriage are gradually replaced by cold, cruel reality. There is a certain grim conviction that the marriage could never have worked and that it was foolish to prolong it as long as it was prolonged.

Some helpful suggestions in reconstructing and readjusting the everyday life of the divorced warrants at least brief attention:

1 Talking the whole business out with someone who listens without praise or blame, who understands and helps but doesn't become involved; in sum, spending hours of counseling until the memories no longer bring numbing pain and can be faced with some objectivity.

[13] For a discussion of this mechanism, see pp. 17–18.

2 Developing new skills which have no associations with the marriage and which can show progress quickly, such as singing, painting, working at certain types of crafts; doing "something you have always wanted to do," in order to balance the accounts with something positive and satisfying.

3 Plunging into professional work with renewed vigor, but not to the exclusion of all social contacts.

4 Picking up social contacts; the person is his own best judge of the number and depth of new contacts he is emotionally able to take.

5 Reorienting oneself in terms of the rest of the universe, and working out a philosophy of life which gives purpose and zest to living.

Now, what have we said about the adjustments preceding and following divorce? The process is necessarily one of conflict, painful and

---

CHECK YOURSELF   Which of the following conclusions are justified in the light of our discussion of the alienation process which precedes divorce? Check those which are correct.

_____ 1 As soon as a couple see that they are incompatible, they should start divorce proceedings and get it over with.

_____ 2 If the couple is interested in preserving their marriage, they should rarely talk about their marital troubles to friends, who might gossip.

_____ 3 Conflicts are followed by periods of comparative peace, even among couples who eventually separate.

_____ 4 Alienation proceeds through a series of destructive quarrels in which the ego, rather than issues, is attacked.

_____ 5 Few divorced persons ever desire to return to their mates once the decree is granted.

_____ 6 It's all a matter of will power; couples who divorce don't really try to get along.

_____ 7 Sexual relations are one of the last habits to be renounced by the alienated couple.

_____ 8 The blow falls hardest on the one who is asked for the divorce. It is he who takes the role of opposing the divorce.

_____ 9 The divorce court proceeding is enjoyed for its drama as well as for the new freedom it gives.

_____ 10 The recently divorced person should be watched for any evidence of depression and encouraged to seek counseling.

_____ 11 Suicides, mental breakdowns, and homicides involving recently divorced persons might be avoided by less hurried divorce and more adequate postdivorce counseling.

★ KEY   Correct: 2, 3, 4, 8, 10, 11

divisive in its results. The timing of needs for sympathy and understanding is wrong; each is too absorbed in his own emotional difficulties to sympathize with the other, and a third party is turned to for sympathy. The process is long-drawn-out and somewhat painful, because the adjustment to the loss of a mate takes place in piecemeal fashion. To move faster in breaking habits of long standing brings danger of damage to personality and possible suicide. It is therefore dangerous to advise couples to divorce quickly.

The readjustment after the divorce consists in reconstructing life anew, developing new habits and new purposes which jibe with life as a single person. Assuming that the predivorce conflicts completely alienated the couple, the postdivorce period needs to be one of talking out problems which continue to arouse uncomfortable emotions and of picking up meaningful activities which will carry the parties back into normal social life.

Do Second Marriages Work?

The remarriage of divorced persons is a phenomenon of marked significance in our society. We have already indicated in Chapter Eight, "Who Gets Married?," that divorced persons remarry at a high rate, only about one fourth in recent years remaining in the divorced status for as long as five years. We have much less information, unfortunately, concerning the success or failure of second marriages. It is argued by those studies which find second marriages more successful than the first that divorced persons have learned a great deal from their experiences and that this can be seen in their second marriages. Goode's discussion of the point for his Detroit cases is quotable:

. . . There is no question now that second marriages are happier than first marriages. I believe that this is not only true when one compares the second marriage with the first unhappy marriage but that the percentage of failures is less among all second marriages than among all first marriages. . . . My sample is not large enough to include the number of "repeaters" which would be necessary for good analysis. There are several bizarre cases of this kind in my group, but most people seem to be couples who simply couldn't adjust to each other at their particular level of growth and experience. Unless you agree that a substantial proportion of the population is emotionally defective, you can't accept the neurosis and personality explanations of divorce. I suspect that most of these people could, after the divorce, adjust happily to their changed spouse — if they could really meet him for the first time, with the unhappy memories expunged.[14]

Less definite in his convictions about the success of second marriages is Harvey J. Locke who matched a married-only-once group of men and women with his sample of remarried couples in which one of the spouses was married for the second time after a divorce. He found divorced *women* good risks in subsequent marriage, but divorced *men* poor risks as compared with persons married only once.[15]

When viewed statistically in terms of "proneness to divorce" the research supports the view that the probability of divorce is greater in a second or subsequent marriage than it is in the first; indeed, one analyst of census data computes the probability as 50 per cent higher for second than for first marriages.[16] No single study has answered the question, "Do Second Marriages Work?" to our satisfaction. As divorce is more generally accepted, it is possible that the divorced group will include more and more well-adjusted individuals who failed largely because of poor matching or other extraneous circumstances related to their early dating experiences. These individuals might in second marriages have high probabilities of marital success.

Divorce Reform

Divorce is not something to fear, but to understand and to make less painful if we can. Prejudice in the past has made the adjustment to divorce doubly hard and painful, because the divorced person has been set in a class apart when he needs most of all to be accepted and assimilated back into social life.

The divorce decree is a perfunctory ceremony which merely signifies the lack of unity in a marriage, just as the wedding ceremony solem-

---

[14] Personal communication to one of the authors from William J. Goode, Columbia University, clarifying generalizations from his Detroit study of 425 divorced women reported for the *Saturday Evening Post* by David G. Wittels, "The Post Reports on Divorce," *Saturday Evening Post*, January 21, 28, and February 4, 11, and 18, 1950.

[15] Harvey J. Locke, *Predicting Adjustment in Marriage: A Comparison of a Divorced and a Happily Married Group* (New York: Holt, 1951), pp. 305–309, reporting on a study conducted with W. J. Klausmer.

[16] Paul Landis, "Sequential Marriage," *Journal of Home Economics* (October, 1950), Vol. 42.

nizes the pair unity which existed before marriage. Judge Paul Alexander has termed the divorce court judge a "public mortician" who buries dead marriages.

There is little justification for the emotional reaction to divorce as divorce. It is only a confirmation of the fact that the couple have separated and are no longer performing the required functions of matrimony, and it merely serves to regularize the matter for the protection of all concerned.

The big problem is not to keep people who want divorce badly from getting relief but to keep more people from wanting divorce. This will involve a complete reversal of policy with respect to the granting of legal separations. Our divorce system has developed out of the importance played by property rights in the marriage contract. In order to protect the respective rights of each party, the law provides a means by which one member might complain of the offenses of the other and, by fixing guilt, obtain a legal release from the contract. Marriage has long since changed in emphasis from property contracts to companionship and affection-giving. Today the question is often not so much one of determining guilt as it is of determining the stage of alienation and estrangement.

Since the National Conference on Family Life in 1948, a committee of the American Bar Association headed by Judge Paul W. Alexander has been actively formulating a new approach to marriage and divorce laws. Their proposals, shown in the charts on the next four pages, depart from a new premise, that divorce is an effect rather than a cause of broken homes. They propose a new kind of court based on a new philosophy sweeping away the "archaic legal philosophy" of punishment for guilt and substituting for it a positive constructive approach which would ask "what is best for the family" and hence best for society. The case would no longer be titled "Jane Doe v. John Doe," but "In the Interest of the John Doe Family." Trained personnel of the court would be used to diagnose, and if possible heal the breach. Divorces would not be easier, but more difficult to obtain. The final decree would be issued, Judge Alexander has written, "only if the investigation plus proper judicial inquiry compelled the conclusion that the marriage could no longer be useful to the spouses, the children, or the state; that the partners could not or would not permit it to fulfill the functions

WHAT

THE PRESENT DIVORCE SYSTEM

Based on Guilt & Punishment

EASY MARRIAGES, No health training or residence requirements

DIVORCE action can be started as SOON after marriage as desired

DIVORCE can be applied for **ANYWHERE —** after setting up temporary residence

GENERAL COURT Hears cases in many fields: criminal, equity, divorce, civil suits

FORMAL QUASI–CRIMINAL ACTION bent on proving guilt in open court

LAWYERS' ROLE To win case

ROTATION OF JUDGES — Each judge hard pressed to keep up with legal aspects of the fields he presides over

SPOUSE'S ROLE — Antagonist trying to prove guilt of mate

GOAL

DIVORCE

IT IS

NEW A.B.A. PROPOSAL
Based on Diagnosis & Treatment

HARD
MARRIAGES —
pre-marital education,
physical exams, no
runaway marriages

DIVORCE action
can't be started until AFTER
3 YEARS of marriage

DIVORCE
can be applied for only
where YOU ACTUALLY
LIVE

FAMILY COURT
Hears only cases in family field:
divorce, annulment, juvenile
delinquency, adoption

PSYCHIATRIST
SOCIAL WORKER
RELIGIOUS LEADER
MARRIAGE COUNSELOR

LAWYERS' ROLE
To salvage family

SPECIALIST
JUDGES
Each judge
gets rounded
non-legal
training, has
staff of
specialists
to help

SPOUSES' ROLE
Patients being treated
for an illness

GOAL

INFORMAL ADMINISTRATIVE PROCEDURE
looking for cause and cure of trouble
in private sessions

WHAT'S BEST FOR
THE FAMILY

Redrawn from chart by GRAPHICS INSTITUTE, N. Y. C., for *Pageant Magazine*

THE PRESENT METHOD

1. Application for divorce is made

2. Public trial — damaging to both parties, and their children

3. Trumped up evidence frequently presented

4. Divorce possible only if one is "proved" guilty of grounds for divorce

5. . . . Both parties are proved guilty of charge

6. . . . It comes out that both parties have cooperated to arrange grounds for divorce

DIVORCE IS NOT GRANTED IF . . . (5, 6, and 7)

7. . . . An attempt — even though non-lasting — at reconciliation has been made

8. Alimony settlement based on bargaining power

WORKS

NEW A.B.A. PROPOSAL

1. Application for help is made

2. Private diagnostic investigation made by Court's specialists

3. Psychological aid to try to solve personality-emotional problems

4. Welfare counseling to try to solve social-economic problems

5. Treatment efforts may last from 2 months to 2 years

6. Report on results made to judge. Will show treatment has succeeded, in some cases

7. Divorce granted only if treatments fail, and judge is convinced case is hopeless

8. Alimony settlement based on real needs and resources

Redrawn from chart by GRAPHICS INSTITUTE, N. Y. C., for *Pageant Magazine*

imposed by the natural law and the civil law; that perpetuation of the bare legal bond would be more harmful than beneficial to all concerned." [17]

The proposals of the American Bar Association's committee are being debated in conferences not only of the legal profession but of many interprofessional groups. An Interprofessional Commission on Marriage and Divorce Laws sponsored by the American Bar Association but representative of all the major professions dealing with marriage and divorce is conducting research and evaluating the many varied proposals for divorce reform likely to come before legislative committees. A model marriage and divorce act is in the making which will be presented to one of the fifty-two jurisdictions in the United States for debate and action.

Possibilities Through Voluntary Agencies

In concluding this chapter on divorce, some account should be taken of the possibilities of rebuilding unhappy marriages into more satisfactory patterns through marital guidance. The increasing availability of family counseling through marriage and family counseling agencies suggests that counseling should be sought as an alternative to divorce in any case.

Persons of their own will can't successfully arrest the process of alienation, but a third party can, if well trained and if he gets the marriage early enough. The work of the family consultant is to rebuild the discordant family, if the matter has gone so far as to need remedial rather than preventive treatment. The marital guidance clinic serves in many ways as a guard against divorce. As a premarital guidance center it assures couples that they are prepared emotionally and physically for marriage. Premarital guidance utilizes careful premarital examination (discussed in Chapter Five, "The Meaning of an Engagement") and instruction given in conferences and class work in preparation for marriage. Later the center enters the picture to aid the couple in understanding the normality and inevitability of conflict, and encourages the development of techniques for resolving their difficulties (see our discussion in Chapter Twelve, "Common Conflicts in Marriage"). Finally, the couple that has failed to use these resources until

[17] *New York Times*, September 17, 1950.

they are well along in the alienation process may turn to the counseling services for help in rebuilding the marriage in a more satisfactory pattern. Thus the work of counseling agencies is in line with our earlier statement of principle with respect to divorce: "The big problem is not to keep people who want divorce from getting it but to keep more people from wanting divorce."

Selected Readings

ALEXANDER, JUDGE PAUL, "Our Legal Horror – Divorce," *Ladies' Home Journal* (October, 1949).

ANONYMOUS, "Can Divorce Be Successful?" *Harper's Magazine* (February, 1938).

ANONYMOUS, "What I Want My Kids to Know," *Saturday Evening Post* (June 24, 1950).

ANONYMOUS DIVORCEE, "Nobody Tells You," *Woman's Home Companion* (January, 1951).

GOODE, WILLIAM J., "Education for Divorce," *Marriage and Family Living* (May, 1947), Vol. 9.

——, "Problems in Postdivorce Adjustment," *American Sociological Review* (June, 1949), Vol. 14.

GROVES, ERNEST R., *Conserving Marriage and the Family: A Realistic Discussion of the Divorce Problem* (New York: Macmillan, 1945).

LANDIS, PAUL, "Sequential Marriage," *Journal of Home Economics* (October, 1950).

MEAD, MARGARET, *Male and Female* (New York: Morrow, 1949), Chap. 17.

ROSENTHAL, HERBERT C., "Painless Divorce," *Pageant* (April, 1952).

WITTELS, DAVID G., "The Post Reports on Divorce," *Saturday Evening Post* (January 21, 28, and February 4, 11, and 18, 1950).

Technical References

BARNETT, JAMES H., *Divorce and the American Divorce Novel, 1858–1937* (Philadelphia: Privately Printed, 1939).

BERGLER, EDMUND, *Unhappy Marriage and Divorce* (New York: International Universities Press, 1946).

"Children of the Divorced," *Law and Contemporary Problems* (Summer, 1944), Vol. 10. A symposium.

DAVIS, KINGSLEY, "Statistical Perspective on Marriage and Divorce," *Annals* (November, 1950).

GLICK, PAUL C., "First Marriages and Remarriages," *American Sociological Review* (December, 1949), Vol. 14.

GOODE, WILLIAM J., "Social Engineering and the Divorce Problem," *Annals* (November, 1950).

———, "Economic Factors and Marital Stability," *American Sociological Review* (December, 1951), Vol. 16, No. 6.

JACOBSON, PAUL H., "Differentials in Divorce by Duration of Marriage and Size of Family," *American Sociological Review* (April, 1950), Vol. 15, pp. 235–245.

LLEWELLYN, K. N., "Behind the Law of Divorce," *Columbia Law Review* (December, 1932 and February, 1933), Vols. 32 and 33.

LOCKE, HARVEY J., *Predicting Adjustment in Marriage: A Comparison of a Divorced and a Happy Married Group* (New York: Holt, 1951).

"Toward Family Stability," *The Annals* (November, 1950), Vol. 272. A symposium.

WALLER, WILLARD, *The Old Love and the New* (New York: Liveright, 1930).

WALLER, WILLARD, AND HILL, REUBEN, *The Family: A Dynamic Interpretation* (New York: Dryden Press, 1951), chaps. 23–24.

CHAPTER FIFTEEN

Courtesy of Syd Hoff

"He's a dope, but he's mine!"

WHAT HOLDS A MARRIAGE TOGETHER?

Will love alone hold a marriage together?

What does sex symbolize in marriage?

What experiences test a marriage?

When is a marriage a partnership?

Why is it that happily married people come to think alike and talk alike?

*T*HIS CHAPTER CLOSES THE DISCUSSION OF WHAT IT MEANS TO BE MARried. The accent in the chapters immediately preceding has been on the crises of marriage and family life, on the divisive forces which operate to break up and test marriage. This chapter emphasizes the forces and bonds which hold marriage together. It is dedicated to the proposition that successful marriages don't just happen, that marriage is what you make it. A happy union takes working at, and its accomplishment is the product of much sweat and toil in the art of getting along.

The Expectation of Success [1]

"We expect our marriage to work" is one of the strongest bonds tying a marriage together at the outset. This conviction supplies the motivation to stick together when the going is rough rather than to run home to mother. It impels the couple to work out the solutions to problems so they won't recur. Honeymooners with the expectation of success are already consciously addressing themselves to the task of building their

[1] We are indebted to Willard Waller for many of the ideas which appear in this chapter; see *The Family: A Dynamic Interpretation* (New York: Dryden Press, 1951), pp. 322–335.

marriage so that it will work. They are saying, "We want to be good for one another and we want to be good parents. Show us how."

In spite of the high divorce rate in America, the standard held up for every couple is successful marriage. If a person can't make a success of marriage he is made to feel inadequate, and his failure is pointed out by members of society to young people about to be married. Along with the personal expectation of success goes the public's expectation of success. The individual couple may feel strongly the necessity of not letting down the friends who have wished them well. Making marriage work is often easier than facing the public with the admission of failure. One of the real forces in tying marriages together, then, is the expectation of success, the ideal of a happy marriage as the only possible outcome of the marriage, and the feeling that the public can't be let down by a break-up.

Friends are admonished in the "whom God hath joined together" formula to keep hands off the marriage and stay out of the sphere of marital interaction.[2] It is not good form to ask how the marriage is going or to inquire as to its health. The assumption in our society is that all marriages are happy until proved otherwise by appearance in a divorce court. It is doubtful if the net effect of this assumption of marital bliss is good, since it makes for hypocrisy and implies that conflict is abnormal and unusual, but the assumption is an additional force in holding many marriages together.

Social Life Organized for Married Pairs

A second reason for sticking together is the system of pairing young people off for social purposes. Most of our social life is organized around married couples or couples about to be married. The development of pair unity in the engagement period was furthered by the public's recognition that the couple did belong together shown by inviting them to social occasions as a pair. This acknowledgment caused the boy and girl to regard themselves differently and thus gave stability to the relationship. The years of married life add to this sense of "we" and further unify the couple. Together they explore the social circles (and are explored by them); together they make friends and choose the sets which they wish to join. Early in the marriage, if not in the en-

[2] *Ibid.*, p. 324.

gagement, a person learns to accept invitations tentatively until he can find out whether or not the other member of the pair is able to go. The public understands because it expects the couple to act as a unit.

Just because society in America is not organized for sexes separately as are some societies, the marital relationships are strengthened. Most of the entertaining in a community centers within the married set and is motivated by the "you invite us and we'll have to return the invitation later on" phenomenon, leaving almost no social activities for bachelors and spinsters and other nonmarried people. Moreover, to invite one member of a married pair and not the other is something of a breach of etiquette. The cards are stacked in favor of married couples sticking together if they want any social life. Two by two they go marching by.

The positive social pressures just described do hold couples together. In addition, the fear of public disapproval, of neighborhood gossip, and the fear of scandal are negative forces of which many couples are conscious. These socially imposed forces, however, are essentially *adhesive*, inasmuch as they are applied externally. They are most effective in a simple agrarian society where everybody knows everybody else, and are less effective within the social sets of the metropolitan centers. Of more importance today are the forces within the couples as individuals, forces which might be termed *cohesive* since they are based on the inner needs of the participants themselves. It is because marriage is welded together both by adhesive and cohesive forces, by external societal pressures and by internal desires and needs, that it is surviving the buffeting of social change in our day.

Marriage Satisfies Basic Adult Needs

One of the cohesive forces holding American marriages together is the power of the marital relationship to meet the basic affectional needs of its members.[3] The American family is built around the husband-wife relationship, and the power of that relation to satisfy the needs of the couple flavors the whole of family life. Children become accustomed to having their needs for affection, companionship, recognition, and response met in the parental family. Moreover, they are conditioned to

---

[3] The important role of satisfying the basic needs in marriage was anticipated in the discussion of the need for love in Chapter One, pp. 13–15.

expect that the phenomenon of love and affection will carry over into a family of their own making. With that expectation, the early courtship activities are surrounded by questions such as, "Does he love me?" "Is she good for me?" "Does he do anything for me?" or in sum, "Will he satisfy my hunger for affection and security permanently?" The history of the courtship is one of finding in the growing relation reciprocal satisfactions and increasing interdependence of one on the other to satisfy these imperious needs.

The adult is, after all, basically the child older grown. In marriage the child, now grown older, has transferred from the parent to the marriage partner his need to give and receive affection and security. The transfer takes place piecemeal, beginning with the first recognition of the capacity to love someone other than the parent, and continuing until the marriage is stabilized as the main source of affection and appreciation.[4]

To be wanted, to be understood, to be appreciated, to be loved, and to belong to someone are fundamental needs which parallel the needs to possess, to love, and to respond to someone. Uniquely met in the intimacies of the marriage relation, these needs should be listed among the main sources of cohesion holding marriages together in America today.

The Growth of Sympathy

As the marriage wears on and the couple come to take for granted the unreserved intimacies of wedded life, there is a growth of sympathy between the mates. The newlywed is all too often downcast when his wife is slightly displeased with him, but the experienced husband knows that she will get over it after a while. He has been all through this before and can predict the method of bringing the affair to a satisfactory conclusion. Here we see a value in some of the features of marriage which the Hollywood script writers have condemned in their "never let your marriage go to seed" attitude. It is disillusioning to a man to see his wife having breakfast in a housecoat with her hair in pins, and unpleasant for a wife to see her husband's unshaved face, but it is comforting to both to realize that such liberties do not seriously threaten the relationship. These are the jolly little coarsenesses which give to

4 See Chapter Two, pp. 28–44.

the marriage relation its unique strength.[5] Shady little sallies between them, the vulgarities which they alone think funny and which before marriage might have shocked them both, these indiscretions also hold a marriage together.

Gradually each member of a pair comes to share the mental states of the other, to live vicariously in the other, and to learn to predict the other. In this state of complete intimacy the members of the pair develop similar tastes and similar aspirations. The wife hears her husband's jokes hundreds of times but enjoys them because they are her jokes, and prods him to "tell that one about when we were in Chicago, dear."

In the growth of sympathy, the sharing of ideas often results in the sharing of depressions and predicting when they will come. Husband and wife learn to handle one another's blues as well as one another's temper tantrums. Each knows if he's put in the doghouse, the other will soon let him out.

Marriage solidarity develops immensely as members of the pair perceive the strength of the relationship. It is seen as they recognize, while fighting, that they care more about the marriage than they do about winning. It comes forcibly to their attention when a crisis like infidelity is met without the wife's running home to her parents as she would have done earlier in the marriage. It is seen in the willingness of the husband to tolerate shoddy household management or sterility of the wife with nary a hint at separation. The relationship has come to have a value in itself. All such incidents may not seem very romantic; indeed, some romantic-minded people would say such marriages had gone to seed. But family unity is built on just such foundations as these: "We have come to take each other for granted; we know we can count on one another"; "She'll see me through thick and thin. What a lucky man I am!"

Family Habits Create Solidarity

The married pair bring to marriage two separate systems of habits formed during life in their respective parental families as well as during the years away from the family. Consciously, at first, they must go about the task of adjusting the differences in the two systems. The

[5] Waller and Hill, *op. cit.*, p. 333.

wife must find out how strong her husband wants his coffee and when he must arise in the morning in order to get to work on time. The husband must learn that to his wife permanent waves are more important than golf equipment and that ashes on the rug are not to be tolerated. After a time the two systems are modified and become an interlocking habit system which is a great deal more stable than that of the single person could ever be; they rest upon the habit of adjusting to the situation created by the real or imaginary demands and expectations of others.

CHECK YOURSELF   Underline the correct alternatives in the following statements.

1 We have a (high, low) divorce rate in America accompanied by a (high, low) standard of success for marriage. (Because of, in spite of) the divorce rate, engaged couples feel they start with (high, only average) chances for happy marriage.

2 Life in American social circles is (as comfortable, not as comfortable) for bachelors and spinsters as it is for married people.

3 According to marriage authorities, it is not only (devastating, not devastating) to the marriage to come to dinner unkempt and unshaven occasionally but it (strengthens, weakens) the marriage permanently because it proves (how much, how little) the marriage means to the married pair.

★ KEY   much how ;strengthens ;devastating not 3   able
-comfort as not 2   ;high ;of spite in ;high ;high 1

Consider the following illustration of habits at work in a typical urban home:

. . . the husband used to laugh when the wife referred to ant-hills as ants' houses, but now he does not laugh any more; in fact he sometimes uses the expression himself. Each individual member of a family has made certain habit adjustments to the physical setting in which the family lives; each knows at just what height to insert the key in the lock of the front door and each has acquired the knack of giving a little twist to the key which makes the door open easily; each one is able to enter any of the rooms in the darkness and to find the switches for the lights without any difficulty; each knows where to sit on hot afternoons in August, and how to descend the rickety cellar stairs. And each one, likewise, has made a multitude of adjustments to the presence of others in the house. In the morning the father of the family gets up and starts the furnace. He walks carefully in order not to disturb the others, but there is no need of this, for the others have adjusted to his early morning noise and do not hear him. A little later the mother gets up and calls the children, perhaps a number of times, for they may have made an adjustment to her habitual technique and have shifted the responsibility entirely upon her; they have, perhaps, developed mother deafness. She then gets breakfast, sets the table, and calls the family. Father has been reading the paper, which is now split into sections. Each one eats his breakfast in his customary way; there is the usual interchange of pleasantries and the usual grumbling and complaining. Then ensues the morning crisis of getting the children off to school and helping father to catch the eight-thirty train, the struggle over the bathroom, the effort to find things, the examination of shirts to see whether they will do for another day, and all the myriad adjustments which arise from a civilization which demands neatness and promptness. Then all the members of the family but one leave the home, pausing a moment to say good-bye to mother and to pet the dog.[6]

This is just a small part of the family day and misses many of the habits of family living reflected in conversation and gestures. It does serve to illustrate, however, the intermeshing of social habits of family members. Once you become a part of a cooperative enterprise in which your behavior is habitually determined by the responses and helps of others, it is highly inconvenient to separate yourself. We will discuss this point more in detail when we come to the inertia to change which exists in all families.

As the pair become accustomed to each other and dependent upon one another for the sharing of family habits, they cease to operate in the family as individuals and come to take on a family personality. This is the reason married people in time come to talk alike, think alike, plan alike, and in some instances even to look alike. Back of the common gestures and facial expressions are common attitudes and beliefs. These habits serve as an additional source of solidarity in marriage.

Couples find that one of the techniques for making marriage work is to enter wholeheartedly into the business of building common habits. They may lose some of their premarriage individuality and independence, but they gain a more satisfying personality in the process.

Habits and Resistance to Change

In any marriage, after the initial adjustments to personal idiosyncrasies have been made and routines established, a level is reached at which the married pair feels comfortable. Decisions have been reached concern-

[6] *Ibid.*, pp. 328–329.

ing the division of duties, and the time schedule for each day has been committed to memory. The routines are fast becoming habits through repetition and the achievement of satisfying results. The major needs are being met, the major drives satisfied. The fact that habits are established makes experimentation less and less necessary. The couple are finding the grooves, and married life is gradually reaching an optimum level of interaction.

These routines act for the marriage as a gyroscope acts for a ship, pulling it back on an even keel when it is about to go over. It sometimes seems inevitable that a particular marriage should break up in divorce or desertion. Conflicts arise which seem impossible to resolve, but somehow equilibrium is restored, and things go on very much as before. Sometimes, too, a series of fortunate events makes it look as if a marriage were going to reach a level of impossible happiness — but that also passes.

An illustration may help to explain the tendency to stabilize marriage at a given level. When there is a "blow-up" each person is conscious of the cultural standards (that is, what is right in the situation) and of the fact that friends and families would disapprove if the truth were known. To add to their sense of guilt the couple may hear a sermon, or read a story, or hear a bit of gossip about a recently divorced couple which reminds them of the cultural norm. Discussion and reconciliation follow and the marriage is restored to its normal level. Thereafter the couple is tempted to let sleeping dogs lie. Ways are found for settling conflicts with a minimum of disturbance.[7]

Another explanation of marriage stabilization lies in an understandable reluctance to change a mutually satisfying relation in favor of something new or unknown. The collective habits of a married pair are solidly based on the needs and motives of both parties — or at least they were originally built up to satisfy the couple's needs. As long as these needs are satisfied there is inertia to change. Another kind of reluctance to change arises from the inability of either partner to know the mind of the other and the consequent difficulty of getting together on any ground other than that they now share.

In sum, one of the forces holding marriages together is the reluctance to give up "a good thing." The marriage may not be perfect, but to break habits is painful. They become vested interests, active in their

7 Adapted from Waller, op. cit., p. 331.

own perpetuation, as anyone knows who has tried to quit smoking or doodling.

Working toward a Common Goal

Dick is a medical student just beginning his four-year course and would like to get married, but he is afraid it is impossible for about six years. He has his M.D. to get first, followed by an internship and residence work. Marie suggests that there are things a girl would dislike more than working jointly with a man for an M.D. It would be *their* M.D., and they would share the experiences and sacrifices together, if they were married.

In the struggle to reach a common goal, a new feeling arises, a sense of having fought and bled together. Pride in common achievement, the sense of superiority which common accomplishments bring, or the feeling of struggling together against misfortune — such experiences are basic to marriage solidarity. They form a backlog to hold the marriage together in the crises which follow later in family life. The reference to "leaner" days, the technique of reminiscing together, reminders of the history of the relation, these can be called up when trouble arises on the home front.

In Chapter Twenty, "Marriage Isn't What It Used to Be," it will be pointed out that the family has lost many of the old-time economic functions which made it a partnership. In the old-style family, making a living was a common enterprise which tied the family members together. Today it is more typical that the man earn and the woman spend the living. In the modern family, mutual interdependence arises largely out of husband and wife's sharing the budgeting and planning of expenditures, the joint consumption rather than the joint production of economic goods. In addition, it must be admitted that the division of familial duties between man and wife makes for interdependence, as any husband will find who is forced by circumstances to take over the task of managing the home while his wife is gone. One harried husband found, thanks to his rich parental family training, that he had been given some background for all except one of the wifely homemaking duties. Can you guess what it was? Braiding his daughter's hair! Even so, this husband's life was immeasurably brighter when his wife returned, and the balance of duties was established once again.

Another phase of partnership centers around buying furniture and setting up a home. The things you buy are often bought after much deliberation. You scrimped and saved for each stick of furniture. Each item brings to memory a multitude of associations which solidify marriage. In the divorce process the most painful step of all is breaking up housekeeping and distributing the furniture. The converse of breaking up housekeeping is the solidifying function of building a home by self-sacrifice and hard work. The good family person comes to talk about his accomplishments and his possessions as "ours": "*our* degree," "This is *our* chance," "When *we* bought this, Jane was just a baby," "*We* saved for six months for *our* coffee table."

Another evidence of partnership as a binding force in marriage is seen in the unselfish goals which a pair will set for themselves. Many marriages are initiated and grow as the participants strive to serve humanity in specific ways. The ideal of alleviating the lot of the sick and the lame, of leaving society the better for their marriage, unifies many modern couples. An age-old ideal is that of rearing healthy, useful children, and this appears to be positively related to marital happiness. Couples are drawn together and their marriage is given meaning as a partnership by the wider interests and services which they care about.

The Role of Love

Not to discuss the role of love in holding a marriage together would be an oversight. We have tried to show first that there are other forces working to this same end: the forces of public approval, the meeting of basic needs of affection and security, habits of living together, interests and intimate jokes in common, experiences in working toward a common goal, interdependence because of duties performed, and inertia to change, all of which have a part in maintaining the integrity of a marriage. It is difficult to know exactly what role love plays in the whole picture.

We are sure of one thing, that the romantic dogma has been a major source of premature break-ups through its brittle philosophy, "if you really loved me you wouldn't do this." Not helpful to marriage solidarity are the following romantic notions: that a marriage will ride through on love alone, that it doesn't take working at, and that true love always runs smoothly. Every marriage faces bumps and jolts —

to pretend otherwise is fantastic. The all too frequent example of the woman who runs out on a marriage before it really gets started just because her husband acts like a human being instead of a Prince Charming derives support from the romantic love philosophy. Marriages based mainly on romantic love are precariously set up, because they weaken as the emotion itself changes.

Conjugal love is quite another emotion. It grows as the marriage progresses, thrives on companionship, common experiences, and the number of happy episodes which are scattered through a rich marriage. Conjugal love builds on the familiar, the mementos, the souvenirs, and waxes stronger with each additional year of marriage. Unlike romantic love, conjugal love is impossible for newly acquainted young people, since it requires time to form and grows from continuous association. Romantic love is greatest where each party knows least about the other — you see, reality gets in the way of romance. This is the love that is blind.

As conjugal love comes to the fore in marriage the relationship is strengthened. Few marriages in America persist over any length of time without developing conjugal love sentiments, because they are based on companionship and common interests which intertwine the experiences of established marriages. In contrast, romantic love gradually disappears in the companionable marriage except for the lip service paid it in the exaggerated moments of bliss which occasionally occur throughout married life. Romantic love as a solidifying factor in marriage gives way to conjugal love, which is more mature and more compatible with the companionable features of contemporary marriages.

The Two Shall Be One

Married love, which we have called conjugal love, finds expression in many day-by-day experiences. None of these is more effective as a unifying force than regular, satisfying sex intercourse. The regular release of tension in coitus is extremely satisfying in the purely physical sense, and in addition it serves as an expression of fulfillment for the entire relationship.

Fred and Mabel are examples of happily married people. Fred comes home from a busy day at the plant full of the doings of his day. He tells Mabel about how grouchy the boss is, how green his new assistant is, how much progress he is making on his new machine, what he had for lunch, and what a funny duck he got to talking to on the way home on the bus. This conversation takes up most of the dinner hour; it leaves Fred relaxed at having spilled his day's experiences and gives Mabel the feeling that she has been a part of Fred's day.

Mabel too has things to relate. She wants to share excerpts of the letter she has just received from her folks. She is eager to discuss with Fred what they will do with her mother when her father goes (this last letter tells of another heart attack, and both Fred and Mabel know that some day soon there will be one too many of them). Although they don't reach a final decision, Mabel senses that Fred is back of her, whatever happens, and she feels a sudden burst of affection for her good old dependable Fred right there while they are finishing dessert. She gets confidence to confess that she has been running over her budget for the month, which they talk over with some heat. They end up with an understanding of the financial situation, and the atmosphere is cleared, leaving them both relieved.

After supper they do the dishes together. Fred drops and breaks the jelly dish. Mabel starts to fuss and then admits that she hated the thing anyway. They got it last Christmas from Aunt Harriet, whom she always has disliked. Fred grins and says he can't stand her either, as he kisses the back of Mabel's neck. She leans against him for a moment and observes that this is one thing she likes about him: they both dislike the same people.

Aunt Harriet gets a going over by both of them as they move into the living room and turn on the radio. Their favorite mystery couple comes on for a half hour, leaving them feeling as if they too had been out on an adventure. Fred puts on some records that they both enjoy and goes over his paper once more, and Mabel sews in front of the fire. The clock strikes ten as the symphony hour comes on. They are both tired but agree to stay up until the program is over. Mabel puts up her sewing and stretches out on the sofa. Fred drops his paper and comes over to sit beside her. As a favorite passage of music flows into the room, Fred squeezes Mabel's hand and smiles into her eyes.

By bedtime there has developed a strong sense of belonging to each other, a feeling of true unity. Sex intercourse then becomes not just a physical release, but a symbol of the whole relationship. Into it flow the meanings and the feeling tones of the broken jelly dish and the music and Fred's boss and Mabel's mother and all the security that has come from working it all through together.

Next morning Fred gets up feeling like a million, and leaves for work with the conviction that it would take a dozen bosses to get him down today. Mabel goes out to shop with a tune on her lips, and in her mind a resolution to economize. Both face the new day with more poise, more peace, more strength and courage, because the two are one.

The accompanying diagram shows roughly what the sex relationship has meant to Fred and Mabel in symbolizing their sense of unity.

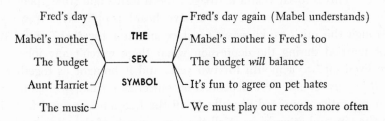

Making Marriage Fun

When the peace of the household has been broken and the offending party finds himself in the doghouse, he may utilize any number of devices to restore the *status quo*, one of the most effective being the use of humor. There is something funny about almost every marital crisis if the participants don't take themselves too seriously. A mate with a funnybone is an asset to any partnership and has saved many a marriage from cracking up.

Conciliatory devices become extremely handy to "save face" in a tense situation and are most often learned in the parental family in the process of growing up. In our culture we have developed a repertoire of techniques which most of us recognize when they are used on us, but which enable us to save face and make up if we really want to. These devices are no cure for fundamental alienation, but they tide over many a marriage in the early stages of conflict to the point where a workable balance is attainable. Every couple should be familiar with these techniques and should learn to use them to advantage. They are: 1. humor twists, such as punning, kidding, infantilisms; 2. storytelling; 3. compliments and flattery; 4. tension-dispelling devices, such as walking, swearing, crying; 5. appeals to the past history of the relationship;

6. displacing hostility onto a pet peeve common to both; 7. apologies, resolutions to improve, statements of plans for the future, etc.

Weathering the Storms

No marriage can be called a strong marriage at the outset. It is untried, untested; only after experiences with normal conflict and only after meeting such crises as war separations, depressions, unemployment, or serious illness can we be assured of the fundamental solidarity of a marriage. This is to say that a marriage is both tested and strengthened by the crises it has overcome. We have heard people say, "If we get through this crisis we know we can face anything together," and, "We got married during the depression when there weren't any jobs, and we lived on $50 a month for two years and it brought us together as nothing else could. We depended on ourselves for moral support, and our recreation consisted of walks to all the free museums and factories in the city and attendance at all the free concerts of the city symphony orchestra. We shall never be afraid of facing impoverishment, because we know from experience we can take it!"

Some of the forces we usually think of as making for break-ups also make for solidarity. It is a source of security to a married couple to have been through enough conflicts to learn how to handle them. The pair need no longer be afraid if tensions build up to a high pitch; a blow-up might clear the air. A good fight defines the issues, and leaves the combatants knowing that they are still loved and can get away with airing their differences. Over a period of time grievances accumulate and tension arises. There is a quarrel, and the grievances are expressed. Both persons experience a purging of their souls, and then settle back into the accustomed level of routine interaction. Crises, conflict, and illnesses, mastered and assimilated, act as forces to hold marriage together.

Why People Stay Married

Much has been written about marital conflict but relatively little about marital solidarity. The happily married pair have until recently kept their secrets locked up — only the alienated and the divorced have spilled for research workers. As far as we have gone in our discussion of marital solidarity, we are on firm ground, however. We have drawn largely from materials on well-adjusted families obtained from shrewd observers of family life and from the files of marital guidance clinics, which deal with both marital failures and marital successes.

What are the factors which hold marriages together in America to-day?

1 Couples begin marriage with the expectation of success, and this ideal of solidarity holds them together.

2 Much of social life is organized around married pairs — there is no satisfactory provision for the single person, unmarried, widowed, or divorced.

3 Couples find uniquely supplied in the marriage relationship the satisfaction of many basic adult needs: the desire for affection, companionship, security, recognition, response, and understanding.

4 Common interests, family jokes, and common experiences hold marriage together.

5 Marriage becomes a habit which is painful to break; the interdependence which develops because of duties performed solidifies marriage.

6 In the struggle for a common goal a new feeling of unity arises, a sense of having fought and bled together.

7 Conjugal love is a tying factor which grows as marriage progresses, thrives on companionship, common experiences, and the memory of things familiar.

8 The meeting of sexual needs comes to symbolize for the couple the sense of growing unity in the marriage relationship.

9 The use of tension-dispelling devices tides over many marriages in the early stages of conflict to the point where a workable balance is attainable.

10 Crises such as war separations, impoverishment, and serious illnesses test and may strengthen the untried marriage.

Selected Readings

BOWMAN, HENRY A., *Marriage for Moderns* (New York: McGraw-Hill, 1948), Chap. 10.

LANDIS, JUDSON T., AND LANDIS, MARY, *Building A Successful Marriage* (New York: Prentice-Hall, 1948), chaps. 10–14.

LEVY, JOHN, AND MUNROE, RUTH, *The Happy Family* (New York: Knopf, 1938), Chap. 5.

MAYO, ELTON, "Should Marriage Be Monotonous?" *Harper's* Magazine (September, 1925), Vol. 151, pp. 420–427.

MERRILL, FRANCIS E., *Courtship and Marriage* (New York: Sloane, 1949), chaps. 13–14.

WALLER, WILLARD, AND HILL, REUBEN, *The Family: A Dynamic Interpretation* (New York: Dryden Press, 1951), chaps. 14–16.

Technical References

BURGESS, ERNEST W., AND LOCKE, HARVEY, *The Family: From Institution to Companionship* (New York: American Book, 1945), Chap. 11, "Family Unity."

FISHBEIN, MORRIS, AND BURGESS, ERNEST W. (EDS.), *Successful Marriage* (Philadelphia: Blakiston, 1949), Chap. 8, "Psychological Factors in Marital Adjustments."

FOLSOM, JOSEPH K., *The Family and Democratic Society* (New York: Wiley, 1943), Chap. 12, "Personality and Marital Happiness."

MAGOUN, F. A., *Love and Marriage* (New York: Harper, 1948), Chap. 2, "The Nature of Marriage."

WINCH, ROBERT F., *The Modern Family* (New York: Holt, 1952), Chap. 15, "Companionship Love and Marriage: A Theory of Complementary Needs."

PART 3

THE MAKING OF A FAMILY

CHAPTER SIXTEEN

"And he looks just like his dad . . ."

WHERE BABIES COME FROM

Will your children be just like you?

Just what happens during the period before birth?

Why can't some couples have babies?

How much does a baby owe to heredity?

*T*HERE ARE NO CHILDLESS FAMILIES, JUST CHILDLESS MARRIAGES, BE-cause it takes a baby to make a family out of a marriage. This chapter is devoted to the discussion of what it takes to bring a baby into the world, the process of embryonic growth from fertilized ovum to finished product. Each baby that is born has a history which starts long before its squeal is heard in the delivery room. To tell that story is our present assignment.

How Much Do You Know about Heredity?

In reviewing where babies come from we look first at the endowments each starts with, his inheritances. What do you know about heredity? Try yourself out on the following test by Dr. Amram Scheinfeld.[1] Mark each statement true or false. Check your answers with those of Dr. Scheinfeld, which follow immediately after the test. Give yourself ten points for each right answer. Then add up your score and see how you stand; 80 to 100 is excellent, 60 to 80 is good, 40 to 60 is average, 20 to 40 means that you will learn a lot from this chapter that you never knew before.

[1] Reprinted by special permission of the Curtis Publishing Company; see Amram Scheinfeld, "How Much Do You Know about Heredity?" *Ladies' Home Journal*, November, 1941, pp. 121–123.

_____ 1 A child's sex is determined by the father.

_____ 2 A son born to a man of seventy will be weaker than one he fathered at thirty.

_____ 3 A pregnant mother can in no way improve the future character of her child by keeping her thoughts pure, listening to good music, reading inspiring books, and so on.

_____ 4 The mother contributes more to her son's heredity than does the father.

_____ 5 Redheads are by nature more passionate than blondes.

_____ 6 In a blood transfusion, a mother's blood is safest for her child.

_____ 7 A Negro child may be born to an apparently white couple if one of them had a Negro ancestor.

_____ 8 Members of certain human races cannot reproduce if mated with members of a widely different race.

_____ 9 Women have just as much native intelligence as men.

_____ 10 There are no human "thoroughbred" families.

Here are the facts:

1 (*True.*) The human male produces two kinds of sperm which differ in a minute degree with respect to sex-determining properties. The egg produced by the mother is "neutral." Thus if one type of sperm (containing an "X" chromosome) fertilizes the egg, the result will be a girl; if the other type (containing a "Y" chromosome), a boy results.

2 (*False.*) Neither the age nor the condition of the father can change the nature of the chromosomes (hereditary factors) which he transmits to a child.

3 (*True.*) Any hereditary factors bearing on the child's character are in it the moment it is conceived. Not until after it is born can the mother influence the child's character for the better.

4 (*True.*) While their contributions to a child's heredity are in all other respects equal, the sex chromosome ("X") contributed by mother to son contains many additional "genes" not present in the sex chromosome ("Y") from the father. Thus, certain defects — such as hemophilia — are passed on to sons only by their mothers, because the genes for them occur only in the sex chromosome they get from her.

5 (*False.*) The hereditary factors producing hair coloring (and eye coloring as well) are not linked with those making for any specific type of personality. Any kind of coloring may go with any kind of temperament.

6 (*False.*) A mother's blood may often be as different from her child's and as dangerous to transfuse as that of some total stranger. Blood types are inherited through a combination of factors from both parents, and it is just as possible for a child and parent to have different blood types as to have different-colored eyes.

7 (*False.*) Only if both parents have Negro blood, and in a considerable degree, can a Negro baby appear. Stories to the contrary are either myths or cases of doubtful paternity.

8 (*False.*) All human beings belong to the same species, Homo sapiens, and are fertile with one another.

9 (*True.*) All intelligence tests now indicate that women have as much mental capacity as men, but that any intellectual inferiority on their part is due to less opportunity to develop themselves.

10 (*True.*) To produce human thoroughbreds, as in domestic animals, would have required the closest inbreeding between mothers and sons, fathers and daughters, brothers and sisters. As matters stand, all humans, even members of royalty, are biologically mongrels.

No One Else Just Like You! You are somebody very special. There never has been anyone like you. There isn't one chance in 300,000,000,-000,000 of there ever being another person just like you! Yet you were not a haphazard accident that could happen only once in the history of mankind. You were rather the result of a complete new deal of human characteristics. Every one of your children, and your grandchildren, and their children will be quite as unique — yet they will be your progeny and draw from the same general pool of inheritance that produced you. With Nature emphasizing uniqueness so strongly, how does she do it? What is the process by which you became you in the first place?

The fact that your father chose your mother (or the other way around) brought together two streams of heredity that had been branching out in similar twosomes since the beginning of time. And then out of the hundreds of human ova produced by your mother and the hundreds of millions of sperm available from your father, the fusion of the particular egg with the particular sperm that started you off was something that never could happen twice the same way.

You began with the union of one of your mother's human eggs which, though no bigger than a fraction of a dot on this paper, carried the full deal of her side of the family to you, and the microscopic sperm which brought you everything that had been dealt out for you from your father's side of the house. The microscopic miracle that carried all your characteristics and inherent tendencies in this union of two germ cells was an elaborate and highly exact arrangement of ultra-minute packets of hereditary determiners called *genes*. For each characteristic that was inherited there was a pair of genes (one from father, one from mother). The color of your eyes, the shape of your nose, the set-up of your body, the length of your fingers, the tendency to freckle or not, to sing on key or not, and to have twins or not, these and all of your other characteristics were to be found in potential form in the genes somewhere in the fertilized ovum which, in time, was to be you.

These genes are strung like beads on a string, each one exactly matching in position the parallel gene of every other germ cell, and separated at convenient lengths in tiny bodies called *chromosomes*. Military drill has nothing on chromosome formation. There are always the same number when they line up for review, each one in its place.

Deep in your reproductive organs is a cluster of cells that exist for the sole purpose of transmitting your particular line-up of genes and chromosomes to your children. These *germ cells* (produced in the ovaries of the girl and in the testes of the boy) coast along through childhood without much activity. At adolescence the ovaries and testes begin their business of turning out at regular intervals the germ cells that have the capacity of making a parent of you — an ovum every month in the girl, hundreds of millions of sperm every few days in the boy. Whether you marry or not, these germ cells are produced with a faithful regularity throughout your active adulthood. In germ cell production, instead of each chromosome splitting to form 48 new ones for each cell, each *pair of chromosomes* separates and one goes into each new cell, so that the final germ cell has just half of the original twenty-four pairs, twenty-four singles. Twenty-four singles from the mother plus twenty-four singles from the father equal twenty-four new pairs when they unite to form the beginnings of a new baby. Twenty-four pairs of chromosomes, each with its own gene determiners, now struggle for dominance. Some characteristics cover up others, in the same way that darker colors cover lighter ones on a canvas. A gene for dark hair, for instance, finding itself paired off with a gene for blond locks, has the right of way and wins the race for expression in the new individual. This tendency for some genes to win over others in the expression of characteristics is called *dominance* and works according to the well-known laws of heredity. The characteristic that is there but doesn't show in the new individual is said to be *recessive* (blond hair coloring in the illustration above is recessive . . . it doesn't show in this person, but paired off with another blond gene in the next generation might result in a true goldilocks). A monk by the name of Mendel, studying many generations of flowers in his garden during the last

This is what makes all the differences there are
between a woman and a man:

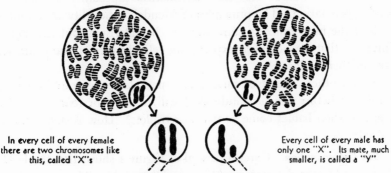

In every cell of every female
there are two chromosomes like
this, called "X"s

Every cell of every male has
only one "X". Its mate, much
smaller, is called a "Y"

X X   X Y

For reproduction, a female forms eggs, a male sperms,
to each of which they contribute only HALF their quota
of chromosomes, or just one from every pair

Since a female has TWO "X"s, each egg gets one
"X", so in this respect every egg is the same:

But as the male has only ONE "X", paired with
a "Y", he forms TWO kinds of sperms:

 ----- X

HALF WITH
AN "X"

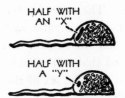

HALF WITH
A "Y"

Thus: If an "X"-bearing sperm enters the egg,
the result is an individual with TWO "X"s

   =   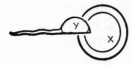   A GIRL

. . . If a "Y"-bearing sperm enters the egg,
the result is an "XY" individual, or

    =   A BOY

FIG. 1 How Sex Is Determined

century, discovered this tendency of some genes to cover the expression of others, and worked out the mathematical expectancy in each succeeding generation. The principles of Mendelian heredity are found to work in the inheritance of some human characteristics, but it is not as simple as that, so not even experts can reliably predict the characteristics of their children.[2]

Certain other aspects of inheritance may challenge you: What determines whether the new individual will be male or female? What happens when babies come as twins or triplets? How is skin color inherited?

Sex Determination. Careful perusal of Figure 1 shows that the father is responsible for determining the sex of his child. There are apparently two kinds of spermatozoa, and the sex of the child is determined by the type which enters the Fallopian tubes first and fertilizes the egg. There are hundreds of millions of sperm in each ejaculation of semen and it is pretty much a matter of chance which type of sperm reaches the egg first. Since a few more boys than girls are conceived, there would seem to be a slight advantage in favor of the male-determining sperm. The normal ratio of 105 boy babies to 100 girls at birth in the U.S.A. varies slightly with race and age of mothers,[3] but no one has been able to explain satisfactorily just why. Nor has any method emerged that will reliably select which type of sperm will fertilize the egg, so that the sex of the child-to-be remains a mystery until the baby is born.

Twinning. Twinning seems to run in families, and there has been a great deal of speculation on just how the tendency is inherited. No definitely reliable findings are available that will guarantee the production of twins — nor give insurance against their arrival in any given union! Like almost all of the other products of gene shuffling there is a new deal for each new child, and prediction of twins is difficult.

Figure 2 points to the following generalizations concerning twins: 1. there are two kinds of twins, identical and fraternal; 2. identical twins come from the *same* fertilized egg; 3. identical twins are always of the same sex and share the same heredity; 4. fraternal twins come

---

[2] Amram Scheinfeld, *The New You and Heredity* (Philadelphia: Lippincott, 1950).

[3] C. A. McMahan, "An Empirical Test of Three Hypotheses concerning the Human Sex Ratio at Birth in the United States, 1915–1948," *Milbank Memorial Fund Quarterly* (July, 1951), pp. 273–93.

IDENTICAL TWINS
Are products of

A single
sperm

and

A single
egg

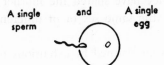

In an early stage
the embryo divides

The halves go
on to become
separate
individuals

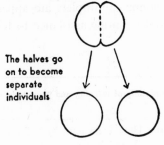

Usually — but not always — identical
twins share the same placenta and
fetal sac

But regardless of how they develop,
they carry the same genes and are
therefore

Always of the same sex — two boys
or two girls

FRATERNAL TWINS
Are products of TWO different eggs
fertilized by TWO different sperms

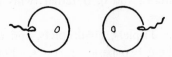

They have different genes and may
develop in different ways, usually—
but not always — having separate
placentas and separate fetal sacs

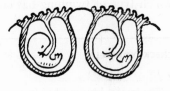

Also, as they are totally different individuals, they may be

Both
of the
same sex

Two boys

—or two girls

—Or a
mixed
pair

One
boy

One
girl

From Amram Scheinfeld, *You and Heredity* (Lippincott)

FIG. 2 How Twins Are Produced

from *two* different fertilized eggs, that is, two eggs and two sperm; 5. fraternal twins have no more in common in their heredity than other brothers and sisters, except that they have shared the mother's uterus; and 6. fraternal twins may be of the same sex or of different sexes.

Triplets, quadruplets, and quintuplets are formed by extensions of these two basic processes. For instance, triplets may be all fraternal (three fertilized ova), or all identical (one fertilized ovum with two divisions and separations), or partially identical and partially fraternal (one pair of identical twins and a fraternal third individual conceived and delivered together). The famous Dionne quintuplets are apparently identical. Often it is difficult without scientific assistance to tell which type of twinning has occurred.

CHECK YOURSELF   Fill in the blanks from your reading of twinning and your study of Figure 2.

---

1 The Joneses have just had twins, a boy and a girl. These twins must be _____.
2 Two boys, one blond and blue-eyed, the other dark and brown-eyed, were born of the same mother at the same time. They are probably _____ twins.
3 Two girls just exactly alike have been born of the same mother at the same time. They are not twins. Therefore they must be _____.
4 Twin girls marry twin boys. It is _____ that they will have twins.
5 Identical twins are always of the _____ sex.

★ KEY   1 Fraternal   2 Fraternal   3 Two of a set of triplets or more   4 Possible   5 Same

---

How Skin Color Is Inherited. The facts about skin color are not widely known. Especially is there public confusion about the inheritance of skin color in interracial unions. The materials presented in Figure 3 cover only two types of skin color genes, but there are probably more. Some of the facts on skin color inheritance implied from this chart are worthy of restatement: 1. two full-blooded Negroes could not have a white child; 2. two pure whites could not have a Negro baby; 3. two parents from mixed Negro-white stock *might have* a white child; 4. two parents from mixed Negro-white stock *could have* a dark-skinned child, even though they were relatively light-skinned themselves; 5. in respect to skin color, the mulatto is always of mixed

IF A NEGRO MATES WITH A WHITE:

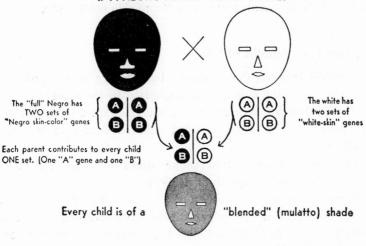

The "full" Negro has TWO sets of "Negro skin-color" genes

The white has two sets of "white-skin" genes

Each parent contributes to every child ONE set. (One "A" gene and one "B")

Every child is of a   "blended" (mulatto) shade

WHEN TWO MULATTOS (like child above) MATE:

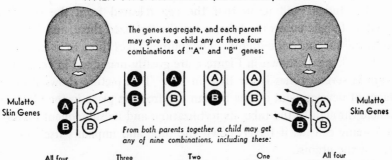

The genes segregate, and each parent may give to a child any of these four combinations of "A" and "B" genes:

Mulatto Skin Genes   Mulatto Skin Genes

From both parents together a child may get any of nine combinations, including these:

All four "Negro" genes:	Three "Negro" genes:	Two "Negro" genes:	One "Negro" gene:	All four "White" genes:

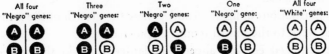

PRODUCING CHILDREN OF VARIOUS SHADES:

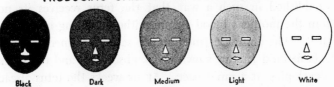

Black   Dark   Medium   Light   White

(NOTE: Only two types of skin color genes are shown, but there probably are more)

From Amram Scheinfeld, *You and Heredity* (Lippincott)

FIG. 3 Skin Color

heredity, Negro and white; and 6. a true black-skinned child can occur only if *both* parents carry some Negro skin color genes.

The First Nine Months of Life

That period between the moment when the egg is fertilized and the
time when the baby is born is characterized by the most rapid growth
and the greatest differentiation of the whole life span, yet few of us have
the opportunity for studying what happens during these first nine
months of life.

The accompanying pictorial presentations show the development of
the baby from conception through birth.

Figure 4 shows a cross section of a uterus, a Fallopian tube, and an
ovary. To check his familiarity with the items shown in the chart, the
reader might try to locate and label the following: ovary, Graafian follicle (there are three or four in the ovary section), Fallopian tube,
uterus, body of uterus, and cervix of uterus.

The student will recall that the egg released from the ruptured
Graafian follicle enters the tube, is usually fertilized there, and journeys
down the tube into the uterus. The journey takes three to five days.

The elements shown in Figure 5 are greatly magnified in size. The
ovum is several times larger than in life. This picture shows thirteen
stages of development of one human egg from its place in the Graafian
follicle through to the tube, its fertilization, and its subsequent division
into many cells as it travels down the tube and implants itself in the
wall of the uterus.

The illustrations in figures 6 and 7 show the growth of the fetus from
the sixth week to the fourth month of pregnancy.

The fertilized egg has already implanted itself in the wall of the
uterus. The placenta has long since been formed and the baby's circulation established in such a way that the fetus receives its nourish-
ment from the mother's blood stream without coming into direct contact with it. The amniotic (membrane) sac has formed, in which the
baby floats in fluid (nature's own shock absorber), and the fetus itself
is now developing at a rapid pace. At six weeks the fetus already has
a definite shape, although it cannot yet be said to look very human! By
four weeks a careful student may be able to identify the arm and leg
buds, the spinal column which ends in a true-to-life tail, and the large

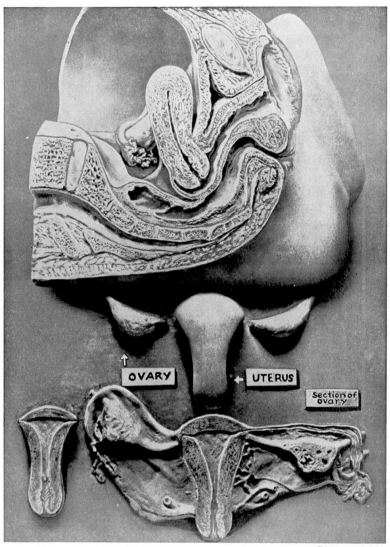

Dickinson-Belskie

FIG. 4 Cross Section of Uterus and Related Organs
Below: Before and After Pregnancy

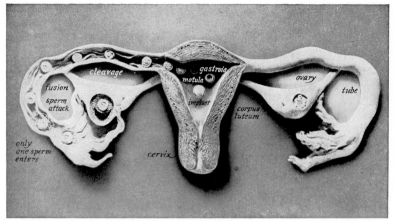

FIG. 5 Travel of Egg: Ovulation to Nidation

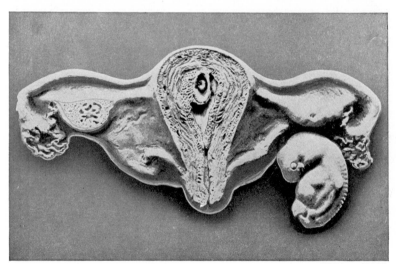

FIG. 6 Fetus at Six Weeks

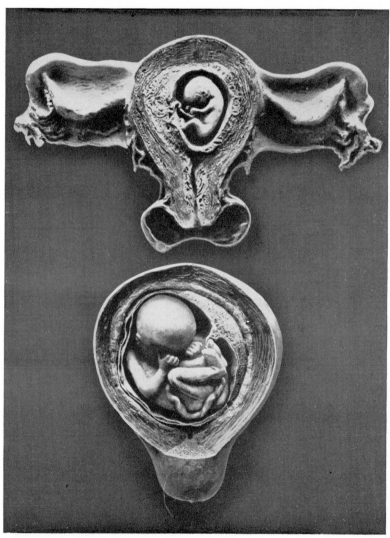

Dickinson-Belskie

FIG. 7 Fetus at 2½ Months and 3½ Months

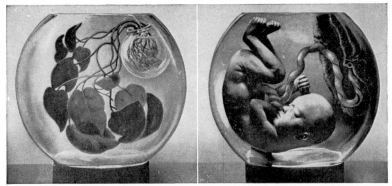

FIG. 8 Baby Grows Like the Plant

FIG. 9 Before Labor

head with the beginnings of the eyes and mouth. By three and one half months (about fourteen weeks) the fetus is several inches long and is beginning to look like a real baby. Although it weighs only about two ounces, it is already complete with fingers and toes and a very shapely ear.

The two pictures in Figure 8 are arranged to show how the fetus is fed through the umbilical cord and the placenta in much the same way as a plant is nourished through its stem and root system. In the case of the fetus, the blood vessels of the mother and those of the baby lie close to each other within the placenta, and the exchange of food (from the mother's blood to the baby's) and waste (from the baby to the mother) takes place through the membranes of the blood vessels. The mother's blood does *not* enter the baby. Blood from the placenta is conveyed by blood vessels in the cord to the baby.

Figure 9 shows the baby in the uterus just before labor begins. The baby is full term and is ready to be born. Now it weighs seven and one half pounds, more or less, and is about twenty inches long. The baby is in the best position for birth with the head against the cervix. See if you can find the following landmarks of the mother's anatomy: the bladder (squeezed between the baby's head and the bone in front), the colon, the vagina, the pubic symphysis, the end of the mother's spinal column.

Figure 10 shows the cervix dilating (notice how much thinner it is than in Figure 9). The mother is now in labor. The *first stage of labor,* in which the cervix dilates enough to let the baby through, usually lasts about sixteen hours for a first baby (less for subsequent children) and is characterized by rhythmic pains that increase in intensity and frequency until the cervix is completely open. It is early in the first stage that the woman usually notifies her physician of labor pains. She will be ordered to the hospital when the interval between pains is from ten to fifteen minutes.

Figure 11 shows the cervix completely open. One thin portion of the cervix shows just at the baby's right ear lobe, the other high on the forehead. The mother is now in the *second stage of labor,* in which the pains come frequently and with great intensity. The pains now have a bearing-down quality as the uterine muscles attempt to expel the baby. This stage of labor lasts for an hour or two and is usually made endurable for the woman by anesthetic or analgesic.

In Figure 12 we see the baby's head already born and the doctor assisting in the birth of the shoulders. The uterine and abdominal muscles are contracting vigorously now. Note how the baby's shoulders turn to fit the size of the birth passage. Not all babies are born with head and shoulders first, although that is the most frequent position. The so-called breech presentation, buttocks first, is not an infrequent occurrence.

In Figure 13 we see the *third stage of labor*. The placenta is separating from the uterine wall and will soon be expelled along with the membranes and umbilical cord that is still attached to it. The other end of the cord has been tied and cut close to the baby's body. This expulsion of afterbirth and cord is the third stage of labor. It usually lasts only a few minutes and is felt by the mother as a series of pains similar to those which caused the birth of the baby. They bring about the final separation of the placenta from the uterine wall. The doctor examines the materials carefully to make sure that the placenta has been completely expelled after the birth of the baby, because of complications which might otherwise arise.

Abortions and Miscarriages

The emptying of the uterus before *full term* (nine months) is not uncommon, occurring in one out of every five pregnancies. The popular term *miscarriage* refers to the accidental or spontaneous emptying of the pregnant uterus, while an *abortion* is generally held to mean the act of artificially relieving the pregnant uterus of its contents. In medical language an abortion is the expulsion of the fetus and placenta for any cause between the time of conception and the twenty-eighth week of pregnancy. Between this period and full term, expulsion of the baby is called *premature labor*.

The cause of most miscarriages is unknown. Some may be due to defective germ plasm (bad eggs or sperms). Other causes are maternal diseases, such as chronic kidney disease or syphilis, and abnormalities, such as tumors of the uterus. Injuries and shock to the mother are not usually sufficient in themselves to precipitate a miscarriage.

Occasionally it is necessary for a physician to terminate a pregnancy to save a mother's life. This is called a *therapeutic abortion* and is done only under the most favorable conditions. It must be medically justi-

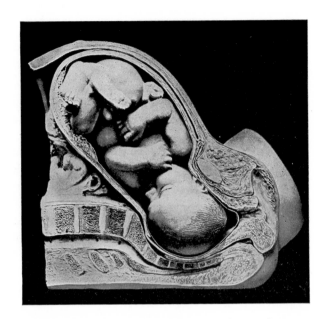

FIG. 10   Labor: Cervix Dilating and Bag of Waters

FIG. 11   Full Dilation, Cervix High, Head Deep in Pelvis

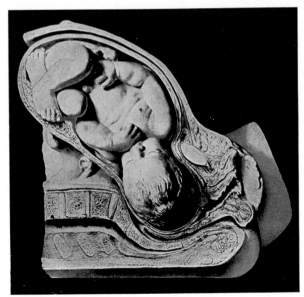

Photos by Dickinson-Belskie

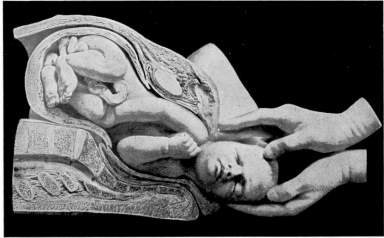

FIG. 12 Birth of Shoulders Rotation

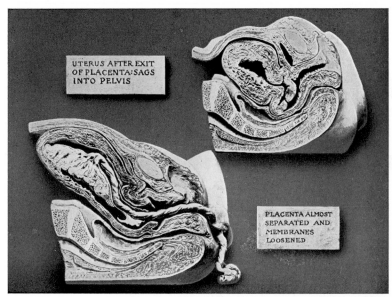

UTERUS AFTER EXIT OF PLACENTA: SAGS INTO PELVIS

PLACENTA ALMOST SEPARATED AND MEMBRANES LOOSENED

FIG. 13 Third Stage of Labor

fied and officially authorized. Unless carried out in a recognized hospital by a competent physician under the conditions just specified, interrupting a pregnancy by destroying the fetus is legally forbidden in most states, and known as *criminal abortion*. The dangers of *infection* and *hemorrhage* are great, since criminal abortions are usually performed under most unfortunate conditions by practitioners of questionable skill and training. Since there is no known medication which when taken by mouth will empty the uterus of its contents without grave danger to the woman, the abortionist must resort to surgical procedures. These are usually performed without complete antiseptic safeguards and they exact a heavy toll of maternal lives. If you or any of your friends are considering an abortion — stop! Talk it over with your family doctor. It's a privilege to have children, and some women may become pregnant only once in their life span.[4]

The Rh Factor [5]

Since 1941, when it was first discovered, there have been hundreds of articles on the Rh factor in the blood. Many of these discuss the possible damage that may be done to the fetus in the mother whose Rh blood type is incompatible with that of the father.

Approximately 85 per cent of the white population of the United States have Rh positive blood. That is, they have blood containing one or more Rh factors. The other 15 per cent have Rh negative blood containing no Rh factor. Actually there are several varieties in the Rh family, but the above is roughly correct.

When both father and mother have the same Rh blood type there is no difficulty. Or if the mother is Rh positive, all goes well. But when an Rh positive man and an Rh negative woman have an Rh positive child, then the Rh positive blood cells from the fetal circulation *may* escape into the mother's blood stream. There they stimulate the mother's blood to produce antibodies capable of destroying the Rh positive blood cells. These antibodies enter the fetal circulation and attack the baby's blood cells, producing *erythroblastosis*, or *hemolytic disease*. Some of the usual symptoms of this disease are jaundice, anemia, and

---

[4] See *How Does Your Baby Grow?* (New York: Maternity Center Association, 1942), p. 12.

[5] From Evelyn Duvall, *Facts of Life and Love* (New York: Association Press, 1950), pp. 70–71.

general edema, or swelling, in the baby. Such babies may die as they near term, or soon after birth, or they may survive and be perfectly normal children.

In spite of all the public concern, this disease is not very common. Out of 80,000 births in Chicago in 1948, only twenty infant deaths were known to be from erythroblastosis, according to Dr. Edith Potter, pathologist at Chicago Lying-In Hospital. One reason why this is a much lower incidence than might be expected (when 15 per cent of the white women are Rh negative) is that other conditions besides the Rh factor must be present in order for the disease to develop. For instance, this difficulty is not usual in the first-born. It is after antibodies have been built up in the mother's blood by previous pregnancies that the baby may be affected. Secondly, there must be some leakage in the fetal and maternal circulations in the placenta in order for the red blood cells of the baby to reach the mother's blood stream. Usually the circulation of blood in the baby and in the mother is kept separate, each within its own blood vessels.

Therefore, although some doctors will give tests for the Rh factor in the blood of couples about to be married, this is not yet usual practice. The reason is that the discovery of incompatible blood types is not necessarily a prognosis of Rh trouble in pregnancy, as we have seen above, and therefore should not be a deterrent for the marriage or the parenthood of the couple involved.

Blood studies for the Rh factor may be personally reassuring to some couples with personal fears about it (because of difficulties with it among family or friends, or the anxiety produced by wide-spread publicity of it), since the chances are very much in the direction of a favorable combination of Rh blood types in any individual couple.

Infertility and Sterility

One out of every ten couples who want children are unable to have them. This inability to conceive is called *infertility*, which is treatable, or *sterility*, if the inability is permanent, and may be due to many causes. Sometimes the male sperms are not numerous enough or sufficiently active to reach and fertilize the egg. Rest, improved health, and medical treatment may correct the condition sufficiently for conception to take place. In the woman the cause may be 1) immature or infertile sex organs, 2) a tilted uterus, 3) obstructions of the cervix, 4) unfavorable vaginal secretions which affect the sperms' motility, 5) glandular deficiencies, or 6) closed tubes which make it impossible for the sperm and the egg to meet. *Infertility clinics* in our larger maternity hospitals are successfully treating many couples who desire their own children, with many responding favorably to treatment.

Test Tube Babies. Modern science is not yet able to grow babies in a test tube, but some advance has been made in helping couples who want babies to have them. Sometimes the treatment of the physician or of the infertility clinic is not enough to assure the couple of conception. When the man has insufficient or inadequate sperm, and remedial treatment does not correct his condition, the only way his wife may become pregnant is through impregnation with other sperm. The careful physician makes sure that the use of other sperm will be acceptable psychologically to both members of the couple, then selects a semen donor whose health and heredity are acceptable and compatible, and with a syringe deposits the semen donation in the upper end of the vagina, or directly into the uterus at the time of the month most favorable to conception. Legal tangles (the baby is not the husband's), religious, social, and psychological problems, and difficulties of matching donors to recipients without the knowledge of either keep artificial insemination from becoming widely accepted. It has promise, however, for the many couples who would otherwise be childless, and is mentioned in the recent literature as a possibility for some couples whose Rh blood types are incompatible and who have in previous pregnancies faced the frustration of miscarriage or fetal death. Some eugenists favor artificial insemination as a means of improving the human stock, as has been common practice in animal husbandry for many years, but to date the practice remains more of an intriguing possibility than an actuality for the average couple.

Eugenics

The science of improving human stock by influencing the hereditary process is called eugenics. The methods suggested vary all the way from encouraging biologically superior people to have more children (by subsidizing "good" families, improving maternal and infant care, etc.) to sterilizing the biologically unfit, so that they cannot reproduce their kind. Each individual concerns himself with eugenics when he considers the factors in his own and his mate's family background which may affect the children of the marriage. Such questions as the following might be asked: What hereditary weaknesses occur in either of our families? What chances are there that an aunt's insanity or a brother's epilepsy or an uncle's hemophilia might appear in our children? These are technical questions, the answers to which are best worked out with a professional investigator through detailed study of the individual case.

Healthy babies born of good stock to couples who intelligently plan for their arrival are the hope of the nation and the joy of their parents.

Selected Readings

BROWN, FRED, AND KEMPTON, RUDOLF, Sex Questions and Answers (New York: McGraw-Hill, 1950).

DICKINSON, ROBERT, AND BELSKIE, ABRAM, Birth Atlas, Second Edition (New York: Maternity Center Association, 1943).

DUVALL, EVELYN, Facts of Life and Love (New York: Association Press, 1950), Chap. 3.

EASTMAN, NICHOLSON, Expectant Motherhood (Boston: Little, Brown, 1940).

ETS, MARIE HALL, The Story of a Baby (New York: Viking, 1939).

FISHBEIN, MORRIS, AND BURGESS, ERNEST (EDS.), Successful Marriage (Garden City: Doubleday, 1947), Part II, Chap. 10; Part III, chaps. 1–5.

GILBERT, MARGARET, Biography of the Unborn (Baltimore: Williams and Wilkins, 1938).

GOODRICH, FREDERICK W., JR., Natural Childbirth, A Manual for Expectant Parents (New York: Prentice-Hall, 1950).

GUTTMACHER, ALAN, Having a Baby: A Guide for Expectant Parents (New York: Signet, 1947).

——, The Story of Human Birth (New York: Pelican, 1947).

LANDIS, JUDSON, AND LANDIS, MARY, Building a Successful Marriage (New York: Prentice-Hall, 1948), Chap. 18.

MUSEUM OF SCIENCE AND INDUSTRY, The Miracle of Growth (Urbana: University of Illinois Press, 1950).

SCHEINFELD, AMRAM, The New You and Heredity (Philadelphia: Lippincott, 1950).

VAN BLARCOM, CAROLYN, AND CORBIN, HAZEL, Getting Ready to Be a Mother (New York: Macmillan, 1940).

Technical References

NEWMAN, H. H., Multiple Human Births (Garden City: Doubleday, 1940).

OSBORN, FREDERICK, Preface to Eugenics, Revised Edition (New York: Harper, 1951).

PARSHLEY, H. M., *The Science of Human Reproduction* (New York: Norton, 1933).

POTTER, EDITH, *Fundamentals of Human Reproduction* (New York: McGraw-Hill, 1948).

——, *Rh* (Chicago: Yearbook Publishers, 1947).

SCHATKIN, S. B., "Artificial Insemination: Legal Aspects (human)," *Human Fertility* (June, 1948).

SNYDER, L. H., "The Genetic Approach to Human Individuality," *Science Monthly* (March, 1949).

STERN, CURT, "The 'Black Baby of White Parents' Myth," *Journal of Heredity* (August, 1945).

STRANDSKOV, H. H.; ROTH, J. A.; AND BISACCIA, HENRY, "Sex Ratio of Human Stillbirths," *American Journal of Physical Anthropology* (1949), No. 7, pp. 1, 2.

WIENER, A. S., AND OTHERS, "Heredity of the 'Rh' Blood Types," *American Journal of Human Genetics* (December, 1949).

CHAPTER SEVENTEEN

"Why didn't someone tell me?"

GETTING READY TO BE PARENTS

How soon after marriage should the first baby be planned for?

How painful is childbirth?

How does it feel to be a father?

Why is prenatal care important?

*W*ANTING A CHILD IS AS NATURAL AS WANTING A MATE AND IS a normal manifestation of our growth as persons. For the couple ready for this step, having a baby is a supremely satisfying experience. There is more to having a child than just wanting it, however. This chapter is concerned with the preparations and adjustments couples make in readying themselves for parenthood.

Why Have Babies?

We have babies because we want them. Powerful physical, psychological, and social forces drive us into the experience of parenthood. No substitute has been devised to return satisfactions equal to those received from bearing and rearing children. One expert summarizes the fundamental gratification of pregnancy, childbirth, and child rearing for women when he writes: "The bearing and rearing of children is woman's greatest achievement and the climax of her erotic expression . . . not only her greatest joy, but the source of her greatest power." [1] Having a family is a fulfillment of a couple's desire to establish a home of their own.

[1] Karl Menninger, *Love against Hate* (New York: Harcourt, Brace, 1942), p. 52.

Studies of both college and noncollege young people indicate that they are looking forward eagerly to parenthood. Increasingly both boys and girls are signing up for courses in child care and are becoming intellectually interested in parenthood long before they are ready chronologically to become parents.

How do we explain such interest in having babies? One explanation is that each one of us has played the role of parent in childhood play groups and in his daydreams for years. When we marry it seems only right and natural that we should have children in our family. This expectation is derived from having been reared in a family and having learned so satisfyingly the parental roles.

Social pressures add their weight to bring couples around to starting a family. It is the thing to do after a few months of marriage. Other couples married about the same time blossom forth with baby carriages and beaming smiles, leaving laggards feeling strangely empty and fruitless. Bridge table and back-yard discussion among women, and golf and office conversation among men, center on first teeth, bright sayings, and recent accomplishments of babies. Parents of the newly married are reminded of their desire to become grandparents and may exert their influence in that direction. Attractive advertisements in magazines and

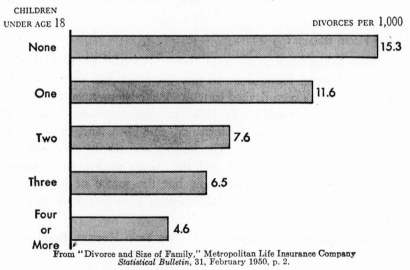

DIVORCES PER 1000 MARRIED COUPLES, ACCORDING TO
SIZE OF FAMILY. UNITED STATES, 1948

CHILDREN
UNDER AGE 18   DIVORCES PER 1,000

None — 15.3

One — 11.6

Two — 7.6

Three — 6.5

Four
or — 4.6
More

From "Divorce and Size of Family," Metropolitan Life Insurance Company
Statistical Bulletin, 31, February 1950, p. 2.

daily papers are another insidious force in stimulating interest — picture after picture shows winsome cherubs clothed in beguiling infant-wear, eating healthful cereal, and sleeping under downy quilts. No wonder the childless couple conclude that "all the world is having babies and we should have one too."

"More divorces have been prevented by a youngster's cry or smile than by any legislation," writes an eminent psychiatrist.[2] The fewer children, the higher the divorce rate, as seen in the chart above.[3] For couples without children the divorce rate in 1948 was 15.3 per 1,000. Where one child was present the rate was 11.6 per 1,000. The figure steadily decreases until we find in families with four or more children, a rate of 4.6. These findings indicate that the relative frequency of divorce is greater for families without children than for families with children. Yet, the presence of children is not necessarily a deterrent to divorce. It is possible that in most cases both divorce and childlessness result from more fundamental factors in the marital relationship. Conversely, children seem to be symbolic of the permanence of the marriage.

Time to Have the Baby

Many couples need time to work out the adjustments of a new marriage before adding pregnancy and its complications. First, the couple needs to adjust to living as two, to work out the routines of marriage and establish firmly the unity of the relation. All told, this process may take several months.

There are dangers, however, in postponing the first baby too long. The couple should not wait until they have enough money to take care of a child. Furniture, automobile, travel, can easily become an established part of the budget, so that children may never find a place. The young wife who works to save money for a family may find that her earnings serve only to advance the couple to a plane of living which they are reluctant to relinquish in favor of a baby.

Recent studies of Dr. Nicholson Eastman at Johns Hopkins Univer-

[2] John Levy and Ruth Munroe, *The Happy Family* (New York: Knopf, 1938), p. 240.
[3] See also Paul H. Jacobson, "Differentials in Divorce by Duration of Marriage and Size of Family," *American Sociological Review* (April, 1950), Vol. 15, pp. 235–244.

sity indicate conclusively that the age of the mother is of great importance in the bearing and delivering of babies. The decade between twenty and thirty in the woman's life is the optimum period for childbearing. The older the mother above thirty, the more dangerous is childbearing both for her and for the child.

Another important factor to consider is the readiness of the mother for a baby. A teen-age girl is rarely sufficiently grown up herself to sincerely want a baby and to be able to love it and care for it properly. The older woman likewise faces emotional difficulties in relating herself to her first baby. If she has wanted one for years, her final joy in having it may make for more possessive attachment than is good for the child. If she has been long postponing the baby's arrival, she may not really want one when it does arrive. Her ways may be fixed and her life routinized along other channels which may make it difficult to accept a child fully into the household.

The time of year may be a factor to consider in deciding when to have a baby. Since babies are especially susceptible to respiratory diseases and food infections during the first year of life, the autumn is a more desirable season than midsummer or winter. The Children's Bureau finds that the death rate of tiny babies is highest during July and August, especially in those parts of the country where refrigeration is not universally available. When the couple is prepared to provide adequate care for the infant, the seasonal factor may be of less importance than other matters of personal and family convenience.

The time to have a baby is when you want it! More important than all external factors is the genuine desire of both husband and wife for the baby. Child development studies have shown without doubt that being wanted is of primary importance in the well-being of the child. When a couple is ready and eager for children, then is the time to have them.

How Much Do Children Cost?

Children are expensive. They may have been an economic asset back on the farm where "a kid could earn his keep around the place." Today children are an economic liability in most families. Yet, they are not "luxury goods" that only the rich can afford! On the contrary, as you study the chart on page 443 you will see that most children are in low and moderate income families.

The cost of rearing a child in higher income families is proportionally higher than in more modest brackets. The Metropolitan Life Insurance Company, using data for the most part issued by the National Resources Planning Board and the Bureau of Labor Statistics, has carefully compared the item by item costs of rearing a child to the age of eighteen in two types of American families: those having an income of $2,500 a year, and those with an income of from $5,000 to $10,000 a year. As will be seen by studying the table below, every item but food shows a considerable proportionate increase, while expenditures for education, medical care, transportation, and recreation show the greatest increases. If interest on the investment and cost of burial are added, this study concludes, "the total cost of bringing up a child to the age of eighteen in families with an income of $5,000 to $10,000 a year averages $20,785. This figure does not, however, include the cost of public education and other services furnished by the community, nor the value of the personal services of the mother." [4]

EXPENDITURES TO BRING UP A CHILD TO AGE EIGHTEEN
ACCORDING TO 1935–36 PRICE LEVELS *

TYPE OF EXPENDITURE	AMOUNT		PERCENTAGE	
	$2,500	$5,000–10,000	$2,500	$5,000–10,000
Cost of being born	$ 300	$ 750	3.9	4.6
Food	2,272	3,628	29.3	22.2
Clothing	710	1,697	9.1	10.4
Shelter	2,648	5,774	34.1	35.3
	. . . . .	. . . . .	. . . .	. . . .
Clothing and shelter	3,358	7,471	43.2	45.7
Education	82	283	1.1	1.7
Medical care	297	846	3.8	5.2
Transportation and recreation	1,127	2,787	14.5	17.1
Sundries	327	572	4.2	3.5
Total	$7,763	$16,337	100.0	100.0

* By type of expenditure and family income

[4] *Statistical Bulletin* (New York: Metropolitan Life Insurance Company), January, 1944. NOTE: Since these figures, the most recent available (according to a personal communication from Louis Dublin, Second Vice-President and Statistician, the Metropolitan Life Insurance Company), are for 1935–36 price levels, and so markedly below those at midcentury, we read with interest from the same authority that, with a fixed income in a period of rising costs, the cost of bringing up a child will be raised by only a relatively small amount. Louis I. Dublin and Alfred Lotka, *The Money Value of a Man* (New York: Ronald Press, 1946), p. 57, footnote.

MOTHERS ARE HAVING MORE BABIES TODAY

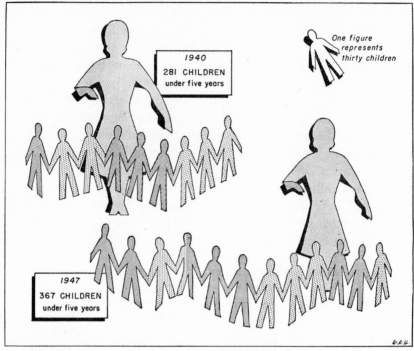

1940
281 CHILDREN
under five years

One figure
represents
thirty children

1947
367 CHILDREN
under five years

Children under five years per 1000 women of childbearing age (15–44 yrs), 1940 and 1947.
U. S. Bureau of the Census.

In addition to costing money, babies make drastic changes in the pattern of daily living, especially for those young people who heretofore have been relatively foot-loose and fancy free. If the couple wish to rationalize postponement, they can find reasons aplenty for dodging the restrictions and responsibilities that babies inevitably bring. Husbands accustomed to the undivided attention of a wife will be unwilling to share with the newcomer. Wives who enjoy the role of "just keeping my husband happy" will rebel at the prospects of long lines of diapers.

Moreover, the children of today are rarely financial assets except on a farm, where they may render some economic service and may be housed without strain. City dwellers find it extremely difficult to find apartment space if they are handicapped by little children. Landlords don't want them, in peacetime or wartime. An advertisement in a large city newspaper in June, 1944, reflects the desperation of many young couples with babies who have tried to persuade landlords to accept them as tenants:

> WANTED — A place to live by couple with
> five months old baby of great sentimental
> value. Prefer to keep child if possible. Will
> drown if necessary to get roof over our heads.

Discouraging as all these factors of cost and disrupted routines and housing would seem to be, the fact is that a great many people do still have children. Interestingly, new babies come in larger numbers with the threat of war and the increase of prosperity. The fertility rate for this country increased considerably during the 1940's as the comparative data depicted at top of page 344 so clearly shows.

Children may be expensive, but it looks as though they are here to stay — a vital part of the American way of life.

Pregnancy

Not every sex intercourse results in pregnancy. A couple may be married for some time before conditions are just right for conception to take place. Both sperm and egg must be right. The pathways that bring them together must be clear. And the timing of copulation must be such that the sperm reaches the egg while it is still in the tube (less than one full day's acceptance each month) in order for impregnation to take place.

Presumptive Signs. The woman may diagnose pregnancy herself by the appearance of a certain combination of symptoms. No symptom is conclusive by itself, but taken together they give her the basis for seeking definite confirmation in a medical examination.

The cessation of menstruation is usually the earliest and most important sign of pregnancy. When a healthy married woman who has been menstruating regularly suddenly misses a period, it is a good indication that pregnancy may have occurred. Occasionally a woman has one or two scanty menstrual periods after conception has taken place. More frequently, the menstrual period may be delayed by a variety of causes — change in climate, certain diseases, nervous tension, fear of or extreme desire for pregnancy.

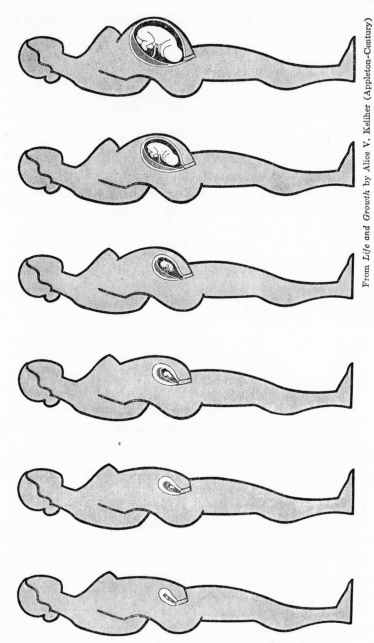

From *Life and Growth* by Alice V. Keliher (Appleton-Century)

PREGNANCY

Another symptom which appears in about two thirds of all women in early pregnancy is morning sickness. The pregnant woman will experience waves of nausea for a few hours in the morning, but even this symptom may be caused by other conditions and is only a presumptive sign of pregnancy.

A third symptom is a change in the breasts of the woman. Many women sense a fullness and tenderness of the breasts early in pregnancy, accompanied by a change in pigmentation of the nipple.

Frequency of urination is also an early presumptive sign of pregnancy. The tendency diminishes as the uterus rises in the pelvis and the bladder is no longer so closely associated with the enlarging uterus.

The married woman who experiences a missed menstrual period, who feels nauseated for a while in the morning, who is aware of changes in her breasts, and who feels the urge to urinate frequently may well presume that she is pregnant.

Pregnancy Tests. The woman may receive definite confirmation or denial of her condition from her physician, who will conduct certain tests before making a diagnosis. He will note changes in the uterus and changes in the coloring of the vaginal lining, and he may use one of several standard urine tests to establish the fact of pregnancy. These tests are based upon the changes in the hormonal excretions in the urine of the pregnant woman which affect noticeably the development of the sex apparatus or function in small animals, such as frogs, rats, mice, or rabbits. The great advantage of these tests is that they are remarkably reliable very early in pregnancy. They are well worth the extra cost if the wife needs to be sure of her condition early in pregnancy, e.g., if she is a professional woman under contract for twelve months. In most cases the urine tests are unnecessary for diagnosis; the experienced physician can usually detect pregnancy reliably by the other signs, but not as early, not before 8 weeks usually.

Positive Signs. As the pregnancy continues, many other confirming signs appear. Changes in the abdomen, the cervix, the vagina, and the uterus become apparent. By the middle of the pregnancy the fetal heart sounds may be heard. Fetal movements within the uterus may be felt from the fifth month on. X-ray pictures show the outlines of the fetal skeleton after the twentieth week and are positive proof of pregnancy.

When Will the Baby Come? As soon as the fact of pregnancy is established, the question inevitably arises as to just when the baby can be expected. Labor usually occurs about 280 days from the first day of the last menstruation. The rule in most frequent use is the following: determine the first day of the last menstruation, add seven days, and count ahead nine months. The date arrived at, however, is only approximate.

CHECK YOURSELF   Check every answer that is correct in the following list.

The first signs of pregnancy are:

_____ 1 Swelling of the abdomen   _____ 4 Bursting of the bag of waters
_____ 2 Lack of sexual desire   _____ 5 Changes in the breasts
_____ 3 A missed menstrual period   _____ 6 Movement of the baby in the womb

★ KEY   Only 3 and 5 are correct.

There may be a leeway of two weeks either way. As one obstetrician put it, "If I could know exactly when babies would arrive, I could take my vacations like a normal man, and I could catch up on my sleep. An obstetrician leads the life of a fire chief, constantly on call."

Maternal Care

Since maternal care became universal in America, having a baby is no longer the dangerous experience that it once was. The chief causes of maternal death are infection, hemorrhage, and toxemia, and can be avoided today by early diagnosis and regular supervision of the pregnancy and birth as well as of the post partum period. That is why there is such a striking decrease in maternal mortality associated with births in hospitals, as is vividly shown in the twin graphs on page 349.

When Should Maternal Care Start? Ideally the couple should have gone to a physician for a thorough physical examination before marriage (remember the premarital conference described in chapters Five and Six). The physician would note at that time any remedial operation which might need to be performed before children should be conceived. If some time elapses between marriage and the time the couple is ready to conceive, another visit should be arranged with the physician. His go-ahead sign is based on a careful check-up paralleling the investigations which took place in the premarital examination. As soon as the woman suspects that she may be pregnant she should again put herself under the care of a reliable physician. After making a thorough physical examination from head to feet, he will take pelvic measurements to see if normal delivery or Caesarian section may be indicated by the position and size of the opening between the pelvic bones. Periodically through the pregnancy he will check the patient's blood, urine, rate of gain in weight, heart rate, and blood pressure. He will note the progress of the baby's growth even though his major concern is to keep track of the mother's health. These are factors which are all-important for the well-being of both the mother and the baby. Maternal care starts, then, before conception takes place and ends after the baby has been delivered and checked over, and the mother is back on her feet again.

You and Your Doctor

Selecting a doctor whose education, training, and experience will assure both mother and baby of the kind of care they need is not easy for the

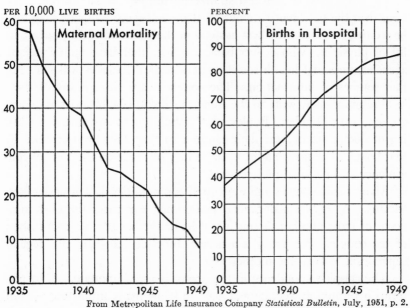

**MATERNAL MORTALITY AND HOSPITALIZATION OF BIRTHS
UNITED STATES, 1935-1949**

From Metropolitan Life Insurance Company *Statistical Bulletin*, July, 1951, p. 2.

THE FIRST YEAR OF LIFE HAS BECOME MUCH SAFER

Mortality in the first week of life now presents the greatest challenge

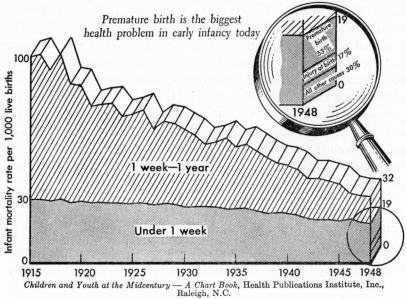

Premature birth is the biggest
health problem in early infancy today

Premature birth
53%
17%
Injury at birth
All other causes 30%

1948

1 week—1 year

Under 1 week

Infant mortality rate per 1,000 live births

1915   1920   1925   1930   1935   1940   1945   1948

Children and Youth at the Midcentury — *A Chart Book*, Health Publications Institute, Inc., Raleigh, N.C.

couple newly established in a strange town. Neighbors' recommendations over the back fence are not reliable. Far more adequate help may be secured by calling the best hospital in the community and getting its list of physicians who deliver babies. Cities that have family welfare agencies, maternal health societies, and medical societies will offer further sources of information. The couple unable to tap any of these local resources may write to the American Board of Obstetrics and Gynecology, 1015 Highland Boulevard, Pittsburgh, Pennsylvania, for a listing of doctors in or near their community that have been certified by that board. From such a list a choice may be made on the basis of convenience and personal preference.

Many smaller towns and most rural communities do not have obstetricians. A well-trained general practitioner can meet the obstetrical needs of most families successfully if he or she has the full cooperation of the couple. Pregnancy is a normal function requiring only regular supervision to keep the mother well.

The couple's confidence in the doctor is very important. If he performs his function well, he will need to know many intimate details of the couple's life together and will want to advise them about many of their daily habits, including eating, resting, recreation, vacations, sex relations, etc. The wife will need to trust her doctor implicitly so that she will eagerly follow his directions as her pregnancy progresses. It is helpful, however, to understand the reasons for the advice given by the physician. The husband must recognize that this relationship between his wife and the doctor does not exist to deprive him of his wife's full companionship, but to insure her health. Whenever possible, it is helpful for the husband to go with his wife on the first visit to the doctor, so that he may have a part in the general arrangements. At that time he may ask the doctor what the cost will be and agree on the payments to be made. The couple may want to ask about such things as:

1 The general condition of the wife and prognosis for the pregnancy.
2 The time when the baby may be expected.
3 Advice about diet, exercise, clothing, sex intercourse, bathing, rest, trips, etc.
4 Frequency of the wife's visits to the doctor during her pregnancy.
5 The hospital the physician takes his patients to, and how arrangements there are made.
6 Anesthetics that the doctor uses to relieve pain at birth.

One outstanding obstetrician [5] gives his expectant mothers a little manual of directions in which he specifies the conditions under which he is to be called:

Notify Your Physician at Once in Case of:

1 Bleeding or brownish discharge from the vagina.
2 Cramps.
3 Excessive vomiting.
4 Severe pain in lower abdomen.
5 Headaches.
6 Disturbances of vision.
7 Swelling of feet and, particularly, of face and hands.
8 Scanty urine or bloody urine.
9 Persistent constipation.
10 Sore throat or cough.
11 Marked shortness of breath.
12 Chills and fever.
13 Sudden escape of fluid from vagina.

[5] Arthur K. Koff, M.D., Chicago.

Some of the general questions about the nature of pregnancy and childbirth may be discussed. The doctor will be glad to explain why a mother's experiences cannot affect her unborn child, why certain infrequent abnormalities and markings are unavoidable, why no one can accurately predict the sex of the child before its birth or determine its sex before conception, and why the mother's attitude and feelings are important for her health and well-being.

Does Childbirth Have to Be Painful?   Childbirth is painful. The pains which result from the contractions that open the cervix are sharp and increase in intensity and duration for several hours. The pains which mark the expulsive contractions of the uterus are intense, probably the most excruciating pain women ever experience. The knowledge that the pains are helping her bring forth her own baby helps the woman bear the suffering and to forget its agony soon after delivery. Although through the years ways of relieving the pain of childbirth have been sought, no completely satisfactory, safe, and universally applicable method has yet been found. Some of the newer methods such as caudal anesthesia, hypnosis, twilight sleep, etc., may present hazards to mother or child under certain conditions. The wise couple discusses the question with their doctor who makes the final decision.

Natural Childbirth.   Childbirth is a normal, natural process. Some doctors [6] believe that much of the mother's labor pain is the result of muscular tension associated with fear. The expectant mother is trained for "natural childbirth" by instruction in what to expect (thus relieving unfounded anxieties), and by supervised exercise in the relaxation and control of pertinent muscle groups so that she may cooperate in the birth process more effectively.

Pregnancy Is a Family Affair

The man who said, "We are pregnant at our house," expressed the "we" feeling that is so important for both husband and wife during their period of expectancy. Pregnancy is a social condition quite as much as a biological state. It involves the adjustment of both the husband and the wife, their relatives, their children already born as well as

[6] Grantly Dick Read, *Children without Fear* (New York: Harper, 1944).

those yet to come. Yes, even more, pregnancy is of importance to the community and to the state. We find more and more laws introduced to assert the interest of the commonwealth in healthy, robust families.

Pregnancy and childbirth can be a strain on immature young folk, but the experience can be and usually is a happy adventure for emotionally and socially mature people. They show it in many ways. The husband who learns early how he may help will find that his role is not the anxious one portrayed in the cartoons of fathers nervously pacing waiting rooms. He may assume certain responsibilities of helping with the housework, plan recreational jaunts that are possible for his wife, make furniture for the new arrival, cooperate in maintaining the diet that the doctor has prescribed, and provide many other personal attentions that do much to ease the wife's burdens and to help him share more fully the experience.

More important than anything that the husband does is how he feels about the pregnancy and his expectant wife. If he is happy about it and proud of his wife, if he treats her as a real person and not as an invalid, he will be giving her the support she needs from him. The pregnant woman may become self-conscious about her figure and general awkwardness as the pregnancy continues and may need her husband's reassurance of his continuing love and admiration. Jealousies and oversensitiveness about her husband's activities outside the family are frequent and may be recognized as resulting from the restrictions imposed by her pregnancy. Even though his wife is not able to participate freely in the activities he enjoys, the mature man will show that he values her companionship. Her silhouette may not be what it once was, but their pride and pleasure in being "in a family way" compensate to both for some of the temporary cumbersomeness of the pregnancy.

Many couples openly enjoy their expectancy and take pleasure in thinking of themselves as parents-to-be. Men as well as women are eager to learn how babies are born and reared and cared for today. Classes for expectant parents are proving popular in many communities. Books on the subject of parenthood are read with new interest. Expectant parents are most receptive to teaching and find that study adds to their enjoyment of anticipation.

The husband who understands best his role during pregnancy is one who:

_____ 1 Completely ignores his wife.

_____ 2 Pokes fun at his wife's figure to make her laugh.

_____ 3 Plans with his wife for the coming child.

_____ 4 Is ashamed to take his wife out in public.

_____ 5 Reassures his wife that he doesn't mind her changing silhouette and demonstrates his eagerness for the baby.

_____ 6 Treats his wife with solicitude as if she were ill.

_____ 7 Accepts pregnancy as a normal, natural function.

_____ 8 Impresses his wife with his lore of stories about mishaps and difficulties at birth.

_____ 9 Does what he can to make life pleasant and happy for both of them.

★ **KEY**   6 ʻ⁊ ʻϛ ʻᘓ :ʇɔǝɹɹoϽ

Having a Baby with Its Father Absent. It is sometimes necessary for the husband to be away from home during his wife's pregnancy. Unfortunate as this situation is, the mature couple can find much satisfaction in letters. Sharing the eagerness of anticipation, expressing the dreams of family reunion and the baby's future, choosing the baby's name, discussing detailed plans for the confinement and the care of the baby for the first few weeks until the mother is able to undertake its full care herself — all these bring a sense of partnership to the couple even though they are separated. The prospective mother can reassure her husband about her condition by relaying accounts of her trips to the doctor, telling him what the prognosis is, how she is spending her time, and how she looks forward to her husband's return and the baby's arrival so that they can all be a real family.

Adopting Children

Not all marriages are blessed with children. Estimates indicate that roughly one marriage in ten is infertile for one reason or another. If the couple is truly ready for parenthood, emotionally mature enough to enjoy its privileges and responsibilities, and to accept the "chosen child" as their own, then adoption is a possibility.[7]

[7] Lee and Evelyn Brooks, *Adventuring in Adoption* (Chapel Hill: University of North Carolina Press, 1939).

Where to find a child available for adoption is a big question in many localities. It is not that there are not enough children needing homes. One child out of every eight in the United States is not living with both parents.[8] In 1948, about two million children under eighteen years of age were living with neither parent, and nearly four million children with only one parent. In 1947, the National Office of Vital Statistics estimated some 132,000 babies born outside of marriage (30,000 of them to girls seventeen years of age or younger). The rate of infants born to unmarried women 15–44 years of age was nearly 80 per cent higher in 1948 than in 1940.[9]

1940 ▶ *71 infants born outside of marriage per 10,000 unmarried mothers*

1948 ▶ *127 infants born outside of marriage per 10,000 unmarried mothers*

Without proper controls all these babies form a potential black market in adoption. The "baby farm" offering babies for a price, or a "contribution" of several hundred to more than a thousand dollars, should be assiduously avoided. Such unscrupulous outfits rarely offer the vital records, birth certificates, and other controls that should come with adoption. The well-staffed state-licensed agency, public or private, places a child for adoption only after a thorough study has been made to safeguard the future of the child and the foster parents. Such an agency can be located through the state or local welfare department. *Adoption laws* are built upon three important objectives.[10]

1 To protect the child from unnecessary separation from parents who might give him a good home and loving care if sufficient help and guidance were available to them; from adoption by persons unfit to have responsibility for rearing a child; and from interference after he has been happily established in his adoptive home by his natural parents, who may have some legal claim because of defects in the adoptive procedure.

[8] Bureau of the Census, as quoted in Chart 13, *A Chart Book, op. cit.*
[9] National Office of Vital Statistics, as quoted in Chart 14, *A Chart Book, op. cit.*
[10] Adapted from *Essentials of Adoption Law and Procedure*, Children's Bureau Publication Number 331 (Federal Security Agency, Washington, D.C., 1949), pp. 2, 3.

TOO MANY CHILDREN ARE ADOPTED WITHOUT ADEQUATE SAFEGUARDS!

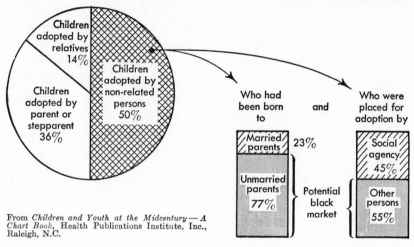

From *Children and Youth at the Midcentury — A Chart Book*, Health Publications Institute, Inc., Raleigh, N.C.

2 To protect the natural parents from hurried decisions to give up the child, made under strain and anxiety.

3 To protect the adopting parents from taking responsibility for children about whose heredity or capacity for physical and mental development they know nothing; and from later disturbance of their relationship to the child by natural parents whose legal rights had not been given full consideration.

Once the approved procedures for adoption have been followed, the parents may relax and bring up their chosen children as their own. Not all the answers in the heredity-environment controversy are in, but there is evidence that children tend to resemble their adoptive parents in many characteristics more closely than they do their biological parents.[11] From what we know of personality development, we would expect this to be generally true. Surely one's "own baby" is not as carefully selected from the grab bag of genes as is the chosen baby at adoption! Parents mature enough to be ready to adopt a child take it as a privilege and a challenge, very much as emotionally mature parents have welcomed their babies from time immemorial.

[11] See especially references by Freeman, et al.; Newman, et al.; Roe; Skeels; Skodak; and Woodworth in *Technical References* at end of chapter.

Marrying a Ready-made Family

One way to become a parent is to marry one. In these days when re-marriage is common, it is not unusual for a man to find himself with not only a wife, but with a child or more as well, when he marries their mother. The stepmother so cruel and heartless in the fairy tale often turns out today to be a lovely person trying her best to win a place in the lives of the children of the man she married.

Being a stepparent is not easy. After all, the others were there first. The children may be expected to cling to their original parent and to accept the new parent in a full-fledged parental status only after he or she has proven worthy. Jealousy and sibling rivalry that in other homes are but irksome interludes are apt in the stepparent's eyes to be un-surmountable obstacles, green-eyed monsters that will not be tamed. Discipline ministered with a casual hand by the "real parent" may seem like a threatening form of hostility or rejection in the hand of the step-mother or father.

"Time is on your side" was never more true. Patience, understand-ing, and a willingness to wait and not force affection brings rewards of new family ties and renewed solidarity. Even teen-aged young people grow up and learn to love their stepparents; in fact that may be a good index of their growing maturity. As soon as parents and children seem ready, steps may be taken to adopt the stepchildren legally so that "your children" may be "our children" in the fullest, final sense.

Grandparents and the New Baby

Family solidarity at this time is often enhanced by the attention of the other relatives. Grandparents-to-be are especially interested in the new-comer. There is a sense of fulfillment in anticipating one's grand-children that even parenthood is said to miss. It is fortunate that the American trend toward excluding members of the extended family from the intimate father-mother-child constellation has been reversed with the increase in births under wartime conditions. Wisely managed, as-sorted grandparents are real assets to the new family. When help is hard to hire, a visiting grandmother who sees the new family through the birth and the confinement is a godsend. When new habits must be established around the new little family member, the going will be rough for the inexperienced parents. The perspective and the practical help of a grandmother who knows the way through the routine of bathing and feeding schedules is a real boon. When the new father and mother feel swamped with their new responsibilities, it is comforting to be able to lean for a bit on parents and to take advantage of their presence to slip out for an evening's fun as a couple once again.

THE WAY OUT [12]

If baby-sitters charge a lot,
For services they render,
Call Grandma in to mind the tot,
For she's the legal tender.

M. M. PARRISH

To be sure, grandparents do have limitations and should be used sparingly. Child training methods do change. But if grandma rocks the baby there are some child care specialists who will support her. The couple do want to feel that they are on their own and that they can manage their own family in their own way. But there are few in-law problems if the family members are well-adjusted persons. Modern grandmothers are as eager as their daughters and daughters-in-law to follow modern methods of child care. Together the two generations can greet the newcomer with a united front that promises well for his future.

Having babies is just about the most exciting and satisfying thing that can happen to a family. The more it is shared and enjoyed and enhanced by intelligent planning, the more satisfying it will become.

Selected Readings

ALDRICH, C. ANDERSON, AND ALDRICH, MARY, *Babies Are Human Beings* (New York: Macmillan, 1941).

BECKER, HOWARD, AND HILL, REUBEN (EDS.), *Family, Marriage, and Parenthood* (Boston: Heath, 1948), Chap. 15.

BOWMAN, HENRY, *Marriage for Moderns* (New York: McGraw-Hill, 1948), Chap. 15.

BROOKS, LEE, AND BROOKS, EVELYN, *Adventuring in Adoption* (Chapel Hill: University of North Carolina Press, 1939).

CHILDREN'S BUREAU, *Essentials of Adoption Law and Procedure* (Washington, D.C.: Federal Security Agency, 1949), Publication #331.

[12] From *The Saturday Evening Post*, April 28, 1951.

CORBIN, HAZEL, *Getting Ready to Be a Father* (New York: Macmillan, 1939).

FISHBEIN, MORRIS, AND BURGESS, ERNEST (EDS.), *Successful Marriage* (Garden City: Doubleday, 1947), Part IV, chaps. 3, 4.

LANDIS, JUDSON, AND LANDIS, MARY, *Building a Successful Marriage* (New York: Prentice-Hall, 1948), chaps. 17, 19.

LOCKBRIDGE, FRANCES, *Adopting a Child* (New York: Greenberg, 1947).

MERRILL, FRANCIS, *Courtship and Marriage* (New York: Sloane, 1949), Chap. 11.

NIMKOFF, MEYER, *Marriage and the Family* (Boston: Houghton Mifflin, 1947), Chap. 16.

PRENTICE, CAROL, *An Adopted Child Looks at Adoption* (New York: Appleton, 1940).

RAUTMAN, ARTHUR, "Adoptive Parents Need Help Too," *Mental Hygiene* (July, 1949).

VAN BLARCOM, CAROLYN, AND CORBIN, HAZEL, *Getting Ready to Be a Mother* (New York: Macmillan, 1940).

WALLER, WILLARD, AND HILL, REUBEN, *The Family: A Dynamic Interpretation, Revised Edition* (New York: Dryden, 1951), Chap. 18.

WASSON, VALENTINA, *The Chosen Baby* (Philadelphia: Lippincott, 1939).

ZABRISKIE, LOUISE, *Mother and Baby Care in Pictures*, Third Edition (Philadelphia: Lippincott, 1946).

Technical References

BISKIND, LEONARD, "Alleviation of Anxiety during Pregnancy," *Modern Medicine* (May, 1946), pp. 3–11.

BURKE, BERTHA, "Nutrition during Pregnancy," *Connecticut State Medical Journal* (September, 1946), pp. 744–753.

FREEMAN, F. N.; HOLZINGER, K. J.; AND MITCHELL, B. C., "The Influence of Environment on the Intelligence, School Achievement, and Conduct of Foster Children," *27th Yearbook of the National Society for the Study of Education* (1928), Part I, pp. 103–217.

JACOBSON, PAUL, "Differentials in Divorce by Duration of Marriage and Size of Family," *American Sociological Review* (April, 1950), pp. 235–244.

KAVINOKY, NADINA, "Marital Adjustments during Pregnancy and the Year After," *Medical Woman's Journal* (October, 1949).

KISER, CLYDE, AND WHELPTON, P. K., "Social and Psychological Factors Affecting Fertility," *Milbank Fund Quarterly* (January, 1951), XI: The Interrelation of Fertility, Fertility Planning, and Feeling of Economic Security.

LANDIS, JUDSON; POFFENBERGER, THOMAS; AND POFFENBERGER, SHIRLEY, "The Effects of First Pregnancy upon the Sexual Adjustment of 212 Couples," *American Sociological Review* (December, 1950), pp. 767–772.

Midcentury White House Conference on Children and Youth, *Children and Youth at the Midcentury: A Chart Book* (Raleigh, North Carolina: Health Publications Institute, Inc., 1951).

NEWMAN, H. H.; FREEMAN, F. N.; AND HOLZINGER, K. J., *Twins: A Study of Heredity and Environment* (Chicago: University of Chicago Press, 1937).

REED, ROBERT, "The Interrelationship of Marital Adjustment, Fertility Control, and Size of Family," *Milbank Fund Quarterly* (October, 1947), pp. 382–425.

ROE, ANNE, AND BURKS, BARBARA, *Adult Adjustment of Foster Children of Alcoholic and Psychotic Parentage and the Influence of the Foster Home* (New Haven: Yale University Section on Alcohol Studies, 1945).

SKEELS, HAROLD, "Mental Development of Children in Foster Homes," *Journal of Consulting Psychology* (1938), Vol. 2, pp. 33–43.

SKODAK, MARIE, "Intellectual Development of Children in Foster Homes," in *Child Behavior and Development* by Barker, Kounin, and Wright, eds. (New York: McGraw-Hill, 1943), Chap. 16.

STUART, H. C., "Findings on Examinations of Newborn Infants and Infants during the Neo-Natal Period Which Appear to Have a Relationship to the Diets of Their Mothers during Pregnancy," *Federation Proceedings* (September, 1945), Vol. 4, No. 3, pp. 271–281.

TEAGARDEN, FLORENCE, *Child Psychology for Professional Workers* (New York: Prentice-Hall, 1946), Chap. 3.

WOODWORTH, R. S., "Heredity and Environment: A Critical Survey of Recently Published Material on Twins and Foster Children," *Social Science Research Council Bulletin* (New York, 1941).

CHAPTER EIGHTEEN

It's Fun to Be Parents

WHAT IT MEANS TO BE PARENTS

Do parents always have mixed feelings about their children?

What does a baby do to the husband and wife relationship?

Is adolescence always difficult?

Are there methods of discipline that really work?

Can parents be people too?

EVERY TIME A NEW BABY IS BORN THERE IS A BRAND NEW MOTHER and a brand new father. Each must learn his or her new role in the family. Each now has new privileges and new responsibilities. Previous relationships change as each member of the family adapts and adjusts to the newcomer. Even the family of many children realigns itself every time another baby enters the circle. This stretching of the family ties is satisfying and challenging. But it is strenuous too.

When the First Baby Comes

There are at least three stages in getting used to a new baby. The first is the flowers and pink ribbons stage. Mother is in her glory bedecked in her best bed jacket, with roses on her table and solicitous friends and family asking after her and the little newcomer. Father, who has felt like a fifth wheel during the long days of the pregnancy and the interminable hours of labor and birth, now comes into his own as exuberant herald to all the world of the miracle that has happened. He passes cigars to all the boys and showers this wonderful woman of his with tokens of his undying affection. Everybody is happy. The parents are thrilled. Life is wonderful — too wonderful to last.

Not long after mother and baby have returned from the hospital, the second stage of parent-child relations is apparent. The exuberance of the first flush of parenthood gives way under the weight of daily diapers, lusty cries at 2:00 A.M., and the cleaning woman who didn't come. The insistent demands of a hungry baby break into the tenderest moments of husband and wife. The mother's preoccupation with feedings and daily baths often seems to take precedence over diversions previously enjoyed by the couple. Let a friend suggest a movie or an evening out, and the chorus sounds from new mother and father alike, "What will we do with the baby?" Babies bring new responsibilities thick and fast, sometimes so fast that it takes quite a bit of readapting before things run smoothly around the little newcomer and his family.

Before very long the family has a helper or two. Aunt Molly is willing to come in and stay with the baby occasionally. Or a trustworthy baby-sitter has been found who allows the new mother and father an occasional evening out to themselves. The routines which at first seemed so exacting settle down into comfortable schedules. Baby gets used to its food and sleeps straight through the night without a whimper. Mother begins to feel more like herself now that she is around the house and doing her own work without getting too tired. It is fun wheeling baby to the store and back. Bath time has become a frolic for both mother and baby. Life is good again. The new family is really under way.

This characteristic cycle reappears in various forms again and again in the lifetime of the family. Enthusiasm and the sense of being in on a wonderful miracle of life occurs many times as parents take pride in their children. But the heavy weight of responsibility is constantly present; children *are* a responsibility. It takes many years to work through the ways and means of handling these obligations effectively and comfortably, but time is a great educator. And then comes the quiet satisfaction of being a family, the happy contentment so characteristic of parenthood.

Parents Are People

Parents are people first of all. Long before the arrival of their children, and long after the children have grown and gone, they will be people, persons in their own right. To hear some talk, one would think a mother and father were born and brought up as parents. Unfortunately, few gave much concern or time to the business of being parents before they found themselves with their own children to rear. No preparatory training period was required before children were allowed to come into the home. No license was necessary before practicing parenthood. Only the barest of biological essentials and social sanction were required.

As one of the authors has said elsewhere,

Parents represent the last stand of the amateur. Every other trade and profession has developed standards, has required study and practice and licensing before releasing the student into his work. Before a girl can wave my hair or tint my nails she must have gone to school a specified number of hours, she must have apprenticed successfully under a qualified operator and she must have passed a state examination and become duly licensed. Nursing, social work, teaching, law, medicine, welding, mechanics, plumbers and plumber's helpers all must come up to standards appropriate to their successful performance. Only one profession remains untutored and untrained — the bearing and rearing of our children.[1]

There was a time when families were large. Then little girls learned how to take care of babies by helping care for younger brothers and sisters under the watchful eye of mother or big sister. There was a time when family ways were stable. Then girls learned to bake bread and make candles and churn butter and discipline children by watching and helping their mothers do these things, which they in turn would be expected to do when they grew up. Likewise, boys followed their fathers around the barn and shop and learned through years of apprenticing to play the roles they were to play later in their own homes. Now each generation finds itself in situations so strange that the learnings of childhood only partially carry over into adult usefulness. Families now spend more and more of their time in complex business transactions and community activities which remain mysteries to the children. Only the most fundamental tasks remain in the home — washing dishes, laundering, cooking, and bedmaking.

Parents have learned to be parents by being parents! Step by step as the children grow up the parents develop too; skills for handling situations are perfected; what to expect becomes clearer. By the time the

[1] Evelyn Millis Duvall, "Growing Edges in Family Life Education," *Marriage and Family Living*, May, 1944, p. 22.

children are grown, most parents have some pretty good ideas about what they would do differently if they could start all over again. But by that time their children are out starting in all over again, for themselves.

Parents start with their own particular concepts of what they may expect of a child. These ideas are gleaned from the expectations of the people with whom they have grown up. Although there are some common denominators, true for all levels of society, as to what constitutes a good child, most parents follow the demands and expectations of their particular set in their judgment of what must be expected of children. Recent studies at the University of Chicago indicate that there are significant differences between racial groupings, and particularly between the various socio-economic classes, in what is expected of children.[2]

These specific judgments of what a child should and should not do are gathered from neighbors and friends who exert pressure upon parents to exact behavior of one kind or another from their children. "What will the neighbors say if I let him . . . ?" is a powerful factor in the disciplining of many a child. These social pressures tend to strengthen and to modify the earlier learning of childhood as to what is appropriate and inappropriate behavior.

Parents tend to reproduce or to repudiate their own childhood training in the bringing up of children. It is a frequent experience for a parent to find himself involved in a situation almost identical with one he experienced as a child. He suddenly finds himself acting out the role his parent played. It may not be a pleasant role; it may not even be a comfortable one for him; but somehow, it suddenly appears full-blown in an actual situation.

Consider the case of Mrs. C. She is a modern mother, trying to bring up her child in a progressive manner. But one day in a burst of anger at her son's use of a vile phrase she found herself washing out his mouth with soap in exactly the way her mother had done when she had used unseemly language. Mrs. C. didn't believe in such harsh discipline. The methods which she was consciously putting into practice were more studied and less impulsive. But in the heat of the actual

---

[2] W. Allison Davis and Robert Havighurst, *Father of the Man* (Boston: Houghton Mifflin, 1947); W. Lloyd Warner, Robert Havighurst, and Martin Loeb, *Who Shall Be Educated?* (New York: Harper, 1944); and Evelyn Millis Duvall, "Conceptions of Parenthood," *American Journal of Sociology* (November, 1946), pp. 193–203. See Chap. I, p. 6.

situation she reverted to what her mother had found effective. She was so identified with her own mother that in a crisis she reproduced her mother's method of discipline even though it was not her own!

At other times parents find themselves just as vigorously repudiating the patterns of their own parents. There is John Q., for instance. His father was a harsh man, quick to use the strap or hairbrush where it would do the most good, if any of his children disobeyed or defied him. John grew up vowing that he would never lay a hand on one of his own children. No matter what they do to provoke him, he insists on reasoning it out with them. Never once in his life has he raised his voice or his hand to his children. Because his father was harsh, he cannot be. Insightful parents learn to spot these compulsive responses and to understand their causes.

Parents Who Live through Their Children. Mothers and fathers who live vicariously through their children are doomed to disappointment. No one can live the life of another, not even of one's own child. But because of frustrations in their own youth, parents often insist on trying to find satisfaction through their children. Alice T. always wanted to

"You're so disobedient, stubborn, contrary . . . Mother's proud of you."

take violin lessons when she was a little girl. Her parents refused to allow this extra extravagance until she had mastered the piano. That day never arrived for her. Now she stands over her seven-year-old son insisting that he practice on his violin. He unfortunately doesn't share her enthusiasm for violin playing and is rebelling with all the fury of an active seven-year-old. So the mother is disappointed and despairing, while the son learns how to resist her efforts to live his life. Many parents are so eager that their children should enjoy all the satisfactions which they have been denied that they try to live through the child rather than with him.

Parents Who Grow Up with Their Children. The secret of successful parenthood seems to lie in the ability of the parents to keep on growing. Parents who continue to find joy in learning show by their enthusiasm and interest that learning is fun. By being the kind of people who live eagerly, they show their youngsters how worth while it all is.

Mary Ellen, like Alice T., always wanted to play the violin. She didn't get a chance until after she was married and had reared her three children past the diaper stage. Then she hunted up a first-rate teacher and began her musical education. She took her practicing seriously and was faithful in her lessons; she shared her little triumphs and failures with the family; she nodded understandingly when the children ran into snags with their lessons, for she knew what it was to unravel tangles. The children admired their mother's growing skill and co-operated actively in getting ready for the friends that she sometimes had in to play with her. When these little affairs grew into an informal chamber music group, the two older children begged to be admitted with their instruments. Today the whole family enjoys music together. Practicing is not a matter of parent-child tension but an accepted part of the whole pattern of family life.

Of course not every family finds its satisfaction in music. It may be books in some homes; or scientific explorations in others; or shop work and household decoration in another. But whatever the parents find absorbing, these things the children will find interesting. Yes, more than that, parents who continue to cultivate their interests are appreciated and enjoyed by their children as real people.

A father of five children put it neatly when he said, "It's more important that children admire their parents than it is for parents to admire their children." When parents continue to grow and to find life challenging, the children are led rather than driven into the good things of life. Discipline is relatively simple, because the parents are getting their own satisfactions for themselves, and because they are freer to understand and to deal with the children's problems as they arise. The development of the individuality of the child is assured when each member of the family is encouraged to develop his own interests at his own pace, without the stifling burden of having to satisfy the needs of another by the excellence of his performance.

How Parents Affect Children

Children are not chips off the old block. They are developing human beings with needs to satisfy and tasks to accomplish. Because parents are the people the child first knows and loves, because they are so all-powerful in satisfying his early hungers and funneling through to him the things he needs, the impressions they leave are lifelong. Just how this influence works in the life of any individual is seen only by careful study of his own particular life history. But certain aspects of parent-child interaction are so general that it may be helpful to consider them here.

Meeting Basic Needs. Present-day knowledge of the basic needs of children comes out of a rich background of years of insightful experience in learning how children grow and in learning what affects, for better and for worse, their development through the years. These findings have come relatively late in man's history. Many generations ago people generally knew that a horse which had been mistreated would probably be vicious. Centuries ago common people knew that living things required certain basic essentials of food, light, air, and favorable atmospheric conditions. When these elements necessary for growth were provided in proper amounts and at the times when they were needed, the organism, be it cow, corn, or human being, grew strong and sturdy, and thrived. When these essentials were lacking or delayed, the plant withered and died, the animal wasted away and became progressively unhappy, disagreeable, and listless. But it took the twentieth century to bring the scientific investigations and points of view which allow us to see children as dynamically growing, living organisms affected by understandable laws of growth which must be obeyed if life is to develop at its best.

These new findings have competed successfully with many theories and platitudes about child nature that have been handed down from generation to generation by people trying to make sense out of human conduct and development. The earlier efforts to understand youngsters were well-meaning but not well founded and have had to be repudiated or reformed in the light of more valid insights. Such time-honored sayings as the following are being revised:

- Spare the rod and spoil the child.
- Like father, like son.
- Chip off the old block.
- Children should be seen and not heard.
- Mother is always right.
- Cleanliness is next to godliness.
- A child is but a miniature adult . . . "little men," "little women."
- Just like his uncle Jim.
- A bad boy through and through.
- Treat a boy soft and you'll make a sissy out of him.
- You can't teach an old dog new tricks.
- Give a child an inch and he'll take an ell.
- Kill him with kindness.
- She's the spit an' image of her mother.
- Grandmothers always spoil children by being too good to them.
- If you are nice to a child, he'll take advantage of you.
- The school of hard knocks is the best teacher.
- Born under a lucky star.

Some of these principles are so unsound that their influence is seriously harmful. Many of these statements are just not true and clutter our thinking with fallacies that must soon give way to more valid findings. Some are but partially true, needing considerably more qualification and modification than is implied. They all need to be examined carefully and revised or rejected in terms of the more valid findings shown in the table on pp. 372–373. Most of us are in the stage of clearing up our thinking about ourselves and getting the basis for understanding our children that will help us supply their needs. Examination of this table shows the specific ways in which these human needs for security, love, response, and achievement may be met.

Discipline Makes a Difference. Discipline which promotes the development of the child has six characteristics: 1. it is firm, reliable, and kind; 2. it shows the child what others expect of him; 3. it encourages the child and promotes a feeling of faith in himself; 4. it strengthens the child's skills for better future performance; 5. it does not sever the child's sense of belonging to the group; and 6. it comes from mature, lovable adults worthy of being emulated.

All too often discipline is a means through which parents express their irritation and annoyance. Children often act in ways which annoy adults, it is true. The love of dirt and of noise and of endless exploration so characteristic of childhood is an affront to the values of adults. There is nevertheless little justification for calling scolding and punishment in such situations good discipline.

Haphazard techniques of discipline are likely to affect the child's feeling of personal worth, and his responses to other people may be adversely affected. Harsh, cruel punishment blocks and distorts the child's feelings for others and shakes his faith in himself. Discipline which alienates and isolates the child casts him outside the group and forbids him the privilege of being loved just when he needs it most! Lax and inconsistent treatment, on the other hand, fails to teach the growing youngster the necessary controls of society, so that he ends up like a ship without a rudder. To be effective, discipline must be administered by adults whose example is worthy of emulation and it should be firm and predictable. To treat a child otherwise is to play fast and loose with his emotions.

Terman's study reveals that firm, but not harsh, discipline accompanied by a close relationship with parents is related to later marriage success.[3] Marriage adjustments are but elaborations and modifications of the relationships built up in childhood.

Look at Alvin, for instance. He is the product of inconsistent discipline. He was the only child of an over-protective widowed mother. At times he felt overwhelmed by her heavy expectations. He spent most of his childhood dodging her passes and demands. He developed

[3] Lewis M. Terman and associates, *Psychological Factors in Marital Happiness* (New York: McGraw-Hill, 1938), pp. 228–231.

elaborate deceits and subterfuges. Then at other times he could get away with anything. He would just creep back into her arms for cuddling whenever one of his escapades had been discovered. His wife must now cope with the weaknesses resulting from the earlier inconsistent discipline. He keeps her frantic with worry, as he did his mother, as he flies from one affair to another, always returning with the little-boy winsomeness that was so effective in dealing with his mother's concern. He has carried over into his marriage the adjustment patterns he developed in his boyhood.

Sally developed quite a different attitude toward people in her childhood. Her parents were fond of her and in love with each other. She was brought up to know what was right and was given opportunities to perfect her skills in being a good girl. Her parents rejoiced in her growth and were understanding and sympathetic when she made mistakes. She and her father were fond of each other. She loved her mother and wanted to be like her when she grew up. By the time she was in her teens she was treated like a young adult in the household, and she thought of her father and mother as persons rather than just as parents. She married a man as emotionally mature as she, and her married life is the natural extension of the fine adjustment she made as a growing girl.

Discipline makes a difference!

EMOTIONAL SATISFACTIONS DESIRED BY HUMAN BEINGS *

AFFECTIONAL, WARM, SECURITY-GIVING SATISFACTIONS

For the infant they come mainly through

Affection. Being cuddled.† Given physical closeness, fondling, etc.

Response. Being attended to when in pain or uncomfortable. Being fussed over, talked to, given attention, etc.

Belongingness. Being cuddled and given physical closeness.†

For the young child they come mainly through

Affection. Continuing cuddling, etc. Verbal as well as tactual demonstrativeness.

Response. (Same as infant response.)

Belongingness. Acceptance by his mother (and closeness to her and later to father).† Having a safe family unit to belong to (i.e., parents harmonious, so that belongingness is not continually threatened).† Being given support when in trouble or doubt (in such a way as to let him feel he still belongs no matter what).†

For the adult they come mainly through

Affection. Tactual demonstrativeness. Verbal demonstrativeness. Being loved.

Response. Friendships — being liked for what one is rather than for what one does. Loyalty. Sympathy. Understanding. Consideration, etc.

Belongingness. Having a place in society at large, i.e., status (which involves likeness with others and differences).

FUNDAMENTAL SENSORY GRATIFICATIONS

For the infant they come mainly through

Sucking.† Cuddling.† General bodily comfort. (Hunger satisfied *without* a prolonged period of waiting.†)

For the young child they come mainly through

Sucking.† Pleasure and interest in elimination: messing.† Masturbation.† General bodily comfort.

For the adult they come mainly through

Satisfying sexual experiences. General bodily comfort.

SELF-ENLARGING, EGO-BUILDING, ADEQUACY-GIVING SATISFACTIONS

For the infant they come mainly through

Achievement. Gaining satisfying response by crying when in pain or when uncomfortable.† Progressively developing body activities.

Recognition. Being admired, having developments noted, etc.

For the young child they come mainly through

Achievement. Self-direction: maintaining independence in regulating own voluntary physiological activities, especially eating and defecation; exploring the environment with all sense modalities carrying through to immediate goals the impulses of the moment. Learning to talk and communicate (progressive symbolization). Being able to accomplish *comfortably* what his parents demand. Physical efficiency.

Recognition. (Same as infant recognition.) Having all accomplishments approved.

For the adult they come mainly through

Achievement. Vocational and/or avocational activities which can be successfully carried through to satisfying goals. Self-direction: being able to take responsibility and to make independent choices. Developing an individuality which one can think well of in spite of a realistic facing of weak spots.

Recognition. Having what one does appreciated and thought well of, admired, followed, etc.

* Adapted with permission from Lee E. Travis and Dorothy W. Baruch, *Personal Problems of Everyday Life* (New York: Appleton-Century, 1941), pp. 80–82.

† Items frequently frustrated in our culture.

CHECK YOURSELF   With the understanding of the basic needs of children gleaned
from the table on page 372, indicate what should be done in each
of the following situations. Mark the course of action you feel would most satisfactorily meet
the child's needs and help him to be stronger in a similar situation next time. Place a (1)
for the action which you feel is the *best choice*. Put a (2) for the courses of action which you
feel *might* work. Mark the statement with an (X) if you feel that the action might be *harmful*,
or *not effective.*

SITUATION 1. *Junior, aged six months, sucks his thumb.*

a _____ Tie his hands down to the mattress so he can't get his fingers to his mouth.

b _____ Let him have a little longer time at the bottle or breast.

c _____ Put a metal thumb guard on his thumb.

d _____ Splint his arm so that he can't bend his elbow.

e _____ Give him a piece of zwieback or toast to suck when he is tired or hungry.

f _____ Scold him severely every time you catch him with his thumb in his mouth.

g _____ Slap his hands every time they go near his mouth.

h _____ Ignore it. Most babies suck their thumbs. He'll outgrow it soon.

i _____ Cuddle him a bit when he is tired and restless.

j _____ Hold him in your arms when you feed him.

k _____ Put bitter aloes on his thumb.

l _____ Take up the matter with your doctor or child guidance specialist.

m _____ Ask your mother what she did.

n _____ Try a little of everything. Something is sure to work.

SITUATION 2. *Sally, aged fifteen, stayed out a whole hour later than she was supposed to last evening.*

a _____ Give her a good bawling out. She should know better.

b _____ Ignore it. She probably didn't realize the time.

c _____ Make her stay in every night this month as punishment.

d _____ Find out whom she was out with and forbid her from seeing him (or them)
again.

e _____ Buy her a good watch.

f _____ Try to find out why she was so late. Listen to her story.

g _____ See what she suggests for getting in on time after this.

h _____ Tell her she can't go out again in the evening until she's big enough to get
back on time.

i _____ Thrash her. You can't let girls roam the streets at all hours of the night.

j _____ Call up the young man who kept her out so long and give him a good talking to.

k _____ Discuss it calmly with her and work out some understanding about future
nights out.

l _____ Say nothing now, but next time she is ready to leave the house remind her
that you expect her in on time.

m _____ Give her an opportunity to help set the hour at which she feels she should
return.

SITUATION 3. *Nineteen-year-old son George, away at school, wants to marry the girl he has been going with the past two years.*

a _____ Absolutely forbid it. He's too young to know his own mind.

b _____ Pretend you don't care whether he does or not.

c _____ Go and visit the girl and get better acquainted with her.

d _____ Write George a letter giving him all the reasons why he should wait.

e _____ Wait until he gets home and then find out how he feels about it.

f _____ Let him do what he thinks best. He's old enough to know his own mind.

g _____ Go right down to visit him and put a finish to the whole affair.

h _____ Tell him if he marries now it will break his mother's heart.

i _____ Talk it over with a sympathetic counselor if it bothers you.

★ KEY

SITUATION 1. Harmful (X): a, c, d, g; Might work (2): n h, k, f; Best choice (1): m, l, i, e, b

SITUATION 2. Harmful (X): a, c, d, h; Might work (2): b, l; Best choice (1): i, h, e, g, f

SITUATION 3. Harmful (X): a, b, g, h; Might work (2): e, d, c; Best choice (1): i, f

Sex Education Is Important Too. Little children learn by watching, imitating, and exploring. This is as true in learning about how their bodies are made and function as in any other area. To get the facts they desire about themselves and others, little children explore 1. by asking questions and talking about how their bodies work, 2. by watching and imitating adults, 3. by looking at the bodies of others, and 4. by feeling and rubbing genitalia. Now it happens, in our culture, that all four of these activities are considered taboo by some adults. Parents are sometimes uncomfortable at seeing little girls running about in abbreviated sunsuits and are shocked to see nursery school children looking at each other at toilet time. A great many parents and teachers have been so frightened by false stories of the evils of masturbation that they severely punish and shame little children who touch their genitalia. Too many adults still are embarrassed by the searching questions and interest of intelligent children naturally concerned about their origin, the functions of their bodies, and the happenings in human and animal families around them. Consequently many children are left at an early age with the impression that there is something dirty and shameful about the sex organs, and something wrong about sexual sensations. Adult embarrassment, uneasiness, and fear are transferred to the child almost without his being aware of it. As he grows older, sex references continue to bring feelings of guilt and shame. Dirty stories,

"Dad, will you bring me home a baby sister like Mom did?"

giggles, and other indirect outlets are found to take the place of the more normal, complete responses of sex love. Feelings of personal unworthiness make it difficult to fall in love with desirable love objects, and control of the powerful sex urges becomes difficult.

Parents who are more wholesomely conditioned and more aware of their own limitations clamor for guidance in the sex education of their children. Few topics are more popular in child study, parent education, and teacher training classes. Books like the following are basic.

SELECTED STARTER LIBRARY IN SEX EDUCATION

Books for Children

BIBBY, CYRIL, *How Life is Handed On* (New York: Emerson, 1947).

DE SCHWEINITZ, KARL, *Growing Up*, Revised Edition (New York: Macmillan, 1949).

EMERSON, VICTORIA, AND THOMPSON, JAMES, *Into the World* (New York: Woman's Press, 1950).

FAEGRE, MARION, *Your Own Story* (Minneapolis: University of Minnesota Press, 1943).

LEVINE, MILTON, AND SELIGMANN, J. H., *The Wonder of Life* (New York: Simon and Schuster, 1940).

STRAIN, FRANCES BRUCE, *Being Born* (New York: Appleton-Century, 1938).

Books for Young People

BECK, LESTER, *Human Growth* (New York: Harcourt, Brace, 1949).

DICKERSON, ROY, *So Youth May Know*, Revised Edition (New York: Association Press, 1948).

DUVALL, EVELYN MILLIS, *Facts of Life and Love* (New York: Association Press, 1950).

KELIHER, ALICE, *Life and Growth* (New York: Appleton-Century, 1938).

MUSEUM OF SCIENCE AND INDUSTRY, *The Miracle of Growth* (Urbana: University of Illinois Press, 1950).

Books for Parents and Teachers

BIESTER, LILLIAN; GRIFFITHS, WILLIAM; AND PEARCE, N. O., *Units in Personal Health and Human Relations* (Minneapolis: University of Minnesota Press, 1947).

GRUENBERG, SIDONIE M., *The Wonderful Story of How You Were Born* (Garden City, N.Y.: Hanover House, 1952).

KIRKENDALL, LESTER, *Sex Education as Human Relations* (New York: Inor Publishing, 1950).

STRAIN, FRANCES BRUCE, *New Patterns in Sex Teaching*, Revised Edition (New York: Appleton-Century-Crofts, 1951).

——, *Sex Guidance in Family Life Education* (New York: Macmillan, 1948).

——, *The Normal Sex Interests of Children* (New York: Appleton-Century-Crofts, 1948).

Gradually the old taboos are breaking down; parents and children alike are becoming comfortable about sex. The next generation of young people will not have to put up with obstacles now that the paths have been cleared.

Adolescent Parent Interaction [4]

Adolescence is almost as hard for parents as it is for the youngsters themselves. Psychologists have been dealing with the problems of the growing young person for years, but only recently have parents felt free

[4] This discussion is adapted from an article by Evelyn Millis Duvall, "Our Children Are Growing up," *The Christian Home*, December, 1944: a parents' magazine published by The Methodist Publishing House. Used by permission.

enough to study the magnitude of the adjustments they must make as their children grow up.

Mary Alice's mother smiled as she started to lengthen another of Mary Alice's skirts. "My, how this child is growing," she commented to her husband, who was just settling down to read the paper.

"Wish she'd learn to pick up her things," he mumbled as he pulled out the tennis ball he had sat down on.

"But she's really quite mature in many ways; why just yesterday . . . ," mother began again.

"Yes, I know, I know. And last Sunday's supper was a masterpiece. Shows she can do things when she really wants to. What gets me is that she's so unreliable, a child one minute and more grown-up than either of us the next. Ho hum, that's life I suppose."

Yes, that is life, especially when children are growing up fast, full of contradictions as well as unreliability, full of mixed feelings for both parents, full of problems and puzzles and new ways of living and looking at life. But the mixed feelings that Mary Alice's parents share about her are only a sample of the typical mixture of emotions which most parents have toward their growing children.

Pride and admiration loom large for most parents. That this child of theirs, so recently a helpless infant, a clumsy toddler, is now a creature of size and strength is an overwhelming reality to face. The proud father and mother cannot help but feel pride in the skills and achievements which unfold so rapidly as growing children get a feeling of what they can do; admiration for the way they open up new outlets for their interests; satisfaction in the promotions and the honors that come along; pleasure in the open admiration of friends and often of total strangers. These are familiar feelings to most parents of growing youth.

Bewilderment, annoyance, and some irritation are not rare among the parents of adolescents. Mary Alice's father is right. When they are honest with themselves parents admit considerable irritation over the spottiness of their youngsters' behavior, annoyance over the almost complete disregard of adult values — the noise and the untidiness and the crudity are difficult to bear. Parents are annoyed at the inconsistency and the unreliability of youth — pajamas on the floor in a heap six days out of seven, and then the one day when the room is immaculate, a decorator's dream (Jimmy is expected over at four). The bathroom can be a mess four tubs out of five, and then such scouring for a chit of a scout leader who is dropping by to leave a package! Mary Alice may be too tired to study or help with the dishes — but when Henry calls she's so peppy and full of life that one wonders at the source of all the extra vitality. Weeks without any real studying can be interrupted by a sudden burst that lasts for days and results in a stunning fifty-page report for a new science teacher. Thoughtlessness of everybody may be relieved by a devoted dedication to a particularly difficult task to please the family. *Bewildering* is the word for adolescent behavior.

Wise parents realize that adolescence is the time for trying out adult roles. Old familiar tasks, like picking up clothes and wiping dishes and studying the same old stuff, have lost much of their appeal because they have already been mastered. Greater challenges are needed and, when recognized, are pounced upon eagerly. By careful observation of adolescent behavior, experts have discovered the tasks which young people strive to perform.[5] Parents too will see some reason for their champing at the bit. Adolescents are in a big hurry to grow up and do big things.

All this recognition of the nature of adolescent cravings goes just so far in helping parents. Because parents are persons with their own needs for appreciation and recognition, the collision of wishes is bound to be frequent and stormy. Parents really don't think their way through their youngsters' adolescence; they feel and storm their way through it with the adolescents themselves.

Parents could probably take the mixture of admiration and bewilderment and frustration which adolescents bring them if their own needs for love and affection were not so hopelessly entangled in the family web. Time was when this same adolescent would rush in to be loved with the vigor of an affectionate puppy; then hurts could be kissed away. Cuddled in a lap, he could pour out tales of woe; troubles could be talked over and worked out. But now that he is older the problems are sometimes fought out without the benefit of parental counsel. The kids in the neighborhood may hear of defeats and tragedies before parents do. The youngster is too big to be cuddled, too big to be fondled and petted and tucked into bed, too big to be held in the lap or to be kissed as he liked to be once, and too big for the babying the parents so enjoyed. There is no longer the same overt love, the same respect and

---

[5] Robert J. Havighurst, *Developmental Tasks and Education* (Chicago: University of Chicago Press, 1948).

obedience. The authority held over the child has changed, and parents must change with it. New satisfactions must replace the old.

Much has been said of the problem of discipline and guidance for these older children. At a time when he needs his parents most, when he is facing serious problems, making important decisions, meeting new hazards — at this of all times he insists on his independence.[6]

"If only he would listen to reason," the harassed parent cries, but knows that now more than ever reason and the experience of his elders will carry the adolescent just so far; his own experiences must take him the rest of the way.

Actually, the insistence of parents on the continued supervision of growing youth is derived only partially from their anxiety for his welfare, real as this often is. It is an expression of the emotional lag of parents who do not yet recognize the needs of the adolescent for independence. He was only a baby yesterday, and now. . . .

The mother whose public kiss is rebuffed feels it deeply. She may feel hurt and humiliated and deprived of affection by this little person to whom she has given so much and who now withdraws so curtly. She can, all unconsciously, react by clamping down on the child's privileges — a sort of "well if you don't love your mother you'll be sorry" retaliation. Or she may, if she is unusually mature and loving as a woman, rejoice that her young hopeful is growing up so fast, and quickly adjust her feelings to match the child's appraisal of his changing relationship to her. Mothers ought not to be surprised to find elements of all three reactions within themselves. After all, mothers are human too, with lots of feelings, especially where their children are concerned.

Nor should father remain crushed when he finds others sharing his daughter's attention and affection. Some fathers are so openly hostile to their daughter's visiting swains that even the youngsters notice the jealousy that colors his severity. Other dads withdraw still further into the emotional doghouse so easily occupied by parents of budding youth,

---

[6] The author discusses in a high school text for adolescents the following:

DEVELOPMENTAL TASKS OF ADOLESCENTS

1 Adjustment to a changing body.
2 New orientation to age mates of both sexes.
3 Establishing independence from family.
4 Achieving adult economic and social status.
5 Development of the self.

Evelyn Millis Duvall, *Family Living* (New York: Macmillan, 1950), p. 84.

while still others take their new places in their stride and find some real satisfaction in sharing grown-up thoughts and plans and problems with the bright new adults within the family.

Of course, some families take emotional growing pains more easily than do others. The home where father has been boss or where mother has been always right for eight or ten or a dozen years will need to have some pretty extensive remodeling of its family patterns when the youngsters begin to want things their way. But the family in which the children have been respected as real people through the years, with rights and responsibilities in line with their strengths and abilities, can slip through adolescence without an emotional upheaval. That family is ready for growth because it has been promoting it all along; that family can adjust its feelings to change because it has had years of happy experience in doing precisely that; that family can provide growing youngsters with the experiences so much needed by youth, and stand back satisfied that the children will not abuse their privileges. The pajamas in a heap will not worry that family, because it is aware that motivation for picking things up is around the corner now that the children are feeling more on a par with adults and their values. Irritations and bewilderment will be balanced with the pride and admiration which accompany them, because the family knows that they go together and that growth of both parents and children holds promise. The family can let little annoyances ride, because there are bigger things at stake in a world which calls for democratic living. Such a family is so busy putting its principles to work within the community that mother hasn't time to nurse her own hurt feelings, and dad hasn't time to bemoan the thoughtlessness of youth.

When the Children Have Grown [7]

With a nervous twitch Mrs. Brown stirs the fire in the fireplace. "My, how quiet the house is tonight!" she murmurs to her husband as she settles herself with her knitting beside him.

Yes, it is quiet, too quiet. Mr. and Mrs. Brown are living in an

[7] Two thoughtful articles on the adjustments of parents in the empty-nest stage are available to the reader: Robert M. Dinkel, "Parent-Child Conflict in Minnesota Families," *American Sociological Review*, August, 1943, pp. 412–419; and Robert M. Dinkel, "Attitudes of Children toward Supporting Aged Parents," *American Sociological Review*, August, 1944, pp. 370–379.

empty nest. One by one the children have grown and gone off to college, to work, and to homes of their own. At first there was a peculiar pleasure in being a couple again. The Browns took to fixing up the house and yard, things they couldn't afford to do while there were clothes to buy and tuition to pay for. Now that the house is as they wanted it, it seems but an empty shell. Too bad that it couldn't have been this way when the children were here to enjoy it, that this leisure so anticipated a few years ago has such a taste of dry ashes! Yet that is life, as much a part of life as the bustling days of infancy or the turbulence of adolescence. So, what now, mom and dad?

Two things won't work. You can't follow your children. They have their own lives to live, their own adjustments, their own problems, their own families to raise. When crises come, the old folks will be welcome for a while. But healthy young folks want to be on their own. You can't live in the past without slipping out of today's realities. Memories warm for a while, but the embers die and the gray ashes are cold solace for an empty heart. Fingering old baby shoes and making scrapbooks of the children's past landmarks are week-end busywork, but such fare is pretty thin gruel for the hearty appetites developed through the years of family living.

The only way open is forward. You can't go back. You can't follow the youngsters. You can't stand still. You must go on. Now is the time when you who have been developing interests outside your children go on cultivating them as you always have done. Now there is time for all the things you've always wanted to do . . . to pick up that course, to train for this thing or that, to work for a cause or a movement, to open up a business or take a fling at art!

As we close this section on parenthood it seems fitting to quote from America's Pledge to Children at the Midcentury, a pledge to *all* children from the Midcentury White House Conference on Children and Youth:

PLEDGE TO CHILDREN

TO YOU, our children, who hold within you our most cherished hopes, we the members of the Midcentury White House Conference on Children and Youth, relying on your full response, make this pledge:

From your earliest infancy we give you our love, so that you may grow with trust in yourself and in others.

We will recognize your worth as a person and we will help you to strengthen your sense of belonging.

We will respect your right to be yourself and at the same time help you to understand the rights of others, so that you may experience cooperative living.

We will help you to develop initiative and imagination, so that you may have the opportunity freely to create.

We will encourage your curiosity and your pride in workmanship, so that you may have the satisfaction that comes from achievement.

We will provide the conditions for wholesome play that will add to your learning, to your social experience, and to your happiness.

We will illustrate by precept and example the value of integrity and the importance of moral courage.

We will encourage you always to seek the truth.

We will provide you with all opportunities possible to develop your own faith in God.

We will open the way for you to enjoy the arts and to use them for deepening your understanding of life.

We will work to rid ourselves of prejudice and discrimination, so that together we may achieve a truly democratic society.

We will work to lift the standard of living and to improve our economic practices, so that you may have the material basis for a full life.

We will provide you with rewarding educational opportunities, so that you may develop your talents and contribute to a better world.

We will protect you against exploitation and undue hazards and help you grow in health and strength.

We will work to conserve and improve family life and, as needed, to provide foster care according to your inherent rights.

We will intensify our search for new knowledge in order to guide you more effectively as you develop your potentialities.

As you grow from child to youth to adult, establishing a family life of your own and accepting larger social responsibilities, we will work with you to improve conditions for all children and youth.

SO MAY YOU grow in joy, in faith in God and in man, and in those qualities of vision and of the spirit that will sustain us all and give us new hope for the future.

Aware that these promises to you cannot be fully met in a world at war, we ask you to join us in a firm dedication to the building of a world society based on freedom, justice, and mutual respect.

Selected Readings

BARUCH, DOROTHY, *New Ways in Discipline* (New York: Whittlesey House, 1949).

ENGLISH, O. SPURGEON, AND FOSTER, CONSTANCE J., *Fathers Are Parents, Too* (New York: Putnam, 1951).

FRANK, LAWRENCE, AND FRANK, MARY, *How to Help Your Child in School* (New York: Viking, 1950).

GESELL, ARNOLD, AND ILG, FRANCES, *The Child from Five to Ten* (New York: Harper, 1946).

GROSSMAN, JEAN SCHICK, *Life with Family* (New York: Appleton-Century-Crofts, 1948).

GRUENBERG, SIDONIE, *Your Child and You* (New York: Fawcett Publications, 1950).

LANDIS, JUDSON, AND LANDIS, MARY, *Building a Successful Marriage* (New York: Prentice-Hall, 1948), chaps. 20, 21.

MERRILL, FRANCIS, *Courtship and Marriage* (New York: Sloane, 1949), Chap. 12.

RIDENOUR, NINA, *Some Special Problems of Children* (Philadelphia: National Mental Health Foundation, 1947).

SPOCK, BENJAMIN, *The Pocket Book of Baby and Child Care* (New York: Pocket Books, 1946).

TAYLOR, KATHARINE WHITESIDE, "The Opportunities of Parenthood," in Becker and Hill (eds.), *Family, Marriage, and Parenthood* (Boston: Heath, 1948), Chap. 16.

WALLER, WILLARD, AND HILL, REUBEN, *The Family: A Dynamic Interpretation*, Revised Edition (New York: Dryden, 1951), chaps. 19, 20.

Technical References

BOSSARD, JAMES, AND BOLL, ELEANOR, *Ritual in Family Living* (Philadelphia: University of Pennsylvania Press, 1950).

DAVIS, W. ALLISON, AND HAVIGHURST, ROBERT, *Father of the Man* (Boston: Houghton Mifflin, 1947).

DUVALL, EVELYN MILLIS, "Conceptions of Parenthood," *American Journal of Sociology* (November, 1946), pp. 193–203.

ELDER, RACHEL ANN, "Traditional and Developmental Conceptions of Fatherhood," *Marriage and Family Living* (August, 1949), pp. 98–101.

LANGDON, GRACE, AND STOUT, IRVING, *These Well-Adjusted Children* (New York: John Day, 1951).

NATIONAL MIDCENTURY COMMITTEE FOR CHILDREN AND YOUTH, *Reports; Progress Bulletins* (160 Broadway, New York).

NYE, IVAN, "Adolescent-Parent Adjustment — Socio-Economic Level as a Variable," *American Sociological Review* (June, 1951), pp. 341–349.

ROY, KATHARINE, "Parents' Attitudes toward Their Children," *Journal of Home Economics*, Vol. 42, No. 8, pp. 652–653.

CHAPTER NINETEEN

We give Thee thanks . . .

FAMILY LIFE AND RELIGIOUS LIVING

When do interfaith marriages work?

What kind of religion should you teach your children?

What is the place of religion in the modern family?

In what way are families and religion interdependent?

"NEITHER JOHN NOR I EVER GO TO CHURCH, SO I GUESS THIS chapter does not concern us." This may be the response of some readers; but they are wrong. For whether or not they think that they have anything directly to do with religion and the church they are inescapably involved. In the first place, all of us live in a society in which religious institutions and ideas are prominent and powerful. Sunday may not be devoted to religious purposes, but it is a religious holiday. So also are Christmas, Easter, and Thanksgiving. A large proportion of all marriage ceremonies are performed by clergy. Our ideas and ideals of family relationships reflect to a very considerable extent the influence of the church.[1] However, a family without church connections is not thereby to be regarded as irreligious. Every individual and every family has some kind of religion, good or bad, whether they know it or not. For religion, contrary to widespread misconceptions, is not the same as the church. In fact, some faiths, such as Mohammedanism and Confucianism, do not have church organizations as we understand them. In many societies there is no separate church, as religion is co-terminus with the tribe or state. In our culture there is much that is genuinely religious quite outside the church, for religion is basically

[1] For the sake of brevity the term "church" will be used in this chapter to designate all types of religious agencies and groups, Jewish as well as Christian.

what a man believes in and lives by. Every individual and every family must have some kind of faith, however limited and inadequate. Therefore we all face such questions as: What kind of religion do we now have, and how sound and satisfactory is it? How deliberate shall be our pursuit of religious goals? Through what institutions and practices can our basic values be most effectively achieved? Fundamental in the answering of each of these questions is the query, "What do we as a couple start with?" We shall begin our discussion, then, with the problem of interfaith marriages.

The Question of Interfaith Marriages

Most authorities in the field of marriage including Catholic, Protestant, and Jewish leaders are agreed that interfaith marriage is risky, if not undesirable. But young people themselves are increasingly disregarding these warnings. An extensive study by John L. Thomas discovers an increase for the 132 parishes included in the East and Middle East of the United States.[2] Roughly 30 per cent of all marriages sanctioned by the Roman Catholic Church were interfaith, and his figures show the proportion to have increased since 1910.[3] Furthermore, these interfaith marriages were only about 60 per cent of all unions between Catholics and non-Catholics.[4] If these figures are correct, nearly half of all Catholics who marry in this country take non-Catholic mates.

Objections to Interfaith Marriage. The attitudes which the major religious faiths have had historically toward interfaith marriages are briefly summarized in Barron's *People Who Intermarry*.[5] The main reasons for their opposition can be stated briefly as follows:

[2] "The Factor of Religion in the Selection of Marriage Mates," *American Sociological Review* (August, 1951), pp. 487–491.

[3] Two studies in intermarriage in New Haven, Connecticut, find that marriages of Catholics and non-Catholics have slightly declined. Ruby J. R. Kennedy, "Single or Triple Melting-Pot? Intermarriage Trends in New Haven, 1870–1940," *American Journal of Sociology* (January, 1944), pp. 331–339, and A. B. Hollingshead, "Cultural Factors in the Selection of Marriage Mates," *American Sociological Review* (October, 1950), pp. 619–627.

[4] Other studies of Catholic intermarriage are those of C. S. Mihanovitch, *Family Life* (December, 1948), p. 6, which indicated 25 per cent, and Judson Landis' study of 4108 families of college students, where he found an interfaith marriage percentage of 23 per cent, *American Sociological Review* (June, 1949), pp. 402 ff.

[5] Milton L. Barron, *People Who Intermarry* (Syracuse: Syracuse University Press, 1946), and "Research on Intermarriage: A Survey of Accomplishments and Prospects," *American Journal of Sociology* (November, 1951).

Catholic. Catholics regard their religion as the only true faith, the only form of Christianity which is both complete and without error. If a Catholic marries a non-Catholic, he is not to permit the ceremony to be performed by someone other than a Catholic priest. If he does, he is automatically dropped from the Church and lost to the "true faith." If the non-Catholic signs an agreement to bring up all children in the Catholic faith, the priest will perform the ceremony. Even then, the non-Catholic may fail to live up to his agreement. Or, by the very fact of not being himself a Catholic, he may weaken the faith of his children.

Protestant. Many Protestants regard the Catholic religion as being in serious theological error. Those of "sound faith" ought not to run the risk of becoming led astray by "false teaching," or of risking the exposure of their children to it.

Ideological objections are far more common. Many Protestants regard Catholics as being under the domination of an ecclesiastical dictatorship. Unless the Catholic is willing to give up his church, the non-Catholic must agree to bring up his children in a religion which he regards as a relentless foe of his democratic ideals. He feels that no parent has a right to sign away the rights of his children to grow up as free men and women in such arbitrary fashion.

Jewish. Orthodox Judaism regards the preservation of Jewish tradition and practices of utmost importance. Intermarriage threatens the purity and strength of the Jewish faith. Nehemiah, in the Bible, felt so strongly that he cursed, struck, and pulled the hair of Jews married to foreign women. Ezra agonized over this same situation, and finally led a movement to require all Jewish people to divorce foreigners to whom they were married. Many liberal Jews, however, feel quite differently.

All faiths fear what is fairly well proved, that people of mixed marriages are less loyal to any faith than those in which both are members of the same faith.[6]

Religious Difference and Marriage Success

Most people who marry, however, are not religious leaders, nor are they too much concerned about the effects of their marriage upon their church. They want to know, "What will union with a member of another faith do to my marriage?" Let us look at this problem!

The first essential is clearly to understand what an interfaith marriage is. We usually understand that a Catholic–non-Catholic, or a Jewish-

[6] See the results of a study conducted by Murray Leiffer reported in *Time* (January 31, 1949), p. 64.

Gentile marriage is interfaith (although the latter may be primarily intercultural). We know too, that the larger Protestant bodies are so similar that marriage across such lines rarely presents a serious problem. But the teachings and expectations of certain smaller groups, such as Jehovah's Witnesses, Mennonites, and Seventh-Day Adventists, are so much at variance with those of other Protestant groups that intermarriage can cause serious difficulties. Yet marriage to one of the same denomination may also be an interfaith marriage. If one is ultraconservative and the other liberal, if one regards church as very important and the other as not important, serious clashes over religion may result.

How do such differences affect marriage success? On the whole, differences in religion tend to make success more difficult. All the studies made indicate that the greater the similarity of religious background, the greater the chances of success. The greater the differences, the greater the risks of failure.[7] (For supporting data see the chart, "Religion and Broken Homes.")

Yet mixed marriage can succeed. Many do. If your marriage is mixed, you may have to work harder to make a go of it. But it is by no means doomed to failure. Church affiliation is but one out of a number of factors which can make for failure or success. Far more important are such qualities as character, mental health, and the attitude which you both take toward your differences, religious or otherwise.

The major problem of interfaith marriage will probably emerge when children arrive. Then your church may step in, not only in the person of the priest or minister, but also in the form of Grandma, or even Uncle Jim. Usually the children follow the religion of the mother, regardless of signed agreements or other factors, unless one of the couple is especially strong in his convictions. But in the final analysis, the decision is, or should be, yours. We who write books can do little more than help you know what to expect. Here are some points which you will wish to examine with especial care.

---

[7] E. W. Burgess and Leonard S. Cottrell, Jr., *Predicting Success or Failure in Marriage* (New York: Prentice-Hall, 1939), pp. 50–51, 122–126; L. M. Terman and associates, *Psychological Factors in Marital Happiness* (New York: McGraw-Hill, 1938), p. 109; Howard M. Bell, *Youth Tell Their Story* (Washington: American Council on Education, 1938), p. 21; H. Ashley Weeks, "Differential Divorce Rates by Occupation," *Social Forces* (March, 1943), p. 336; and Judson T. Landis, *op. cit.*, p. 404.

1 *How intense is the loyalty of each to his own religious group?*
Mary was a Catholic and Jim was a Methodist, but neither of them
cared anything about church nor had attended for some time. They
were married by a justice of the peace, and after their marriage both
continued to stay away from church, even as they had before. Their
families made no attempt to interfere. In consequence their differences caused almost no problem.

On the other hand, Bill and Sally, who belonged to two different
and extremely narrow sects, each regarded the teachings of his or her
church as the only true religious faith, and felt that the other lived in
darkness and sin. They had agreed beforehand that each was to go his
separate way, but after marriage neither could bear to see the loved one
going to hell. Therefore each made ardent efforts to convert the other,
in which their families heartily joined. Bill and Sally never divorced or
separated, but the constant tension which developed between them em-
bittered the whole relationship and had an especially unfortunate effect
upon their children.

RELIGION AND BROKEN HOMES

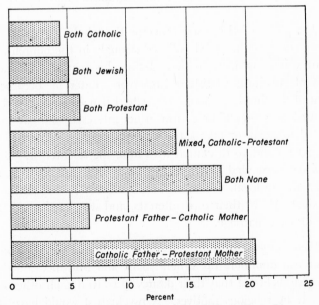

Percentage of Marriages of Mixed and Nonmixed Religious Faiths Ending in Divorce or Separation,
4108 Couples in Michigan, "Marriages of Mixed and Nonmixed Religious Faith" by Judson T.
Landis, *American Sociological Review* (June, 1949), Table 1, p. 403.

2 *How many complicating factors are there, such as relatives and influential friends?* The church is not merely a religious body. Specifically it is Mama, Papa, and Uncle Bill. If they object to the faith of the married partner, it is natural that they should bring considerable pressure on behalf of their church, especially as the children are born. Remember that many parents give up their children with considerable reluctance and sometimes welcome any chance to keep a hold on the life of the young adult. Zealous friends and members of the clergy are often eager to push the claims of their church, even when it means bringing serious discord into the marriage.

3 *What aspects of religion does each feel most strongly about?* Some Christians regard dancing or attending movies on the Sabbath as a sin, whereas others openly encourage such activities. Among Jewish groups the conflict between those who observe Kosher and other orthodox regulations and those who disregard them may prove to be painful. Seeing the person to whom you are married freely indulge in activities which you have been brought up to regard as immoral is inevitably a strain on the whole relationship. Differences in theology indicated by such terms as "modernism" and "fundamentalism" may also cause difficulties.

Another phase of this issue concerns the whole matter of actively supporting the church. Fred believed strongly in the church and was an ardent worker in its activities. Before his marriage he had been president of the local Christian Endeavor. Later he became superintendent of the Sunday school. His wife, Ellen, belonged to the same church but was decidedly lukewarm in her interests. Sunday mornings she wanted to sleep, or take a trip into the country. If Fred insisted that she get up and go to church with him, she resented it. On a few occasions she persuaded him to skip church and visit relatives, and he felt guilty and disloyal. As time went on, each found other persons more sympathetic to their own interests, and wondered about the desirability of their marriage.

4 *Is there danger that religious differences will be used as a means by which one can dominate the other?* Sally and Bill, mentioned above, both honestly believed that their desires to convert each other were inspired solely by religious motives. A psychiatrist would have thought differently; he would have seen in their efforts subconscious attempts to dominate, with their religious ardor used as a smoke screen behind which to conceal their desire to control. So it often is, as we have suggested, with interfering family members.

5 *Are there other strong bonds to compensate for the religious difference?* Doris was a highly educated Catholic of the liberal group. Jacob was a reformed Jew. Both, however, regarded their respective religious groups primarily as social institutions designed to perform social functions. Both were vitally interested in good housing, the improvement of government, and all efforts for social welfare. The children, when they came, were given a social interpretation of the religious groups, and as they grew up were encouraged to choose their own affiliations. This breadth of attitude made possible not only a harmonious, but an enriched relationship which brought them close together. Their marriage was successful because both were actually of the same religion: the religion of humanity. When the fundamental values of each are similar, the religious label is of little importance.

6 *What compromises are both willing to make to solve the problem?* The church relationships of many people are nominal. They have no serious emotional attachments to any denomination or group. If this is true of both members of the couple and also of their families, a difference of denomination may represent little difficulty. They will probably solve the problem by belonging to no church at all. When a marriage partnership consists of one member who is very devout while the other has no strongly held religious convictions or antipathies, the problem is also not impossible. The indifferent one will just turn the whole matter over to the other. If the two have real and conflicting convictions, or if their families have, the problem can seldom be easily solved. Sometimes one will yield to the extent of agreeing to bring up the children in the faith of the other, as non-Catholics who are married by a Catholic priest are required to do. One member of the couple may adopt the faith of the other. Neither of these solutions is likely to prove happy. However sincere the individual making the change may be, there is an element of duress involved. "She" would not have changed had it not been necessary in order to get her husband. Religion is largely a matter of early emotional experiences, powerfully related to family loyalties. One cannot change these as he would a garment. After marriage both husband and wife find that the one who supposedly

changed is still what he was brought up to be and that it is impossible for him to be anything else.

Young people can hardly be expected to be more rational in religion than they are in other matters related to marriage. Emotional factors will pull them on, for weal or for woe. Those who are determined to cross faith lines, however, can increase the likelihood of success by frankly facing the situation and coming to some agreements *before the marriage*. These should involve specific and definite decisions on such questions as the following:

1 Who, if either, will change his church relationships? If this is done at all it should be done before the wedding.
2 If each retains his separate faith, where will they attend church, if at all?
3 In what faith, if any, will the children be brought up?
4 Are parents and relatives to be consulted? This is one of the most crucial and difficult problems, since parental approval is significantly related to later success of the marriage. Shall we keep our parents informed as we go along, or just keep quiet about the whole matter, marry, and let them howl about a *fait accompli*? The latter policy has in some instances proved to be the less difficult. It also has its risks.

Religion and Family Living

Although church groups have always been interested in families, in recent years this interest has increased remarkably. At first such interest was scattered and often negative. Clergy denounced and "viewed with alarm" the increase in divorce. Then here and there a minister began to take a more constructive attitude, and to do "marriage counseling" on a sounder basis. The increased interest of church groups became evident in the widespread adoption of "Mother's Day," which was in time expanded into National Family Week. The letter from President Truman suggests the cooperative approach of this interest.

In recent years, denominational groups have established extensive programs. Departments of the Christian Family have been established, and an increasing literature developed. The Roman Catholic Church has an extensive program for training its members for marriage and family living, in the Cana and pre-Cana conferences. The Methodists have held national conferences on family life which have been attended by thousands. Jewish groups have given increasing attention

January 30, 1951

My dear Friends:

With deep and sincere conviction I endorse the efforts of the Jewish, Catholic and Protestant faiths to emphasize the strengthening of spiritual life in American homes through the ninth annual observance of National Family Week, May 6 to 13, 1951. This work provides evidence of the value Americans place on the role which the family must play in preserving faith in our religious and democratic principles. It also demonstrates the spirit of brotherhood and mutual responsibility in which the three major faiths in this country work together for the benefit of all citizens.

During our heroic national effort, members of many families may be temporarily separated from one another by the requirements of the armed services and defense industries. Such dislocations will not interrupt the basic unity of a family bound together by love and a mutual faith in God. The guiding principles which the child has acquired in a truly religious family will give him moral strength and courage to face with confidence the uncertainties of the future.

National Family Week gives each of us an opportunity to examine our own lives and see how we may further contribute to the type of family life which underlies the moral strength of our Nation. In the uncertain days that lie ahead, America's spiritual strength will be a positive force in determining that the good and the right shall prevail.

Very sincerely yours,

Harry Truman

Reverend Richard E. Lentz,
National Council of the Churches of Christ in the U.S.A.,

Rabbi Hirsch E. L. Freund,
Synagogue Council of America,

Reverend Edgar M. Schmiedeler, O.S.B.,
National Catholic Welfare Conference.

to what has always been the center of their religious program: family life.

This rising concern has good basis in past religious traditions. Marriage, baptism, and the burial of the dead are religious rites which indicate the length and the depth of the concern of religion with families. Clergy have always counseled with, and given support to families as a regular part of their duties. The theology of religious faith has made extensive use of family terms, such as the Fatherhood of God and the Brotherhood of Man. Yes, the relationship between religion and family life has been central and prolonged. Why?

The Church Needs the Family. With few exceptions, people belong to and support churches because they have been taught to do so by their parents. Some parents contribute considerably to the religious education of their children. They read them Bible stories, or drill them in the catechism. In Judaism the main responsibility for the teaching of religion belongs to the family, not to the synagogue. A recent report states that in present-day Poland, every rabbi has been killed, yet the Jewish religion survives because it is being carried on by the families. Most Christians in America depend upon churches for the teaching of religion to their children. Yet it is the parents who largely support these churches, and develop loyalties in their children for them. Without such family support, no church could long continue without crippling losses. These facts are well understood. Less well understood is the relationship of family life to the central teachings of religion.

Families Lay the Basis for Religious Teaching. Religion has not only a knowledge, but an emotional or feeling aspect. The knowledges of religion can probably be taught better by specially trained teachers than by most parents. But for some teachings (including some of the knowledges) experience in family living seems essential. A church may teach that God is Love. But love can have meaning only for those who have already experienced it. Most people, especially children, are not likely to have had such experience outside their families. And how can a child understand about trust and faith in God, unless he has had experiences with people whom he could trust, and in whom he had faith? How many teachings of religion can be understood, only by those who have had a background of appropriate experiences in their own families!

So it is with religious loyalties. Religion will be important for most children only if they see that it is important to their parents. Parents may be able to give their children some *knowledge* about religion, merely by sending them to a church school where they will be taught by someone else. But religious attitudes and loyalties are usually learned only from parents who participate in and themselves support church activities.

What Shall We Teach Our Children? This question has in part already been answered. Our example teaches them much, whether we will or no. In the matter of direct instruction, those who belong to conservative groups have the simpler task. Their denomination usually has clear statements of its doctrines, often printed in a catechism. The task of the parent is to help the children memorize these statements. But for parents who hold "liberal" views, the task is often difficult. The impact of a scientific point of view makes them uncertain about religious doctrines. They see sincerely religious people who make messes of their lives and those of their children. They find it hard to see how religion has contributed materially to a solution of important social problems, such as war. They sense that there is something important in religion which their children should have. But what is this "something"? Because of their own uncertainties, they either do not try to teach their children anything about religion, or they are so "wobbly" and tentative in their teaching that nothing much results. Often they feel quite guilty about their failures. But what can they do? After all, you can hardly teach your children what you do not have yourself! The discussion which follows is intended to help those who are bewildered, as well as those who feel more confident.

What Is a Religious Family?

Many people define a religious family as a nice, ordinary, respectable family with a religious "plus." This "plus" usually includes beliefs (as in God, Christ, the Bible, or the Church), practices (church going, prayers, and Bible reading), and probably a rather high moral standard. This, however, is a family with religion, not a religious family. (See the diagram, p. 398, which illustrates the difference.) Religion at its best is not an addition to life, but a transformation of life. A religious family does not merely add a religious "plus." It is a family organized around religious ideals. This religious core relates all aspects of life

FAMILY AND RELIGION

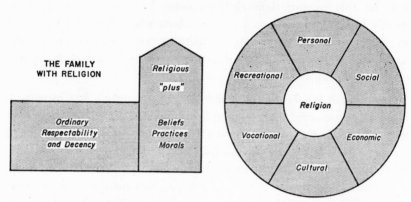

THE RELIGIOUS FAMILY

meaningfully to each other, and transfuses them with religious ideals. As a result, life is unified and takes on new meaning and basic worth. For the religious family, religion is not a set of often burdensome obligations. It gives to family life meaning and purpose, and is a source of wisdom, insight, and power.

Living Religion in the Family. The religious quality of a family is not to be judged by the fidelity with which parents teach their religious views to their children. Neither is it to be determined by the forms and ceremonies observed. Some will find prayers, especially at mealtime, to be a natural and helpful expression of religious faith. But whatever the form, we may expect considerable variation.

Prayer, for instance, has come down through the ages in a multitude of forms. For some it is formalized and structured, the very words being prescribed, yet for others it may be exceedingly spontaneous. A little girl shocked her formally religious parents by bursting out in her anxiety one evening with the prayer, "Oh, God, be with us, don't leave us now. If you do we're sunk." Surprising as this was to her parents who were accustomed to other ways of addressing the deity, the child's words had many of the elements which have caused prayer to persist so long as a satisfying form of religious expression.

Man's sense of his dependence upon forces outside of himself has led him from time to time to clarify his situation, analyze himself, unify his efforts, and solve his problems with capacities that emerge out of the dynamics of the prayerful attitude. Aside from supernatural implications, this approach is still sound, whether the rite be fixed or flexible. Similarly, other rites and practices of religion have their roots in human need and satisfaction and continue to have meaning for people to the extent to which they have been found effective.

But religion is not primarily a matter of beliefs, practices, or institutional relationships. It is primarily a matter of inner response. The type of religion to which a man can respond depends primarily upon the previous development of his own inner life. Crude, spiritually undeveloped persons will necessarily have a primitive and often tribal religion, regardless of what it is called. In reading of wars of religion or persecutions made in the name of religious faith, we have often thought, "How could religious people do such things?" The reason is that their religious faith was an expression of the kind of persons they were inside, and the label of "Christian" or whatever had little to do with their actions. We have often bewailed the distortion of Christian teachings by its avowed followers, but we need not be surprised. Exalted spiritual teachings can be understood only by those spiritually ready for them. If offered to others, they must inevitably be either rejected or distorted. Love can have meaning only for those who have experienced it. And for most, a sufficient experience can come only within the family circle. So it is with ideals of brotherhood, truth, and honor, even with the very concept of spirituality itself. Religion is like a skillful woodworker: he can make great and beautiful things only if he has the wood. The spiritual life can be built only if the materials for it already exist. The significance of the home for a truly spiritual religion is most important. So far as most people are concerned, only in the home can the inner attitudes develop which make a truly spiritual religion even possible.

In the development of religion within the family, the truly important consideration is the spirit which dominates all relationships. If religious teaching is to be effective, it must be inculcated into children as a normal result of the processes of living. In the final analysis the problem is not the teaching of religion in the family; it is rather to make the family religious.

The religious family derives its meaning and significance from purposes beyond itself. Many young people think of marriage in terms of their own personal satisfactions. When they think of an ideal situation they see a lovely house in the suburbs surrounded by shrubs; they think of a good social status, a suitable car, and a salary big enough to keep all these going without pinching. "We'll build a sweet little nest, somewhere in the West, and let the rest of the world go by," is a popular sentiment, but it is not religious. The truly religious person thinks of marriage rather in terms of establishing a cooperative unit of human relationships for the purpose of fulfilling religious objectives. This means, to begin with, that the family will be so conducted as best to satisfy the personality needs of its members. Husband and wife will give each other, and their children, that security of relationship which is a normal need of all.

The religious family will not, and cannot, remain isolated or complete within itself. Of necessity it will reach out into the community in wholesome and constructive activities. Religious parents will be active not only in personal social contacts, but in efforts to promote the well-being of the community. Children will take it for granted that their parents will participate in worth-while enterprises. One of the best descriptions of such religious family activities is to be found in the following testimony of Pearl Buck:

. . . I know my mother loved her children with all her heart, but certainly she never loved us with all her time. But we shared everything with her. She took us to her religious meetings and we went with her when she dispensed food and money to the poor and we helped her with her clinics and her housekeeping equally. We were pressed into every sort of service — not in her case for any obvious training of us, but simply because she had to have help. She was deeply involved in life and she involved us with her. We were early familiar with the sight of hunger and death and we knew because we had heard them the life problems of our surroundings. The result was that without knowing it I grew up hating sorrow and hardship but not afraid of either. I learned so early how to look on death that I cannot remember horror at a dead face. By the time I was grown a lot of the clutter of childhood was out of the way and without personal pain or even knowledge that I was learning I had learned what life is.

. . . The realities of life are not sad or dreary. Life is good to the very last drop, and evil and sorrow and grief are part of the whole. For the person whose home had been a part of the world the balance is never afterwards wrong. He will never be hopeless or despairing because he knows from the moment that he knows anything that there is evil and sorrow as there is also good and happiness, and he is not frightened as he would be if for all his childhood years he had been taught that real life was happiness and plenty and then found out that it is not. The anxiety with which so many of us face life and live life comes from the longing to get back into what we were taught as children, that happiness is the normal, the real atmosphere — that plenty and safety and security are to be expected. The truth is that nothing in life can be expected — the joy of living is to take what comes and fight against it or accept it — but live, and not try all the time to escape living and get away into some romantic refuge where everything ends happily.[8]

Community activities, if overdone, may indicate a basic dissatisfaction with the home and a desire to escape from its responsibilities. On the other hand, unless both parents get out to some extent (and this means the wife as well as the husband) they will not have much to contribute to the more intimate personal relationships of the family. Religious parents try to keep a sound balance between chasing around so much that family relationships are neglected, and sticking around so closely that they become dull and uninteresting, and constantly in the way. This balance is a natural consequence of recognizing that the meaning and significance of the family lies in values which exist outside and beyond itself.

The family, like the individual, finds its life in losing it in the large world. Just as the church steeple stands as a symbol of religion in the community, so the religious family stands out as a center of strength in every neighborhood. The family that is genuinely stable and secure within itself does more than spiritually nourish its own members. It finds itself called upon to share these strengths with neighbors and friends. Good families are the living cells of society: its sustaining pillars and its strength.

Selected Readings

ANDERSON, WILLIAM K., *Making the Gospel Effective* (Nashville: The Methodist Church, 1945), Chap. VII.

BECKER, HOWARD, AND HILL, REUBEN (EDS.), *Family, Marriage, and Parenthood* (Boston: Heath, 1948), Chap. 20.

BOSSARD, JAMES H. S., AND BOLL, ELEANOR, *Ritual in Family Living* (Philadelphia: University of Pennsylvania Press, 1950).

BRO, MARGUERITE H., *When Children Ask* (Chicago: Willett, Clark, 1940).

CHAPLIN, DORA P., *Children and Religion* (New York: Scribner, 1948).

DUVALL, SYLVANUS M., *Men, Women, and Morals* (New York: Association Press, 1952), chaps. 14, 16.

[8] Pearl S. Buck, "At Home in the World," *Marriage and Family Living*, February, 1942.

FALLAW, WESNER, *The Modern Parent and the Teaching Church* (New York: Macmillan, 1946).

GROVES, ERNEST R., *Christianity and the Family* (New York: Macmillan, 1943).

WIEMAN, REGINA WESTCOTT, *The Family Lives Its Religion* (New York: Harper, 1941).

PART

4

FAMILY LIFE YESTERDAY, TODAY, AND TOMORROW

MARRIAGE ISN'T WHAT IT USED TO BE

FAMILIES IN AN UNEASY WORLD

CHAPTER TWENTY

Marriage Isn't What It Used to Be

MARRIAGE ISN'T WHAT IT USED TO BE

Why was grandfather boss in the good old days?

Should a man be the head of the house now?

Is woman's place in the home?

Are modern children given too much freedom?

*A*MERICA'S GREAT-GRANDFATHERS, ASIATIC, AFRICAN, AND EURO-
pean, each brought a pattern of family life to the shores of North
America, but the struggle to survive in the new land necessitated rapid
changes in their traditional theories of who did what in the home. The
sharp changes in social and political conditions which occurred as America grew up from a frontier agricultural nation into an urban industrial-
ized country also forced changes in the institution of the family to meet
new demands. The social climate, the very atmosphere around us today, differs sharply from the setting of family life in bygone days.

The Changing Family

Yes, the family has changed. All of us, no matter how young we are,
know this from what we read, from our own memories, from what older
people say. And sometimes we worry about these changes because
we've heard so often: Modern families are breaking down — Fathers and
mothers do not stay home as much anymore — Children are spoiled —
Young people are running wild — The good old days are gone — City life
is the trouble — Working wives are the trouble — Too small families are
the trouble. How much of this is true? What are the facts?

Family life has changed because most of the conditions of life have

AMERICAN COLONIAL FAMILY TRAITS *
(New England Puritan — Southern English)

Community Life and Values

Compact village settlements and outlying isolated farms; no large estates
Large estates with slaves, later with laborers and tenants; small crossroads hamlets

Manual work and skill dignified, combined with brain work
Manual work regarded more or less servile, hence less manual skill developed

No great class stratification
Wealthy aristocracy, with leisure and cultured manners; poor whites; slaves

Emphasis on thrift
Less emphasis on thrift

Strict Sabbath

Marital and Sexual Relations

Marriage by civil magistrate only, at first; later modified, but marriage regarded as secular
Marriage ceremony by Church of England clergy only

Divorce rare but permissible
Divorce practically nonexistent

Strong social pressure to marry; bachelors taxed and penalized; fairly balanced sex ratio
High sex ratio at first, with women later imported for marriage

Widows and spinsters often fell under witchcraft persecutions
Girls often married at 12; considerable illegitimacy through race mixture

Severe public punishment and church confession for premarital and extramarital intercourse, yet many violations
Double-standard sex mores

No recognized class of prostitutes

Bundling in courtship

No intermarriage with Indians

Some intermarriage with Indians; none with Negroes although sex relations common

Primogeniture abolished at outset

Social Roles and Interrelations of the Sexes	Women devoting time to homemaking and farm chores, but also following other occupations such as trade and teaching at early date

Women's work dependent upon social class, upper class doing less homemaking and few chores, lower class more menial labor than in North

Chivalrous, playful attitude of men toward women in upper class

Discipline of Children	Strict discipline and Spartan treatment of children, early inculcation of industrious habits and fear of hell; theoretical death penalty for rebellious sons over 16 in Connecticut

Compulsory education of some degree by 1649

Universal education late in developing

* Adapted with permission from Joseph K. Folsom, *The Family and Democratic Society* (New York: Wiley, 1943), p. 117.

CHECK YOURSELF   Before each of the following family activities indicate by an *i* if there has been an increase in this family activity since pioneer family days, by a *d* if this activity has decreased within the family.

_____	1 Churning butter	_____	11 Baking bread
_____	2 Attending PTA meetings	_____	12 Preserving
_____	3 Weaving cloth	_____	13 Manufacture of ice
_____	4 Family vacations	_____	14 Soap making
_____	5 Raising poultry	_____	15 Visiting museums
_____	6 Making garments	_____	16 Enjoying sports
_____	7 Cobbling shoes	_____	17 Knitting stockings
_____	8 Listening to music	_____	18 Grinding meal
_____	9 Curing meat	_____	19 Listening to children
_____	10 Drying fruits	_____	20 Caring for the sick

★ KEY   20 d, 19 i, 18 d, 17 d, 16 i, 15 i, 14 d

13 i, 12 d, 11 d, 10 d, 9 i, 8 d, 7 d, 6 d, 5 i, 4 i, 3 d, 2 i, 1 d

changed in the past fifty years. The home didn't change first. It changed as a result of these other forces to which each family had to adapt. Undoubtedly we face still further changes in the next twenty-five years. Need we be alarmed?

Change isn't anything to fear. It's a condition of human life. To exchange one thing for another, to enter upon a new phase of living, is a challenge to our ingenuity, to our ability to see things as they are.

Before we make up our minds about present-day family life in general or the kind of family life we want in particular, let's look at some of the facts. The establishing of families in America was accomplished by progressive people from other countries who did not like the old ways and who came here to break away from old traditions. These early pioneers founded small communities, where they lived for the survival of all by the usefulness of each. People were esteemed for their economic contributions to the family rather than for their beauty or their family background. Great-grandmother was an asset to her family. She cooked the food, kept the house, cared for aged parents, nursed the sick, made the clothing and household linens from materials grown on the land, besides producing a large family. Great-grandfather welcomed children as helpers. Indeed, he needed a large family to keep the wolf from the door, to clear the land, plant and gather the crops, grind the grain, and build shelters. He was boss of the family as well as the foreman of the big job of getting the family settled.

These pioneer families measured success and wealth in terms of numbers, whether they were numbers of acres of land, of horses, of cows, of pigs, or the number of children in the family. In 1675 the average size of the New England household was *nine*. The motivation to marry centered in the economic advantages first; the satisfactions of love came later, if there was time! Family relations were not unusually warm, since affection of the child for parents was colored with the dull gray of an attitude of duty. In the table on page 406 the details of family life among the colonials throw into relief the attitudes and values of these early American families.

Pioneers of New Horizons

These pioneer families produced children who, as they struggled to survive, dreamed dreams which made them even greater pioneers than their fathers. This next generation sought freedom from the arduous labors of their fathers; they invented machines which would do the work in less time, with less energy. But these changes brought frustration to the older people because their sons and daughters were taken away from home into factories and cities. The young people were more receptive to these creative changes and saw in them the solution of the human needs of their generation. They also had visions of the hardships which their children could be saved if better ways of doing things were only encouraged. And as the dreams of each succeeding generation became realistic, many changes occurred which affected family life, necessitating adjustments for the individual and for the family as a group. Indeed, the ability to accept scientific, social, and political changes has become one criterion for measuring family stability in latter-day American life.[1]

Midcentury American Families [2]

Family life certainly isn't what it used to be. Sweeping changes have taken place during the twentieth century, and back of them is the rapid growth of our industrial civilization. Machines have affected, directly and indirectly, every phase of our lives, including our most basic institution — the family.

Families Live in Cities. One of the most direct effects of our machine economy on the family has been its influence in determining where the family shall live. We see, in the accompanying chart, that in 1890 64 per cent of all households in the United States lived on farms. By 1948, only 17 per cent were still on farms. The picture is clear: more and more "machine" jobs have lured increasing numbers of families to cities; the growth of industry and cities has gone hand in hand.

Families Buy Their Goods. At the turn of the century most of the goods and services needed by the family were produced in the home. At midcentury, most families had become units of consumption, buying almost all that was needed. What had formerly been homemade now was produced on assembly lines as "big business" production increased

[1] Robert C. Angell, *The Family Encounters the Depression* (New York: Scribner, 1936), pp. 44–45, 263, and Reuben Hill, *Families under Stress* (New York: Harper, 1949).
[2] See Chart "Twentieth Century Changes in American Family Life," pp. 416–417.

PREPARING BREAKFAST | WORKS ALL DAY | RUSHING HOME AT FIVE

FEEDING FAMILY | CLEANING HOUSE | OTHER HOUSEWORK

From *An Economic Challenge to American Women* by Florence M. Schneider

OVERWORK AND

five-fold between 1900 and 1950. Machines have provided families with literally hundreds of time- and labor-saving devices, from electric toasters, grinders, and mixers to electric stoves, washing machines, refrigerators, air conditioners, and television. And in addition to all the modern home conveniences, a great deal of work formerly done at home is now done outside in bakeries, dairies, packing houses, canneries, laundries, etc.

Families Are Small. The average American family at midcentury consisted of 3.6 persons. Families are smaller than they used to be, not only in the smaller number of children but also in that fewer extended family members (Grandma, Aunt Celia, Uncle Tim) now make their homes with them. Now that homes are not as busy making things, these "extra" adults are not as welcome with their married relatives.

Families are smaller for two reasons. 1. Children and other relatives were an asset in the days when so many things had to be done in the home; they were especially valuable to farm families. Today they are usually a financial liability. 2. City life is not conducive to large families. Couples with several children have difficulty renting a dwelling large enough and cheap enough; they often must rent an old house

BREAKFAST | TIDYING UP APARTMENT | READING PAPERS & MAGAZINES

A CHAT | A KITCHENETTE SUPPER | A CARD GAME

(National Federation of Business and Professional Women's Clubs)

UNDERWORK — AN URBAN SAMPLE

or one in an undesirable neighborhood, since many landlords object to children.

Families Have High Standard of Living. The figures in the table on page 416 show vividly that family members at midcentury were better educated, enjoyed more leisure, ate better food, traveled farther and faster, spent more for luxuries and comforts, and had an income per family member that was twice that at the turn of the century.

More Marry at Younger Ages. With the higher standard of living has come the ability of young people to marry at younger ages, and a far higher percentage of the population marry than was possible at the beginning of the twentieth century.

Families Less Stable. Our machine civilization has brought about, indirectly, more instability in homes. City life has made divorce more feasible because of: 1. greater mobility of the family, relieving people from community criticism and taboos; 2. greater financial independence of women (today a woman with few or no children and all sorts of job possibilities does not have to continue living with a husband she does not love just for financial support); 3. wider contacts at younger ages, increasing possibilities of mate selection and of remarriage.

Thus far the discussion has been primarily on the outward changes in family life, those which lend themselves to statistics. Let us now turn to the internal changes as revealed in activities and attitudes, a story which cannot be told in figures but which is nonetheless vital.

Internal Changes. More democratic family practices are accepted today than fifty years ago. Then the family was still patriarchal; the husband and father was the dictator whose authority was final, whose judgment was infallible. Children were taught to regard their parents with reverence and never to talk back; punishment was severe, usually physical. More of today's parents try to be companions of their children, as human beings who make mistakes and have to "beg pardon" occasionally. Parents and children are bridging the old chasm between the child world and adult world by being pals, playing and working together, trying to understand each other.

The older Puritanical sex attitudes have given way to a more wholesome acceptance of the sex side of life and to more realistic efforts in sex education. The rigid rules, regulations and "cover up" of the nineteenth century are rapidly disappearing as many of today's families attempt to exchange blind conformity for exploration of what will be wise and best.

Mother's place in this new family has changed greatly. The modern mother with few and widely spaced children, with her many mechanical devices, can spend much less time and energy at *housekeeping* and much more time at *homemaking*. She has time to study diets, budgeting, and child training. She can spend more time with the children, helping them develop hobbies and cultural interests. And, if she is wise, she also keeps up her own intellectual and social interests. Thus her service to her family is less physical, more mental and spiritual.

The family today has more time, resources, and facilities than ever before for real unity through recreation, fun, and cultural activities. The family isn't what it used to be, but it has innumerable opportunities for becoming much better than it ever has been.

The Rising Status of Women

A generation ago a portrait of an old lady, seated with her hands folded, was painted by Whistler. This became the ideal picture of mother. A portrait of mother in serviceable slacks might be more appropriate today. These extremes of complacency and action in women depict the startling social and economic changes which families have absorbed in the last fifty years.

Before the foot that rocked the cradle worked a pedal on a machine, many changes took place, including the discovery that babies slept better in a stationary bed that could not be rocked. Obviously a man can't get a girl just like father used to have. Girls don't grow up with the same ideas any more. But it's equally true that neither the vote nor greasy overalls have changed Mary's essential femininity. Heads still turn and pulses beat for her; she still gets into ruffles when she can; she spends more time and money than ever before to make herself attractive, she still wants and plans and works for a home, a husband, and a family.

The changed world which is responsible for the new Mary has also made changes in the techniques of getting and caring for and keeping a home, husband, and family. Mary is trying to adapt her nature to new conditions. What are they? Why does she want to wear overalls?

Should Women Work? They always have. In the old days, when marriage was their only possible career, it afforded them plenty of work. When all food was prepared at home,

WHY MARRIED WOMEN WORK

MOST because of urgent family need

SOME to raise standard of living

FEW for a career

From *Public Affairs Pamphlet* No. 49, Public Affairs Committee. Drawn by Pictograph Corporation

cooking, baking, and preserving for a big family were almost a job in themselves, and added to this was a house to keep in order, a new baby every year or two, sewing, washing, ironing, and gardening. The only leisure problem a woman had then was how to get any leisure. The reward which she reaped for her labors was the knowledge that she was needed, essential to her family's existence and comfort, and her pride at managing so many jobs pretty well.

Then conditions changed. The machine age arrived. Bakeries took over the baking of her bread, canneries the preserving of her food, factories the making of the family's clothes. The increase in commercial production, with opportunities for more jobs and higher wages, brought more and more families to the city. Children went to school more regularly and stayed in school years longer. People generally became more prosperous, bought more articles and services, performed less physical work.

In the course of these changes the wife and mother lost many of her former jobs. She either sent the laundry out or used a washing machine. Milk was delivered at her door daily; the grocery boy brought the food. She had fewer children. Formerly, with a multitude of daily chores to perform on the farm or in the home, children had been not only an act of God but an economic advantage. Now they became an expense. Shelter cost more, living conditions were more crowded, and neighbors objected to noise. In order to get good jobs when they grew up, children had to have more education. Going to high school and college became the accepted instead of the extraordinary thing to do. Money was required for lunches, carfare, books, for more clothes, for tuition for the children. So, many people tended to have fewer children, and to spend more on those they had.

Where did all these changing conditions leave the housewife? The average woman had less to do in the home than ever before, but at the same time the economic pressure became greater. Father spent long hours at his work (though not as long as his father before him) in order to earn the constantly increasing amount of money needed. In contrast, except for the few years when the children were small, the city

INCREASE IN MARRIED WOMEN WORKERS

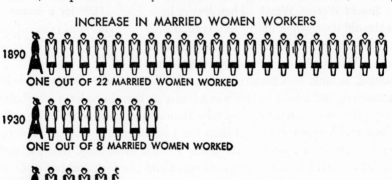

1890
ONE OUT OF 22 MARRIED WOMEN WORKED

1930
ONE OUT OF 8 MARRIED WOMEN WORKED

1940
EST
ONE OUT OF 5 OR 6 MARRIED WOMEN WORKS

From *Public Affairs Pamphlet* No. 49. Drawn by Pictograph Corporation

housewife's work in the home required considerably less time and energy.

In most cases, as statistics show, women work because of financial need, or to raise the living standard of the family. In other words, most women have not left their proper sphere, but their sphere has changed. Earning money has become a part of their service to their family, as performing more direct services once was.

During the last fifty years the number of married women working outside the home has steadily increased. In 1890, less than one million married women and three million single women were at work. In 1910 the figures were two million married women and five and a half million unmarried women; in 1930, three million married women and seven and a half million unmarried women. The increase since 1940 continues very rapid. Young people marry at younger ages today, partly because of the ability and the willingness of the woman to continue working after marriage.

There is another side to this story. Mothers who have left the home to work have been missed! Even smaller living quarters with all the conveniences require some work and time. Children always need the loving attention of their parents, and mothers are needed especially in infancy. A home with unmade beds, unwashed dishes, delicatessen meals, children left with hired help all day or actually neglected is a heavy price to pay for any economic advantage.

Some of this upheaval is inevitable in periods of transition. It seems that changes in women's status and services have come so fast in our day that we have not had time to revamp our mores or customs. Our present culture exemplifies several conflicting ideas as to what women should be or do. The situation is admittedly confusing for everyone. However, there are many partial solutions hovering on the horizon; community kitchens, community nursery schools, shorter working days, new household conveniences, and education for new roles are some of them.

Studies indicate that women who have had some work experience before marriage tend to make better marriage partners than those with none.[3] Other statistical and clinical studies tell us that women can work outside the home and carry on their functions as wives and moth-

[3] Ernest W. Burgess and Leonard S. Cottrell, Jr., *Predicting Success and Failure in Marriage* (New York: Prentice-Hall, 1939), pp. 150–152.

TWENTIETH CENTURY CHANGES IN AMERICAN FAMILY LIFE
(At the Turn of the Century – At Midcentury)

Rural: 64% households on farms, 1890
Urban: 17% households on farms, 1948 [1]

Homes producing units: raise food, preserve, bake, cook, sew, cobble shoes, etc.
Families consumers: "big business" production increase five-fold, 1900–1950.[2]

Large family: average 5 persons in 1890
Small family: average 3.6 persons in 1948 [1]

Few divorces: .54 divorced per 100 married persons, 1890
More divorces: 2.82 divorced per 100 married persons, 1949 [1]

Few women work outside home: 1 out of 22 married women work outside home in 1890
More women work outside home: 1 out of 4 married women work outside home in 1949 [1]

Fewer women marry: 51.8% women 20–24 years single in 1890
More women marry: 30.8% women 20–24 years single in 1949 [1]

Fewer ever marry: 63.1% population ever married in 1890
More ever marry: 78.6% population ever married in 1949 [1]

Marry late: median age first marriage for men 26.1, for women 22 in 1890
Marry early: median age first marriage for men 22.7, for women 20.3 in 1949 [1]

Education limited: modal man leaves school at 14; in 17 states no school attendance requirement at all, 1900
Educated longer: modal man leaves school at 18; all states require school attendance at least up to 16, some to 18, 1950 [3]

Education for domestic roles implicit in apprenticeship of child to adult in home
Education for marriage and family life becoming explicit in formal and informal programs in home, school, community [4]

Family is provincial: limited to horse and some train travel; few telephones, few automobiles; no radio, TV, or airplanes
Family becomes at home in the world: airplane, automobile travel common; radio, TV, news of world events hourly into homes [4]

Long hours: work week 59 hours in 1900
More leisure: work week 40 hours in 1950 [5]

Family income small: $520 per family member (1948 purchasing power
dollars) in 1901
Income per family member doubled: $1085 (1948 purchasing power dol-
lars), 1948 [5]

Few luxuries: 17% family income spent on things other than necessities,
1901
More luxuries: 41% family income spent on things other than necessities,
1948 [5]

Family diet heavy in grains and potatoes: 42% more in 1900 than 1949
Families eat more protective foods: 273% more citrus fruits, 43% more
vegetables, 30% more eggs, 29% more milk in 1949 than in 1900 [6]

More babies die first year of life: 100 per 1000 live births, 1915
Infant mortality rates reduced to one third: 32 per 1000 live births, 1948 [7]

More mothers die in childbirth: 60 per 10,000 live births, 1915
Childbearing five times safer: 12 per 10,000 live births, 1948 [7]

Patriarchal, autocratic control
Democratic, equalitarian controls gaining [4]

Children raised by rule and "chores"
Child study, mental hygiene, psychology help parents guide personality
growth [4]

Roles of men, women, and children tend to be fixed and rigid
Flexible roles of men, women, and children are accepted and widely practiced [4]

Families stay put: residence rarely changes, little separation of family
members
Families on the move: many change residence; much travel as families and
individuals [4]

Puritanical attitudes on sex; double standard of morality; little sex education
Acceptance of sex side of life general; trends toward single standard of morality; many efforts toward sex education [4]

Definite standards of right and wrong with strong social buttressing
Tolerant acceptance of deviations general, fewer black and white judgments
by fewer "Mrs. Grundies" [4]

[1] Bureau of Census.
[2] Council of Economic Advisors, Bureau of Census.
[3] Bureau of Labor Standards.
[4] Observation.
[5] Bureau of Labor Statistics.
[6] Bureau of Human Nutrition; Bureau of Agriculture Economics.
[7] National Office of Vital Statistics.

ers as well, with no serious damage to their husbands' happiness, their children's welfare, or their own adjustment.[4] As we said in Chapter Eleven, "Money Matters in Marriage," there are many different kinds of women, some of whom are so constituted and trained that finding creative outlets is their only assurance of making a good adjustment to their environment. Even though they are married, they fail to find the challenge they need within the confines of the modern home. After their children have grown up, many women find that the stimulus of work to be done outside the home makes them dissatisfied with the enforced leisure of the typical housewife. These women see themselves as citizens in a growing society, as people with a contribution to make, as personalities with a need to feel needed and to be living a worth-while life. Such fulfillment adds much to the vitality and richness of a marriage. But in spite of all the changes with which the modern woman finds herself confronted, there are still many services which she alone can provide her family. These services are the core of women's work and underlie family life today: affection giving, day-by-day companionship, guidance of children, and building personalities of family members.

As we indicated in detail in our opening chapter, the processes of personality development are extremely complex, and exceedingly important both for individual happiness and for the good of the social whole. The family is the most important single influence in personality development. Until recently the meeting of the personality needs of the growing persons in the family has been incidental to the housekeeping and production functions of family life. Now with the time-consuming tasks taken care of outside the home, men and women alike will have time to focus their attention upon the building of persons who will emerge as the real products of family life. It is against this background of shifting functions of the family — from a unit for production of *things* to a center for production of *persons* — that we should see, in our times, the changing role of women, of children, and of men.

[4] Mary S. Fisher, *Conflicts Which Face Women Today* (unpublished study); see also John Levy and Ruth Munroe, *The Happy Family* (New York: Knopf, 1938), p. 268, and Harvey Locke, *Predicting Adjustment in Marriage* (New York: Holt, 1951), pp. 288–297.

The Child as a Personality

Today, Junior, obviously just a baby, lying in his crib, pink-toed and kicking, represents something more to his parents than Juniors formerly represented. They see him not as a replica of themselves, or a mere helpless, lovable bundle, but as an individual-in-the-making, with the making largely up to them.

This new concept represents a tremendous change in our outlook on child rearing. In the past, most mothers and fathers felt that they had done everything possible if they provided shelter, food, clothes, and admonitions with regard to manners and morals. Frequent childhood illnesses and tragically frequent infant deaths were simply to be accepted, while any deviations in behavior from what was regarded as desirable were to be spanked out. Today the job of parenthood is more cheerful, but more complicated.

With the realization that the child is an individual came the corollary that he should be guided to develop his own powers and aptitudes rather than coerced into simulating those of his parents. As obstetricians and pediatricians provided modern mothers and fathers with healthier babies than ever before, parents acquired a great respect for the newer, more scientific methods of child care.

Yesterday's child lived under the rule of absolute authority, with the switch not infrequently used to enforce his obedience or quiet his questionings. Today's child lives in a home that is becoming a democracy, where he too is considered an important individual, with rights as well as duties. Fathers and mothers no longer want their children to be afraid of them. They value the confidence and frankness of their growing sons and daughters as a more than adequate substitute for the more superficial respect their grandparents received. They make requests instead of giving orders; they try to make discipline meet the needs of the child, and they go to some trouble to find out what causes a misdeed without immediately attributing it to the natural perversity of children.

With all due respect to devotees of the new psychology, there are nevertheless individual cases in which the results are anything but happy. Children have become absolute monarchs in some homes, wielding the authority of a spoiled ego over worried and too eager-to-please parents. Such literal-minded parents have slipped off the beam of moderation.

They have gone too far in the direction of license for their children; they have forgotten or ignored the fact that we must all accept duties, boring routines, and some authority as a part of our adult lives. But such individual family failures do not detract from the many beneficial results which have come from conceiving of the child as a personality.

As Junior has become more important in the family, he has also become more expensive to rear. In addition to the little garments mother made and the help of a skillful neighbor woman we must now use a long line of articles and services, from hospital and pediatrician to cribs, carriages, and play pens, ready-made layettes, special food, bathing and sterilizing equipment — even diaper services. Parents get their reward for this outlay as Junior gains more than the requisite number of inches and ounces, and avoids croup, colic, diphtheria, and smallpox, the former "inevitable" infant and child ailments. Undoubtedly infancy isn't as painful an experience to the baby as it used to be; but the

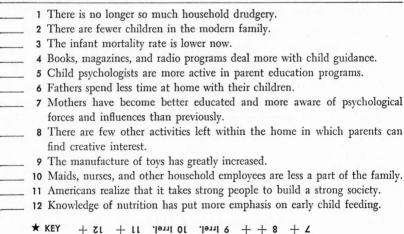

CHECK YOURSELF   The following is a list of statements concerning the reasons for the interest of parents becoming more focused on their growing children as personalities than was true in the "children should be seen and not heard" era. Some of these statements express more basic causes than do others. Some are irrelevant. Go through the listing, indicating by a double plus sign those which you feel are especially significant, by a single plus sign those which you feel must be related. Leave blank those which are irrelevant to the question of why modern parents focus more attention upon their growing children.

_____ 1 There is no longer so much household drudgery.
_____ 2 There are fewer children in the modern family.
_____ 3 The infant mortality rate is lower now.
_____ 4 Books, magazines, and radio programs deal more with child guidance.
_____ 5 Child psychologists are more active in parent education programs.
_____ 6 Fathers spend less time at home with their children.
_____ 7 Mothers have become better educated and more aware of psychological forces and influences than previously.
_____ 8 There are few other activities left within the home in which parents can find creative interest.
_____ 9 The manufacture of toys has greatly increased.
_____ 10 Maids, nurses, and other household employees are less a part of the family.
_____ 11 Americans realize that it takes strong people to build a strong society.
_____ 12 Knowledge of nutrition has put more emphasis on early child feeding.

★ KEY   + 12   + 11   10 Irrel.   9 Irrel.   + + 8   + 7
+ + 6   + 5   4 Irrel.   3 Irrel.   + + 2   + + 1

fact remains that each individual child costs more to produce and rear. Responsible parents whose incomes are limited have to limit the size of their families too.

By throwing out the expensive frills we should be able to retain all the essentials of scientific care and still have more children. In many cases a new brother or sister would do more for Junior than a private school or an insurance policy planned for his college education. This emphasis on quality rather than quantity is a part of a larger social trend. Dr. Brock Chisholm, head of the World Health Organization, put it vividly when he said, "Our children must be better than we are, for we are the kind of folks who go to war every few years." Our best hope for peace, for the good life men have always envisaged, lies in the everyday lives of our families where men are made. "The loss of extrinsic functions, such as economic production, education, religious training . . . enables the family to specialize in the functions of giving and receiving affection, bearing and rearing children, and personality development." [5]

Life for Father

With mother admittedly an individual and often a wage earner, and the child acquiring new dignity and rights in the home, what becomes of father?

Traditionally he was the family's sole source of support and the family boss. If the children objected to his despotism they were personally escorted to the woodshed; if mother objected — well, she just didn't! It was beneath father's dignity ever to help in the house except in dire emergency; not only business but the whole world outside the home was assumed to be his sphere alone, from which Olympian height he occasionally let drop jewels of wisdom.

This stereotyped description of father, a paragon of male pride, self-sufficiency, and petulance, never existed in the flesh. He is but a composite picture of the yearnings of males frustrated by actual wives, children, businesses, and bosses. He is a stereotype; but since we human beings tend to base our wishes and patterns of conduct on stereotypes instead of facts, his influence is still felt by fathers and mothers in their efforts to adjust to a streamlined family life.

[5] Charles S. Johnson, "New Forces in Family Living: Social Reorientation," *Journal of Social Casework* (February, 1949), p. 50.

All the men and women and children composing those homes of fifty or sixty years ago were individuals, and each reacted differently to authority. Some men who were lordly in public had their minds changed for them privately by mother at home. Having to ask for every cent of cash they needed made some women dependent, some secretly resentful; others became experts at chiseling on the grocery or dressmaker's bill. Where the stereotyped roles were played, it is probably safe to say that there was a minimum of honesty, frankness, and understanding.

Father is less of a boss, even theoretically, today. He is more than an earner and supplier of the good things of life. He is, ideally, a husband, companion, and partner to his wife; a friend, guide, protector, and playmate to his children. The home is becoming a democracy with rights of free speech for every member; allowances and joint checking accounts have become commonplace. In this less materialistic family set-up there is less fear, more freedom to be oneself, increased emphasis on the enduring values of home life, on loving rearing of children, on the deep companionship of shared experiences. What has father gained in this new home?

For one thing, today's father has won the confidence of his children, their joyous acceptance of him as a person. For another, he has discovered the ability to relax and act foolish when he feels like it without sacrificing his family's respect for him, because that respect is no longer founded on his maintenance of unbroken dignity (impossible in a four-room flat, anyway). For another, he now enjoys increased understanding and intelligent cooperation from his wife, to whom his business and outside interests no longer need be a mystery or a bore. Finally, he has found greater security in weathering the vicissitudes with his wife and family now that he is accepted as a partner in their joint enterprise, a home.

Now that father is becoming a person, just as mother is, just as Junior is, isn't there a boss, or at least a head of the family? Of course there is. In pointing out any social change, the hardest factor to emphasize is the extent of the transformation. Conditions never change absolutely, or wholly, and individual families differ widely in the degree to which they reflect any particular social change.

That men are still in the ascendancy in many homes is understandable. The average husband still tends to be older than his wife, and to have more life experience. Furthermore, since many men and women grow up in homes where patterns of male dominance prevail, they may tend to expect and to assume it as "right" in their own marriages. As more and more wives come to marriage with an education equivalent to that of their husbands, and ready to share economic responsibilities, more cooperative living is inevitable.

Man's Attitude toward Women's Work. Father is not hurt today if mother takes a job outside the home; his dignity is not damaged by occasionally pinning on a diaper, or cooking a meal. He may be a university professor or a corporation lawyer, but he has acquired a sense of humor and a sense of proportion. As long as he knows that his wife loves him, trusts him, and is trustable, as long as his children run to greet him with shining faces and come to him confidingly with scraped knees and hurt feelings to fix, he is a success at home and has lost no prestige.[6] The following analysis constitutes one of the best statements in print of the problems of the modern family man:

One often hears that "a man cannot keep his self-respect and allow his wife to work." This is true if, because she works, he takes no responsibility for the family support. But his attitude may indicate that he has not recognized that women have always contributed to the support of the family; he may be unwilling to admit that work away from home may not be so arduous or monotonous as is work within the home. Or it may only mean that he has not yet given thought to the new adjustments which must be made by his generation in contrast with the accepted role of his mother.

Again, it is sometimes held by men that a woman cannot respect a man who cannot support his family. But too often in the past the man's apparent magnanimity in insisting upon supporting his wife and family has been accompanied by subjection and domination. Many of the chivalrous clichés about women are sentimental coverings for lack of intellectual honesty and of emotional integrity. Woman's "priceless position" in a price society is not always an enviable situation. Likewise those things done for "love" have often become the basis of demands and exactions disastrous to the relationship between husband and wife. Often a boy makes the statement that he will not marry a girl until he can support her. This ought at least to be a mutual decision; for if he does not marry her, she may have to work anyway and should have some part in deciding whether she would rather work when married to him or as an unmarried woman.

Certain readjustments in family life are necessary if the home under modern conditions is to be successful. If both husband and wife work outside the home, it would seem to follow that both would share in the work of the home. Too often in any arrangement where the wife worked out of the home

_____
6 Do not miss O. Spurgeon English and Constance Foster, *Fathers Are Parents, Too* (New York: Putnam, 1951).

it has been assumed that she carried in addition the work inside it. Many a woman has not been able to stand the physical and emotional demands of the two jobs. In any arrangement it will probably be necessary for her to carry a major part of the responsibility for the management of the home. But if she as well as her husband works outside the home, there should be a sharing of the work inside or else provision in the family budget to cover part of the homework.

This sharing of home responsibilities by husband and wife has been difficult to secure because of the extent to which the roles of men and women have been fixed as if there were an impassable gulf between them, and as if no man without loss of self-respect could do what has been designated as woman's work. But aptitude for most of the work of the home would seem to be rather a matter of individual than of sex difference. There is no real reason to assume that cooking is inherently woman's work when all of the highest paid chefs are men, or that sewing can be done only by women when the highest paid designers and tailors are men. Neither does there seem to be a valid reason for assuming that washing and ironing, scrubbing and sweeping are better fitted to women's physical capacities than to men's. Boys in many progressive schools, where the old assumptions are not made, prefer to take cooking rather than "shop" while many of the girls choose the shop. Many a man might stay at home more willingly if he ate his own instead of his wife's cooking. Many a home would be more tastily furnished if the man had chosen the furniture and the color scheme for the decoration. Many children would be more becomingly dressed if their fathers chose their clothes. An eye for line and color is an individual rather than a sex difference. In the new partnership between men and women, there must be joint planning and joint responsibility for the things in the home that are the outward and visible signs of inner unity.[7]

At Home in a Larger World

Once the family's horizons were limited to the clearing around the cabin with the forest beyond, or to the village with its few familiar streets. Now its world is literally the entire globe! Parents are finding that the home can no longer be an independent unit. Families today are tied up irrevocably with the world around them. The election of a president or of a school board member may be of more importance in the life of the family in the years to come than all the domestic duties and job routines carried out that year. An incident in a tiny town in the Balkans several decades ago started a war from which we have not yet completely recovered. Militarism brewing through the years in Japan was climaxed in the attack on Pearl Harbor, which until then

[7] "The Home in Transition," *Social Action*, October 15, 1937, pp. 17–19.

was unheard of by many of us. Economic depressions delay marriages, put father out of work, break off sister's college education, and keep the whole family from enjoying a new roof. Study has indicated that such periodic disasters as wars, depressions, and political intrigue are not the result of inevitable forces of evil, but rather the misfortunes that occur when the common people are not intelligent enough and interested enough to utilize the resources at hand to deal with everyday problems effectively. Obviously the difficulty of electing a leader or voting on a bill in these complex times is much greater than in the old days of the New England town meeting when everyone knew everyone else, and the issues were clear-cut and familiar. But the new avenues of communication today, the radio, the daily paper, the study groups and trained interpreters, make feasible the task of modern citizenship.

Mother has a role on this world citizenship stage. Men have stopped laughing at women for not bringing the millennium when they were given the vote; we know that women are only people, with wisdom limited to their experience. We should hardly have expected the world to be remade overnight when women went out to vote if we hadn't been so eager to poke fun at the dear, funny, valiant suffragettes. Men in America have been at the game of community and world affairs for a longer period of time. While women were still tied to their spinning wheels, men were stumping the country for their favorite candidates and rushing off to the state legislatures to back a new bill. The old cracker barrel at the crossroads store saw some straight shooting of tobacco juice and some not too crooked shooting off of new ideas of democracy as a way of life.

Now that women have the educational background, the leisure to study, and sufficient interest to join the League of Women Voters and become active in the Public Affairs Committee of the YWCA, as well as in councils for social action in the churches and the auxiliaries of political parties, they too can find their way around in the maze of current socio-economic problems.

What we need right now is a merging of these two bodies of experience. Men and women work together on the problems facing the world today. They need each other to assure real progress. Man's new role will be to encourage and back his wife as she delves into the facts of social life, and learn with her how to perfect the complex machinery that runs our social organizations.

Families are living cells of our emerging democracy. Father may, by his attitude and interest, do a great deal to guide the children into experiences which will round out their understandings. His attitude toward his wife's interests, his indignation over a miscarriage of justice, his alignment with causes and movements, do more to educate the children in the family than all the civics courses they will get this side of college. Parents who participate in civic activities and projects set the stage for children as they play out the roles for themselves. Introducing members of the family into their responsibilities in their world is all part of father's role in the family, a part not as well defined as the one in which he wielded a big stick and hung onto the purse strings, but no less challenging in its implications for the future.

"This is a wonderful time to be a parent. Our children are growing up in the greatest era we have ever known, though a greater one may be just around the corner. There are some people in every generation who keep looking backward because the future is always full of fear. But there are other people who keep looking ahead. They see new things coming constantly into the world. They take hold of those things; they turn them to the good of their time and their generation." [8]

There's No Place Like Home

Home as great-grandmother knew it no longer exists. It never can return. We move forward into a new type of family life that none of us, men, women, or children, have ever experienced before. Modern society is adjusting to changes and will undoubtedly face many more which will affect family life. Down through the ages the family has been buffeted about by social change, but it has been well ballasted. It has survived countless wars and catastrophes. It has made many adjustments, but through it all the central core of family life has remained.

What the family will be like tomorrow is another question which we will take up in the very last chapter. What your family and mine is like today is the result of generations of adapting human relations to changing conditions. We cannot cut ourselves off from our roots. They provide stability in a changing world. But we have seen appear in our day a body of knowledge about family life and personality development, and we have seen its validity proved in real life situations.

[8] John Harvey Furbay, "The One World Is Here," *National Parent-Teacher* (October, 1950), p. 18.

Adding this knowledge to that already learned from family life in other times gives us the perspective to draft our own design for a more workable family for tomorrow.

Marriage isn't what it used to be, but to the student of family life it shows promise of being much better.

Selected Readings

BUCK, PEARL, "At Home in the World," *Marriage and Family Living* (February, 1942), pp. 1–4.

CLOSE, KATHRYN, "Young Families in 1950," *The Survey* (January, 1950).

COMPTON, ARTHUR, "Effect of the New Scientific Age on Family Life," *Journal of Home Economics* (September, 1947), pp. 387–390.

ENGLISH, O. SPURGEON, AND FOSTER, CONSTANCE, *Fathers Are Parents, Too* (New York: Putnam, 1951).

FRANK, LAWRENCE K., "Yes, Families Are Changing," *The Survey* (December, 1949).

FURBAY, JOHN HARVEY, "The One World Is Here," *National Parent-Teacher* (October, 1950), pp. 18–20.

JOHNSON, CHARLES S., "New Forces in Family Living: Social Reorientation," *Journal of Social Casework* (February, 1949), pp. 47–50.

LANGMUIR, MARY FISHER, "Wife Trouble? Get Her a Job!" *American Magazine* (February, 1950), pp. 36–37, 90–93.

MEAD, MARGARET, *Male and Female: A Study of the Sexes in a Changing World* (New York: Morrow, 1949).

——, "What is Happening to the American Family?" *Journal of Social Case-Work* (November, 1947), pp. 323–330.

Technical References

BERNARD, JESSIE, *American Family Behavior* (New York: Harper, 1942), chaps. 1–9.

BURGESS, ERNEST, AND LOCKE, HARVEY, *The Family: from Institution to Companionship* (New York: American Book, 1945), Chap. 16.

FOLSOM, JOSEPH, *The Family and Democratic Society* (New York: Wiley, 1943), chaps. 3–7.

LEE, ALFRED, AND LEE, ELIZABETH, *Social Problems in America: A Source Book* (New York: Holt, 1949), Chap. 3.

LOCKE, HARVEY, AND MACKEPRANG, MURIEL, "Marital Adjustment and the Employed Wife," *American Journal of Sociology* (May, 1949), pp. 536–538.

RIESMAN, DAVID, *The Lonely Crowd: A Study of the Changing American Character* (New Haven: Yale University Press, 1950).

TRUXAL, ANDREW, AND MERRILL, FRANCIS, *The Family in American Culture* (New York: Prentice-Hall, 1947).

CHAPTER TWENTY—ONE

Coming Home — to What?

FAMILIES IN AN UNEASY WORLD

What happens to families in wartime?

Do war marriages work out all right?

What about all these war babies?

What place does the family have in America's future?

Does education for family life make sense?

THE GREAT DEVELOPMENTS OF THE TWENTIETH CENTURY IN TRANS-portation and communication have made possible the linking of nations, states, regions, communities, and neighborhoods into one highly interconnected and interdependent world. With the channels of communication open, news of events can be transmitted to every part of the world in a matter of minutes. The impact of specific events will also be felt in every sector of our highly interdependent societies. If events are disruptive, the disruption travels through the political structures, affects the economic systems, and ultimately reaches individual families.

Major catastrophes like wars, depressions, revolutions, technological developments, and the ideological accompaniments of these movements reach into everyday family discussion, arguments, and agreements. The family is a bottleneck through which flows the everyday life of almost all individuals in society. As such it becomes the sounding board for most of the problems occurring in the lives of millions in the workaday world. The family has been called the great ventilator of society, since so many of the problems brought by breadwinners and school children are carried to the family table for airing, discussing, and rephrasing. Decisions to act are often reached within the family milieu which in turn have repercussions on economic and political policies. Wars are planned, bond drives launched, and price controls tightened by people with power operating on the basis of the convictions, sometimes erroneously reached, that the great bulk of family people are behind the proposed actions. How families react to economic conditions in the cashing of savings bonds, how they respond to excessive marking up of retail prices on goods, and how they turn out for elections — all these actions make a difference in the planning that goes on in the economic and political systems of the country. Ours is a highly interrelated society with no part of it isolated or independent of any other part.

In recent years the trends in marrying, divorcing, and reproductive behavior of families have been characterized by short-run fluctuations integrally related to the economic and political fluctuations of our economy and polity. Marriage and birth rates are greatly affected by wars and threats of war, by depressions and prosperity cycles. The effects of war on family behavior deserve special attention.

What Wars Do to Marriage

When war comes, millions of families are disrupted as young men are drafted from their parental families or from their young families of procreation. Millions of women, many of them married and having children, enter the labor force to replace their men. Whole family units migrate to war production areas, bringing to a boil communities already overflowing. Romance is stepped up before couples are torn apart by the call to duty. A desperate urgency to live life to its fullest while there is yet time seizes young and old alike and gives rise to new behavior patterns.

Marriage Rate Increases. The marriage rate during the nineteen forties was greatly influenced by World War II and its aftermath. The effects of the war were most pronounced in the occupied countries and in those which participated actively in the hostilities. In the neutral countries of Europe, on the other hand, the marriage rates were relatively little affected.

The high points in the English-speaking countries came in the early period of the war — 1939 to 1942 — and again in 1946, with a trough in between. In the United States the marriage rate increased from an an-

MORE MARRIAGES ARE TAKING PLACE

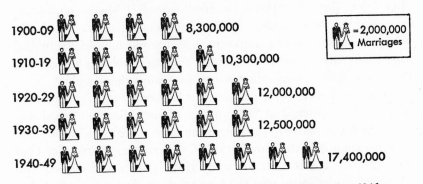

1900-09   8,300,000

1910-19   10,300,000

1920-29   12,000,000

1930-39   12,500,000

1940-49   17,400,000

= 2,000,000 Marriages

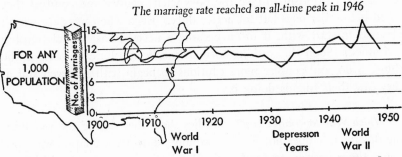

The marriage rate reached an all-time peak in 1946

FOR ANY
1,000
POPULATION

No. of Marriages

15
12
9
6
3
0

1900   1910   1920   1930   1940   1950
World   Depression   World
War I   Years   War II

From *Children and Youth at the Midcentury — A Chart Book*, Health Publications Institute, Inc.,
Raleigh, N.C.

nual average of 10.7 per 1,000 in the period 1935–1938, to 12.2 in 1936–
1942. In the next two years, as our armed forces expanded and large
numbers went overseas, the rate declined, falling to a low of 10.5 in
1944. Following the return to civilian life of servicemen the rate swung
upward and reached a peak of 16.2 marriages per 1000 population in
1946. This was not only the highest rate in our country's history but
also above that recorded in any other country during the postwar period.
Since then the marriage rate has dropped close to its prewar level except for a small increase in 1950 which reflected the war in Korea.[1]

Why is it that Cupid accompanies Wars? Why, of all times, should
people rush into marriage during war and immediately after? The in-

[1] "Recent International Marriage Trends," *Statistical Bulletin* (June, 1951),
Vol. 32, Number 6, pp. 1–3. Most overrun European countries suffered severely depressed marriage rates during the later years of the war. The rates of Belgium,
France, Italy, Luxembourg, and Romania were continually below the prewar level
up through 1944; rates at a level of about 5 per 1000 were not uncommon. A rebound came after the war, in France almost doubling 1944–1946.

dividual reasons are many — almost as numerous as the couples themselves — but they are apparently good enough. Many couples are stampeded in their decision by the impending disaster. With the pick-up of business and of employment in new war industrial activities, many young folk can afford for the first time to establish a home. The fears of separation precipitate marriage for many other couples.

As men left their home communities in larger and larger numbers, girls became frightened at the prospect of remaining unmarried and often took the initiative in speeding up an affair. The popular song that swept the country in the early forties, "Get Your Man, Sister, Get Your Man," became a battle cry for many girls. Others were moved with feelings of patriotism to give the boys what security and comfort they could before the boys left for active duty. Even when marriage wasn't planned to start with, it often became a necessity as the relationship continued. Soon this rushing to marriage license bureaus became the thing to do, and couples more cautious to begin with followed suit as they saw their friends doing it.

Which War Marriages Last? Studies show that during the war itself the divorce rate does not increase rapidly. For many couples war postpones their decision to break up. While they are separated they can stick it out. Then, too, there are dollars-and-cents reasons for women remaining married for the duration. Allowances and allotments assure a service wife a steady income and a backlog of security at a time when the general man shortage gives her few better alternatives. Public sentiment adds its weight to discourage wartime divorce by making it difficult for a girl to get a legal separation from a man in service. But after the war is over, the breaks come painfully fast. Couples who were married while they were still practically strangers never did get a chance to become acquainted, and reunion proves not the haven of refuge of which each had dreamed, but a painful realization of having made a poor choice. Much of the unhappiness in these wartime marriages results from the haste with which they were consummated, the short time allowed for getting settled before being separated, the general impulsiveness, the lack of such stabilizing forces as a house and furniture of one's own, the rapid changes in people's attitudes toward themselves and each other, the new ways of living that war inevitably brings, and the strain of long, enforced separation. Although a great many marriages do weather the actual period of the war, they face the bitter battle of divorce soon after hostilities cease.[2] There are authorities who question whether many war marriages are worth salvaging — it may be best to get divorced and get back into circulation. Many couples, who do not separate, face a task of reconstruction that will require earnest effort, time, intelligence, and adequate skills.

Those whose marriages took place after a real period of acquaintance and mutual planning for life together find that their rediscovery of each other after the war is a pleasure rather than a disillusionment. Which war marriages last? Those couples who were truly ready for marriage, who were mature enough to know what they wanted and who planned for it intelligently, who were weaned from their childhood dependence on family, and who were already launched on a way of life that was truly their own stand a good chance of picking up family life again and making a go of it. Couples who were able to keep closely in touch with each other throughout the long periods of separation find that the experience of living together again is stimulating and satisfying, while other couples, less successful in bridging the miles and the months that separated them, find their reunion strangely baffling and disillusioning.

These contrasts lead us to distinguish sharply between two varieties of marriages that occur in wartime. There are the *war marriages*, characterized by haste and impulsiveness and urgency; and there are the *marriages in wartime*, which are the marriages that would properly have taken place, war or no war. These more considered unions, though buffeted by wartime forces, may be expected to last in far greater numbers than the others, which were so hastily thrown together. Happiness will grow out of living, as partners achieve the satisfactions that are earned through devoted effort.

Babies Born in Wartime and After

As marriage rates increase so do birth rates. With the larger number of war marriages comes a wave of babies about a year later. This is particularly true of the birth rates of first babies. A glance at the figure demonstrates the sensitivity of the birth rate to fluctuations in economic and

---

[2] Divorce rates increased over 50 per cent from 1939 to 1946; veterans had rates twice those of nonveterans. Since 1946 the divorce rate has declined to a point in 1951 about 20 per cent higher than prewar years.

political climates, in Germany and in the United States. The birth rate in the United States remained relatively stable during World War I, but the German birth rate was almost cut in half. It dropped from 27 per thousand population in 1914 to 14 in 1917. Following a postwar spurt the rates of both nations declined to a depression low point in

FLUCTUATIONS IN THE BIRTH RATE IN THE U.S. AND GERMANY

Through the Two World Wars and the Intervening Depression

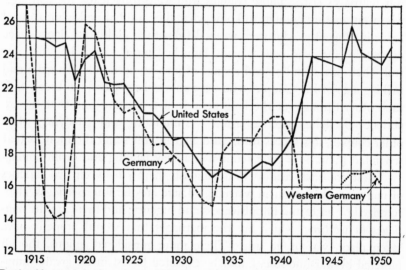

Reprinted by permission from chart by U. B. Hauser in *Fortune*, March, 1943, supplemented from the *Statistical Bulletin*, December, 1943, and from releases of the U. S. Bureau of the Census, 1951.

1933. The German rate rose rapidly as economic conditions improved and as the Nazi anti-abortion policy went into effect. The upswing in the United States occurred with the advent of the New Deal and increased steadily until the outbreak of World War II when a rapid change upward occurred. Only during the period that great numbers of servicemen were overseas did reproduction falter, and it picked up again to reach the highest point in over thirty years in 1947. Germany's rate in contrast was depressed by World War II; and when data were again available, although for Western Germany only, the birth rates of the late forties were shown to have been relatively low compared with the period following World War I.

During the early upswing of birth rates in the United States the increase was largely in first babies, somewhat less in second and third

BABY BOOM BRINGS BABIES TO ALL SIZED FAMILIES

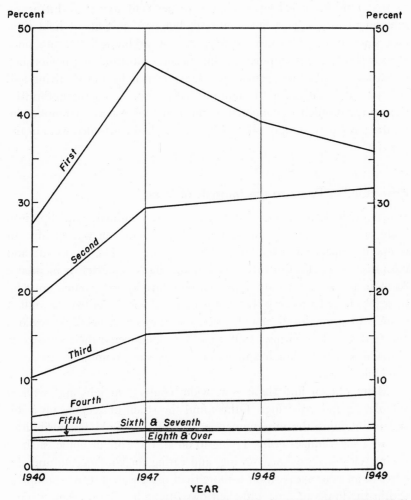

Live Births by Birth Order per 1000 female population, 15–44 years of age, U. S., 1940, 1947–49. Federal Security Agency.

babies. By the fifties it was apparent that the increased birth rates were a fact also for higher orders of births. From 1940 to 1947 the number of first births almost doubled, but declined from this peak about 20 per cent by 1950. Second births increased almost two thirds from 1940 to 1947 and continued to increase about 6 per cent up to 1950. Third births increased 50 per cent the first seven years, and increased again about 7 per cent, 1947–1950. Fourth births increased 27 per cent, 1940 to 1947, and increased again almost 10 per cent to 1950. Fifth and subsequent orders have not increased, but have just about held their own since 1940. This reversal of a steadily declining birth rate since 1870 is perplexing to population statisticians, and troubling to housing, educational, and other agencies whose concern is to provide living and educational facilities for the bumper baby crop. To some authorities the continued high reproductive performance of American families indicates a revival of family values which many had concluded were in the discard.

How Families React to the Impacts of War

When we have total war that touches every continent and dips into every sea, we can hardly expect that any institution or way of life can escape its impacts; and the family is no exception. The immediate and most disrupting effect of this war on home life is to scatter its members. As more and more men are drawn into military service, women must fill their jobs in order to keep the wolf from the door. Over twenty million women were employed in industries, government agencies, professions and trades, and on farms. Other millions volunteered their services to Red Cross, USO, church and welfare programs, community agencies, and child care centers.

Many women find these new, wider contacts in jobs and services stimulating and satisfying. Others find the strain of keeping up a job and maintaining the minimum essentials of household responsibilities almost a superhuman task. Trying to do all the work at home, such as baking, cleaning, cooking, sewing, and caring for children, around the edges of an exacting position is more than most women can accomplish within the limits of time and their own strength. Relinquishing some of these tasks to other agencies in the community is but a partial answer to the problem; laundries are unable to absorb the swollen demands for their service at the time when the labor shortage is so critical; processed foods and prepared articles are scarce and expensive; shopping becomes more and more time-absorbing, especially for the woman who must do her buying at the tag end of the day when all the preceding shoppers have had their pick.

Most difficult of all is obtaining adequate care for children who need almost constant supervision. When parents are engaged in essential war work outside their homes, some provision must be made for their children. Child care centers set up in many communities attempted to help by providing day care for children of working mothers. Parents in many towns and cities were reluctant to take full advantage of these centers, however. They often found the burden of getting the children dressed and transported over long distances to the nearest child care center just one thing too much in the work-heavy day. Makeshift arrangements with neighbors and relatives were a far more frequent solution to the problem, especially for the mother who felt uneasy about leaving home every day and who got some sense of satisfaction in knowing that the children were there anyway. Communities wise enough to call upon mothers in the planning and organizing of child care were more successful in providing facilities acceptable both to the children and to their mothers than those in which professional workers tried to run the whole program. Cooperative plans for community child care which grew out of the war era have been extended in a number of communities with local financial support both for the sake of those women whose interests carry them naturally into larger community affairs and for the good of the children, who benefit by systematic care and socialization.

The net effect of war on the family has been to focus attention on the dispersal of its members and to accelerate the trends for supplementing family functions with some outside help in the form of child care centers, nursery schools, and day nurseries.

Juvenile Delinquency. Older children, too, become objects of general concern as families disrupted by the war leave them to run the streets with door keys around their necks and money jingling in their pockets. The increase in juvenile delinquency in wartime is widely attributed to the preoccupation of the adult members of the family and the resulting letdown in supervision of older children. Other factors in the wartime community contribute their share to the increase in the troubles of teen-age youngsters through the war period:

1 The emotional chaos of war with its simultaneous bombardment of fears, excitement, anxiety, hates, and loves hits the growing child and the budding adolescent in his most vulnerable spot, his emotions. When the rest of the world is going in for wholesale bombing of civilian population, it must be expected that the small fry will break a few windows and whack some of their fellows occasionally.

2 School programs with traditional emphasis on academic learning can hardly compete with the adventurous goings-on in the world outside. Youngsters filled with an eagerness to do something about the war, to become actively identified with the mass mobilization they see all about them, often find the stereotyped school program sterile. Truancy is a first step to further mischief. The dilution of school personnel, as the money-conscious teachers leave for more lucrative wartime positions while the pool of teachers in training is drained dry by industrial and war programs, makes for weak teaching at the very time that the children are most in need of strong, able school leadership. In urban areas where increases in population greatly exceed the available facilities not only teachers but physical accommodations are inadequate. There were schools in which three separate shifts of children were staggered into every school day. Some students arrived at eight to stay until twelve; others came at twelve to stay until four, while the third shift overlapped by coming at ten and staying until two. What these children did with the rest of the day outside of these hurried four hours in crowded classrooms was nobody's business, as the behavior of the children themselves so eloquently indicated.

3 Child labor and youth employment have mixed effects upon young people. On the one hand, jobs at which youth feels needed and feels responsibility for doing a real piece of work are a boon to the many young people who seriously need just such a place in the larger society into which they are so eager to be inducted. Increase in home responsibilities helps many children get a new sense of what being a family member means, and they take their places beside their parents with insight and eagerness.

But, also, jobs that pay considerable money to children who have never before earned or spent more than a few dimes tend to make it difficult for young people to conduct themselves wisely. Money is hardly the root of all evil, but it can cause a lot of trouble when it is in the hands of youngsters with few controls and with little opportunity for learning to use money wisely. This situation is aggravated by the lack, in most communities, of wholesome youth activities.

4 American towns and cities have grown up so rapidly around the industries and businesses which brought them into being that few have had time to provide adequately for leisure activities. The scattered playgrounds are available to only a small number of children and are usually restricted to the lower age levels. Vacant lots where boys may play ball are few and far between in the congested urban areas where teen troubles occur most frequently. Beyond these resources there are only the tavern, the pool hall, and the movie theatre to absorb the time and the earnings of young America. Churches have but very recently discovered that their facilities may be used for the play of young people as well as the glory of God. YM's and YW's have been pegging away at the problem with increasing effectiveness, but they cannot be everywhere. The Boy Scouts and Girl Scouts have tended thus far to draw members largely from the comfortable neighborhoods where parents already provide constructive activities for their growing children. The "bad eggs" of town, the no-accounts, the tough guys, and the wild girls, still are not participating in the better recreational facilities in most American communities. These are the very youngsters who need constructive and creative outlets for the emotions that have been built up by years of resentment and hostility. These are the children who have been left out of school functions, who are not too sure of the home base and have nothing else to tie to. Progressive communities have responded to the need in some instances with well-placed and wisely guided recreational programs, teen towns, dry night clubs, and similar hang-outs.

5 Girls get into trouble in many communities. During wartime the increase in delinquency occurs more generally among young teen-age girls than among young men and boys. There are at least two reasons for this: first, the young men are under military control and discipline, as war has drafted and recruited them right out of high schools into military service; and second, girls, feeling the threat of a manless world, with all the frustrations it brings to romantic dreams of love,

marriage, and a home of their own, react with a peculiar urgency to get as much attention as they can while there is still a chance. Few of these girls have developed skills that will let them explore and experiment without getting seriously involved in affairs beyond their depth. They cannot help it that the war has caught them just out of pigtails; with too few of the knowledges and abilities of women, they can think of little else to do than swarm over army camps and down the main streets of boom towns in hope that something exciting will happen. The present generation of mothers and teachers cannot be held completely responsible for not giving these girls the guidance and teaching that would have built the needed skills before it was too late; for these mothers and teachers were only yesterday little girls, brought up to believe in innocence and in a philosophy of "you will know all you need to know when the time comes." Tomorrow's girls may have enough education for life to meet their needs effectively and with less distress and disaster. In the meantime, war has focused attention on our present-day shortcomings in educating girls in what it means to be women, and emphasizes the need for strengthening our resources for bringing up women and girls to face the realities of the world and to fulfill their human needs in ways that are personally satisfying and socially desirable.

War Quickens Family Tempo. Further impacts of war on home life are seen as families move toward war production areas or join their menfolk near military posts. The life of the mushroom community with its trailer camps and crowded housing, with all its strains and stresses on the routines of eating three times a day, keeping clean, resting and playing and getting off to work on time, uncovers old weaknesses in our community planning. A new impetus is given to housing projects, recreational centers, community clinics, cooperative laundries and kitchens which, too new and too few to meet wartime deficiencies, gather momentum to carry on into the postwar period. The increased tempo of living necessitated when more must be done in less time with fewer hands and resources piles up strains and tensions, and increases both the satisfactions and the disappointments of life in double-quick time. Educators find that material can be covered in a few months which, with outmoded techniques, used to take years. Earning and spending are speeded up for all families by the increasing demand for employees, and are complicated by the establishment of rationing and price ceilings. Habits of eating and sleeping have to be changed to meet the speed-up system of industry. New work schedules which follow the clock around, new types of recreation to release wartime tensions, new contacts with a bewildering variety of people, more living in less time, characterize war's influence on American family life.

And so families torn and disrupted and dislocated by war pick themselves up, mobilize their resources, and undertake the larger task of unifying and solidifying themselves, while the world continues to seethe in the postwar cauldron of social chaos. Many tasks are still undone; the decades ahead will see some progress, but the extent to which they are well done depends on the development of the knowledges, the skills, and the appreciations that make possible creative interpersonal relationships. We turn now to a consideration of one of those tasks, the building of democratic companionship type families.

The Emergence of the Family as a Companionship

One effect of war has been to accelerate the trend to the companionship type of family characterized by equality of the sexes and democratic procedures in the home. The biggest change in this connection is the further rise in the status of women. World War I gave women the outward symbols of equality with men, that is, the right to drink and smoke and wear bobbed hair and short skirts. World War II has given more of the actual substance of equality, perhaps because of its longer duration and perhaps because of the continued improvement in woman's status during the interim between wars. The making of WACs and WAVEs and Marines part of the armed forces rather than auxiliary corps was symbolic of the new role conceded to women. For the first time in history some industries have given women equal pay for equal work, and many employers hire women for positions previously held by men only. This enhanced social status and increased economic independence has been reflected in the growing equality of women in the home. The effect of war in terms of family organization, then, has been to add momentum to the formation of a democratic family out of the vanishing semipatriarchal family of the past.

In general, the effects of the war on the functions performed by the family have been as follows: those functions which were losing ground to industry, the school, the church, and the state have continued to move out of the family at an even faster rate, and those functions which the family performs without serious competition have become further entrenched as uniquely family activities. The family has lost its historic functions of economic production for the market and for home consumption, care of the sick, education, and protection of its members, recreation, and the direction of religious rites. The surge of women into industry has meant fewer economic activities in the home, more reliance upon other institutions for health care, a great expansion in day nurseries for the care of young children, more reliance upon community and commercial recreation facilities, and fewer hours for the mother to spend in the education and religious development of her children.

The companionship type of family performs best the functions which remain, namely, the giving and receiving of affection by its members, and the bearing, rearing, and informal education of the children. The insecurity created by a world at war and the difficulties of achieving a permanent peace have further emphasized the security-giving functions of the companionship family. Those families which adequately perform this function provide the best protection for the growing child that society has yet devised.

War and its aftermath have added to the instability of the family in its transition from an institutional semipatriarchal type to the new democratic companionship type. We are living participants in this transition and should recognize that much of the uncertainty concerning the family of the present and of the future rests on the fact that we can't follow the exact patterns of our parents in dealing with family situations.

Inequities of the Contemporary Family System

Our system of rearing children in families gives some a far better start than others. Today it is family income and education that open doors or limit opportunities for child growth and development. The fact that children are reared in homes varying widely in socio-economic resources means they have varying social inheritances as well. This is reflected in their intelligence, their personalities, their health, their occupational choice, their opportunities in the industrial order — in short, in almost every conceivable aspect of their lives.

MOST CHILDREN ARE IN LOW AND MODERATE INCOME FAMILIES

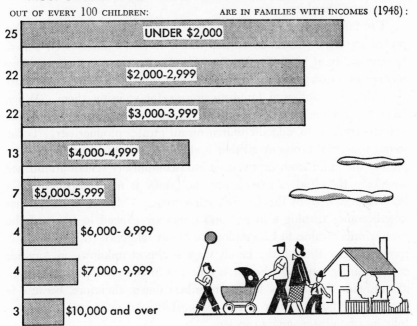

OUT OF EVERY 100 CHILDREN: ARE IN FAMILIES WITH INCOMES (1948):

25	UNDER $2,000
22	$2,000-2,999
22	$3,000-3,999
13	$4,000-4,999
7	$5,000-5,999
4	$6,000- 6,999
4	$7,000-9,999
3	$10,000 and over

From *Children and Youth at the Midcentury — A Chart Book*, Health Publications Institute, Inc., Raleigh, North Carolina

There is not much doubt that the family system fails to provide the necessities of life equally for all children. It is the great creator and perpetuator of inequalities of opportunity.[3] Moreover, the family is also the conservator of status inequalities because the child starts life with the status provided by his family. Little wonder that many children seek to dissociate themselves from their family beginnings and establish themselves in more favorable statuses; particularly children of the foreign born, of minority groups, and of the unskilled occupational groups.

In America the family has become a buffer between the state and the individual and between the economic order and the individual. The state has held the family responsible for the upbringing and support of children and has interfered only when the welfare of the child was seriously endangered. The struggle for existence has been waged, not by individuals, but by family groups. The rugged individualism of early America was really "rugged familism." It is only in recent

[3] Jessie Bernard, *American Family Behavior* (New York: Harper, 1942), p. 544.

years that the burden of breadwinning has been exclusively placed on the parents' shoulders.

The family fails to provide the good life primarily because it is expected to carry out functions for which it is no longer well suited. Responsibility or blame is placed on families for provision of protective services of medical care, nutrition, shelter, and guardianship in a society that has outlawed familistic means for securing them. When "making a living" was family centered and all members except the toddlers could help, added children meant greater productivity. Today in our industrial economy all that is changed. Child labor laws rightly protect the child from exploitation, and compulsory school attendance laws keep the child in school, but the family is not compensated for his withdrawal from the family's labor force. "Making a living" has now become "earning a living" and wages are gauged in terms of the breadwinner's value to his employer without reference to his family responsibilities. Indeed, the family wage is almost unknown in America except during wartime when it is reflected in the family allotments to servicemen. The family lets its members down, therefore, because it is still being held to most of the responsibilities it once carried successfully in a familistic agrarian society.

Most of the factors affecting family income and expenditures are now outside the control of individual families. Wage levels vary, not with added dependents in families, but with the business cycle. Inflation, in turn, is quite likely to render family income inadequate. Economic opportunities open up and recede locally, unemployment increases and decreases, and technological changes make obsolete formerly useful skills in response to changes in the social order which family heads not only cannot control but may even find difficult to understand. The social insurances in the Social Security Act are calculated to spread the risks of unemployment and death of the breadwinner, but they too ignore the number of dependents the lost income is expected to serve.

For too long American families have been called upon to take up the slack in a poorly integrated social order. If fiscal policies are bungled, producing inflation, the family purse strings are tightened; if depressions bring sudden impoverishment, family savings and the family's capacity to restrict consumption to subsistence levels are drawn upon, with subsequent threats to child health and growth; if real estate and building interests fail to provide housing, families must adapt themselves to broken down, obsolete dwellings or double up with other families. For too long the family has been ignored in social planning and the strains are telling.

If we are committed to the family system of child care and guidance we must establish a national policy for families that supports its role as the great burden carrier of the social order. The rights for children embodied in The Children's Charter prepared by the 1930 White House Conference have been largely nullified so long as families are unable to secure for their charges the basic elements for health, education, and growth.

The inequality features of the family system are not intrinsic but extrinsic. One of the challenges we now face is to devise ways of reducing the unnecessary pressures on those families which are burdened with more than their fair share of responsibility.

The modern family lives in a greater state of tension than yesterday because it is the major burden carrier of a social order undergoing rapid social change. Problems outnumber solutions in many sectors of society, and the resulting uncertainties are absorbed by all of us, who are for the most part also members of families. Because the family is the bottleneck through which all troubles pass, no other association so reflects the strains and stresses of life. With few exceptions persons in workaday America return to rehearse within the family their daily frustrations, and hope to get the necessary understanding and resilience to return tomorrow to the fray.

Thus, the good family today is not only the focal point of frustrations and tensions but also the source for resolving frustrations and releasing tensions. A good family has become one in which a person can be his worst without risking permanent ostracism (another instance of the family's role as buffer between the individual and the outside society). No longer effective as a producer of domestic goods, the modern family elaborates other functions concerned more intimately with the production and preservation of personality. Through its capacity for sympathy, understanding, and unlimited loyal support, the family rehabilitates personalities bruised in the course of competitive daily living.

If we wish to implement mental health for America's children and youth, we shall do well to consider what we can do by concerted effort to help all families, not as a sentimental movement but as a basic need for personal stability and social order. The capacity of families to take up the slack in the social order is approaching an upper limit. Their tremendous resilience and recuperative strengths must be fostered and conserved. A national policy which deals with American families as a precious national resource in social organization is badly needed.

A Movement for Strengthening Family Life

The National Conference on Family Life, in the White House in 1948, was the first attempt at national planning looking toward a set of national and domestic policies for family life. Perhaps the most significant factor in the movement for the improvement of family life is that the impetus has come from family members themselves. In much the same way that pioneers got together for the raising of the frame of a new dwelling or pooled their resources for harvesting, our present-day families have banded together to meet their needs. The fact that these contemporary needs are child guidance and social security rather than house building and husking bees does not destroy the parallel.

For several decades there has been a growing movement on the part of parents to join forces in the guidance and welfare of their children. The parent-teacher movement has developed as a result of the desire of the parents to have a part in the education of their children. Child study groups and mothers' circles and parent federations have come into being, not so much as a result of the supersalesmanship of child psychologists and guidance experts as from the drive of parents to obtain help. Likewise, in more recent years the development of programs of education for marriage has followed the demands of young people for knowledge and guidance in preparation for marriage. The movement for the improvement of marriage and family living has had all the vigor of a true folk movement, which accounts in part for the vitality and rapidity of its growth. It is not a case of the family's passively accepting help. Family members are the participants, the lobbyists, and legislators who are influencing changes which encourage family independence.[4]

---

[4] See Evelyn M. Duvall, "Growing Edges in Family Life Education," *Marriage and Family Living*, Vol. 6 (May, 1944); and Lawrence K. Frank, "Opportunities in a Program of Education for Marriage and Family Life," *Mental Hygiene*, Vol. 24 (1940), pp. 578–594. See also the Symposium on Family Stability, *The Annals of the American Academy of Political and Social Science*, Vol. 272 (November, 1950).

Child Care and Training. The movement for child care and training arose out of the distress of mothers who found themselves unable to provide all the services of the rural family in the cramped urban apartment quarters of cities. No chores to do, no long walks into the woods for recreation, and no fishing hole to while away a child's summer — these were just some of the deficiencies of city living which prompted mothers to band together into child study groups. Children with time on their hands and no place to run became problem children, and mothers in need of help pooled their resources to get specialists to tell them what to do about Johnny who runs away, and Jimmie who eats dirt, and Sally who has temper tantrums over nothing at all.

The child guidance and parent-teacher movement spread countrywide but changed its emphasis from asking questions of specialists and getting answers, to working out cooperatively the division of labor between school, community, and family, so that these institutions might perform more adequately their common functions of socialization, education, and recreation. Individual families derive support from knowing that their methods of discipline and of teaching in the home coincide with the methods used in the classroom and on the playground, and that their objectives of releasing and fulfilling personalities are common to the school and the community.

Family Life Education. Educational programs have come into being wherever there has been an eager constituency of family folk together with some kind of leadership and organizational channel. The variety is as impressive as it is confusing.

1 Churches have developed family-life institutes, training schools for parents and leaders, marriage courses for young people, and a multitude of informal programs to meet the requests of their members. Denominational bodies have developed family-life departments, issued materials, published periodicals, and trained leaders for this work. National interdenominational bodies have similarly given their assistance by coordinating and stimulating efforts to help families meet their common needs.

2 Community agencies such as the YWCA, the YMCA, settlement houses, housing projects, social agencies, and youth groups have found their constituents clamoring for work in marriage and family life. Programs go all the way from teen-agers discussing boy-girl relationships to grandmothers' clubs taking refresher courses in child guidance. Most

"We had the usual thing today, reading, writing, and sex education."

agencies still meet these needs with the help of scattered resources within the community, using doctors, nurses, psychologists, and so on. Some few communities have been fortunate in the establishing of a central agency in education for marriage and family life from which the needed leadership and materials and guidance emanate. The Association for Family Living in Chicago is illustrative of this method of a central resource agency and is being widely emulated through the country.

3 Government agencies are doing much to encourage the development of these local resources. The Children's Bureau issues valuable material and shares its well-qualified leadership. The Office of Education through its demonstration projects in communities across the country is stimulating interest and showing how local resources may be coordinated to meet local needs in family-life education. The extension service of the Department of Agriculture carries on family-life education programs through its home economics extension specialists in several states and reaches rural communities untouched by other agencies.

4 Formal education programs start in the nursery school and extend through elementary school, high school, and college into adult education programs for married adults. With education compulsory up to the age of eighteen in many states, it has been possible to accomplish a great deal through this medium.

The nursery school and elementary school concentrate in three areas of family-life education particularly: 1) They aid the child to understand his home and appreciate its place as a part of life. 2) They help parents to understand the growing child through frequent conferences with teachers. 3) They carry on the program of socialization started by the family, so necessary to later parenthood.

At the high school level, education for family living comes chiefly through classes in home economics, biology, social science, and mental hygiene. Although such course work reaches as yet only a small percentage of high school students, it is during this period that formal preparation for marriage will need to receive greatest attention. The high school is more nearly than any other the universal school for all youth.[5]

College courses in marriage and the family are offered at most of the institutions of higher learning in the country, and are increasingly functional in their adaptation to the needs of the students. A significant publication of the American Council on Education outlines a full course in marriage and family adjustments based on a functional approach.[6]

Luther E. Woodward has recently reviewed the history of family life education in the United States and has identified eight significant trends:

1 There has been a shift from complete preoccupation with the interests and needs of parents to include those of the aged, the newly married, the unmarried, the teen-age boy and girl, and even younger children.

2 In parent education there has been a shift from an emphasis on habit training and techniques of discipline to attention to parent-child relationships, the emotional aspects of family life, and the importance of affection as compared with habits and skills. . . . There has been a comparable

---

[5] For a much more complete discussion of formal education for family living, see Bess Goodykoontz and others, *Family Living and Our Schools* (New York: Appleton-Century, 1941); and *Education for Family Life* (Washington: American Association of Administrators, 1942).

[6] *Design for General Education* (Washington: American Council on Education, 1944).

trend in home economics. Cooking, home management, and other household arts are giving way slightly to increased attention to the dynamic aspects of family relations.

3 Sex education has received a great deal of attention in recent years, but its focus is changing rapidly. Emphasis on the biological factors of life is yielding to an emphasis on the emotional and social factors in family living. We are now well aware that the emotional concomitants accompanying instruction are likely to be more significant than the facts presented. The current trend therefore is to integrate sex education, in a narrow sense, with the total of family living and to impart such information to children as they may want and need it, as their curiosity is naturally aroused.

4 There is a further tendency to place emphasis on the affectional relationships in the family, since these so largely determine each person's ability to give and accept love in a mature way.

5 In family life education fathers are coming into their own. In some cities classes for expectant fathers are fairly common, and in all parent education work the significance of the father's role is being more and more appreciated. . . . Fathers are needed for the psychosexual maturing of the boy and the girl as well as to participate in the everyday discipline, control, and guidance of the children.

6 The strength of cultural pressures on the family is being more and more recognized. It is a common observation that most of the psychological mistakes that parents frequently make are committed out of deference to culture patterns which they dare not overlook or violate lest they bring down on themselves unbearable criticism from relatives and neighbors.

7 The trend of family life education is away from utilizing primarily clinical, pathological materials toward a more positive emphasis which parents and married couples find essentially reassuring. Instead of scaring parents and mates by accounts of the dire things that will happen if they do not do thus and so, they are given positive images of desirable outcomes and are helped to acquire the necessary "know-how" to achieve them.

8 There is today a trend toward evaluation of the results of various family life educational programs and marriage and family counseling programs. It is, of course, clear that in this field education is much more than the giving of information; that in many instances nothing less than an emotional re-education is required; and that this involves either personal counseling or a dynamic kind of group thinking and self-discovery.[7]

Family Counseling. From all these hundreds of thousands of people studying sensible ways of meeting the everyday problems of living come increased demands for family counseling services.

There was a time when a troubled mother would talk over a family

---

[7] Luther E. Woodward, "Family Life Education," *Social Work Yearbook,* 1950 (New York: American Association of Social Workers, 1951).

problem with the next-door neighbor or an older relative. As families have become more mobile, it has been increasingly difficult to maintain such confiding relationships. Furthermore, new skills and knowledges have arisen that are recognized as more effective than the trial and error approaches of the well-meaning layman. As health education has done much to teach us what to eat and how to be well and when to call a doctor, family-life education is teaching us about our relationships with other people in the family. The trained counselor is able to take the troubled person far enough in discussion for him to understand what it is that is bothering him. Counseling agencies have built up a clientele of satisfied customers that insure the success of family counseling.

Commercial efforts to exploit this vast reservoir of human need have been numerous. Radio programs run by people of dubious background compete with magazine and newspaper columns in giving advice to the lovelorn. Their admonitions can rarely be helpful even when the motivation is not primarily commercial, since those responsible for them lack the necessary training and essential skills for successful counseling. The existence of such a mass of questionable material, plus the true-life periodical trash, is evidence of the need for still further expansion of legitimate and reputable counseling services.

The criteria for distinguishing the authentic from the spurious counseling service were outlined in detail in Chapter Twelve, "Common Conflicts in Marriage." Such family counseling agencies as may be relied upon are usually to be found in connection with reputable medical, educational, or social agencies, and are subject to professional standards of practice. New developments in this field are numerous, and they will undoubtedly expand rapidly to serve the family of tomorrow.

We have selected for discussion here only three of the many disparate movements which have merged to form a general movement for improving family life. Independently organized, several movements such as those for maternal health, social hygiene, family welfare, eugenics, birth control, as well as those discussed (parent education and child study, family-life education, and family counseling) are now finding common ground and becoming integrated into one driving force with common aims and objectives — the improvement of family life through the critical utilization of social and psychological science and social action.

The Family of the Future

You have covered a large territory since your first reading of the opening chapter, "What You Bring to Marriage." You should be more confident in facing the prospects of marriage and family life from having exposed yourself to the findings of research and clinical experiences recorded here. We might be expected to say, "It's up to you, now," but we won't, because you should return again and again to what you have read here as you get an opportunity to work its principles out in practice. Besides, you are going to have a chance to go over the whole subject several times with the one you marry. You both need insight and understanding of the forces which operate to hold marriages together and which enable parents and children to grow with each other.

One study of successful marriages revealed that the majority of the adjustments are made by the wife. The professor reporting the study suggested the need for equal understanding on the part of both men and women if democratic families are to be produced.[8] Undoubtedly the hundreds of thousands of men studying books of this sort will contribute to change the situation. If the family of the future is to be a democratic family, there should certainly be no monopoly on the understanding of marriage and family relationships.

Families of the future will profit from the mistakes of the past. Several pages of this book have been devoted to refuting the common-sense solutions in practice today. These horse-sense remedies are like the herbs of grandmother's closet, some harmless, some helpful because of the attention given along with the herbs, and some actually harmful. The traditional methods of child rearing employed by the family of yesterday and sanctioned by authority deliberately terrorized, brutalized, and humiliated the child. We can see the anxiety and guilt and life-long resentment and hostility in the lives of unhappy, antisocial individuals today. Unless we break with the past by carefully evaluating our family practices in terms of modern science, we may continue the cycle in our own homes.

The family of the future will need to examine critically the cultural traditions now guiding families in rearing children, to evaluate those traditions, especially the ethical and moral instruction, in terms of the

[8] Ernest W. Burgess and Leonard S. Cottrell, Jr., *Predicting Success or Failure in Marriage* (New York: Prentice-Hall, 1939), pp. 325–327.

"I thought this television would bring the family together!"

social life and the personalities they produce. Ours is a day of transition in which change is not only permissible but encouraged. It is a day of image breaking for which we pay a price in social disorganization and breakdown. One of the changes now underway is the final break with the patriarchal, man-dominated home of the past, with its obsolescent ideas and beliefs and destructive practices.

Men and women together must find new satisfactions in building a companionship family in which the integrity of every individual may be recognized and conserved. This is the major challenge of our time: to break with the belief that any one person may rule the family, and to build a family life which will bring about the releasing and fulfilling of personality. This involves paying more attention to giving and receiving of affection in the family, more attention to the emotional needs and hungers of family members. It includes providing a home in which the experiences of democratic living are satisfying and growth-promoting. These are the challenges of the family of the future, and the leads for meeting them are scattered throughout the pages of this book.

The Long-Time View. What lies ahead? Innumerable changes in industry, government, and social life. It is a rough testing ground for families. Divorce may be expected to increase for some time to come, until better means of bringing together compatible couples in marriage are devised. Marriage will continue to be popular in the future despite the mounting divorce figures, both because it fills a need and because couples are not easily dissuaded from marriage by the failures of others. Childless marriages may be expected to continue to constitute a significant proportion of our population, since they are better equipped to meet the hazards of economic depression and unemployment than marriages burdened with children.

Families of the future will draw more heavily than families of the past on the services they have devised to keep themselves well, such as associations for family living, recreation centers, child guidance centers, family counseling centers, well baby clinics, and so on. These should act constructively to protect individual families against many of the crises which they are unable to handle themselves.

Suppose we summarize the shift of values we perceive ahead, taking the long-time view. The family of the future as we see it will be:

- More democratic than patriarchal
- More affectionate than economically productive
- More adaptable than rigidly loyal to family traditions and protocol
- More versatile in the performance of family tasks
- More concerned with homemaking than housekeeping
- More person-centered than work-centered

The family of the future will be made by our generation. If we can recognize now that democratic family living, and by that token democracy itself, depends upon how children are nurtured and socialized by the family, we can get some glimpse of the importance of our task. There are unlimited opportunities ahead in family life for creation of a better culture and a more livable society if we foster sane, integrated personalities who will not be compelled to defeat and destroy others or themselves because of deficiencies in childhood teachings and experiences. This is the supreme challenge of family members in a world of change and promise.

Selected Readings

BARUCH, DOROTHY W., *You . . . Your Children . . . and War* (New York: Appleton-Century, 1942), Chap. 12.

BECKER, HOWARD, AND HILL, REUBEN (EDS.), *Family, Marriage, and Parenthood* (Boston: Heath, 1948), chaps. 24, 26.

CUBER, JOHN F., *Marriage Counseling Practice* (New York: Appleton, 1948).

DUVALL, EVELYN M., "Loneliness and the Serviceman's Wife," *Marriage and Family Living* (Autumn, 1945), pp. 77–81.

FRANK, LAWRENCE K., "A National Policy for the Family," *Marriage and Family Living* (February, 1948), Vol. X, No. 1, pp. 1–4.

HAVIGHURST, ROBERT J., AND OTHERS, *The American Veteran Back Home* (New York: Longmans, Green, 1951).

HAVIGHURST, ROBERT J., AND MORGAN, H. GERTHON, *The Social History of a Warboom Community* (New York: Longmans, Green, 1951).

HILL, REUBEN, *Love and Marriage in Wartime and After* (New York: Association Press, 1944).

HOLLIS, FLORENCE, *Women in Marital Conflict* (New York: Family Service Association of America, 1949).

MEAD, MARGARET, *Male and Female* (New York: Morrow, 1949), Chap. 18.

WALLER, WILLARD, *The Veteran Comes Back* (New York: Dryden, 1944).

Technical References

AMERICAN ASSOCIATION OF SCHOOL ADMINISTRATORS, *Education for Family Life*, The Nineteenth Yearbook (Washington: National Education Association, 1941).

"The American Family in World War II," and "Toward Family Stability," two symposia, *The Annals of the American Academy of Political and Social Science* (September, 1943), Vol. 229; and (November, 1950), Vol. 272, respectively.

FOLSOM, JOSEPH K., *The Family and Democratic Society* (New York: Wiley, 1943), especially chaps. 18–20.

GOODYKOONTZ, BESS, AND OTHERS, *Family Living and Our Schools* (New York: Appleton-Century, 1941).

HILL, REUBEN, *Families Under Stress: Adjustment to the Crises of War Separation and Reunion* (New York: Harper, 1949), Chap. 10.

MUDD, EMILY H., *The Practice of Marriage Counseling* (New York: Association Press, 1951).

MYRDAL, ALVA, *National and Family: The Swedish Experiment in Democratic Family and Population Policy* (New York: Harper, 1941).

STOLZ, LOIS MEEK, "The Effect of Mobilization and War on Children," *Social Casework* (April, 1951), Vol. XXXII, No. 4, pp. 143–148.

WALLER, WILLARD, AND HILL, REUBEN, *The Family: A Dynamic Interpretation*, Revised Edition (New York: Dryden, 1951), Chap. 25.